Web Matrix
Developer's Guide

JOHN PAUL MUELLER

Apress™

Web Matrix Developer's Guide

ISBN (pbk): 1-59059-092-9

Printed and bound in the United States of America 12345678910

Trademarked names may appear in this book. Rather than use a trademark symbol with every occurrence of a trademarked name, we use the names only in an editorial fashion and to the benefit of the trademark owner, with no intention of infringement of the trademark.

Technical Reviewers: Shawn Nandi, Russ Mullen
Editorial Directors: Dan Appleman, Gary Cornell, Jason Gilmore, Simon Hayes, Karen Watterson, John Zukowski
Managing Editor: Grace Wong
Project Manager: Tracy Brown Collins
Copy Editor: Ami Knox
Compositor: Impressions Book and Journal Services, Inc.
Artist and Cover Designer: Kurt Krames
Indexer: Valerie Robbins
Production Manager: Kari Brooks
Manufacturing Manager: Tom Debolski

Distributed to the book trade in the United States by Springer-Verlag New York, Inc., 175 Fifth Avenue, New York, NY, 10010 and outside the United States by Springer-Verlag GmbH & Co. KG, Tiergartenstr. 17, 69112 Heidelberg, Germany.

In the United States, phone 1-800-SPRINGER, email orders@springer-ny.com, or visit http://www.springer-ny.com.

Outside the United States, fax +49 6221 345229, email orders@springer.de, or visit http://www.springer.de.

For information on translations, please contact Apress directly at 2560 9th Street, Suite 219, Berkeley, CA 94710. Phone 510-549-5930, fax 510-549-5939, email info@apress.com, or visit http://www.apress.com.

The information in this book is distributed on an "as is" basis, without warranty. Although every precaution has been taken in the preparation of this work, neither the author nor Apress shall have any liability to any person or entity with respect to any loss or damage caused or alleged to be caused directly or indirectly by the information contained in this work.

The source code for this book is available to readers at http://www.apress.com in the Downloads section.

This book is dedicated to the latest addition to our family, Sugar Plum. May her life be filled with as much joy as she has already given us.

Contents at a Glance

Contents

About the Author

 **John Mueller** is a freelance author and technical editor. He has writing in his blood, having produced 56 books and over 200 articles to date. The topics range from networking to artificial intelligence and from database management to heads-down programming. Some of his current books include a C# developer guide, a small business and home office networking guide, and several Windows XP user guides. His technical editing skills have helped over 31 authors refine the content of their manuscripts. John has provided technical editing services to both *Data Based Advisor* and *Coast Compute* magazines. He's also contributed articles to magazines like *SQL Server Professional, Visual C++ Developer,* and *Visual Basic Developer*. He's currently the editor of *.NET eXTRA eNewsletter* for Pinnacle Publishing. (Subscribe at http://www.freeenewsletters.com/.)

When John isn't working at the computer, you can find him in his workshop. He's an avid woodworker and candle maker. On any given afternoon, you can find him working at a lathe or putting the finishing touches on a bookcase. One of his newest craft projects is glycerin soap making, which comes in handy for gift baskets. You can reach John on the Internet at JMueller@mwt.net. John is also setting up a Web site at http://www.mwt.net/~jmueller/. Feel free to look and make suggestions on how he can improve it. One of his current projects is creating book FAQ sheets that should help you find the book information you need much faster.

About the Technical Reviewer

 **Russ Mullen** has been involved in the computer field since the early days of MS-DOS. He has technically edited or coauthored more than 40 titles. He has been a Web developer for a large international company and the IT manager for an insurance adjusting company. Russ has a consulting/application development firm that does Web site design and application development (see http://www.whoyouare.com for more information). He enjoys getting up very early in the morning and coding with coffee in hand long before the sun rises, and then retiring early to prepare for the next day's activities. You can reach Russ by e-mail rmullen@bellsouth.net.

Acknowledgments

Thanks to my wife, Rebecca, for working with me to get this book completed during an exceptionally difficult time. I really don't know what I would have done without her help in researching and compiling some of the information that appears in this book (especially the glossary). She also did a fine job of proofreading my rough draft and page proofing the final result.

Russ Mullen and Shawn Nandi deserve thanks for their technical edit of this book. Both editors greatly added to the accuracy and depth of the material you see here. I really appreciated the time the technical editors devoted to checking my code for accuracy—especially the last minute checks of test utilities. Russ also supplied some of the URLs you see in the book as well as other helpful tips and hints.

Finally, I would like to thank Karen Watterson, Tracy Brown, Ami Knox, and the rest of the production staff at Apress for their assistance in bringing this book to print. It's always nice to work with such a great group of professionals.

Introduction

"It's free!" That phrase emblazons many products. Everything from coupons in your local grocery store to the trade paper you read this morning use that phrase. Web Matrix is another product that uses the phrase "It's free!" However, unlike many products for which free also means nonuseful, Web Matrix is an extremely useful product. This is the editor you've always wanted on your desktop, but never had before. By the time you finish this book, Web Matrix will likely find a permanent place in your toolbox because it does so many tasks well.

This book provides a complete view of Web Matrix—everything from generating simple Web pages, to developing Web Services, to performing database development, and on to creating mobile applications. You'll learn how to use Web Matrix to perform a variety of tasks and how to extend it to meet needs that the original developers might not have envisioned. You'll also learn about places where Web Matrix isn't the right tool for the job. This book presents an honest evaluation of how you can use Web Matrix to improve your development environment. As with many tools, Web Matrix helps you perform some tasks well, but doesn't perform well in other areas.

Instead of taking a Microsoft-specific view of the product, I provide you with a generic (you can use this for anything) view when appropriate. For example, you'll learn how to add your custom controls and components to Web Matrix and develop applications using the same resources that you've always used. In addition, you'll learn how to add new templates to Web Matrix and even create an environment where you can edit files created by other language products on other platforms. In short, you'll learn just how flexible Web Matrix is and why you should participate in the community effort to improve it.

What's in This Book

What will you get from this book? The following descriptions tell you how *Web Matrix Developer's Guide* will improve your Web Matrix experience. More importantly, you'll learn a few tantalizing details about Web Matrix that you might not have known about in the past.

Chapter 1: An Overview of Web Matrix

This chapter introduces you to Web Matrix. We'll discuss what Web Matrix can and can't do for you. You'll also learn about features in the IDE. Finally, this chapter shows you how to create a test setup that you'll find not only works with Web Matrix, but proves useful for other types of development projects, as well.

Chapter 2: Using Web Matrix

This chapter begins with some installation details for Web Matrix and other utilities that I think you'll find helpful. You'll learn a little more about the IDE elements and then we get to work. First, you'll find out how to use the Web Matrix workspace. Web Matrix offers advantages that full-fledged products don't for performing some tasks very quickly. You'll also learn how to connect to the Internet to modify your projects online, and we'll discuss how to download components and controls from the Online Component Gallery.

Chapter 3: Building a Simple Web Site

Although Web Matrix was originally designed for teaching new developers how to create ASP.NET applications, it includes a lot of support for standard HTML. You can create a Web site that relies on standard HTML using just Web Matrix. This chapter shows how you to create a simple HTML-based Web site. We also discuss Cascading Style Sheets (CSS). This chapter presents a number of new Web Matrix features such as how to use code snippets. Finally, this chapter shows your first ASP.NET application and some of the support files it uses such as WEB.CONFIG.

Chapter 4: Web Matrix and Security

Security is essential on Web sites today. Fortunately, Web Matrix provides a number of solutions in this area, and this chapter discusses them all. Not only will you learn about the two specialty pages that Web Matrix provides for logging into and out of Web sites, but you'll also learn about other options that you have for securing your Web server.

Chapter 5: Web Matrix Database Development

Database management is a keystone of every business. In fact, I'm often surprised at how many home users rely heavily on databases as well. This chapter provides a discussion of several types of database development. You'll learn how to create a form view and a grid view, along with the reports that most people need. This chapter also discusses the limits of creating database applications in Web Matrix. You might be surprised at just how far this product can go, but it's also important to realize it can't do everything.

Chapter 6: Applications with Custom Components and Controls

This chapter helps you understand how to work with components and controls in Web Matrix. First, we look at the tools you'll need to make working with components and controls possible. All of these tools come with the .NET Framework, so you already have them installed on your machine. Next, we'll discuss how to work with both unmanaged and managed components and controls. Unmanaged components and controls are those created with pre-.NET technology—managed components and controls rely on the .NET Framework. This chapter also introduces you to a new tool, the ActiveX Control Pad. This utility is another free download from Microsoft.

Chapter 7: Web Matrix and XML

You may not know that XML is used for a number of purposes other than pure data transmission. One of those purposes is the presentation of data online at Web sites. This chapter shows you how to work with XML in a number of ways. We'll discuss how it's used to create Web sites, display data from databases, transmit data, and store user configuration settings. This chapter also introduces you to Microsoft's XML Notepad—a great utility that helps you work with XML files (and another free download).

Chapter 8: Web Matrix and Web Services

Web services provide a means for companies to share resources with partners or to make code available for general use. This chapter helps you understand the potential of Web services and shows you how to use Web Matrix to implement Web service solutions. We'll discuss the Simple Object Access Protocol (SOAP)—a technology based on XML, which is used to describe programming interfaces and acts as a data transmission package. You'll also learn about one of the performance solutions that Web Matrix provides along with a wealth of additional free tools (including one that validates your SOAP messages).

Chapter 9: Web Matrix Mobile Applications

Everyone wants to access their data on the road today. The devices used to access this information get smaller all the time. Unfortunately, most developers are accustomed to creating desktop applications. This chapter helps you understand the requirements for creating mobile applications, shows you how to use emulators to develop your applications, and then helps you develop several mobile applications using Web Matrix.

Chapter 10: Improving Performance with Web Matrix

For many developers, performance is everything. They continue to tweak an application until it speeds along like a racecar. Web Matrix offers two methods for tuning your applications so they run faster. First, you can use special controls to make the user interface friendlier and faster to use. Speeding up the user's access to the application enhances the performance of the application as a whole. Second, you can change the way that the Web server interacts with the application—enhancing the handling of application data. This chapter discusses how Web server performance ultimately helps the client see better application performance.

Glossary

The glossary includes all the terms and acronyms used in the book.

Appendix: 52 Ways to Improve the Web Matrix Experience

This appendix shows you 52 unique ways to make your Web Matrix experience better. Each tip is an essential nugget of information that you can use to change the way you view Web Matrix and what it can do for you. There's one tip for each week of the year so that you can enhance your Web Matrix experience over time.

Who Is the Audience for This Book?

This book has two audiences. The primary audience is developers who want to learn more about ASP.NET. Web Matrix was originally designed to help developers learn about ASP.NET without having to purchase Visual Studio .NET. Web Matrix provides a GUI similar to the one found in Visual Studio .NET (with important limitations we'll discuss in the book). I'm assuming that you've already read some information about ASP.NET and know how to use a language such as C# or Visual Basic. This book is focused on intermediate to advanced developers. Developers who want a tool that can perform quick edits fast will also want to read this book. I provide a wealth of hints and tips on how Web Matrix can help you become more productive. More importantly, I show you how Web Matrix can bridge gaps. Instead of opening a multitude of development environments to fix problems with your Web site, you can open this one text editor and still have an incredibly friendly IDE. With the addition of a few templates, you can also perform a limited amount of Web site development with Web Matrix.

What You Need

Chapter 1 will tell you about the setup that I've used to write the book and why I think that setup works so well for my development needs. Theoretically, all you need is a machine running a version of Windows with the .NET Framework installed. You don't need to buy anything—all of the products used in this book are free for the price of a download. That's right, every tool in this book is accessible from a Web site, and all you need to do is download them to use them. Some products are shareware or crippleware, which means the product authors would love it if you purchased their product. I encourage you to try all of the products so you can see what a great environment Web Matrix provides for some development needs.

Conventions Used in This Book

It always helps to know what the special text means in a book. In this section, we'll cover usage conventions. This book uses the following conventions:

CONVENTION	DESCRIPTION
`Inline Code`	Some code will appear in the text of the book to help explain application functionality. The code appears in a special font that makes it easy to see it. This monospaced font also makes the code easier to read.
[Filename]	When you see square brackets around a value, switch, or command, it means that this is an optional component. You don't have to include it as part of the command line or dialog field unless you want the additional functionality that the value, switch, or command provides.
<Filename>	A variable name is a value that you need to replace with something else. For example, you might need to provide the name of your server as part of a command line argument. Because I don't know the name of your server, I'll provide a variable name instead. The variable name you'll see usually provides a clue as to what kind of information you need to supply. In this case, you'll need to provide a filename.
File ➢ Open	Menus and the selections on them appear with the right arrow symbol. "File ➢ Open" means "Access the File menu and choose Open."
URLs	URLs will normally appear highlighted so that you can see them with greater ease. The URLs in this book provide sources of additional information designed to make your development experience better. URL s often provide sources of interesting information as well.
Input	All user input is in bold type to make it easy for you to see. If you see some text in bold type, make sure you type it precisely as shown in the book.
Term	Sometimes you'll run across a special term in the book. Such terms appear in italic type so that you can see them easier and find them faster the next time you want to locate them. Whenever you see a term in italics, pay special attention to it.

Icons

This book contains many icons that help you identify certain types of information. The following paragraphs describe the purpose of each icon.

 NOTE   *Notes tell you about interesting facts that don't necessarily affect your ability to use the other information in the book. I use notes to give you bits of information that I've picked up while using Web Matrix, ASP.NET, C#, Visual Basic .NET, Windows 9x, Windows 2000, or Windows XP.*

 TIP   *Everyone likes tips because they tell you new ways of doing things that you might not have thought about before. Tips also provide an alternative way of doing something that you might like better than the first approach I provided. In most cases, you'll find newsgroup and Web site URLs in tips as well. These URLs are especially important because they usually lead to products or information that help you perform tasks faster.*

 CAUTION   *The Caution icon means watch out! Cautions almost always tell you about some kind of system or data damage that'll occur if you perform a certain action (or fail to perform others). Make sure you understand a caution thoroughly before you follow any instructions that come after it.*

Part One

Using Web Matrix

CHAPTER 1

An Overview of Web Matrix

In This Chapter

- Discover What Web Matrix Can Do for You

- Learn How You Can Use Web Matrix in Your Next Project

- Learn About Web Matrix Limitations

- Obtain an Overview of the Web Matrix Features

- Create a Development Server Setup

- Create a Development Client Setup

Web Matrix may very well be the best piece of free software that you'll ever see produced by Microsoft. Just in case you haven't downloaded this product yet, you can get it from http://www.asp.net/webmatrix/default.aspx.

NOTE *All URLs, Web references, newsgroups, and help topic references in this book are accurate as of the time of writing. However, these references could change over time. If an URL doesn't work, check my Web site at http://www.mwt.net/~jmueller/ for a changed URL. If you don't see the changed URL there, you can usually find it using Google (http://www.google.com/). If you report the changed URL to me at JMueller@mwt.net, I'll add it to a table of changed URLs on my Web site so that everyone can benefit.*

The first thing you'll notice is how small and fast Web Matrix is. A small download nets you a very capable editor.

This chapter provides an overview of Web Matrix. We'll discuss issues such as what Web Matrix is and why you'd want to use it. Given the nature of Web Matrix, we'll also discuss some of the things you can't do with it. Any expectation that Web Matrix will provide the same functionality as a large product such as Visual Studio is going to result in disappointment. However, I think you'll find that the positive features of Web Matrix far outweigh any negatives. With this in mind, we'll discuss the features that Web Matrix does provide.

In the final section of this chapter, I'll show you how to create a client and a server setup for Web testing. Some developers attempt to create and test their Web applications using a single server. When they move the applications to real-world environments, they often find that the applications that used to work on one machine have problems when tested on two. The best setup is to create and test your applications on a two-machine setup from the outset to avoid the heartbreak of moving pains later.

> **NOTE** *Web Matrix, like most of the applications demonstrated in this book, is a free download. In general, this means that the vendor doesn't provide direct support for the product. For example, Web Matrix is supported as a community effort. If you want a tool that's fully supported by the vendor, you'll need to purchase a product like Visual Studio .NET.*

What Is Web Matrix?

Web Matrix is an exciting new Integrated Development Environment (IDE) created as a community project[1] by some of the folks at Microsoft. The whole IDE is a relatively small 1.2 MB download, which is something I haven't seen for something this original since the days of DOS. The IDE uses a format similar to Visual Studio .NET, as shown in Figure 1-1, but that's where the similarities end. Web Matrix truly is a different concept from Visual Studio .NET. Throughout this book, you'll learn just how different Web Matrix really is. I think that you'll be pleasantly surprised when you learn about the extreme flexibility this product offers and see how it helps you create great applications faster.

In some respects, Web Matrix is a proof-of-concept product. It answers the question "How fast and efficient can you can make a .NET application?" That's right, the development team wrote this svelte IDE using C# and the .NET

---

1. "Community project?" Well, yes. Remember that it's a "product" that's been created by Microsoft employees. Some folks refer to it (flatteringly) as a sort of "skunkworks" product; others as a product created in the spirit of the open source movement. Of course, spirit only, since the source isn't available.

Framework. However, you'd never know it from the way the application works. This IDE is fast and efficient.

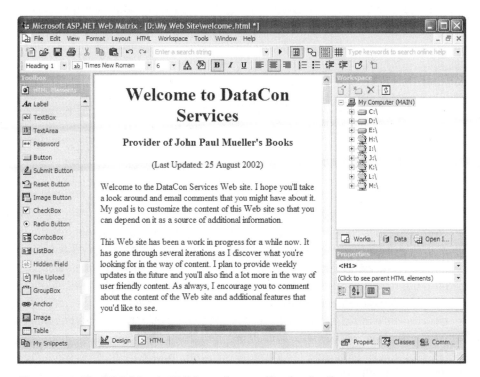

Figure 1-1. The Web Matrix IDE has a lot to offer the developer.

The name "Web Matrix" tells you a little about the product. This application helps you design and create Web applications. However, unlike many other products in this market, Web Matrix uses a file-oriented approach for working with applications. You won't see a project file included with Web Matrix because it's designed to edit individual files. However, this feature actually works out to your benefit in many situations. For example, you might need to tweak an existing Web site. The file-oriented nature of Web Matrix makes the change simple, and you don't need to load a large IDE to do it.

TIP *Web Matrix has an interesting history that you might want to know about. It seems that even the name went through a few changes before the developers working on the project decided on Web Matrix. You can learn more about the Web Matrix project at* http://www.asp.net/webmatrix/AboutProject.aspx.

Some developers might view Web Matrix as a standalone product. You definitely don't need Visual Studio .NET installed to use it, and I've used it for one standalone project already. However, Web Matrix also shines as a Visual Studio .NET "companion." It actually fills in a few gaps that you might have found in the Visual Studio .NET environment. The two products are complimentary in many ways.

Most developers will find that Web Matrix also extends the Visual Studio .NET IDE in a few important ways. The most important form of extension is the fact that you can use it to modify files created by other applications on other platforms. Using the File Transmission Protocol (FTP) connection method enabled me to change some of the HTML files on a Linux Web server. (We'll discuss FTP and other connectivity options in the "Using the Workspace" section of Chapter 2.) I was able to change some eXtensible Markup Language (XML) files on a NetWare server using the same technique. Although it's possible that you could do the same thing with Visual Studio .NET, it wouldn't be nearly as easy as it is when using Web Matrix.

In sum, Web Matrix is a standalone IDE that helps you perform tasks that aren't necessarily easy to do with Visual Studio .NET. The small design makes it easy to use on just about any platform that also supports the .NET Framework. You can use it for project and nonproject files. It enables you to work with files created by other tools on other platforms without noticing many difference. Web Matrix is a "must-have" utility that every developer needs in their toolkit because it provides so much and asks for so little in return.

Web Matrix is also a great learning tool for those who want to learn more about ASP.NET without incurring the cost for Visual Studio .NET at the outset. It helps you discover how ASP.NET can help your organization at the lowest cost possible. You can also use the online tutorial as a training aid. (The tutorial is found on the Web Matrix site.) And, in case you didn't guess, this book will also help you learn a lot more about ASP.NET.

Why Use Web Matrix?

Now that you have a better idea of what Web Matrix is, you have to consider why you'd want to use it. In the following sections, I describe a few of the reasons you'll find Web Matrix helpful.

It Enables You to Work Fast, on Single Files

Web Matrix is good for situations when you need to edit a single file or work with just a few files. Yes, you can use it to create projects, but Web Matrix doesn't support an actual project file in the sense that Visual Basic or Visual Studio .NET programmers might expect. Consequently, it provides a fast way to work with single files in a manner that some projects actually prevent.[2]

It's Community-Based

Another reason I like Web Matrix is the sense of community from the developers who created it. The Web Matrix home page at `http://www.asp.net/webmatrix/default.aspx` appears in Figure 1-2. Notice that the site provides all kinds of links to additional information and help. The authors are justifiably proud of their efforts. The fact that they had a good time putting this product together really shows. All of the fit and finish of a custom application appears in Web Matrix.

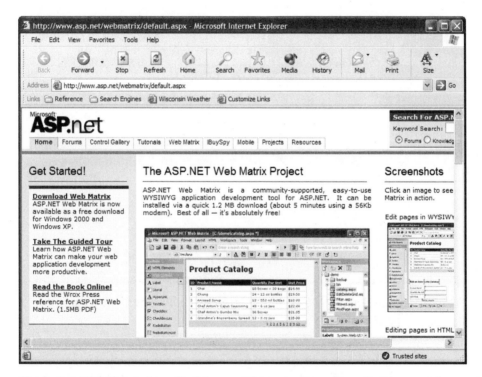

Figure 1-2. Web Matrix has all of the good features of a well-crafted community project.

Speaking of community, check out the discussion group for this product at `http://www.asp.net/Forums/ShowForum.aspx?tabindex=1&ForumID=30`. As shown

---

2.   Its "single file" approach reminds me of Microsoft Access.

in Figure 1-3, you'll find a lot of lively discussion on the newsgroup. The fact that this is an HTML-based newsgroup makes participation a little easier than using a traditional newsgroup. Generally, this first newsgroup handles all of the Web Matrix usage messages, as well as a few development questions. The developers have also supplied a separate bug reporting newsgroup at http://www.asp.net/Forums/ShowForum.aspx?tabindex=1&ForumID=31. The Web Matrix developers monitor both newsgroups, so you can be sure that someone will see your question, suggestion, or bug report.

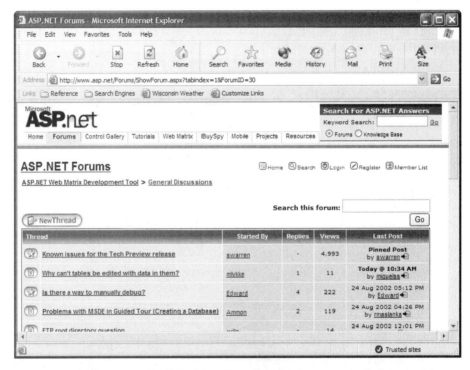

Figure 1-3. Make sure you check the online discussion groups for help using the Web Matrix product.

Most developers will find that they prefer Web Matrix to many other solutions out there—at least those with a similar memory footprint and download size. It's certainly better than using the many notepad editors available on the market. With Notepad, all you get is an editing screen—no controls, no color coding, no designer—none of the features built into Web Matrix. You receive all of the benefits of using a standard IDE to work on your files. In addition, all of the keyword highlighting is in place. It's true that you don't receive some IDE features of advanced products, such as automatic code completion, but there are limits to what you can expect from such a small application.

It's Free!

Somewhere along the way, I have to mention that this product is free. You can download and use it—no one expects you to pay a penny for the benefits Web Matrix provides. Of all the reasons for using Web Matrix, this one probably falls to the bottom of my list. Personally, I'd want a copy even if I had to pay a reasonable price for it. I consider Web Matrix a great tool and I hope that you will, too.

Web Matrix Features

For such a small "utility," Web Matrix boasts an impressive list of features. One of the more impressive features is the range of file types that this utility can view. For example, you can create full ASP.NET pages using this utility alone—no added functionality required. I was also able to open most Web graphics files for viewing (sorry, no editing for these files yet). Of course, Web Matrix provides support for all of the standard Web files such as HTM and HTML.

> **NOTE** *The current version has an interesting problem. When viewing files with an HTML extension, you can't change the properties for the page because the Properties window isn't active. However, files with an HTM extension work as expected. The developers will likely fix this behavior in a future version of the product.*

Now that I've whetted your appetite, let's look at some of the other features that Web Matrix has to offer. The following sections provide a good overview of many of the features Web Matrix provides. Of course, we'll cover many other features in depth as the book progresses.

IDE Features

One of the features I like best is that the IDE isn't a simple text editor. When you open some types of files, you get a tabbed view of the information it contains. For example, Figure 1-4 shows how an ASP.NET file will appear when you open it. Notice that the editing window includes tabs for the Design, Markup, Code, and All (both markup and code) views. In this case, you're seeing the Markup window, which contains the code required to create the user interface elements of the page.

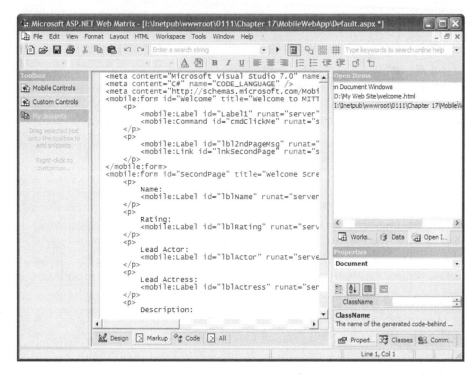

Figure 1-4. The Web Matrix editor provides tabs for the various views required to edit some types of files.

The three code-oriented tabs are an interesting feature. Unlike Visual Studio .NET, you don't have to use a separate file to hold the code for your ASP.NET page. (The use of a separate file to hold the code is called *code behind.*) You can combine code and markup in the same file. Web Matrix displays the two types of code separately, using the Markup and Code windows, or together, using the All window. I actually find it easier to work with ASP.NET files using this technique. This is one of the differences you'll see due to the file-oriented nature of Web Matrix versus the project-oriented nature of Visual Studio .NET.

Database Features

Web Matrix can work with Database Management Systems (DBMSs) directly through the Data window (you'll find in the "When Will You Want to Use Something Else?" section that there are some limits to this support). Currently,

Web Matrix only supports SQL Server and the Microsoft Database Engine (MSDE). You can use the IDE to perform a variety of database-related tasks including

- Editing existing SQL and MSDE databases.

- Creating new databases.

- Adding/editing/deleting tables and stored procedures.

- Editing data content.

- Automatically generating ADO.NET code to execute SQL statements and stored procedures.

One feature you won't find lacking is support for data-bound controls. (A data-bound control is one that has a connection to the data repository and automatically updates as the record position changes.) After you create a connection to a database, you can add data bindings to the various controls provided by Web Matrix. It's easy to create both form-based and grid-based views of data on your system. In fact, we'll build a complete database application using just Web Matrix in Chapter 5. As you'll see, this application will include multiple views, and you'll even build some reports for it. However, you'll still want to use Visual Studio .NET to build large projects, and the content in Chapter 5 will show you why.

In Web Matrix you'll find a new control not found in Visual Studio .NET. It's the MxDataGrid. This particular control offers some unique features, and you may find that you like it better than the one in Visual Studio .NET. However, some developers have experienced problems using it, so Chapter 5 will demonstrate all of the features of this control for you so that you can use it in your next database application.

Web Services Features

Many companies are looking toward Web services as a means for sharing data and code today. A Web service is simply a special component that you make accessible through an Internet connection. Another party requests access to your service using any of a number of methods—the most popular of which is to send an XML-formatted request using the Simple Object Access Protocol (SOAP).

Web Matrix provides the functionality to work with Web services, but not at a low level. For example, you wouldn't want to use Web Matrix to create a utility for changing the security on your server because it doesn't provide the required resources. You have access to both XML and SOAP. In addition, Web Matrix provides what you need to create a component. However, it lacks direct access to a compiler that will turn the component code into something you can deploy. You need to perform this task at the command line. Still, considering everything that Web Matrix does do, this is actually a small limitation.

You can also use Web Matrix to consume Web services. All you need to know is where the Web service is located and build the required files. Some developers will miss the automation that Visual Studio .NET provides, but Web Matrix is quite usable and better than a few other solutions on the market.

Mobile Application Features

As you'll see in Chapter 9, Web Matrix provides some exciting mobile application support features. In fact, this support is nearly on par with the support you'll find for standard Web applications. About the only additional support you'll need is access to an emulator. Chapter 2 will show you how to obtain and install several (free) emulators you can use to experiment with the mobile application examples in the book.

Other Useful Features

Web Matrix provides a few other features of interest. One of the most useful features is a built-in Web server. This lightweight Web server works for most content, including ASP.NET pages and XML. Of course, the Web server doesn't provide the full features of Internet Information Server (IIS) and you'll find that you can't manage it like IIS. In general, this lightweight server provides support for small or simple Web projects. If you want more control over your project, then you need to use IIS.

 NOTE *The Web server provided with Web Matrix does have two advantages that you might not think about initially. First, it provides a test environment in situations where you can't or don't want to install IIS. Second, it doesn't present a security problem because this Web server doesn't serve pages.*

Small businesses normally buy time on a hosted Web server rather than use a local server. The interface for most of these remote Web servers relies on an FTP connection. It's nice to know that you can connect directly to the FTP site using Web Matrix and modify the files without problem (you obviously need to set up permissions to do this with your ISP). The remote server shows up the same as a local workspace in the Workspace window, as shown in Figure 1-5. As you can see, the various folders and files on the FTP site are completely accessible.

Figure 1-5. Accessing online content through an FTP connection is just as easy as accessing local content.

The final feature you'll find helpful is the Community window. It appears as a tab in the lower-right corner of the display. This window includes links for a wealth of resources for using Web Matrix, including special Web sites and newsgroups. Figure 1-6 provides an overview of some of the material contained in this window. The number of links will likely increase as Web Matrix becomes more popular. The Community window also provides an area for related links and another area for contacts. The buttons at the top of the Community window provide access to these other features.

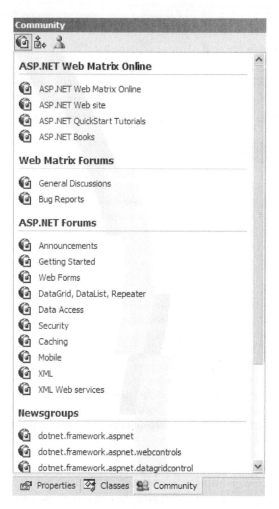

Figure 1-6. Check the Community window to gain access to Web sites, newsgroups, and additional sources of information.

What Web Matrix Can and Can't Do For You

A good programmer, like any professional, has a toolbox full of tools. Each tool has a specific use, and the developer has some favorites that see a lot of use. Web Matrix, like most tools, is good at performing some tasks and lacks the features required to perform other tasks. You should view it as you would any other tool. Web Matrix has a lot to offer, but I don't think you'll ever find a tool that does everything. Still, during the time I've used it, Web Matrix has found a spot in the favorite tool list of my toolbox, and I'm sure you'll find it excels at the tasks it performs as well.

TIP *Web Matrix isn't the only ASP.NET add-on product available. You can find a wealth of other add-on products at* http://www.asp.net/Default.aspx?tabindex=8&tabid=40. *Two of the more interesting add-ons as of this writing are Dreamweaver MX ASP.NET Support* (http://www.macromedia.com/software/trial_download/) *and Borland Delphi ASP.NET Support* (http://www. borland.com/about/press/2002/net_platform.html).

Of course, the problem is to define precisely how you can use Web Matrix to its best advantage. The following two sections describe how I think you can best use Web Matrix with other tools in your toolbox. You might find that you like it in other applications, and that's one of the reasons why tools are such a point of discussion for developers. (I've actually seen tool discussions become wars on the various developer newsgroups.) Everyone has a favorite tool, and not every developer uses every tool for precisely the same reasons. Consider this list a starting point as you work through the examples in the book and develop an opinion of your own.

How Can You Use Web Matrix?

Web Matrix has become my tool of choice for quick edits and creating single files. The fact that I don't have to do very much to connect to an FTP server makes this IDE more practical than other products I've used for the sorts of quick fixes that many developers have to make between major coding sessions. For example, I get simple input from Web site users on problems such as spelling errors. Getting a full product such as Visual Studio .NET out to fix such a simple error doesn't make sense—Web Matrix is faster and easier to use.

In many cases, Web Matrix could be the only IDE that a small business needs. If a small business maintains its own Web site on someone else's server, Web Matrix provides the perfect tool for creating, updating, and maintaining that Web site. Visual Studio .NET is actually overkill in such a situation. Web Matrix provides an ease of use that small business users will love. It makes the process of working with a Web site (at least a simple Web site) easier.

Some developers will find that Web Matrix provides a quick way to experiment. In some cases, you don't really want to set up an entire Web site to see if some new solution will work as anticipated. A simple Web site often does the trick, and using Web Matrix to create it will take less time. The personal Web server included in the package makes it possible to test new ideas without contaminating the code on your production server. Given that most developers are in a constant time crunch today, any technique that saves a little time is going to help. Although you can't develop huge Web sites with Web Matrix, it more than does the job in a pinch.

My favorite use for Web Matrix is checking out code on other platforms. Sometimes it's inconvenient to move to another machine, open another Web development tool, and then make just a few changes. Web Matrix handles most common Web files without regard to platform. It allows you to make simple changes without leaving your desk to go somewhere else to work.

I can see many developers moving Web Matrix to a laptop or other portable machine. The small size and memory footprint makes it possible to place this product on a machine that might not support Visual Studio .NET, or at least not support it very well. Although laptops have become more powerful over the last few years, they still lag behind desktop machines in many ways. In addition, developers who have a top-of-the-line desktop machine can't always count on getting a top-of-the-line laptop as well. An older laptop can probably support Web Matrix even when other solutions fail. Of course, you could always go back to Notepad, but that wouldn't be my first choice.

Getting a Head Start on Web Matrix

The Web Matrix developers have made it possible for you to get started with this product quickly. The walkthrough at http://www.asp.net/webmatrix/tour/getstarted/intro.aspx makes it easy to get going quickly. Generally, you'll find that they provide a quick "hands-on" tour of all the Web Matrix features. Here's what the Web site (and associated topics) looks like.

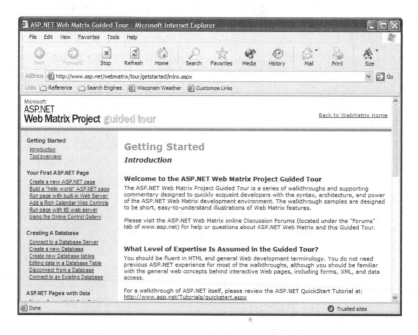

If you want to skip a particular topic or read about a topic a second time, just use the handy links on the left. The Web page will take you to that topic and show you a quick example of how to work with that feature in Web Matrix. None of the examples are earth shattering, but they do help you get started.

This book assumes that you've at least scanned the walkthrough. I wanted to avoid duplicating the efforts of the development staff as much as possible. Of course, we'll cover a little of the ground in the walkthrough a second time to prepare for an advanced example that a section of the walkthrough discusses.

When Will You Want to Use Something Else?

Web Matrix is a phenomenal product. However, it can't do everything for you—it has limitations, just like many other products out there. The most important consideration is that Web Matrix is a light, small editing environment. The features that make it unique and useful also limit the ways in which you can use it. You won't find many of the features of the Visual Studio .NET environment in this product because it's not designed to include those features. For example, Web Matrix truly is a Web application IDE—you can't use it for desktop applications.

As mentioned earlier, Web Matrix is also a single-file editor. Sure, you can open multiple files, but Web Matrix doesn't provide the cohesiveness of a project file. In many ways, the lack of project file restrictions is nice because you don't have to worry constantly about how a change will affect a project as a whole. However, the lack of projects also means you can't use this product for large-scale development. If you want to support the needs of a group of developers, then this isn't the product to use. What you need for group development is a product like Visual Studio .NET.

You won't find an actual compiler in Web Matrix. Although you can create class files, you can't compile them within the IDE. You need to compile them outside the IDE at the command prompt. However, there are ways around this problem that we'll discuss in the "Compiling and Registering the Component" section of Chapter 6. Generally, if you're interested in using a utility-type IDE instead of a full-featured IDE like the one provided in Visual Studio .NET, the need to perform a few tasks manually isn't such a big deal.

Some of the missing features in Web Matrix have a lot to do with the small download file. For example, you won't find a complete help file of the type provided with Visual Studio .NET. Web Matrix does include some helpful tips and tells you about the major classes used for ASP.NET development, but it doesn't include an extensive help file telling you about every feature of the .NET Framework. When you think about the purpose of this product, including a complete help file doesn't make sense. If you need a full-fledged help file, then you'll want a Microsoft Developer Network (MSDN) subscription or the full Visual Studio .NET help file.

TIP *The MSDN library is available online at* http://msdn.microsoft.com/library/. *You can use it in place of a desktop help file whenever necessary. However, the MSDN subscription has a lot more to offer than just a huge help file. For example, you'll have access to all of Microsoft's latest operating system developments. Microsoft offers several levels of MSDN subscription. You can learn more about the MSDN subscription and the features offered at each level at* http://msdn.microsoft.com/subscriptions/.

There are some pieces of automation that I miss from the Visual Studio .NET IDE. For example, you'll find that you actually have to press F2 to hide or show the Toolbox (you can also use the appropriate button on the toolbar). I wouldn't consider this a major omission, it just makes the Web Matrix IDE ever so slightly different from the one found in Visual Studio .NET, which means there's a slight learning curve. Although Web Matrix is an incredibly easy product to learn, the IDE differences could cause problems for some people.

You'll also find a few gaps in the database support for this product. For example, I wasn't able to access any of my "old," MDB-format Access databases natively. Of course, even Visual Studio .NET doesn't provide native Access support, so this particular omission is logical (albeit somewhat inconvenient).

A little more inconvenient is the lack of remote database support. If you want to access SQL Server, you *must* have the DBMS installed on the local machine to see it in the Data window. Fortunately, you can use the MSDE for local development. In fact, you'll find a link to this download on the Data window if you don't have any other DBMS installed, as shown in Figure 1-7. If you need complete database support for an application, you probably need the full version of Visual Studio .NET. In fact, you'll very likely want the "high-end" VS .NET Enterprise Architect Edition so that you don't run into any functionality problems with this product.

Figure 1-7. Web Matrix assumes that you'll want to load MSDE if there isn't any local support for SQL Server on your system.

Designing a Test Setup

Now that you have a better idea of what Web Matrix is and how it can help you develop better applications, you need to set up your system to use it. I have a specific method of working with Web applications that reduces development time, helps me discover errors faster, and increases the chance that the application will work correctly the first time. There's a trend in the computer industry by some vendors to rely on a single-machine setup to test critical applications. These vendors promote the single-machine perspective because using a single machine makes it appear that they're reducing development costs. In addition, using a single-machine setup makes it easier to put examples together that have a good chance of working on the majority of test systems. The problem with this perspective is that a single-machine setup doesn't reflect the real-world scenario. A Web application consists of a minimum of two machines working together. To test a Web application completely, the developer must duplicate the two-machine setup.

Using a single-machine setup does work for testing theories or for learning. However, you should consider such applications temporary and never leave them laying around for others to use. I've actually had vendor examples fail when I attempted to try them on a two-machine setup because the vendor never anticipated that anyone would test the application in this way. The problem is that many developers rely on the vendor applications to test their setup—it's supposedly a "known good" application designed to demonstrate the vendor's wares.

I wrote all of the applications in this book using a two-machine setup to ensure they'll work on your test system. The following sections tell about the setup that I used so that you'll know how I tested the applications. In addition, the sections discuss the minimum setup conditions that I think will work for the examples in this book. You're free to use a single-machine setup or machines with fewer resources, but these sections help you better understand what constitutes a good test setup.

Creating a Single-Machine Setup

Some developers will want to use Web Matrix on a trial basis for experimental purposes. One developer might want to use it to learn how to use ASP.NET. Another might just be in "tire-kicking" mode. In this case, the intent is to produce simple test applications that will never see the light of day as a production application. If you fall into this category and only want to do a quick "check it out" install or just use Web Matrix as a learning tool, then a single-machine setup can work.

Microsoft recommends a minimum of a Windows XP Home Edition setup for Web Matrix when used in a single-machine setup. This book tells you where to download all of the required software that you'll need in addition to the features provided by Windows XP Home Edition. Make sure you have at least a 9 GB hard drive, a minimum of 512 MB of RAM, and a decently fast processor (I tested the setup on a 450 MHz dual processor machine) before installing Web Matrix and the associated software found in this book. Yes, you can get by with a less capable setup, but you'll find that the test applications run very slowly and that you'll have a hard time running some software such as the emulators found in Chapter 9.

I don't recommend the Windows XP Home Edition setup for anyone who wants to create production applications. The reason is simple. A two-machine setup models a real-world client to Web server connection. Using a two-machine setup helps you find errors that a single-machine setup will miss. In addition, I don't recommend Windows XP Home Edition for production work because it lacks access to many of the administrative tools you need to monitor your application. For example, you don't get complete Performance console support—an essential tool if you want to optimize your application.

Even if you create a single-machine setup for testing, evaluation, or learning purposes, make sure you use a machine that you don't need for critical work. An application can fail, a modification might not work as anticipated, or the development environment itself can falter—damaging your system enough that it might require a hard drive format. Always use a machine that you don't mind setting up again.

Creating the Server Setup

As previously mentioned, I used a minimal setup for testing my applications because I didn't know what hardware you'd have in advance. You *must* have a Windows 2000 Server (or you can use a .NET Server when they become available) setup to work with all of the examples in this book. I wrote all of the examples using the standard server product on a dual processor 450 MHz Pentium processor machine with 512 MB of RAM. However, you could probably get by with a single 450 MHz processor machine with 256 MB of RAM installed. I'd recommend a minimum of 9 GB of hard drive space, although more is certainly better considering how much space you'll use for the various programming language additions.

The test server will require access to a number of Windows-specific components if you want the examples in the book to work. All of these tools, except the Microsoft .NET Framework, are easily installed using options in the Add/Remove Programs applet of the Control Panel. The following list summarizes the components that I installed while writing this book:

- Internet Information Server (complete)

- Microsoft .NET Framework

- Management and Monitoring Tools (all) (If you can see all of the tools in the Administrative Tools folder in the Control Panel, you have this feature installed.)

- Message Queuing Services (optional)

- Microsoft Indexing Service

- Networking Services (all)

- Terminal Services (optional)

NOTE *The name of my server is WinServer. Yes, I know it's not a very imaginative name, but it's easy to find in the code and short enough to see well on screen. Throughout the book, you'll see references to my server in the code. You must change these references to the name you've given your server in order to make the test applications run correctly. I'll provide additional information as needed as part of the coding example explanations.*

Once you have your test server up and running, there are some additional programs you'll need in order to work with some of the examples in the book. The number of features that you install depends on which examples you want to work with. Obviously, you'd need a database manager to work with the database examples. The following application list assumes that you want to work with all of the examples.

- SQL Server (version 7.0 or better)

- Microsoft Front Page Server Extensions

- Microsoft Posting Acceptor 2.0

My test server also has a complete copy of Visual Studio .NET Enterprise Architect Edition installed. I installed this product as part of my normal test server setup, but you don't need it to use this book. That's one of the benefits of using Web Matrix; you don't need to install a more expensive product on your system. However, I've found that some Visual Studio .NET features such as remote debugging do come in handy. In many respects, Web Matrix and Visual Studio .NET are complimentary products that work well together. None of the text examples will assume that you have any version of Visual Studio .NET installed on your machine, however.

Creating the Client Setup

To get anywhere in this book, you'll have to have a development workstation. This is where you'll install Windows 2000 or Windows XP, write your code, and perform any desktop-level testing. For the most part, you'll want to avoid using your regular workstation for development for two reasons. First, there's no guarantee that an application is going to work the first time, and you don't want to crash the machine that contains all of your data. Second, you want to create the cleanest possible environment so that you know for sure that any bugs you're seeing are the result of application errors, not compatibility problems.

The version of Windows you install depends on personal taste and the number of machines you plan to use. You'll definitely want to install one of the server versions of Windows 2000 (or .NET Server when it arrives) if you only plan to use one machine as both a development workstation and a server. However, all of the programming examples in this book will work better and demonstrate more if you use two machines. (I'll always assume you have two machines: one with Windows 2000 Professional or Windows XP Professional installed for development purposes and one with Windows 2000 Server installed for the server.)

If you're using two machines, you can set the development workstation up using Windows 2000 Professional or Windows XP Professional. My test system is dual boot—it has both Windows 2000 Professional and Windows XP Professional installed. I'll use both products to test my applications so there's less chance that a version-specific error will creep in. I didn't test any of the examples in this book using any version of Windows 9x, and I don't consider Windows XP Home Edition a good business testing platform. Consequently, I don't guarantee that the examples will work on these systems. The reason you'd want to use a desktop operating system rather than the server version is so you that can get a better idea of how things will actually look from the user's perspective. The server versions include many features that the user won't see, and these features could possibly taint the results of any tests you perform.

For a development workstation that you're going to use exclusively for development and not for testing purposes, make sure you get a reasonably fast processor, a lot of RAM, and even more hard drive space. My test workstation includes 512 MB of RAM, dual 450 MHz Pentium II processors, and a 9 GB hard drive. This setup worked very well for my needs in creating code for this book— you'll obviously need to increase your hard drive space as you add more features and create applications that are more complex. Most developers will want a faster processor, as well, but this addition isn't a requirement.

The development workstation requires the Web Matrix installation, along with the .NET Framework. If you want to work with the mobile applications in this book, you'll very likely need one or more emulators for test purposes. We'll look at installation and various tradeoffs of both of these requirements in Chapter 2. My development workstation also includes a full installation of Visual Studio .NET Enterprise Architect Edition, some business applications (such as Microsoft Office), and a few graphics products (such as Paint Shop Pro). You won't need all of these other additions on your system, but you do need a browser of some type. I tested all of the applications using Internet Explorer.

TIP *You may not think about the font you use to work on your machine very often, but working with monospaced fonts all day can lead to eye strain, bugs (like when you confuse an l and a 1), and other problems. Microsoft's choice of Courier for a monospaced font hasn't been well received by many developers because it doesn't do the job very well. Fortunately, there are alternatives, some of which are free. Paul Neubauer's Web site, at* http://home.bsu.edu/prn/monofont/, *talks about how monospaced fonts are used on a typical Windows system and what replacement fonts are available should you decide you really don't like Courier. This Web site even includes reviews of the various fonts so that you can make a good choice the first time around.*

I initially tested every application on my development machine, then on the server, and, finally, on a test workstation. The test workstation is a 450 MHz Pentium machine with 256 MB of RAM and a 4 GB hard drive running Windows XP Professional Edition. The test workstation you use should reflect the standard issue machine for the environment in which the application will perform. Many enterprise users don't have modern 2.5 GHz systems with huge hard drives and a large amount of memory. The problem is that many developers test using this setup, and then the application fails when they deploy it. A clean test workstation is always a helpful addition to your toolbox.

Summary

This chapter has provided you with an overview of the Web Matrix development environment. We've discussed what this product is, how it can help you, and where you'll probably need to use something else. You've also learned about the basic Web Matrix features. Make sure you download Web Matrix from the Web site mentioned at the beginning of the chapter before you proceed to Chapter 2.

The final portion of this chapter illustrated the need to put a two-machine test environment. We also discussed the minimal requirements for such an environment as part of the test system description. One of the tasks you should perform now is to set up a test system before you proceed with the book.

Make sure you visit the Web sites listed in this chapter. You'll definitely want to check out the other support options for ASP.NET and see what's happening on the various Web Matrix newsgroups. These other sites can really enhance your Web Matrix experience.

Chapter 2 shows how to install and use the Web Matrix product. In addition, you can install the Microsoft Internet Toolkit if you want to work with the mobile examples in Chapter 9. This chapter provides an overview of the Web Matrix IDE. You'll also learn how to perform some basic tasks, such as connecting to the online gallery—an important part of using Web Matrix to its fullest extent.

Using Web Matrix

In This Chapter

- Learn How to Install Web Matrix

- Learn How to Install the Microsoft Mobile Internet Toolkit

- Discover the Web Matrix IDE Elements

- Learn How to Use FTP Workspaces

- Create Pseudo-Project-Oriented Workspaces

- Create Projectless Workspaces

- Discover the Online Component Gallery

- Learn About the Web Matrix File Types

In Chapter 1, we discussed all of the reasons that you might want to use Web Matrix for your next repair or new project. We have a few more preparatory tasks to perform before we begin the discussion of how to use Web Matrix. This chapter discusses the installation and setup of both the Microsoft Mobile Internet Toolkit and Web Matrix itself. You can skip these first two sections if you already have a working Web Matrix installation with all of the features you need.

In this chapter, we'll begin discussing how you use Web Matrix to perform various tasks. We'll start with an overview of the Web Matrix IDE. You'll learn about the various IDE features and see how to configure the environment. This chapter also discusses the various types of workspaces that you can create as part of the IDE discussion.

The latter part of the chapter tells you about the Web Matrix file types. Remember that Web Matrix is file-oriented, not project-oriented. Learning about the various file types is essential because they form the basis of what you can do with Web Matrix. This section also helps you understand which files you can edit from other platforms—one of the better Web Matrix features.

The final section of the chapter shows you the Online Component Gallery. This is where you can download new Web Matrix features. Web Matrix is an ongoing community project, so you can expect to see new additions to it from time to time.

Web Matrix Installation

Normally, you'll install Web Matrix before you install any of the other add-ons discussed in this chapter or the rest of the book. However, nothing I found in the documentation leads me to believe there's a specific order you need to follow. Generally, you'll want to install Web Matrix before you install database support. The following sections begin by showing you how to install Web Matrix.

NOTE *Single-machine developers—those who are using Web Matrix only as a learning tool—can rely on MSDE alone. Experimenters don't need to expend the time and energy to download a copy of SQL Server and install it. Consequently, these developers can skip the "Installing the Evaluation Version of SQL Server 2000" section of the chapter. In addition, a developer who only wants to learn about ASP.NET or Web Matrix can install all of the products on a single machine, rather than installing them on two machines as described throughout the book. As mentioned in the "Creating a Single-Machine Setup" section of Chapter 1, I tested the examples in this book on both single- and two-machine setups.*

Web Matrix actually includes support for both Microsoft Database Engine (MSDE) and SQL Server 2000. Of the two, MSDE has the lightest platform for developing your applications, but it's also the most limited. The most important problem is that MSDE has no interface other than the access provided by Web Matrix. Just a little additional download time will net you the SQL Server 2000 demonstration version, which is good for 120 days—more than sufficient to perform short tests. However, if you already have SQL Server installed on another machine, you'll want to use the MSDE option to create a connection to it. In some cases, you might want to install both products to create a more complete environment. The following sections contain instructions on how to install both products.

NOTE *No matter which database engine you use with Web Matrix, make sure you install the latest service pack for it if you're using the released (not the evaluation) version of the product. At the time of this writing, the most current service pack is SP2. You can download this service pack from* http://www.microsoft.com/sql/downloads/2000/sp2.asp. *The instructions in the following sections will tell you when to install the service pack. SP2 includes three downloads: one for SQL Server 2000, one of the Analysis Services Components, and one for MSDE. Make sure you download the correct service pack components. In addition, SP2 won't work with the evaluation version of either SQL Server 2000 or MSDE.*

General Installation

Download Web Matrix from http://www.asp.net/webmatrix/default.aspx if you haven't done so already. Web Matrix requires 2,565 KB of space on the local drive—you can't install it on a network drive. Make sure your local drive has the required space before you begin the installation. The following steps show you how to perform the Web Matrix installation.

1. Start the Web Matrix installation program. You'll see a Windows Installer dialog box for a few seconds while the installation program initializes. The Welcome dialog box will appear on screen when the initialization process is complete.

2. Click Next. You'll see a License Agreement dialog box.

3. Read the license agreement, select the agree option, and then click Next. (If you disagree with the license agreement, you'll need to exit the installation program at this point.) You'll see the Customer Information dialog box shown in Figure 2-1.

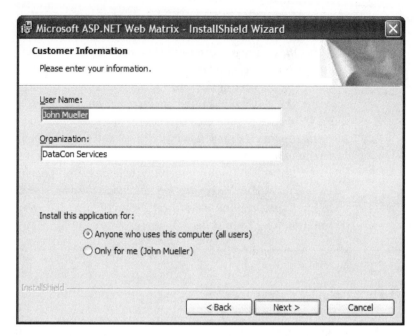

Figure 2-1. Select the appropriate customer options for your system.

4. Verify that the user name and organization (if any) are correct. Also, select an installation option. The default option installs Web Matrix so that everyone who has access to the computer can use it. You also have the option of installing it just for your use.

5. Click Next. You'll see the Custom Setup dialog box shown in Figure 2-2.

> **CAUTION** *If you click Space or Change, it appears that you can install Web Matrix on a network drive. However, if you choose a network drive, the installation program can freeze, forcing you to start the installation process over. Make sure you choose a local drive for installation.*

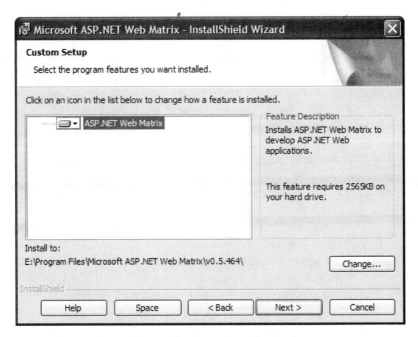

Figure 2-2. Choose an installation location for Web Matrix.

6. Verify that you have enough space to install Web Matrix by clicking Space and viewing the available space on the Disk Space Requirements dialog box. If the current drive doesn't have enough space, select the location you want to use for the installation by clicking Change and choosing the location using the Change Current Destination Folder dialog box.

7. Click Next. You'll see the Ready to Install the Program dialog box.

8. Click Install. The application will install.

9. Click Finish to complete the process.

At this point, Web Matrix is ready to use. If you don't want to work with database applications, you can skip the database installation in the following sections. However, we'll work with database applications in Chapters 5 and 9, so you might want to install one of the database options at least temporarily.

Installing the MSDE

You can get MSDE from a number of locations. For example, there's a link right on the Web Matrix site at http://www.asp.net/msde/default.aspx. The version of MSDE that you obtain from the Web Matrix site is the evaluation version, so you can't update it with SP2. The Web Matrix site also has a short set of MSDE installation instructions. You also get MSDE as part of a number of other products, including SQL Server 2000. The version of MSDE distributed with a released product does allow SP2 to complete. The SQL Server 2000 120-Day Evaluation CD also comes with a copy of MSDE. However, this version of MSDE is an evaluation copy and you can't update it.

NOTE *Many of the downloads in this book tend to be large. Always check the size of the download before you begin to ensure you have enough disk space and want to invest the time. For example, the MSDE download is 33 MB, which would require substantial time to download using a dial-up (56 Kbps) connection.*

Install MSDE even if you have SQL Server installed on another machine. Web Matrix won't allow you to connect to a remote database unless you have MSDE installed. You don't need a copy of MSDE installed if you install a local copy of SQL Server. We'll see how to create the remote connection in Chapter 5. For now, all you need to know is that MSDE is a required part of the Web Matrix database access strategy.

The copy of MSDE on the Web Matrix Web site is current as of the time of writing, but that won't always be true. To ensure you have the most current version of the product, it's best to view the MSDE overview found at http://www.microsoft.com/sql/techinfo/development/2000/MSDE2000.asp. Although this site doesn't include installation instructions, it does provide some good information about MSDE and tells what you can expect from it.

TIP *Generally, MSDE isn't manageable outside of an environment such as Web Matrix—it doesn't include the administration utilities provided by SQL Server. You can overcome this problem with a third-party product named MSDE Administration. Check the write-up at http://www.forward123.co.uk/ for details. You can download this product at http://www.msde.biz/.*

Once you have MSDE downloaded (or you have ordered the SQL Server CD and received it), it's time to install it. The following steps will show you how to install MSDE on your system.

> **NOTE** *The MSI extension stands for Microsoft Installer, so you need to have this product installed on your machine. Newer versions of Windows have the Microsoft Installer included by default. You can get a copy for Windows NT and Windows 2000 at* http://www.microsoft.com/downloads/release. asp?releaseid=32832&area=top&ordinal=8 *and Windows 9x at* http://www.microsoft.com/msdownload/platformsdk/ instmsi.htm?gssnb=1.

1. Unpack the MSDE.MSI file if you've downloaded it from the Internet. Make sure you use a temporary directory that doesn't contain anything else so you can erase the installation files later.

> **NOTE** *Setup provides a number of options that you'll find helpful. To see a full list of installation options, type* **Setup /?** *at the command prompt. If you already have a copy of MSDE installed and would like to install a second copy, then use the INSTANCENAME=<Instance Name> switch.*

2. Double-click SETUP.EXE (either on the SQL Server 2000 CD or in the temporary directory). You'll see a configuration dialog box. This dialog box will remain visible for up to a minute as the installation program configures MSDE.

> **NOTE** *The downloaded version of SP2 only works with the first instance of MSDE. If you have more than one instance of MSDE installed or have installed MSDE on the same machine more than one time, you'll probably need to order the SP2 CD. If you try to use the downloaded version of SP2 on an MSDE installation other than the first instance, you'll receive an error message. The most common error message is, "This installation package could not be opened. Verify that the package exists and that you can access it, or contact the application vendor to verify that this is a valid Windows Installer package."*

3. Double-click SQL2KDESKSP2.EXE (or an updated file) to install the service pack if you're using a released version of MSDE. The service pack will silently install and the installer will then terminate. At this point, MSDE is ready to use. However, you might also want to install the MSDE Administration graphical interface. If so, continue with Step 4.

4. Download MSDE.CAB from `http://www.msde.biz/download.htm` and extract the files into a temporary directory. (The CAB extension designates a cabinet file—a type of archive with features similar to a ZIP file.)

5. Double-click SETUP.MSI. You'll see a Welcome dialog box.

6. Click Next. You'll see an Installation folder dialog box.

7. Select a disk location. Choose between an installation that everyone can use and one that's only available to you. Click Next. You'll see a Confirm Installation dialog box.

8. Click Next. You'll see an Installing MSDE Query dialog box for a few moments. The Installation Complete dialog box will appear.

9. Click Finish. You now have an updated MSDE installation with MSDE Query to use as a configuration and management utility. We'll discuss this utility in detail in Chapter 5.

Testing the Installation

After you get everything installed, you'll probably want to perform a few checks to ensure the installation worked as anticipated. We'll look at how you actually use MSDE in Chapter 5. However, for now you'll want to verify that the MSDE Query works and that the patch you applied worked. The following steps help you verify both requirements.

1. Start MSDE Query. You'll see a license agreement dialog box. Read the agreement, check the Agree checkbox, and click OK. The application will start.

2. Click New on the toolbar. You'll see a Connect to SQL Server dialog box similar to the one shown in Figure 2-3. Notice that this dialog box has the (Local) option selected, which is the MSDE server we just installed. It also has the Windows NT Authentication option selected.

Figure 2-3. Select the (Local) server to make a connection to MSDE.

3. Make the appropriate selections and click OK. You'll see a Query window that includes a query area and a response area.

4. Type **SELECT @@VERSION** in the upper portion of the window. Click Execute. MSDE Query will display the MSDE version number, which you can use to validate the updated status of the product. Figure 2-4 shows a typical result.

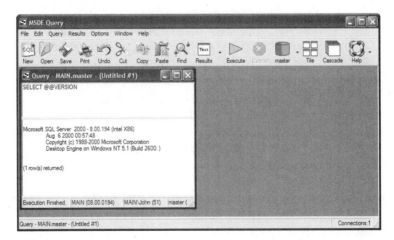

Figure 2-4. Use the Query window to verify the current version of MSDE installed on your system.

As you can see from Figure 2-4, the version number should read 8.00.532 for SP2. Make sure you verify the version number to ensure that your test applications run with the fewest problems. You'll also note that this check would have been impossible without MSDE Query because MSDE doesn't provide the tools to perform the check.

Installing the Evaluation Version of SQL Server 2000

The evaluation version of SQL Server 2000 will work for 120 days. You can use it to evaluate SQL Server and see how it compares to MSDE, which you can continue to use for free. Obviously, SQL Server has a lot more to offer than MSDE, which is a simple DBMS with no interface. However, because there are so many add-on utilities for MSDE, you'll want to spend time evaluating the two—especially if you're a small business owner who doesn't need everything that SQL Server can provide. Some developers are beginning to use MSDE as a less-expensive alternative for SQL Server if the conditions are right.

NOTE *This chapter assumes that you're using the evaluation version of SQL Server 2000. If you're using any other version of SQL Server, please follow the installation instructions that came with the product. Make sure that you install all applicable patches and upgrades before proceeding with the remainder of the chapter. For SQL Server 2000, this means using the SQL2KSP2.EXE service pack file as a minimum and SQL2KASP2.EXE if you have Analysis Services Components installed. You'll also want to download the post SP2 patch for SQL Server 2000 found at* http://www.microsoft.com/technet/treeview/default.asp?url=/technet/security/bulletin/MS02-056.asp. *Remember that SP2 won't install on the 120-day evaluation version of SQL Server 2000.*

Before you can begin this section, you need a copy of SQL Server to install on your test system. You can download or order the trial version from http://www.microsoft.com/sql/evaluation/trial/default.asp. Once you have a copy to install, use the following steps to install it. (Make sure you install SQL Server 2000 on the machine you intend to use as a server for the examples if you plan to follow the two-machine approach described in Chapter 1.)

1. Place the CD in the drive. It should automatically run the initial installation program. If it doesn't, you can start the installation program by double-clicking the AUTORUN.EXE file in the root directory. If you downloaded the SQL Server 2000 evaluation product from the Internet, double-click SETUP.BAT and proceed to Step 3.

2. Click SQL Server 2000 Components. You'll see three choices: Install Database Server, Install Analysis Services, and Install English Query. Select Install Database Server. You'll see the Welcome dialog box.

3. Click Next. You'll see the Computer Name dialog box shown in Figure 2-5. Notice that you can perform a local or remote installation from your computer. This procedure assumes you're performing a local installation on the server machine.

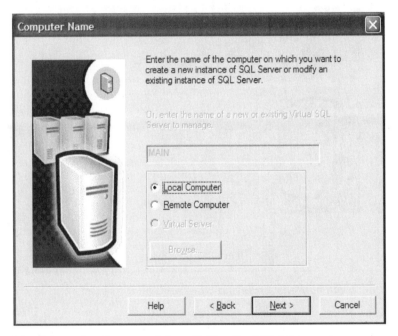

Figure 2-5. Select a local or remote installation for SQL Server.

4. Choose Local Computer and click Next. You'll see the Installation Selection dialog box. The Advanced Options choice gives you more control over the installation process. However, most people find that the default option, Create new instance of SQL Server, works fine for a test server setup.

5. Click Next. You'll see a User Information dialog box.

6. Verify the user information is correct and click Next. You'll see the Software License Agreement dialog box.

7. Read the licensing terms and click Yes. (If you click No at this point, the installation will fail.) You'll see the Installation Definition dialog box shown in Figure 2-6. Notice that this dialog box contains an option for installing just the client components. This feature comes in handy if you want to install the client components on your workstation for remote management of SQL Server.

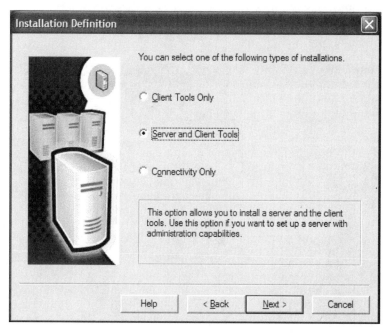

Figure 2-6. Install both the server and client tools on the server.

8. Click Next to choose the Server and Client Tools option. You'll see the Instance Name dialog box. Notice that this dialog box has the Default option checked. Keep this option checked for a single-server installation or you'll find that the SP2 downloaded from the Internet won't work. The downloaded version of SP2 depends on finding a default initial installation on the target machine.

9. Click Next. You'll see the Setup Type dialog box. This dialog box offers a choice of Typical, Minimal, or Custom installations. You can also choose the data paths used to store both the application and the data you generate. To keep this installation procedure simple, this chapter will assume you selected the Typical installation and default installation paths. However, it's worth the extra effort to use the Custom installation for a production server because you gain a lot of flexibility. In addition, a production server might require that you change the path information so SQL Server gains access to a larger data store on another drive.

10. Select Typical and then click Next. You'll see the Services Accounts dialog box. This dialog box can help you set up stronger security for SQL Server by choosing something other than the default account for the services that it offers. Using a custom account means that you can limit the resources that SQL Server can use and consequently the amount of exposure that SQL Server offers a potential cracker. The example will use the default settings because this is a test server. A production system should set the security provided for SQL Server with care in today's computing environment.

11. Click Next. You'll see the Authentication Mode dialog box. This dialog box offers an opportunity to change the SQL Server authentication mode. In general, you'll find that Windows Authentication Mode is a little more secure and simpler. However, it's incompatible with older applications, so you might need to use mixed mode authentication. The book assumes that you're using Windows Authentication Mode because the test server shouldn't have any older applications installed on it.

12. Click Next. You'll see the Start Copying Files dialog box.

13. Click Next. Setup will begin copying the files to your hard drive. When the copying process is complete, you'll see a completion dialog box.

14. Click Finish. The evaluation version of SQL Server 2000 is ready to use.

Microsoft Mobile Internet Toolkit Installation

The Microsoft Mobile Internet Toolkit (MMIT) is a collection of additional projects for your Visual Studio .NET or Web Matrix installation, along with support for certain types of mobile application development. You'd normally install this product after you install Web Matrix; however, there doesn't appear to be a preferred installation sequence in the documentation. MMIT includes support for

- Wireless Markup Language (WML) and Compact HyperText Markup Language (cHTM) cellular telephones

- HTML pagers

- Personal Digital Assistants (PDAs)

NOTE *Microsoft recently renamed MMIT to ASP.NET Mobile Controls. The change hasn't appeared on most of the Microsoft Web sites yet and on none of the third-party Web sites. Because MMIT is still the name that most people know about, I'll use the MMIT acronym throughout the book. However, any reference you see to ASP.NET Mobile Controls also applies to this product.*

It's important to note that MMIT includes support for the projects—the coding portion of the process. MMIT doesn't include any emulators or other test applications. You still need to provide either a real device for testing (preferred) or an emulation. We'll use the emulation option in this book because it's unlikely that we all have the same physical devices and using emulation helps you test more device types. However, you'll still want to test on the physical target device, whenever possible, because emulation doesn't provide a complete mobile environment. We'll discuss emulation more in the "Installing Mobile Device Emulation Support" section of Chapter 9.

As of this writing, you need to perform multiple downloads to obtain a complete copy of MMIT. The first is the main MMIT download at `http://msdn.microsoft.com/downloads/sample.asp?url=/MSDN-FILES/027/001/817/msdncompositedoc.xml`. Second, download the hot fixes for MMIT at `http://msdn.microsoft.com/vstudio/downloads/updates/mobileinternet.asp`. Third, download the set of device updates at `http://msdn.microsoft.com/downloads/sample.asp?url=/msdn-files/027/001/955/msdncompositedoc.xml`. The following steps show you how to install MMIT.

1. Double-click MOBILEIT.EXE to start the MMIT installation. You'll see a Welcome dialog box.

2. Click next. You'll see the licensing dialog box.

3. Read the licensing agreement, select the I accept the terms in the license agreement option, and then click Next. You'll see the Setup Type dialog box. Normally, you'll select the Complete option because there aren't any optional features if you're using Visual Studio .NET. However, if you're using Web Matrix by itself, you can save some disk space by selecting the Custom option and not installing the Mobile Internet Designer for Visual Studio .NET feature shown in Figure 2-7. You must install the Mobile Internet Controls Runtime. The documentation is an important but optional feature. This book assumes that you've performed a complete installation.

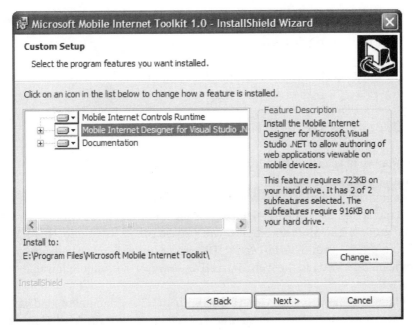

Figure 2-7. Using a custom installation has benefits for the Web Matrix developer.

4. Choose a Complete or Custom installation. Select Custom options if necessary. Click next and you'll see the Ready to Install the Program dialog box.

5. Click Next and the installation process will begin. After a few minutes, you'll see a completion dialog box.

6. Click Finish. You can now perform the first required MMIT patch.

7. Double-click MOBILEITQFE.EXE to start the MMIT hot fix. You'll see a dialog box quickly flit across the screen—you've installed the path. Let's move on to the second patch.

8. Double-click DUPDATE.EXE to start the MMIT update. You'll see the Welcome dialog box.

9. Click Next. You'll see the license dialog box.

10. Read and agree to the license agreement. Click Next. You'll see a Ready to Install Program dialog box.

11. Click Install. The installer will begin installing the update. You'll see a completion dialog box after a few seconds.

12. Click Finish. The MMIT installation is complete.

An Overview of Web Matrix IDE Elements

Now that we have installed everything required to create Web Matrix applications, it's time to look at the IDE. As mentioned in Chapter 1, the Web Matrix IDE is amazingly similar to the one used for Visual Studio .NET. That might not mean much for those who haven't used Visual Studio .NET, so I wrote this section with them in mind. Most developers who've used the Visual Studio .NET IDE will feel comfortable with the Web Matrix IDE almost immediately. There are some significant omissions in the Web Matrix IDE, however, so you might want to read on as well.

Figure 2-8 shows the Web Matrix IDE with an HTML document loaded. The interface is essentially the same no matter what document you load. However, you'll find that some features work with some documents and not with others. For example, you can't add a database connection to a standard HTML page, but you can to an ASP.NET page. The number of tabs will also change. Some documents, such as text files, only have one editing view. As shown in Figure 2-8, HTML pages have both an HTML view and a Design view. ASP.NET pages have the most tabs because they include three levels of coding views and a Design view. We'll explore each view as the book progresses.

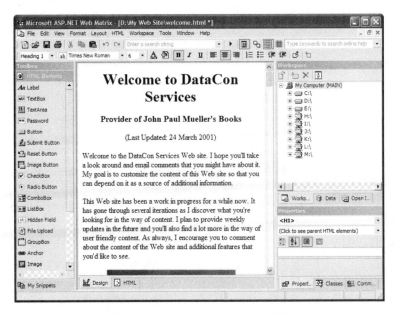

Figure 2-8. Using the Web Matrix IDE is similar to using Visual Studio .NET.

Some of the most important feature differences between the Web Matrix and Visual Studio .NET IDE include the loss of automation and special connectivity. For example, you won't find Solution Explorer in Web Matrix and there's no References folder. This means that any COM component you want to import requires hand coding. The Toolbox includes functionality to add controls, but only to certain tabs. The import feature also assumes the controls provide the required functionality—it displays an error message if they don't. Even so, the Web Matrix IDE is extremely friendly and quite easy to use. Table 2-1 describes the IDE elements.

Table 2-1. Web Matrix IDE Controls

CONTROL	DESCRIPTION
Toolbox	The Toolbox contains the controls you use to build a Web application. Each tab contains a group of controls for specific tasks, such as adding HTML features to the page. Some tabs, such as HTML Elements, won't allow you to add new controls. Other tabs will allow you to add controls from local or online sources, but only if the controls provide some type of Web functionality. You can also use the Toolbox to store code snippets. This feature enables you to create short function elements and then add them to your application with a simple drag and drop.
Editing area with views	The editing area changes according to the type of file you load and the view you choose. All files provide some type of text editing view for code or information. Some files provide multiple coding views and others provide at least one Design view. The Design view helps you create applications quickly because you can drag and drop controls onto it. Generally, you'll find that Web Matrix provides some extra features in this area, such as keyword color coding, but doesn't support all of the features of advanced IDEs, such as automatic code completion.
Menu	You'll find all of the commands for managing, editing, saving, configuring, and otherwise manipulating your project on the menu. We'll discuss the menu commands in detail as the book progresses.
Toolbars	In general, the toolbars contains the commands that the design team thought you'd use most often. Unlike many applications, you can't configure or hide the toolbars. However, most developers will find the list of shortcuts they provide are more than adequate to perform any editing task.
Workspace window	When you start Web Matrix, this window contains a list of your local and network drives. You can use the hierarchical display to select a file to edit. The Workspace window also displays remote connections when you make them. For example, if you connect to an FTP site, the content of this site will appear in the Workspace window, and you can select files from it just as you can locally.

(continued)

Table 2-1. Web Matrix IDE Controls (continued)

CONTROL	DESCRIPTION
Database window	You must install database support before this window becomes active. Once you have either local SQL Server or MSDE support installed, this window helps you create connections to data sources, even those on remote machines. Web Matrix helps you perform an amazing number of database tasks for a product its size. For example, you can create new databases, tables, and other data elements.
Open Items window	Use this window to see which items you have open. This window replicates the functionality of the Window menu to an extent. However, it's easier to use the Window menu if you need to switch between documents quickly.
Properties window	The Properties window contains a list of property values you can change for the currently selected object. You'll use the Properties window to configure a control before you add any code to it. In addition, this window contains a complete set of events for the control, so you can add event handlers to your application quickly. The Properties window contains buttons to arrange the properties in alphabetical order or by category. The bottom of the window contains an explanation of the use of the currently selected property. Some properties also include drop-down list boxes that help you set values. In short, this Properties window works about the same as the Properties window found in any IDE.
Classes window	This is a unique window that you won't find anywhere else. It lists the elements of the .NET Framework including namespaces, classes, and interfaces. Double-clicking an entry displays a synopsis of that element.
Community window	Use this window to learn more about the ASP.NET community in general and the Web Matrix community specifically. The Community window provides access to a wealth of online resources you can use to learn more about Web Matrix. In addition, you'll find discussion groups and sources of additional resources.

(continued)

Table 2-1. Web Matrix IDE Controls (continued)

CONTROL	DESCRIPTION
View Tabs	The view tabs help you switch between different views of the same file. As mentioned earlier, some files only have one view, which means you won't see any view tabs. Any file that provides two or more views will include these view tabs to make it easier to change views.
Toolbox Tab	The number of toolbox tabs you see depends on the file you have open, the view you've selected, and the preferences you have set. Click the tab that you want to see in the toolbox. Unlike other IDEs, you can't add or remove tabs from the toolbox.

We need to discuss a few additional IDE characteristics before the book progresses much further. The first is the Preferences dialog box shown in Figure 2-9. You access this dialog box using the Tools ➢ Preferences command.

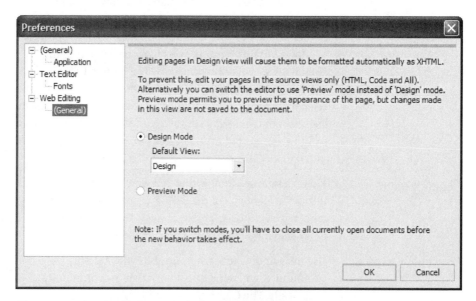

Figure 2-9. Use the Preferences dialog box to control the appearance of the editing and design features of Web Matrix.

The (General)\Application option contains settings that determine if Web Matrix asks to create a new file when you start it and specifies how many entries appear on the Recent Files menu. The Text Editor\Fonts option determines the font used for source code editing and printing. You have separate control over each of these elements.

The Web Editing\(General) option determines the editing mode used for the Web pages. If you choose Design Mode, all of the changes appear as XHTML. Preview Mode enables you to display the page as it will appear on screen, but it doesn't save any changes you make—you have to make the changes in one of the code views. Changing this option won't change the appearance of data on the screen. You must close the document first, and then reopen it to see the change.

Let's discuss the Classes window in a little more detail. As previously mentioned, the Classes window displays a list of namespaces, classes, and other .NET Framework elements. Figure 2-10 shows a typical example of this list. Notice that I've highlighted the MxDataGridField class.

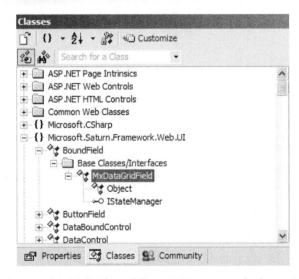

Figure 2-10. A hieriarchical display of the .NET Framework classes in the Classes window

As you can see, the entire Classes window is one large hierarchical display. Figure 2-10 shows the default display. You can also display the elements by assembly. In addition, you can sort the display in various ways to make it easier to find a particular element. For example, you can sort the classes by visibility instead of alphabetical order. The window normally excludes nonpublic classes, but you can choose to display them if wanted. Click the Customize button to add or remove elements from the list.

When you double-click one of the elements, you'll see a display similar to the one shown in Figure 2-11. As you can see, the display provides a short synopsis of the element and details on any other elements it contains, including methods, events, and properties. Notice that the dialog box doesn't actually provide a description of the element. However, you can click one of the links to learn more about the element online and see examples of how to use it.

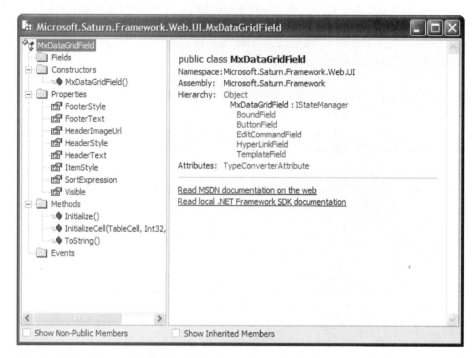

Figure 2-11. Although Web Matrix lacks online help, it does provide this useful display.

At first, it might seem as if the lack of online help would be a problem. However, considering the audience for this product, the development team has hit upon a great way to reduce the footprint of the product and still provide good help information. Many developers will find all they need without going online. Those who don't will probably have an Internet connection anyway because they're working on a Web-based application.

Using the Workspace

The Web Matrix workspace is the focal point of your interaction with the outside world. Every document you can access appears in the Workspace window somewhere. Of course, for the developer, the Workspace window isn't simply a replacement for Windows Explorer—it's actually a replacement for Solution Explorer. The following sections describe how a workspace approach differs from the project approach used by Visual Studio .NET and many other high-end IDEs.

Understanding the Web Matrix Usage Strategy

The Web Matrix usage strategy is the same strategy that developers have used for years—the file is the center of the developer universe. Only recently have vendors decided that developers need complex project files to manage their applications. If you're working on a large application, such an approach is both welcome and required. However, Web Matrix is the tool that lets you do easy things fast, so it uses the file-oriented approach of the past.

Of course, now that we've gotten used to using project files and stuffing multiple applications in one folder, going back to the easy way of managing an application will require a little change in thought patterns. However, there's another element to consider about Web Matrix. This product isn't designed to work on your desktop application—it's designed to work with your Web-based application. The difference between the two environments is interesting because good Web site design dictates using separate folders to contain each page or at least each group of pages.

This issue brings me to a point that some developers miss. I've actually seen Web servers where all of the files for the entire Web site reside in one or two folders—all mixed together and nearly impossible to work with. Web Matrix can actually force you to focus on the organizational problems of your Web site. Using the individual file approach means that the IDE no longer organizes the mess that's a Web server into something the developer can use—the Web site now stays messy.

In short, Web Matrix is a blast to the past and a look at the future. It's a useful tool that helps you see things as they are and enables you to make changes to your Web application quickly. However, as you'll learn throughout the book, Web Matrix also requires a different perspective—it's a tool that forces you to think about some application elements that you might not have considered for quite some time.

FTP

The first way that I used Web Matrix was as a means to connect to an FTP site and make some updates. An FTP workspace doesn't look like a remote connection—it looks like any other workspace you construct on your machine. Figure 2-12 shows a typical example of an FTP workspace. Notice that the FTP site is obvious because it starts at the same level as My Computer in the Workspace window.

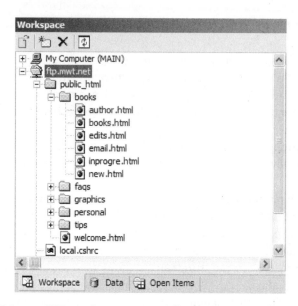

Figure 2-12. Using an FTP workspace is no different from working on a local drive.

FTP sites provide good workspaces for Web Matrix because each user generally has a specific folder to use for their application. In short, each virtual FTP site is a separate Web application. When the user or small business logs in, all they see is a view similar to the one shown in Figure 2-12. The enforced separation of projects on FTP sites is a good start. Of course, nothing forces the user to organize the content of the Web application logically after they log onto the system. However, Web Matrix encourages organization by showing files in easy-to-find groups when the user creates the folders to store them.

Of all the workspace strategies, the FTP approach is the most automatic. This is the only "project" creation technique that's completely automatic. However, as we'll see in the sections that follow, there are other ways to create the appearance of a project in Web Matrix without resorting to using an actual project file.

Pseudo-Project-Oriented

Web Matrix provides the means for creating shortcuts in the Workspace window. Figure 2-13 shows an example of such a shortcut. Notice that the shortcut shows the name of the folder, but you can't access anything above the level of the shortcut in the hierarchy. In short, this is a truncated view of the data at some location.

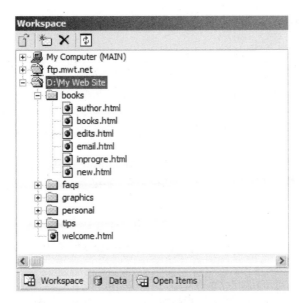

Figure 2-13. Although Web Matrix lacks online help, it does provide this useful display.

So why is the view in Figure 2-13 a pseudo-project? Web Matrix has a file orientation, but as you can see, the Workspace window only displays files in the area of interest when you use a shortcut. Consequently, the folders provide a project container without the use of an actual project file.

Of course, the shortcut only provides an organizational tool. Web Matrix won't load all of the files in a given shortcut if you double-click it. The environment is always the same when you start—Web Matrix makes no attempt to store your IDE configuration from one session to the next.

Some limitations of the pseudo-project are limitations of Web Matrix itself, but these are so minor, I hate to call them such. For example, when you open a project in Visual Studio, you can click a button to compile the project. Web Matrix lacks a compiler, so there wouldn't be any button to push. In addition, most Web applications don't require a compiler unless you plan to create components for them. The lack of compiler support really isn't that big of a problem after all.

We'll use the concept of a pseudo-project throughout the book because it provides an easy way to demonstrate various Web Matrix features without creating a connection to a Web site. As the book progresses, I hope you'll see just how useful the pseudo-project approach is in creating basic Web applications—the type that Web Matrix is best suited to manage.

Projectless

I included a separate section for the projectless workspace because this is what you begin with when you install the project. All you see is the list of drives, folders, and files that you can access from your machine. However, it isn't always necessary to create a project when working with Web Matrix. Sometimes all you need to do is change the content of a single file or create a new file for an existing folder. Developers haven't based the idea that you always have to have a project to build any Web application on any physical limitation. In days gone by, no one used projects and applications still appeared on the market. In the end, project files are a management tool.

Connecting to the Online Component Gallery

Right now, you have a spiffy new copy of Web Matrix installed on your machine and it has a standard set of controls you can use to create basic applications. In fact, the controls you have will create some complex applications too. However, let's assume for a moment that you don't have every control you'll ever need. Few programmers that I know have every control they need. The collection and use of new and unusual controls is almost an obsession with some developers—others display them as trophies on a wall or as a precious set of collectibles.

You have two ways to satisfy your desire for new controls to display as proud additions to your next application. The first technique is to create your own controls. We'll explore that alternative in Chapter 6. However, for now, we'll look at one way to get new controls by acquiring them from someone else. The following steps show you how to gain access to the Online Component Gallery and use it to add new controls to your Toolbox.

1. Create a new ASP.NET document. It doesn't matter what you name it because you'll discard it later.

2. Select the Custom Controls tab of the Toolbox.

> **NOTE**   *You must have an online connection before you proceed to Step 3. Otherwise, Web Matrix won't find any custom controls that you can use.*

3. Right-click in the controls area of the Toolbox and choose Add Online Toolbox Components from the context menu. You'll see an Online Component Gallery dialog box similar to the one shown in Figure 2-14.

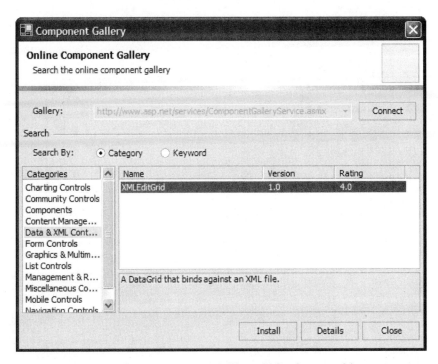

Figure 2-14. Use the Online Component Gallery dialog box to add new custom controls to your Toolbox.

4. Select the component category of interest.

5. Select the control of interest within that category.

6. Click Install. You'll see the Security Warning dialog box shown in Figure 2-15 if you have your machine set up for secure communications.

7. Click Yes if you approve of the vendor supplying the control. Web Matrix will download and install the new control for you. (If you select No, Web Matrix will terminate the download and you won't be able to use the control.) Once Web Matrix completes the download, you'll see the Install to GAC dialog box shown in Figure 2-16. You can use the control locally if you download it and don't install it to the Global Assembly Cache (GAC). If you want to make the control accessible to all applications, then you need to install it in the GAC.

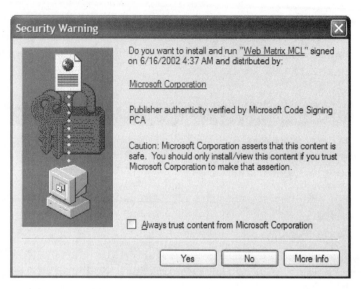

Figure 2-15. Web Matrix displays a Security Warning dialog box if you set your machine up to require this feature.

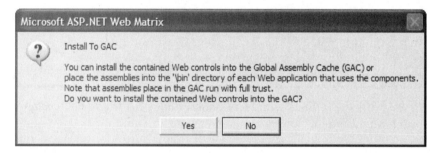

Figure 2-16. Downloading the control means its available for use, but you still need to say where to put it.

TIP *It's generally a good idea to test a control locally if you aren't sure you want it on your machine. Installing it to the GAC means you'll spend extra time trying to get rid of the control if it doesn't provide functionality that you thought it would.*

8. Click Yes or No depending on how you want to install the control. If you choose No, Web Matrix will display the dialog box show in Figure 2-17 that provides instructions on how to use the control locally. Make sure you follow the instructions closely, or your application won't work as anticipated.

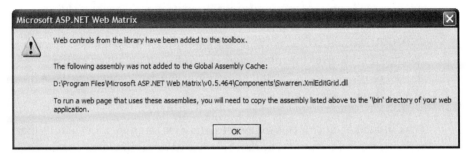

Figure 2-17. Always place a control in local storage, rather than the GAC, if you aren't sure how well it will work.

The Online Component Gallery dialog box currently has one nonoperational field that I hope the development team eventually changes. Notice in Figure 2-14 that the Gallery field is grayed out. This field will eventually allow you to connect to other sources for additional controls.

An Overview of Web Matrix File Types

We'll study the various Web Matrix file types in detail as the book progresses. In fact, just looking at the chapter names will give you a good idea of what types of file support Web Matrix provides. The number of projects you can create is extensive and you can always add to this support by creating templates of your own. It's also a good idea to have an overview of what type of file support you can expect from Web Matrix. The following list provides you with a brief overview of the files that we'll study in detail as the book progresses.

General Web: You'll find support for a number of generic Web pages. The most important of these is the HTML file. However, you'll also find style sheets and even text files as part of the list. Of course, many other generic Web page types use simple text that you could create and edit with Web Matrix. This need is the reason why it's important to know how to create new templates that you might require.

XML: Web Matrix provides a number of XML and XML-related page types provided with Web Matrix. Many developers associate XML with a specific need. For example, you might think that XML data manipulation is the technique used to create Web services. Another developer might view XML as the means for displaying content on screen by using a style sheet to present it. The fact is that XML is used for a lot of reasons today, so this might actually present one of the most used page types in Web Matrix.

ASP.NET: The main focus of Web Matrix is the ASP.NET page, so that's the file type that receives the most attention. Unfortunately, Web Matrix doesn't provide support for ASP directly, but you can always edit these files as standard text files.

Database: Most businesses today use databases for more applications than most are willing to admit. The database has become the indispensable application for every business, no matter how large or small it is. Web Matrix places a special emphasis on database needs. Of course, you'll still find plenty of room for customization, but the default projects provide a good place to start. Not only do you have a variety of data presentation and manipulation pages to choose from, but you also have access to a number of data reports—an essential element for any database application.

Mobile: Some developers are only just beginning to think about mobile applications, but this really is the next area where most developers will spend their time. The problem today is that mobile devices come in so many shapes and sizes that it's hard to create a one-size-fits-all application to meet every need. Web Matrix provides a set of forms that emphasize flexibility to make it easier to develop Web applications. Of course, thorough testing is also a requirement for this application type.

Web Services: You'll find support for all of the standard Web service page types in Web Matrix. For example, Web Matrix includes a special page for sending SOAP messages. You'll also find pages that help make Web service communication more efficient and satisfy standard requirements. We'll explore some customization techniques later in the book that will help you address specific needs as well.

As you can see, Web Matrix supports a broad spectrum of page types that you can use to create relatively complex applications. I've made a special point of looking at every default page type that Web Matrix supports somewhere in this book. By the time you finish, you should know just how far Web Matrix can go in supporting your favorite application.

Summary

This chapter began by showing how to install both Web Matrix and the Microsoft Mobile Internet Toolkit, which contains some additional mobile projects. It's also shown you many of the basic usage details of Web Matrix. You've learned about the various workspace usage techniques and explored the file types that Web Matrix supports. Finally, we discussed how to connect to the Online Component Gallery.

At this point, you'll probably want to check out some of the files you can work with and learn about any limitations that you need to know. You'll also want to explore the Web sites listed in this chapter and begin participating in online discussions.

In Chapter 3, we begin coding a variety of projects. The first project is a simple Web site. This is a good first project because you can start using some of the features that Web Matrix provides in an environment that most developers have worked in before. The project is on the same level as what most small businesses that don't have an online store would use—it's an informational Web site.

Part Two

Developing Applications with Web Matrix

CHAPTER 3

Building a Simple Web Site

In This Chapter

- Learn How to Access Files Using Web Matrix

- Create an HTML Page

- Create a Text File

- Create a Style Sheet

- Develop a Simple HTML Example

- Learn to Use the ASP.NET Page

- Discover the Differences Between Code Behind and Inline Code

- Create a WEB.CONFIG Page

- Create a GLOBAL.ASAX Page

- Learn About the ASP.NET HTTP Handler Page

About now, some of you out there are probably wondering when the book's going to get interesting—after all, you've developed many Web sites in the past, so this chapter can't present much that you haven't seen before. Actually, I hope to surprise you in the new technique area, but that isn't the point of this chapter. This chapter will show you how Web Matrix can help you perform the tasks that you've been doing a lot faster and with fewer hassles.

The point of using Web Matrix is that you don't have to worry about which platform you're working with, at least not when working with the common Web files—those with HTML or XML extensions. It doesn't matter if you normally use FrontPage or Visual Studio .NET to formulate your artistic creations. You don't have to have any ASP or ASP.NET experience to use Web Matrix. I've used this product to access my files on an Apache server and it looks just like Internet Information Server (IIS)—which, by the way, is the Web server we'll use for test purposes in this book. The point is, this is a product for *everyone*—it doesn't matter where you've been before. Consequently, the best way to start learning about Web Matrix is by looking at the applications that everyone understands.

The fact that you can access *anything, anywhere*, with Web Matrix is so important that we'll discuss this topic first in the chapter. You'll find that Web Matrix makes this process so incredibly easy and natural that you'll really feel for anyone who has to use anything else.

The next step is working with some basic files that everyone knows about. We'll start with a text file—how is that for easy? The chapter will move on to HTML files and style sheets. Once you know how to work with these simple files, we'll build a Web site example that uses them. At this point, you might not have learned any new techniques, but you will have learned that Web Matrix can handle common file editing on any type of server you own.

> **NOTE** *You might wonder why the chapter doesn't include an ASP (as opposed to ASP.NET) example. First, Web Matrix doesn't create that type of file directly. You can create an "ASP file" as a standard text file and Web Matrix will edit existing files, but there isn't any special functionality to discuss. Second, many developers are moving on to ASP.NET because it provides so many enhancements over ASP.*

The chapter moves on to ASP.NET at this point. We'll discuss construction of a simple ASP.NET page. You'll notice that the pages in Web Matrix rely on inline code, so we'll discuss that issue next. The next step is creating a simple ASP.NET example that you can test on a server—this is a fully functional example, but it concentrates more on putting a project together, rather than on performing some difficult task.

The final sections of the chapter describe some of the special Web site files you'll use with IIS. You'll learn about the GLOBAL.ASAX and WEB.CONFIG files and how you can modify them with Web Matrix. We'll also discuss the ASP.NET HTTP Handler page. Finally, we'll create a more complex ASP.NET example so you can begin seeing just how well this technology works.

File Access Techniques

Web Matrix helps you access your files, both locally and online, through the Workspace window. As previously mentioned, Web Matrix automatically displays all local and network drives you can access when you start the application. Any FTP site that you want to use will require special configuration. The following sections address the topic of file access.

Accessing Local Files

You can access local files using the Workspace window. As shown in Figure 3-1, this window provides a hierarchical view of your data. This form of local access is available so long as you have Web Matrix open. All you need to do is locate the file you want to open.

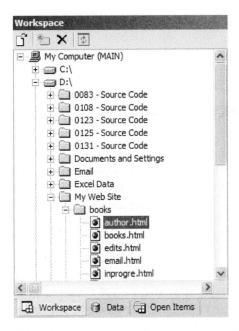

Figure 3-1. Use the Workspace window as needed to locate local resources.

As mentioned in Chapter 2, you can create a shortcut to a particular directory if you want to. This places that directory at the same level as My Computer, making access of a deeply nested resource easier. To create a shortcut, right-click the folder you want to use as the root of the shortcut in the Workspace window and select Custom Actions ➤ Create Shortcut from the context menu. Web Matrix will create the new shortcut for you, as shown in Figure 3-2. You could also use the Workspace ➤ Add Folder Shortcut command to perform this task.

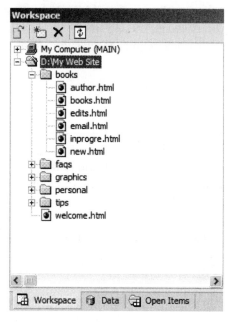

Figure 3-2. Creating shortcuts makes it easier to access projects.

Although the application doesn't add a shortcut to the context menu associated with a file that Web Matrix can open, you can perform this task yourself by modifying the file type configuration. Most versions of Windows make this task easy, but I'll include short instructions for Windows XP.

1. Open a copy of Windows Explorer, and use the Tools ➤ Folder Options command to open the Folder Options dialog box.

2. Locate a file type associated with Web Matrix, such as ASPX, in the Registered File Types list found on the File Types tab.

3. Click Advanced and you'll see an Edit File Type dialog box for the extension that you highlighted.

4. Click New. You'll see a New Action dialog box.

5.	Type a name for the action such as **Edit with Web Matrix**. Use the Browse button to locate your copy of Web Matrix. Type a **"%1"** after the executable filename. You must include the double quotes around the %1. For example, the entry in my Application used to perform action field is

```
"D:\Program Files\Microsoft ASP.NET Web Matrix\WebMatrix.exe" "%1"
```

6.	Check Use DDE. Type **WebMatrix** in the Application field and **System** in the Topic field. Your dialog box should look similar to the one shown in Figure 3-3.

Figure 3-3. Adding Web Matrix to the file extension context menus is easy with this dialog box.

7.	Click OK twice, and then click Close to close the Folder Options dialog box.

You can use this technique to add Web Matrix support to every file type it supports on your system. Now a simple right-click on the file will reveal an Open with Web Matrix option that you can use to start the application and load the file without performing a lot of extra steps.

NOTE *You'll find the FileTypes.REG file in the source code file for Chapter 3, available from the Downloads section on the Apress Web site (http://www.apress.com/book/download.html). Double-click this file to add the Open with Web Matrix option to all supported file extensions with one easy click. The REG file assumes that you've installed Web Matrix to the default C:\Program Files\Microsoft ASP.NET Web Matrix\v0.5.464\ folder. If you haven't, then you'll need to edit the REG file with any pure text editor—don't use a product such as Word because it adds nontext characters. (The REG file doesn't include the graphics file types because Web Matrix can only display these files.)*

Using the FTP Connection

You won't see any FTP connections when you open Web Matrix. This makes sense because no one knows where you'll want to connect. Unfortunately, the connections you create aren't permanent, so you'll need to create the FTP connections you require each time you start Web Matrix. (After spending a while working with the configuration files for Web Matrix, I'm relatively sure you can't add permanent connections by modifying the configuration file.) However, creating an FTP connection is relatively painless. The following steps show you how.

1. Right-click My Computer in the Workspace window and choose New Workspace ➤ Add FTP Connection from the context menu. You'll see the New FTP Connection dialog box shown in Figure 3-4.

2. Type the location of the FTP site in the FTP Site field. You don't need to include the protocol.

3. Verify the port address listed in the Port field. Generally, you'll find that this port works fine. However, the Webmaster for the site that has your Web files on it might use a different port for security reasons.

4. Type your user name and password in the User Name and Password fields. You don't have to type anything in the Web URL field. However, adding an entry to this field enables Web Matrix to go to the Web site to test the changes you make when you use the View ➤ Start command.

New FTP Connection   [X]

FTP Connection
Enter information about the FTP site and your user identity.

FTP Site: [   ]

Port: [21   ]

User Name: [   ]

Password: [   ]

Web URL: [   ]

[OK]   [Cancel]

Figure 3-4. Use this dialog box to describe a new FTP connection.

NOTE   *You might see an odd problem when using the Web URL field in some cases. One ISP that I work with places all of the content for a Web site in a public_html folder. Consequently, the path to the Welcome.HTML file is* `ftp://ftp.mwt.net/public_html/Welcome.HTML`. *When I type the URL for the Web site in the Web URL field (*`http://www.mwt.net/~jmueller/` *as an example), Web Matrix adds the full FTP path information to the starting URL. In this example, the actual starting URL according to Web Matrix is* `http://www.mwt.net/~jmueller/public_html/welcome.html` *when I use the Start ➤ View command. The actual URL is* `http://www.mwt.net/~jmueller/welcome.html`, *so the browser doesn't display the correct information. As you can see, Web Matrix doesn't provide a way to overcome the extra folder level on the FTP site. A minor modification to the URL displayed on the browser's Address field fixes the problem, but you need to be aware of the problem when working with Web Matrix on FTP sites.*

5. Type an entry in the Web URL field, if desired.

6. Click OK. Web Matrix will create the new FTP connection.

Web Matrix caches your FTP information locally as you navigate through the various folders. Consequently, the first access of a folder on an FTP site might take a while (depending on your connection), but subsequent access should be much faster. Of course, the caching effect only lasts for the current session. When you close the FTP connection or Web Matrix, the cached information is gone as well. Even so, the use of a local cache does make working with Web Matrix fast.

Creating New Files

Eventually, you'll want to move from looking at files that already exist to creating some new content of your own. Web Matrix provides a number of ways to create new files. The four most common methods are

- Use the File ➤ New command.

- Click New File on the toolbar.

- Use the Workspace ➤ Add New Item command.

- Right-click a folder in the Workspace window and choose Add New Item from the context menu.

The first two methods will create a new file in the default project folder. Web Matrix defines the default project folder as the folder you have been using for all other new files. The last two methods will create a new file in a specific location—the folder you select using the Workspace window. In both cases, you'll see an Add New File dialog box similar to the one shown in Figure 3-5.

Notice that the left pane contains categories of templates, while the right pane contains the individual templates. A third window contains a description of the template and its purpose.

Depending on the type of file you want to create, you'll see some additional entries on the Add New File dialog box. For example, in Figure 3-5, you'll notice that you can select the language used to program the ASP.NET template. In addition, you can specify the class information used within the resulting file. You can also provide these types of additions when you create custom templates, but you'll find the information more difficult to add because it requires custom programming.

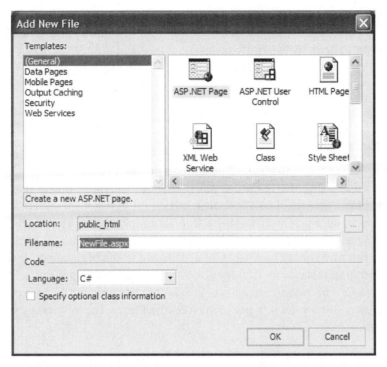

Figure 3-5. Creating a new file means selecting a template from this dialog box.

Using the HTML Page

It's time to learn about the first type of project you can create with Web Matrix—the HTML page. HTML pages are one of the few universal page types you can create—every Web server in the world supports the HTML page. Of course, some Web servers support the HTML extension, while others, such as IIS, support the HTM extension. Web Matrix assumes that you want to create a page with an HTM extension.

NOTE *If you attempt to create a file with an HTML extension, Web Matrix will also add an HTM extension to it. For example, a file that you name Test1.HTML will appear as Test1.HTML.HTM. The only way around this problem is to rename the document after you create it.*

The following sections provide some basic insights into create an HTML page using Web Matrix. The purpose of these sections is to demonstrate the HTML page template, not necessarily to create an example that you'd use on a Web site. We'll create a simple Web site in the "A Simple HTML Example" section later in this chapter.

Designing a Good Update Policy

Normally, I create Web pages on a local drive, and then save them to the production server using an FTP connection. Using this technique means that I always have a backup of my Web site on a local drive. If some nefarious cracker decides to wreak havoc with my Web site, I can simply upload a new copy of the affected pages. In addition, this technique helps me maintain a tape backup of the Web site when I back up my personal drive at the end of each day. Web Matrix doesn't support this update strategy directly, so you'll need to perform a little setup first. One of the best ways to get Web Matrix to cooperate with you is to create a new connection for it to use in My Network Places. The following steps show you how.

1. Open My Network Places and locate the Add Network Place icon. Double-click the Add Network Place icon to start the Add Network Place Wizard. You'll see a Welcome dialog box.

2. Click Next. The wizard will ask where you want to create the network place. You'll normally have a choice of the MSN Communities or another type of connection.

3. Select Choose Another Network Location and click Next. The wizard will ask you to enter the address of the network location.

4. Type the address of the FTP site, such as **ftp://ftp.mwt.net**. Click Next. The wizard will ask you about site security.

5. Clear the Log On Anonymously option. This action will enable you to enter your name in the User Name field. (Notice that you don't enter a password at this point—you'll need to add this information later.) Type your name and click Next. The wizard will ask what you want to name your new location.

6. Type a site name and click Next. You'll see a completion dialog box. This dialog box includes an option for automatically opening the connection you created. It's always a good idea to open the connection to ensure you set it up properly.

7. Click Finish. The Add Network Place Wizard will add the new connection to My Network Places. You should also see the connection open. If not, then you might have to re-create the connection to ensure you entered the location information correctly. Now that you have an FTP connection, you can use it to save your document online.

8. Use the File ➤ Save As command to display the Save Document As dialog box shown in Figure 3-6. Notice that the dialog box includes a My Network Places icon.

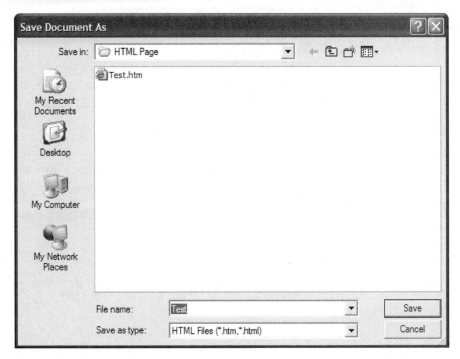

Figure 3-6. Use the Save Document As dialog box to store your document in another location.

9. Click My Network Places. You'll see a list of icons found in the My Network Places folder, including the connection you just created.

10. Double-click the FTP connection. You'll see a Log On As dialog box similar to the one shown in Figure 3-7. Notice that you can use this dialog box to log on anonymously.

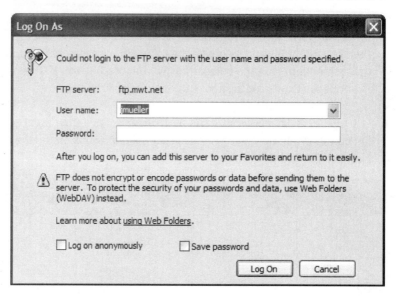

Figure 3-7. Enter your password for an FTP site using this dialog box.

11. Type your password in the Password field. Click Log On. Web Matrix will scan the FTP site and display its contents in the Save Document As dialog box.

CAUTION   *The Log On As dialog box contains an option for Windows to remember your password. Using this feature will open a security hole because anyone with access to your machine can also log on to the FTP site. Always enter your password manually to reduce the probability of cracker interference with your Web site. Of course, it goes without saying that you should take whatever other security steps you can, including the use of WebDAV—a feature explained when you click the link shown in Figure 3-7.*

12. Click Save to complete the process.

Sometimes the Save Document As dialog box will refuse to work as anticipated—the cause might be something as simple as an imperfect connection with the FTP server. In these cases, you can still open the connection in My Network Places or Windows Explorer and transfer the file from your local drive to the FTP site manually. The process takes the same amount of time—you just have to get out of the IDE to do it.

Designing the HTML Page

Most of you have probably created HTML code. However, it's important to understand the Web Matrix way of performing this task. For a product this small, it sure makes the task of creating a Web site fast. First, let's look at the tools you have to use. The Toolbox contains all of the objects shown in Figure 3-8. As you can see, this is a standard list of HTML objects, but you can use them to create most Web page types.

Figure 3-8. Creating a Web site is easy using the objects in the Toolbox.

NOTE *This chapter only discusses applications for desktop machines. Chapter 9 will discuss applications that work on desktop machines and mobile devices, with an emphasis on mobile device development. You'll learn how to create examples that work equally well on PDAs and cellular telephones.*

In addition to the Toolbox objects, you also have the options on the Format and HTML menus shown in Figure 3-9. You can create all of the effects that an HTML page has to offer. For example, you have full access to the recognized heading levels and techniques for creating hyperlinks. These options also help you set the page colors and perform tasks such as wrapping sections in a <DIV> or a <SPAN> tag.

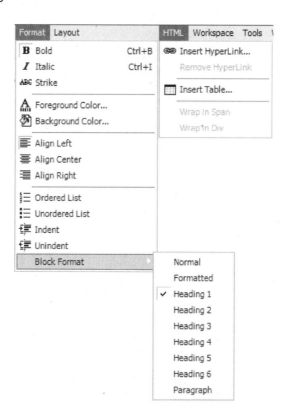

Figure 3-9. Use the Format and HTML menu options as needed to modify the appearance of your document and associated objects.

You can do a lot of the work required to create a simple Web page by dragging and dropping controls onto the Design window. Select the controls to set their properties in the Properties window. Obviously, some of the changes you make to your page will include text, using heading levels, and working with other nonobject design elements. Figure 3-10 shows the simple Web page we'll use for this portion of the example. Notice that I've included some organizational elements, a couple of objects, some plain text, and a few other elements.

Figure 3-10. The example Web page contains a number of elements for testing purposes.

Adding Code to the HTML Page

At this point, you could save the Web page, and all of the user interface elements but the two pushbuttons would work as expected. However, the code is far from complete. The default template doesn't assume much. In fact, the default template contains a few minimal lines of code, as shown in Listing 3-1. Adding text, objects, and other HTML features does little to improve this situation. You can modify the templates so they do begin with some more of the required code in place.

Listing 3-1. The Default Template Code

```
<html>
<head>
</head>
<body>
    <!-- Insert content here -->
</body>
</html>
```

Let's look at the actual code for this example. Listing 3-2 shows the code we'll use to create the Web page in this case. Notice that this example contains a lot of additional code that you might not have seen in the past. The vast majority of this code ensures good access by accessibility software or provides functionality required by the W3C standards.

Listing 3-2. A Simple Web Site Example

```
<!DOCTYPE HTML PUBLIC "-//W3C//DTD HTML 4.01 Transitional//EN"
"http://www.w3.org/TR/html4/loose.dtd">
<html>
<head>
    <title>Test Web Page</title>
    <meta http-equiv="Content-Type" content="text/html; charset=utf-8">
    <meta http-equiv="Content-Script-Type" content="text/tcl">
    <script type="text/JavaScript">
        function btnTest_OnClick()
        {
            txtOutput.value = "Hello World";
        }
    </script>
</head>
<body>
    <h1 align="center">Welcome to the Test Web Page
    </h1>
    <noscript>
        Your browser doesn't support scripts. The only task the scripts on this
        page perform is to display Hello World in the output textbox when the
        user clicks Click Me or remove the text when the user clicks Reset.
    </noscript>
    <p>
        This is some introductory text.<br />
        <font color="red">This text is in <em>RED</em> and the word
        "RED" is in italics.</font>
    </p>
```

```
<p>
    <u>This text is underlined.</u>
</p>
<h2>Here is a Second Level Header
</h2>
<p>
    Output Textbox
    <input id="txtOutput" title="This is the output textbox."
        accesskey="O" type="text" />
</p>
<p>
    <input onkeypress="btnTest_OnClick()" id="btnTest"
        title="Click this button to see a change in the text box."
        accesskey="C" onclick="btnTest_OnClick()" tabindex="1"
        type="button" value="Click Me" />
    <input onkeypress='txtOutput.value=""' id="btnReset"
        title="Click this button to reset the form."
        accesskey="R" onclick='txtOutput.value=""' tabindex="2"
        type="reset" value="Reset" />
</p>
<h2>Here is Another Header
</h2>
<p>
    Click the link to get to the
    <a title=
        "Click this link to visit the DataCon Services Home Page."
        accesskey="H" href="http://www.mwt.net/~jmueller">
    DataCon Home Page</a>.
</p>
</body>
</html>
```

Let's begin at the top of the listing. Web Matrix won't include a <DOCTYPE> tag, but W3C standards require this tag, so you need to add it to the Web page. You can find a list of common <DOCTYPE> entries and associated explanations at http://www.htmlhelp.com/tools/validator/doctype.html. You'll probably want to add this tag to the template so you don't need to add it to every new Web page. Of course, the Web Matrix developers couldn't make this decision for you, so leaving the entry blank was a good decision.

The entries within the <head> tag define specific document elements including some metadata and a script. The two <meta> tags define the content type, character set, and script content type. Most browsers work just fine without this information, but you need the information to comply with W3C requirements and to make the document more accessible. Notice also that the `<script>` tag relies on the type attribute, rather than the language attribute used by older scripts.

The next area of interest is the `<noscript>` tag. Whenever you create a Web page with scripts, you must also include some means of obtaining that information without scripts (or, at least, providing an explanation of what the user would see). This is a requirement of both the Web Accessibility Initiative (WIA) and the government's Section 508 requirements. In this case, I provide a simple text description of what would happen if the user had access to scripting support.

 TIP *If you work with Web pages that could benefit from accessibility features, my book,* Accessibility for Everybody: Understanding the Section 508 Accessibility Requirements *(ISBN: 1-59059-086-4) provides complete details on creating accessible Web sites. You can learn more about this book at* `http://www.apress.com`.

Web Matrix makes all of the entries for the buttons and textbox available in the Properties window. The elements you see in the listing provide various types of support for users, such as balloon help for each of the controls. Notice that the controls provide both keyboard and mouse support. Figure 3-11 shows the output from this Web page.

Figure 3-11. The final output of the test application

Understanding Code Snippets

The previous section showed that Web Matrix often leaves the coding to you, which means that you'll end up typing some text more than once if you're not careful. However, you'll find that Web Matrix also provides a way around this problem: code snippets. You can add a snippet to the Toolbox whenever you think you'll use a particular piece of code more than once.

 NOTE *Make sure you check the Downloads section of the Apress site (*http://www.apress.com*) for source code downloads. You'll also find a Frequently Asked Questions (FAQ) page on my Web site at* http://www.mwt.net/~jmueller.

Creating Code Snippets

To create a code snippet, select the My Snippets tag on the Toolbox. Simply highlight the text in the editor window and drag it. When you drop the code, Web Matrix will assign a name to the new snippet based on the snippet content. In many cases, the name Web Matrix chooses won't be enough to identify the code snippet, so you'll want to change the code snippet name. Right-click the code snippet and choose Rename from the context menu. Type a new descriptive name for the code snippet, and then press Enter—Web Matrix saves your code and makes it ready for reuse.

Saving Code Snippets to Disk

At some point, you'll want to save your code snippets to disk and back them up. You might also want to share your more interesting tidbits with someone else. Web Matrix provides import and export functionality for this purpose. To export one or more of your code snippets, follow these steps.

1. Right-click the Toolbox with the My Snippets area exposed, and choose Export Snippets to a File from the context menu. You'll see the Export Snippets dialog box shown in Figure 3-12. Notice that Web Matrix assumes you'll want to export all of your code snippets, but you're also free to choose which code snippets you export.

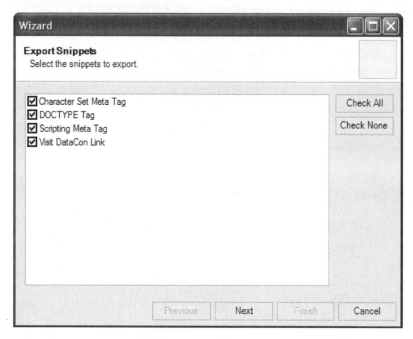

Figure 3-12. Saving your code snippets to disk is easy using the export functionality Web Matrix provides.

2. Select the code snippets you want to save, and then click Next. The wizard will ask you to choose a filename.

3. Type a name and click Finish.

That's all there is to exporting your code snippets. It's interesting to note that the output file uses XML for data storage, so you can use this technique to make small tweaks to your code snippets or simply see what you have stored.

TIP *Microsoft also provides another interesting utility called XML Notepad that you can use to view and edit your XML files. You'll find this helpful utility at* http://msdn.microsoft.com/library/en-us/dnxml/html/ xmlpaddownload.asp. *We'll also discuss this utility in the "Working with Microsoft XML Notepad" section of Chapter 7.*

Importing Code Snippets from Disk

Importing the code snippets is as easy as exporting them. The following steps show you how.

1. Right-click the Toolbox and choose Import Snippets from a File from the context menu. You'll see the Import Snippets Wizard.

2. Type the name of the file containing the code snippets or use the Browse button to locate it. Interestingly enough, although the Export Snippets Wizard doesn't specify a file extension, the Import Snippets Wizard assumes the file has an extension of SNIPPETS.

3. Click Next. You'll see a list of snippets contained within the file.

4. Select the snippets you want to use and click Finish. Web Matrix will import the snippets for you.

Testing the Web Page

At this point, we have a Web page that we can test. In the past, testing consisted of viewing the Web page and ensuring you didn't have any spelling errors. A few Webmasters would even check their creations for subtle programming errors. The emphasis in the past was in looking good, even if the site lacked a few features.

Unfortunately, Web sites of the past often included a healthy sprinkling of broken links and other features that drove users crazy. Scripts, cookies, odd mappings, frames, and endless redirections added to the soup of user discontent. Those days are gone—today you need to perform other types of validation to ensure your Web page meets certain standards. Not only do users view Web sites that don't follow the standards as a nuisance, but the government has stepped in and provided regulation for Web site construction—at least for sites associated with the government (including government vendors).

This section shows a simple method for verifying your Web page will provide the best functionality for all of your users. One of the interesting features of the checks we'll perform in this section is that the tests won't cost anything. I was surprised to find several Web sites that would actually check a given Web site for errors.

You should consider two levels of errors when creating a modern Web site. The first level is the code itself. A correctly coded Web site has a better chance of providing full functionality to a broad range of browsers. The second level is verifying the accessibility requirements of your site. The most commonly enforced accessibility requirement today is the government's Section 508 requirements. Always perform at least these two checks before you contemplate a course of action for your Web site.

The first level of checks will ensure your code is correct. To make this check, go to the W3C HTML Validation Service at `http://validator.w3.org/`. As you can see from Figure 3-13, you begin by entering the Web site URL, selecting any display options, and then click the Validate this page button.

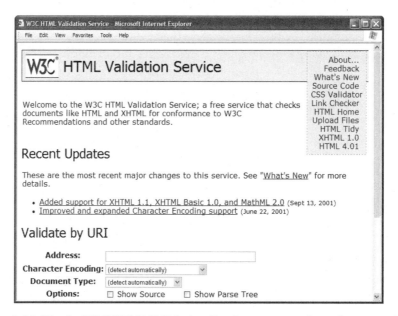

Figure 3-13. Use the W3C HTML Validation Service to ensure the code on your Web page is correct.

Sometimes the Web page won't validate correctly because it lacks a `<!DOCTYPE>` tag or character set entry. See Listing 3-2 for an example of these tags. You can override these problems by selecting a value from the Character Encoding or Document Type fields. However, these selections will skew the results you obtain, and you should add the proper tags to your Web page as soon as possible. After you override the selections, try to validate the page again. If it still won't validate, your Web page has serious problems that you should fix immediately.

NOTE   *This book assumes that you already know how to create HTML code. The purpose of this check is to ensure your page will work as intended. The W3C Web site provides hints and tips you can use to correct your code. You'll also see examples of code that passes all of the requirements in this book that you can use to refine your own code. However, this book won't provide basic HTML coding information, so you'll need to access that information from a third-party source.*

Validating a page doesn't mean it's error free—it simply means that you've fixed enough problems for the tool to tell you about the remaining errors. If you run a page that has errors, the W3C site will point out the exact location of the error and will often provide advice for fixing it. Figure 3-14 shows a report for a page with a few simple errors. This figure concentrates on the errors—you can also view an outline of your Web page, numbered source listing, and a parse tree of the data.

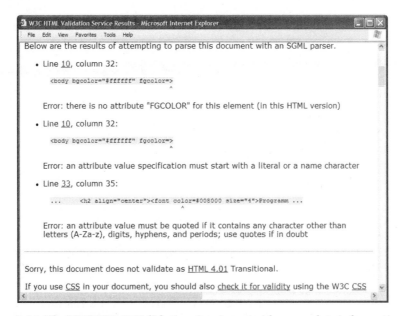

Figure 3-14. The W3C HTML Validation Service provides complete information on the errors on your Web page.

Notice that the output shown in Figure 3-14 shows the precise location of the error as the parser sees it. The output page also includes a brief message on the error and optionally provides some information on how to fix it. Generally, you'll find that this setup works well for simple errors, but doesn't provide enough information to fix complex errors. That's where your training in writing HTML will come into play.

The code in Listing 3-2 is HTML 4.01 compliant. Figure 3-15 shows typical output from the W3C HTML Validation Service for a compliant Web site. The parser tells you that the code appears to follow all of the rules. It does a good job of finding most coding errors, but it still doesn't say anything about the content or usability of your Web site. All that this check will tell you is that the code will work with an HTML 4.01–compliant browser, which is a step in the right direction.

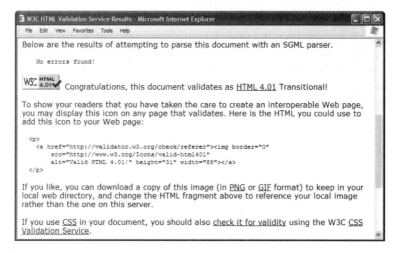

Figure 3-15. Validation of compliant code tells you how to apply the icon to your Web site.

NOTE   *Conformance to a standard doesn't always mean that an HTML page will display on every browser. Each browser vendor must choose the level of standards conformance the browser will provide. With this in mind, you'll also want to check the Webmonkey chart at* `http://hotwired.lycos.com/webmonkey/reference/browser_chart/index.html?tw=eg20001211` *for specific browser compatibility issues.*

Once your code is correct, you can check the Web page for accessibility concerns. Bobby will check a single page of a Web site for free and provide a seal of approval should the Web site pass. You can check out this valuable resource (shown in Figure 3-16) at `http://bobby.watchfire.com/bobby/html/en/index.jsp`. As you can see from Figure 3-16, the Web site performs both Web Content Accessibility Guidelines 1.0 and Section 508 checks on a Web site of your choosing.

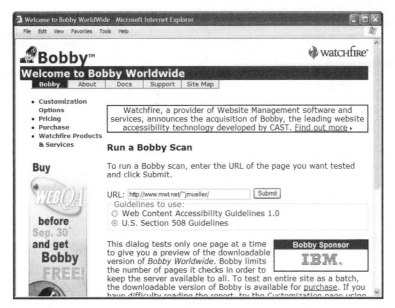

Figure 3-16. Bobby ensures that your Web site meets the required accessibility requirements.

All you need to do is enter a Web site URL, select the test you want to run, and then click Submit. Bobby retrieves the Web site, checks it for errors, and prints a report for you. I actually thought that my pure text Web site would pass on the first try; but, as shown in Figure 3-17, my Web site at `http://www.mwt.net/~jmueller/` still had five glitches to fix. I've since corrected the problems with my Web site and posted an updated version.

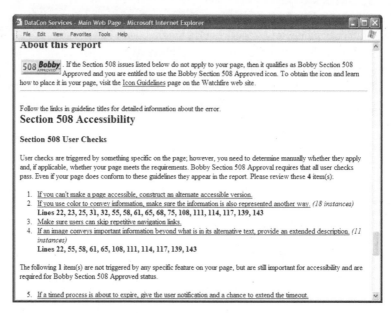

Figure 3-17. Even pure text Web sites can run afoul of Section 508 requirements, as shown in this figure.

> **NOTE** *The Web Content Accessibility Guidelines are much stricter than the Section 508 requirements. If you want the ultimate in accessibility, make your Web site Section 508 compliant first, and then work on the Web Content Accessibility Guideline requirements.*

Notice that all of these errors are *user checks*. A user check error is one that you have to check manually and determine if your site is in compliance. In many cases, Bobby will raise a question that you can answer by saying that your site is in compliance. You can determine the error locations by looking for question marks on the Web page displayed above the report. Every question mark represents an issue that you need to consider, and some locations will contain more than one question mark because they break more than one rule.

Every user check in the report also contains a link you can use to obtain additional information. Generally, the additional information tells you what you need to do in order to correct the error and the rationale behind the rule. In some cases, the help entry also shows short code snippets with generic implementation information. The point is that you can find out the specifics of the problem using your own Web page as a source of the information.

Many people learn by example. I know that I look on other Web sites for ideas on how to resolve issues with my own Web site and those of my customers. Therefore, Bobby can serve another purpose. Before you use a Web site for ideas, check it for Section 508 compliance. I was a little surprised to find that Microsoft's Section 508 Web site at `http://www.microsoft.com/enable/microsoft/section508.htm` had numerous occurrences of 13 Section 508 errors, two of which are major, as shown in Figure 3-18. In fact, I found that none of the Microsoft Web pages I tried would pass the test.

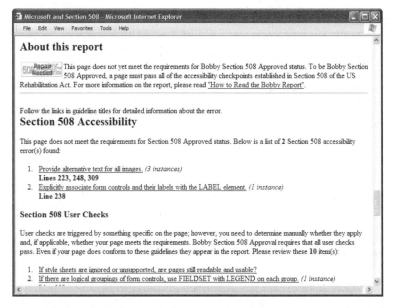

Figure 3-18. Always test Web sites before you trust them as an example of what you should do on your own Web site.

This Web page includes combination of user checks and Section 508 compliance errors. The errors at the top of the report are issues that the Web site must fix in order to bring the Web site into compliance. As with the user checks, the Web site provides links that give you some general information about the problem so that you can make an informed decision about fixing it.

Using a Text File

A simple text file can contain a lot of content in a small amount of space. You don't have to worry about accessibility problems, for the most part, because text files don't contain anything that could cause a screen reader to fail. This type of content also works with any browser on any platform. In short, if you want to provide content to the largest group of people possible, a text file can't fail—at least in theory.

The biggest problem with text files is that you can't format the information. It's in "plain" text and that's it. Sure, you can add a little indention and add double spaces between paragraphs, but that's about it. It doesn't even matter if the text is formatted as 8-bit American National Standards Institute (ANSI) or 16-bit Unicode, text is still text. Consequently, text files aren't the glamour solution to anyone's data presentation needs. You'll find them used by some Web sites—notably educational, governmental, or standards organizations—but they aren't used often anywhere else.

Even if text files aren't popular, Web Matrix provides support for them. You'll find the Text File template in the (General) category. When you create this template, all you need to supply is a filename. Click OK and you'll see a new text file on screen.

One of the features of the editor that I find helpful is that even a text file has line numbers. Figure 3-19 shows how the line numbers come into play. This feature makes it easier to find a particular bit of text or other files when you're editing. Although you might not need this feature when working with text files, it comes in handy for style sheets and other files where you need to perform validity checks. Note that the editor doesn't provide any word wrap or other features for formatting the text—any formatting you want to add requires manual editing.

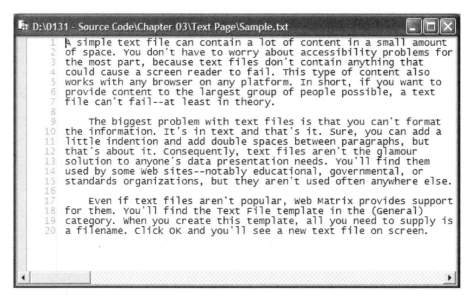

Figure 3-19. The editor window provides line numbers and not much else when editing some files.

Using a Style Sheet

Style sheets help developers create Web pages with a consistent look and feel. In addition, using a style sheet can dramatically reduce the time required to create a page. A few vendors even say that style sheets will help users customize their Web viewing experience in the future because their browser will substitute a custom style sheet for the default entry on the Web page. Accessibility groups like style sheets because they help separate content from presentation—making a Web page more accessible.

 TIP *One of the most interesting places to learn about using Cascading Style Sheets (CSS) is the Glish.com site at* http://www.glish.com/css/. *The interesting feature of this site is that the author is easy to understand. In addition, the author values cross-browser compatibility, which means the techniques you learn won't cause problems on your site. If you don't find what you want on this Web site, the author has an extensive list of other Web sites you can check for information.*

It might sound as if a developer who doesn't use style sheets doesn't understand modern Web site development very well. Unfortunately, the style sheet water is somewhat murky—style sheets also have many detractors. For one thing, using style sheets assumes that the target browser can handle them—some can't. (For a list of browser capabilities, check the Webmonkey site at http://hotwired.lycos.com/webmonkey/reference/browser_chart/index.html.) Some people feel that CSS actually causes compatibility problems and makes it more difficult for those with special needs to access a site. No matter which side of the debate you're on, CSS is here to stay, so it's important to look at what a CSS can do for your site.

Creating the CSS

This book won't teach you how to code CSS, but we'll look at an example of how to create a style sheet using Web Matrix. As with many of the other general files, you'll find the Style Sheet template in the (General) category of the Add New File dialog box. Select the project, type a filename, and click OK to create the new file. Listing 3-3 shows the simple style sheet we'll use for the example Web site that follows.

Listing 3-3. A Typical CSS File

```css
BODY {
    font-size: 100%;
    color: black;
    background-color: white
}


H1 {
    font-size: 200%;
    color: black;
    background-color: white
}


H2 {
    font-size: 150%;
    color: black;
    background-color: white
}


.highlight {
    font-size: 100%;
    color: red;
    background-color: white
}


.highlight-i {
    font-size: 100%;
    color: red;
    font-style: italic;
    background-color: white
}


.underline {
    font-size: 100%;
    color: black;
    text-decoration: underline;
    background-color: white
}
```

As you can see, Listing 3-3 creates the styles used in the example HTML page shown in Listing 3-2. The example in the "A Simple HTML Example" section will combine the two files so that we can achieve a better score on the Bobby test (the page is already completely W3C compliant).

You should notice a few features of this style sheet. The most important feature is that it relies on percentages for the font sizes, rather than precise sizes. Using a percentage means that the user can set the base size for a page and see the remaining elements sized according to the base size. Users with limited vision will appreciate this feature because many Web pages use fonts that are too small for them to see. Likewise, users with great vision will appreciate this setting because they can display more information on screen. It's never a good idea to display fonts in a specific size.

Another feature of this style sheet is that it uses high-contrast color combinations. It's important to consider using high-contrast settings whenever you can. Using a high-contrast display is better because it helps a variety of users get more from your Web site including those with the following needs:

- Low vision

- Using laptops in a sunlit area

- Using alternative input devices such as cellular telephones and PDAs

- Using small font sizes

- Color blindness

The listing also includes one setting that the standards require. Notice that every setting includes a foreground and a background color setting. The standards require this information to ensure the display looks as anticipated.

Testing the CSS

Just as it's important to test the code for your HTML page, it's also important to test the CSS you use for standards compliance. In fact, it might be more important to test this functionality because it has such a big impact on the appearance of your Web site as a whole. The W3C Web site includes the functionality required to test your CSS at `http://jigsaw.w3.org/css-validator/`. In fact, as shown in Figure 3-20, you have four options for testing your CSS.

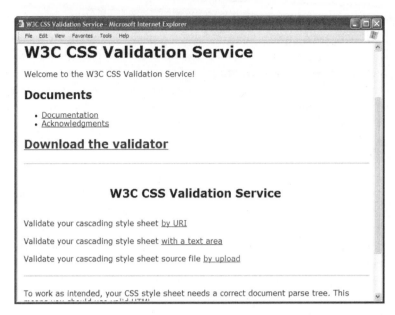

Figure 3-20. Choose any of the four W3C testing options for your CSS.

The option you choose depends on the number of style sheets you have to test, the location of the CSS, and your testing goals. The following list explains the four testing options.

Download the validator: The W3C wants to make testing as easy as possible. If you have many style sheets to test, it might be easier to download the validator, rather than upload each style sheet for separate validation. The validator works essentially the same no matter where you test, so this option simply allows for local testing in place of using the W3C site directly.

By URI: This is the option to use if you have the CSS coded into the HTML page. Some developers use this technique so they don't have to maintain separate Web and CSS pages.

With a text area: Use this option to perform "what if" analysis of style sheet entries or to validate a small style sheet. You'll see a text area where you can type style information. The text area also allows text pasting, so you can copy the style sheet information you want to test from an existing document and paste it.

By upload: In many cases, you'll have a copy of the style sheet you want to test on a local drive. Use this option to upload the style sheet to the W3C Web site and test it. Most developers will use this option because it's the easiest. In fact, we'll use this technique in this section.

This section assumes you only have one style sheet to test, so we'll use the upload method. When you select this method, you'll see a form that asks you to supply the name of the file you want to check, as shown in Figure 3-21. This entry holds the location of the file on your hard drive. If you don't want to reveal this information to a nonsecure Web site, you can still use the text area method.

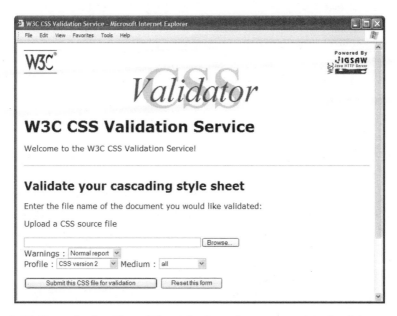

Figure 3-21. Enter the location of the style sheet that you want to check in this form.

Notice that this page contains settings you can use to change the level of the check. It normally pays to set the form to provide you with a complete list of all warnings the style sheet will generate. You'll also want to verify the style sheet against CSS Version 2. The medium is an important setting. If you create a style sheet to answer a particular need, then you should select that medium. For example, you can choose special mediums for handheld devices. Because the style sheet in this example will have to work for all mediums, I set the validator to check all of them. Click Submit this CSS file for validation button and you'll see some output. Figure 3-22 shows the output for the example code shown in Listing 3-3.

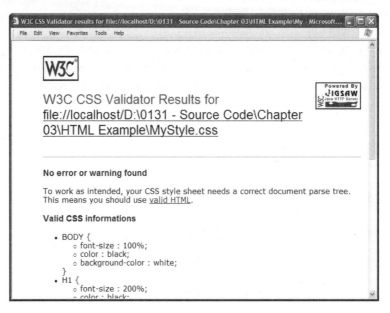

Figure 3-22. Check the output from the validator to learn if you need to make changes to your style sheet.

A Simple HTML Example

At this point, we've discussed several projects you can create with Web Matrix. We actually have enough material put together to create an HTML page with CSS support. Of course, the missing component is linkage between the HTML page and the CSS style sheet. You begin creating this linkage by adding a tag to the heading area of the HTML page, as shown here.

```
<link media="screen" href="MyStyle.css" type="text/css" rel="StyleSheet">
```

This single line of code tells the browser that the styles are found in the MYSTYLE.CSS file. The style sheet automatically adds styles to the general styles we added to the file such as Body and H1 (see Listing 3-3 for details). However, the page also includes the special `.highlight`, `.highlight-i`, and `.underline` styles. We'll begin by addressing the text that appears in red in the original example, as shown here.

```
<span class="highlight">This text is in <span class="highlight-i">RED</span>
and the word "RED" is in italics.</span>
```

As you can see, adding some nested <span> tags takes care of the formatting. The first <span> tag relies on the .highlight class, while the second relies on the .highlight-i class. The result is the same text that we saw earlier. The difference is that the formatting code appears in the style sheet, rather than in the HTML file.

Adding underlined text is similar to changing the text color. The following code adds underline style. In this case, we don't need to use a <span> tag since there's a <p> tag handy.

```
<p class="underline">
    This text is underlined.
</p>
```

That's all you need to do to add the style sheet to the example. It isn't a complex example, but it does demonstrate several important Web Matrix features. You've also learned about some of the checks you should make in order to validate your Web site. As user needs increase, you'll find that these free checks are worth their weight in gold because they make your site more useful and presentable. Of course, you can always purchase the commercial versions of the Watchfire products that validate your site setup, but Bobby is a good place to start.

Using the ASP.NET Page

The ASP.NET page represents one of the more complex projects you can create with Web Matrix because the application provides some additional setup options. The test application relies on C# as the development language, but you can also choose Visual Basic .NET. Figure 3-23 shows the setup for the project. Notice that we'll include the optional class and namespace information. If you don't provide these values, Web Matrix provides a default value for you.

 NOTE *If you decide to use a one-machine setup or decide that you want to perform a quick local test, you can start the Web server provided with Web Matrix using the View ➤ Start command. You can also press F5 to start the server. In either case, you'll see a Start Web Application dialog box. This dialog box contains options for either an ASP.NET Web Matrix Server or an IIS start. (The ASP.NET Web Matrix Server is also referred to as the Casinni Server.) Choose an option and click OK. The application will start.*

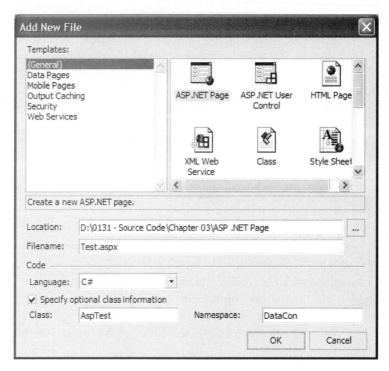

Figure 3-23. Add the optional namespace and class information to your projects to ensure you get a good start.

The example in this section is very simple. (The complexity of the examples will increase as the book progresses.) In this case, the page performs essentially the same tasks that we performed with the HTML example in Listing 3-2. Of course, now we're using ASP.NET to perform the task, so you'll see some major differences in the code, as shown in Listing 3-4.

Listing 3-4. A Simple ASP.NET Example

```
<%@ Page Language="C#" ClassName="AspTest" %>
<script runat="server">

    void btnTest_Click(Object sender, EventArgs e) {
        // Display a new value for the output textbox.
        txtOutput.Text = "Hello World";
    }


    void btnReset_Click(Object sender, EventArgs e) {
        // Reset the output textbox to a blank.
        txtOutput.Text = "";
    }
```

```
</script>
<!DOCTYPE HTML PUBLIC "-//W3C//DTD HTML 4.01 Transitional//EN"
"http://www.w3.org/TR/html4/loose.dtd">
<html lang="EN">
<head>
    <title>Test Web Page</title>
    <meta http-equiv="Content-Type" content="text/html; charset=utf-8">
</head>
<body>
    <form runat="server">
        <h1 align="center">Welcome to the ASP.NET Test Web Page
        </h1>
        <noscript>Your browser doesn't support scripts. The only task
            the scripts on this page perform is to display Hello
            World in the output textbox when the user clicks
            Click Me or remove the text when the user clicks Reset.
        </noscript>
        <p align="left">
            This is some introductory text.<br />
            <font color="red">This text is in <em>RED</em> and the word
            "RED" is in italics.</font>
        </p>
        <p align="left">
            <u><font color="black">This text is underlined.</font></u>
        </p>
        <h2 align="left">This is a Second Level Header
        </h2>
        <p align="left">
            Output Textbox
            <asp:TextBox id="txtOutput" accessKey="O" runat="server"
                ToolTip="This is the output textbox.">Page Output
            </asp:TextBox>
        </p>
        <p align="left">
            <asp:Button id="btnTest" accessKey="C" onclick="btnTest_Click"
                tabIndex="1" runat="server"
                ToolTip="Click this button to see a change in the text box."
                Text="Click Me">
            </asp:Button>
            <asp:Button id="btnReset" accessKey="R" onclick="btnReset_Click"
                tabIndex="2" runat="server"
                ToolTip="Click this button to reset the form."
                Text="Reset">
```

```
            </asp:Button>
        </p>
        <h2 align="left">Here is Another Header
        </h2>
        <p align="left">
            Click the link to get to the
            <asp:HyperLink id="HyperLink1" runat="server"
                ToolTip="Click to visit the DataCon Services Home Page."
                NavigateUrl="http://www.mwt.net/~jmueller">DataCon Home Page
            </asp:HyperLink>
        </p>
    </form>
</body>
</html>
```

Listing 3-4 shows the code as you'd see it on the All tab of the editor window. As you can see, this code works the same as the HTML example we used earlier. The two big differences are that we're using C# for the script language and the server processes all events with the current configuration. The output of this example looks the same as the HTML version. The code does pause longer to change the output textbox because we're using a post back to the server to make the change. The code actually executes on the server, rather than on the client. Using this technique means that the client doesn't have to have as much memory or processing power, but it also means the Web page takes longer to display.

 NOTE *When you finish using the ASP.NET Web Matrix Server for a particular application, stop the server by clicking its icon in the Notification Area and choosing Stop from the context menu. The server icon will disappear when the service stops.*

It's important to note that we have to make some of the same changes in this example that we had to make with the HTML version. For example, you still need to add a <DOCTYPE> tag. It's also important to specify the character set. However, notice that we don't include a scripting tag. That's because none of the script shown in Listing 3-4 actually appears at the client—it only appears on the server. If you use the View | Source command in Internet Explorer, you'll see the same code that the client sees. It doesn't contain any script, which means this page is actually less likely to cause problems with browsers.

Code Behind Versus Inline Code

Look again at Listing 3-4 and you'll notice that the code for this example is inline with the rest of the code used for the HTML page. Visual Studio .NET creates a separate file for HTML and source code. Both Visual Studio .NET and Web Matrix can display the code in separate windows, making it easier to work on. In short, although you see the code in separate windows, the two products handle the code differently at the file level.

In some respects, the use of two file-handling strategies introduce a compatibility problem between Visual Studio .NET and Web Matrix. Both products are using completely legitimate and documented means for storing the code, so the difference is more physical (and philosophical) and real. So, the question is which technique is "better"?

I don't view either technique as better all the time. Visual Studio .NET certainly has the upper hand when it comes to large-scale development because using a separate file for the code means that you can develop your application independently of the code file. The code resides separately—making it easier to move around. In addition, it's theoretically possible for one team member to work on the code for the application while another team member works on the user interface. The separation of code from user interface also nets some gains in making the application easier to understand because the developer doesn't have to interpret HTML that's mixed with code.

The Web Matrix methodology is easier for small application developers to use because everything needed to display a page resides in a single file. The developer doesn't need to worry about a client accidentally removing a file that contains the code for the Web page. In addition, using the single-file approach could have some small storage efficiencies that make it better for businesses on a budget. The use of two small files might waste space on the server and could cause a small performance hit as the server loads two files instead of one. (The performance hit only occurs when ASP.NET needs to recompile the two files—an infrequent occurrence for a production application.) The essential consideration is that a small application is less likely to become complex, so using two files to store the information doesn't provide any benefit to the developer.

Using WEB.CONFIG

The WEB.CONFIG file is important for a number of reasons. You use it to configure the Web-based application for use. Of course, you also need this file in place to enable application debugging. You'll find the WEB.CONFIG project in the (General) project category of the Add New File dialog box. Unlike most of the files we've discussed so far, this one is ready to go almost immediately. The nice part about using the WEB.CONFIG file is that you can make changes to your Web-based application configuration without shutting the server down or recompiling your application. The server automatically notices the change and makes the required modifications to the environment.

The WEB.CONFIG file is in XML, although the numerous comments might make you doubt this fact. The commented material contains entries that you can make in the WEB.CONFIG file. To use an entry, you can either write a custom version or remove the comments from an existing entry. Between the .NET documentation (see the help topic at `http://msdn.microsoft.com/library/en-us/vsdebug/html/vxtskDebugModeInASPNETApplications.asp`) and the WEB.CONFIG file, you have everything need to adjust this file to suit your needs. However, one change that I always make when working on a new application is to add the following line to the configuration/system.web section of the file.

```
<customErrors mode="Off"/>
```

CAUTION   *Setting the* `<customErrors>` *mode to off means that you can see errors from a remote location. However, it also means that everyone else can see the errors from a remote location. Make sure you set the* `<customErrors>` *mode to RemoteOnly before you deploy the application. Otherwise, crackers could gain access to your server by analyzing the detailed information provided by the error messages. In addition, displaying the error information doesn't provide a finished appearance for your application to clients who use it.*

This simple entry helps you learn about errors in your code from your desktop. Otherwise, the application error only appears at the server. Figure 3-24 shows how the WEB.CONFIG file looks in XML Notepad when you add this entry (we'll study XML Notepad in Chapter 7).

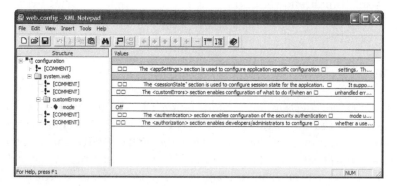

Figure 3-24. Using a product like XML Notepad helps you track entries in a complex WEB.CONFIG file.

TIP *ASP.NET uses the WEB.CONFIG file to perform many configuration tasks with Web applications, so we'll visit this file again as the book progresses. Some areas we won't visit include globalization* (`http://msdn.microsoft.com/library/en-us/vbcon/html/vbtskEditingWebConfigFileForWebFormsGlobalization.asp`) *and the Microsoft Commerce Server* (`http://msdn.microsoft.com/library/en-us/csvr2002/htm/cs_ag_infraconfiguration_uyri.asp`).

Generally, you'll want to use the `<customErrors>` tag for diagnostics only. If you want to display error information for users (so they can report it), using a custom report makes sense. However, the display provided by the standard error reporting page works well, as shown in Figure 3-25. This figure shows a simulated error for the ASP.NET application in Listing 3-4.

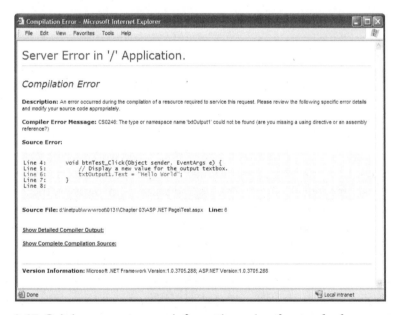

Figure 3-25. Gaining access to error information using the standard error page is easy, but might prove confusing for new users.

Using GLOBAL.ASAX

The GLOBAL.ASAX file is optional for any Web-based application. When you create an application with Visual Studio .NET, the IDE automatically generates a GLOBAL.ASAX file that contains a reference to a file designed to hold global code for the language used with the application. For example, if you use C#, the GLOBAL.ASAX file will typically reference a GLOBAL.ASAX.CS file. This language-specific file contains event handlers for a number of application-level events including

- Application_Start(Object sender, EventArgs e)

- Session_Start(Object sender, EventArgs e)

- Application_BeginRequest(Object sender, EventArgs e)

- Application_EndRequest(Object sender, EventArgs e)

- Application_AuthenticateRequest(Object sender, EventArgs e)

- Application_Error(Object sender, EventArgs e)

- Session_End(Object sender, EventArgs e)

- Application_End(Object sender, EventArgs e)

You don't have to go through all of this effort when working with Web Matrix. Like the ASP.NET page we discussed earlier, you can specify a class name and a namespace for your GLOBAL.ASAX file. You'll also need to specify the language you want to use—the example uses C#, but you can also choose Visual Basic .NET if desired. The resulting file contains a subset of the application-level event handlers found in a Visual Studio .NET setup and relies on a single file. Figure 3-26 shows a typical GLOBAL.ASAX file. You can learn more about the GLOBAL.ASAX file at http://msdn.microsoft.com/library/en-us/cpguide/html/cpcontheglobalasaxfile.asp.

```
1  <%@ Application language="C#" ClassName="AspTest" %>
2
3  <script runat="server">
4
5      public void Application_Start(Object sender, EventArgs e) {
6          // Code that runs on application startup
7      }
8
9      public void Application_End(Object sender, EventArgs e) {
10          // Code that runs on application shutdown
11      }
12
13      public void Application_Error(Object sender, EventArgs e) {
14          // Code that runs when an unhandled error occurs
15      }
16
17      public void Session_Start(Object sender, EventArgs e) {
18          // Code that runs when a new session is started
19      }
20
21      public void Session_End(Object sender, EventArgs e) {
22          // Code that runs when a session ends
23      }
24
25  </script>
```

Figure 3-26. Use the GLOBAL.ASAX file to store application-level event handlers.

Using the ASP.NET HTTP Handler Page

If you've ever created an Internet Server Application Programming Interface (ISAPI) extension, you know that they can require quite a bit of programming. However, creating ISAPI extensions is unavoidable, in some cases, if you want to provide some advanced functionality within your Web-based application. Fortunately, ASP.NET introduces the HTTP Handler page. This project will implement the same IHttpHandler interface used by an ISAPI extension, but with a much simpler interface.

The ASP.NET HTTP Handler project creates an HTTP handler shell for you, including the elements that you must include with the HTTP handler. Unlike an ISAPI extension, you register an HTTP handler with the Web application using the WEB.CONFIG file described earlier in this chapter. You can learn more about HTTP handlers in the help topic at http://msdn.microsoft.com/library/en-us/cpguide/html/cpconhttphandlers.asp. We'll also discuss possible uses for this page as the book progresses.

Summary

This chapter has answered the question of how Web Matrix can help you work with a variety of file formats, no matter where they come from. You've learned how to make connections and create simple Web pages using common Web files. You may have even learned some new techniques in the form of ASP.NET development. However, the important thing is that you've learned that Web Matrix is an extremely flexible tool that can help you in many situations that might have required separate tools in the past.

Now it's time to play with Web Matrix a little. Try making connections to various servers that you can access using any technique that you think will work. The FTP connection seems to work the best on Apache servers, but it helps to try other methods as well. Open a variety of common files to see how they look in Web Matrix. Learn which files Web Matrix handles best and which it only sees as text. Of course, even if you don't see the keyword highlighting that Web Matrix normally provides, the fact you can edit the file without changing applications is a plus.

Chapter 4 examines a topic that every developer needs to consider today—security. In a general sense, Web Matrix can help you check the security of most Web pages. For example, it provides both login and logout pages you can use in your project. However, many of the special features that Web Matrix provides work best on IIS. We'll discuss ways around this problem in the next chapter.

CHAPTER 4

Web Matrix and Security

In This Chapter

- Understand Web Site Security Requirements

- Create a Project with the Login Page

- Create a Project with the Logout Page

- Create a Project with the Config File Page

- Learn Methods for Creating a Better Password Scheme

- Design a General Security Example

- Use Windows-Validated Security

Creating a secure environment for your application is a major concern today. It seems as if every effort developers make is offset by some new security hole or some nefarious plot by crackers intent on making you look bad. I'd love to say that Web Matrix has a solution for every security woe, but the truth is that it's another tool in your arsenal against computer crime. That said, Web Matrix does provide tools to create a reasonably secure Web site so long as you exercise the same caution that you would when building an application with any other tool.

NOTE   *For the purposes of this book, the term* cracker *will always refer to an individual who's breaking into a system on an unauthorized basis. This includes any form of illegal activity on the system. On the other hand, a* hacker *will refer to someone who performs authorized (legal) low-level system activities, including testing system security. In some cases, you need to employ the services of a good hacker to test the security measures you have in place, or suffer the consequences of a break-in. This book will use the term* hacker *to refer to someone who performs these legal forms of service. The best way to view the difference (at least if you like westerns) is that the hacker wears a white hat and the cracker wears a black hat.*

This chapter begins by looking at the three page types (templates) that help create a secure environment. The first two are easy to guess because of their names: the Login Page and Logout Page. The first is a common sight on secure Web sites—many of us enter a user name and password to access Web sites on a daily basis. The Logout Page is something new and interesting because none of the Web sites I've ever visited used one. The third page we'll discuss is the Config File page. Why is this a security issue? Read on and find out—you might be surprised.

NOTE   *The Logout Page is important in many situations— even if you don't regularly use a Web site that features one. The MSDN subscriber Web site does provides a logout option in the upper-right corner of the page if you want to see one implementation of this feature. You'll also find this type of page used with banking Web sites. Consequently, even if you don't think the Logout Page is important at first, you'll probably need to use it sometime in the future.*

After we look at the page types that Web Matrix provides, we'll begin exploring some details on how you can use them to secure your site. We'll move from theoretical knowledge to actual practice by building a secure Web site using the tools that Web Matrix provides. The "A General Security Example" section will rely on some security features from Internet Information Server (IIS) because you can't really build a secure site without some cooperation from the Web server. As part of the example in this section, we'll also address some server configuration issues you should explore.

TIP   *It certainly helps to have as much security information at your fingertips as possible. Of course, you could always try to read every treatment of security on the market, but most developers don't have time to do that. A good place to find the information you need is the Global IT Security Information DATABASE (*`http://www.e-secure-db.us/`*). This site replaces the need to search the Internet and visit numerous sites when performing research into security problems. I wouldn't say that they'll keep you apprised of every new security issue, but it's a good place to quickly find the information you need about a security issue.*

General Requirements for Web Site Security

It's interesting to look at where the media thinks developers are going with the Web and where they actually go with Web applications. Sometimes the two are different. One such example is Web services. Only recently has the media figured out that developers aren't adopting this new technology wholesale. It's a great technology with a lot of potential, so what's the problem? You can make the same statement of Web-based mobile applications. Many companies are still looking at mobile devices to answer a single, non–mission-critical need (a few have gone beyond that point, but not many). Again, this is a technology that companies should use to answer critical business needs, but many simply aren't interested.

The security problems with Web services, Web-based mobile applications, and other Internet technologies are somewhat complex. In some cases, the technologies are new and untested, which means there are bugs to work out and implementation details that aren't clear. In other cases, the developers using the technologies have a hard time adapting to the requirements for using them. New technologies have a learning curve that hinders their initial use. Added to the security problems are issues of intellectual property. Developers don't want to expose their intellectual property over the Internet to potential intellectual theft, and they see other problems with current technology, such as the need to upgrade in a way that leaves existing technology usable. The reasons for not wanting to use Web technologies vary by developer. However, the one reason that all developers agree upon is the lack of good security. Every day brings another revelation of some security leak that some developer found. In addition, many of the coding practices developers employ on Web sites leave a lot to be desired. In sum, creating a Web application is often the same as hanging a sign on your company asking someone to steal not only your application, but maybe even your data.

Consider one development project that I recently heard about from another consultant. In this case, a company wanted to create a secure application that other companies would access externally through a Web site interface. The only problem with this setup is that the company insisted that everyone use the same password for ease of coding and testing. You can't build a secure application if you don't know the people you're working with individually. Even with individual passwords, security is a risky business. Needless to say, the consultant is busy adding clauses to the contract that protects him from the security breach that will almost certainly occur.

NOTE *This chapter can't provide you with a full discussion of Web-based application security. The goal of this chapter is to give an overview of the problems that you'll find and provide you with some answers to resolve them using Web Matrix. I'm assuming that you've consulted a security text and already made plans to secure your application, hardware, users, and network. Of course, making sure the servers that run your application have the latest patches is a requirement.*

Theoretically, Passport (http://www.passport.net/) or the Liberty Alliance (http://www.projectliberty.org/) global password could help resolve a situation where a client doesn't want to implement custom security. However, these technologies are far from finished solutions, and the current user view of these security measures could keep them from ever becoming widely distributed. Consequently, I won't discuss these alternatives in detail in this book. When working with Web Matrix, you'll likely find using Passport easiest. You can learn more about the Passport implementation details at http://msdn.microsoft.com/library/en-us/ppsdk14/Implementation/Passport_Implementation_top.asp. You'll find the Passport SDK at http://msdn.microsoft.com/downloads/sample.asp?url=/MSDN-FILES/027/001/885/msdncompositedoc.xml.

When working with secure applications, you also need to consider using standard Web technologies such as Secure Sockets Layer (SSL). Using SSL to encrypt your data helps keep your applications secure. You've probably used SSL in the past—Web sites that use the HTTPS protocol instead of HTTP rely on SSL to encrypt data. You can learn more about SSL at `http://developer.netscape.com/docs/manuals/security/sslin/contents.htm`. The SSL 3.0 specification appears at `http://wp.netscape.com/eng/ssl3/`.

Web Matrix can't fix your security problems—that's something only you can do with good application design. However, Web Matrix does provide access to functionality that will improve your application's security. Most of these features appear in the Security folder of the Add New File dialog box shown in Figure 4-1. We'll discuss the use of the Login Page and Logout Page projects in this chapter, along with a variety of other security processes you can consider. For example, using an HTTP handler can help increase security by allowing you to examine the requestor more closely. You can also add security settings to the WEB.CONFIG file. In short, you have many resources available.

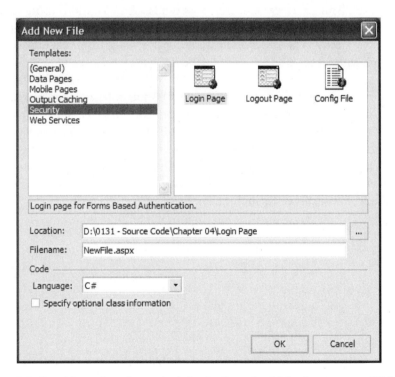

Figure 4-1. Consider using the projects in the Security folder in your next Web application.

NOTE *None of the forms presented in the Security folder contain the settings and code to make them accessibility friendly. We discussed this issue as part of the testing procedures for Chapter 3. If your Web site requires Web Accessibility Initiative (WAI) or Section 508 approval, make sure you change the forms as required.*

It's important to consider the orientation of Web Matrix as a product, however, when building your secure application. At some point, you'll find that you're spending a lot of time reading about security issues, rather than programming, because Web Matrix lacks the automation found in Visual Studio .NET. Web Matrix will help you develop secure applications, but it won't provide the same level of tool-oriented help that Visual Studio .NET does, and this is an important consideration. Yes, you can still build a secure site, but it requires more work. For example, you'll find it harder to learn about WEB.CONFIG options using Web Matrix because it doesn't provide the same level of built-in help as Visual Studio .NET. Web Matrix also lacks Server Explorer support—a feature that makes it easier to work with IIS security from within the IDE as you build your application. As the chapter progresses, we'll discuss areas where Web Matrix excels and those areas where you might want to think about upgrading to Visual Studio .NET.

One problem with the security features provided with Web Matrix is that they're Windows specific. In fact, they're ASP.NET specific to an extent. If you want to exercise another security solution, you'll need to develop it using some other technique. The file types that we explored in Chapter 3 are available for use, but you won't find a security solution that's set up as well as the ASP.NET solution we'll explore in the three files in this chapter.

Using the Login Page

The Login Page project creates a customized login screen for the user to enter a name and password. It also provides some basic password-checking code you can use to validate the user. For the most part, the default project will deter the casual user who bumps into your Web site, but it probably won't work very well with someone who's determined to access the site. Even so, it's better than not having security implemented at all.

One important concept to remember when working with a project such as the Login Page is the relationship between ASP.NET and IIS. IIS is always the first line of security when creating a Web application. Consequently, to create a more secure environment, you would couple the Login Page with IIS-specific security. The ASP.NET runtime checks security after IIS does, so this Login Page project is actually a second line of defense. We'll discuss this issue in greater detail in the "Windows-Validated Security" section of the chapter.

The following sections show you how to work with the Login Page template. Generally, you only need to make a few small changes to provide full functionality for users of this page. The page isn't ready to go as created by Web Matrix.

Creating the Basic Page

The Login Page template is really an ASP.NET project in disguise, so you get all of the usual ASPX file options on the Add New File dialog box. For this example, I used a class name of SecurityTest, but you could use any name you like. The important thing is to make sure you use the same class name across projects so that you don't have to worry about class name conflicts. One element you want to keep is the project name. We'll see later that the name of the file becomes important for redirection purposes, in many cases, so using the default name usually works best unless you want to rewrite the code in other project files. After you create the login page, you'll see a form similar to the one shown in Figure 4-2 in the Design window.

Figure 4-2. The login page consists of a special ASP.NET form.

This form contains a few special features that might not be apparent at first. Figure 4-2 shows that it has two textboxes—one for the user name and another for the password. Next to the two textboxes are two RequiredFieldValidator controls. These controls ensure that the user enters a name and a password as requested.

The standard control settings for the RequiredFieldValidator controls simply display an asterisk when the user fails to enter the required information. The first change you'll want to make is to enter some informative text. Figure 4-3 shows an example of some text you could add to the ErrorMessage property of the control. This new error text will also show up in the Design window, so you don't need to check the property each time you want to check the content.

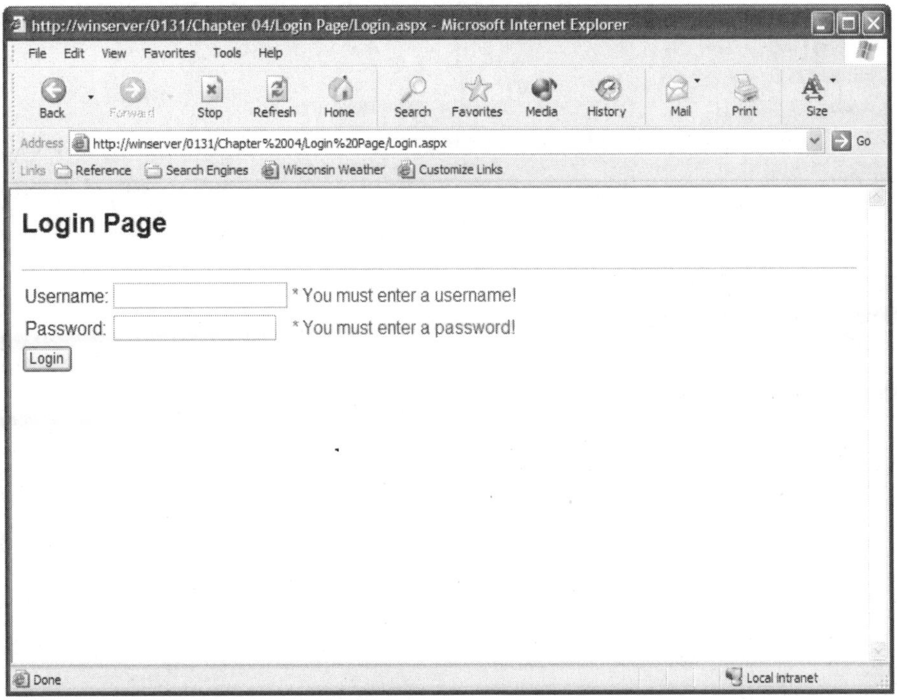

Figure 4-3. Modify the ErrorMessage property of the RequiredFieldValidator control to ensure the user knows what to do.

If the user doesn't enter a name and password, the form displays a message in the area to the right of the appropriate textbox, as shown in Figure 4-3. The presentation of this information means that you can't place anything to the right of the text boxes. Of course, you can always move the RequiredFieldValidator controls to another location on the form to ensure proper placement of the data fields. However, most Web site developers seem to place this information to the right of the control, so don't move the text unless you have a good reason to do so. The rule to remember is that the user has to know what you mean by an error message, which is why placing the message to the right of the textbox works so well.

At some point, the user will provide a user name and password. If they don't provide a correct user name and password, the user will see an error message in the [Msg] label beneath the textboxes, as shown in Figure 4-4. The message label is a standard label. However, it doesn't show up at first because it doesn't contain any text. This makes the field hidden from the user perspective. Theoretically, you can use this label for other error messages or information, but you probably won't need it on this particular page.

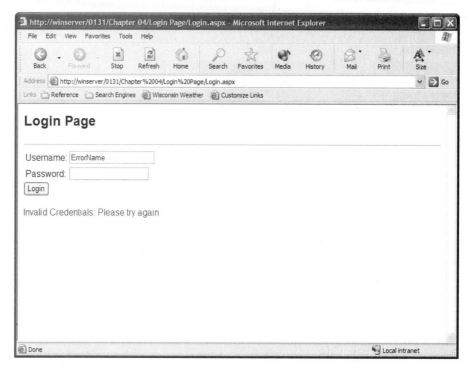

Figure 4-4. Making an error when entering the user name or password produces this error message.

Making a Few Coding Changes

Now that you understand what's going on with the Login Page user interface, let's look at the default code in a little more detail. The form has a single function attached to the Login button. Listing 4-1 shows what it looks like.

Listing 4-1. The Default Login Page Code

```
void LoginBtn_Click(Object sender, EventArgs e) {

    if (Page.IsValid) {
        if ((UserName.Text == "jdoe@somewhere.com") &&
            (UserPass.Text == "password")) {
            FormsAuthentication.RedirectFromLoginPage(UserName.Text, true);
        }
```

```
        else {
            Msg.Text = "Invalid Credentials: Please try again";
        }
    }
}
```

As you can see, the code looks for a specific user name and password, which essentially means that everyone who knows this single user name and password will gain entrance to the Web site. We'll discuss this problem in further detail in the "Devising a Better Password Scheme" section. You've already seen the error message for an incorrect entry in Figure 4-4. However, look at the RedirectFromLoginPage() function call. This function says that the page has authenticated the user and that IIS (or the Cassini Web server that ships with Web Matrix if you use the product in single-machine mode) should redirect the user to the page they originally requested. If the user didn't actually request a page, then the function automatically assumes there's a DEFAULT.ASPX page that the system will use. This call also assumes that you want to store the cookie on the user's machine so they don't have to log in for each request. The server will store the cookie in memory if you set this option to false.

So, how does this system work? The Config File page that we'll discuss later performs the required magic. It contains special entries that tell IIS to redirect the user to the login page, which then tells IIS that the user is authenticated and can have access to the requested page. We'll discuss the various pieces in further detail in the "A General Security Example" section of the chapter.

Using the Logout Page

Unless you want to provide some special content, the Logout Page project is ready to go immediately after you create it. Make sure you give it the same class name and namespace as the Login Page project; otherwise, your application will have a tendency to act strangely during use.

The purpose of the logout page is to allow the user to log out from the system. The forms authentication method used by these pages relies on a cookie for authentication purposes. This page removes the cookie from the user's system so that the user can no longer access the Web site.

You'll normally see the logout page in one of two states. The first tells you that the system hasn't authenticated the user, while the second tells you the user authentication name, as shown in Figure 4-5.

Figure 4-5. Authenticated users will see their name displayed on screen.

I chose to make a few small changes to the logout page to make it more reliable and informative. The original code doesn't provide input if the user is already logged out. It's also a dead end. Therefore, I added a hyperlink that isn't visible until after the user logs out. Listing 4-2 shows the updated version of the code.

Listing 4-2. Logout Page with Added Functionality

```
void Page_Load(Object sender, EventArgs e)
{

    // Display the correct message and enable or disable
    // the button and hyperlink as needed during startup.
    if (Request.IsAuthenticated == true)
    {
        Status.Text = "User " + User.Identity.Name
            + " is currently logged in.";

        // Enable the button so the user can log out.
        LogOffBtn.Visible = true;
        LogOffBtn.Enabled = true;
```

```
        // Disable the hyperlink so the user must log out.
        HyperLink1.Visible = false;
        HyperLink1.Enabled = false;
    }
    else
    {
        Status.Text = "Not authenticated.";

        // Disable the button so it can't be clicked.
        LogOffBtn.Visible = false;
        LogOffBtn.Enabled = false;

        // Enable the hyperlink so the user can log in.
        HyperLink1.Visible = true;
        HyperLink1.Enabled = true;
    }
}

void LogOffBtn_Click(Object sender, EventArgs e)
{
    // Sign the user out and modify the screen text.
    FormsAuthentication.SignOut();
    Status.Text = "Not authenticated.";

    // Disable the button so it can't be clicked twice.
    LogOffBtn.Visible = false;
    LogOffBtn.Enabled = false;

    // Enable the hyperlink so the user can log back in.
    HyperLink1.Visible = true;
    HyperLink1.Enabled = true;
}
```

As you can see, the code isn't overly complex. All it does is make the button or the hyperlink visible as needed. In addition, it enables the desired control. Now when the user logs out, they'll see an option for going back to the home page, as shown in Figure 4-6. It's a small change, but one that most users will appreciate. More importantly, this little addition encourages users to log out because it's not too difficult to log back in to the system afterward.

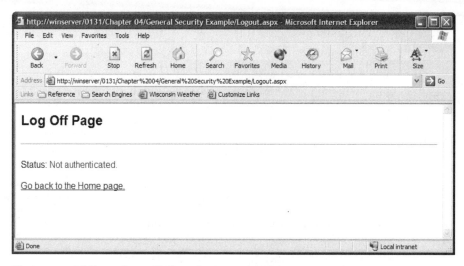

Figure 4-6. Adding a hyperlink to the Logout Page project makes it easier to log back in to the system.

Using the Config File Page

The Config File page is simply a WEB.CONFIG file with a few additional entries set. Figure 4-7 shows the XML Notepad view of this special WEB.CONFIG file. Notice that we have some authentication options set. These options tell IIS to redirect the user to the LOGIN.ASPX file no matter which resource they request from the Web site. After the login page authenticates the user, IIS can redirect them to their originally requested page.

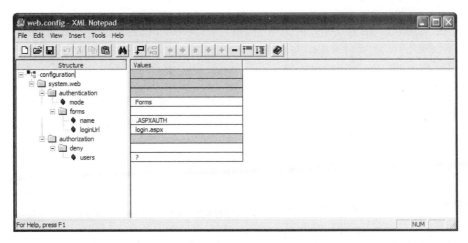

Figure 4-7. Making an error when entering the user name or password produces this error message.

Notice that this file sets the mode attribute of the authentication element to Forms. This attribute indicates that the application will use the forms authentication model. In addition, the forms element contains the name and loginUrl attributes. The name attribute specifies the form that contains the login information for the user. The loginUrl attribute defines the location of the login page. As previously mentioned, you'd need to change one or both of these entries if you changed the name of the Login Page or modified the form in some way.

 TIP *This chapter doesn't look at all of the authentication schemes that ASP.NET supports. We're only looking at the forms authentication because Web Matrix provides special functionality in this area. As a developer, you also have access to Windows, Passport, and custom security options. All of these options rely on entries in the WEB.CONFIG file we'll discuss later in the chapter. You can also learn more about these other schemes in the help topic at* `http://msdn.microsoft.com/library/ en-us/dnbda/html/authaspdotnet.asp.`

Although this page contains more active entries than the example of the WEB.CONFIG file we discussed in Chapter 3, it actually has fewer entries in it. Web Matrix specifically directs this file at providing security for your application. The file lacks the commented entries that you can use for general configuration. In many cases, you'll want to continue using this setup as it currently exists. To maintain the integrity of your application, it's best to place the login page and associated login materials in a separate folder. Using this technique ensures that someone logging in to your system can only see the login page—not the associated application files. Make sure you include the initial page that the user wants to target with the login materials, as shown in the "A General Security Example" section.

Devising a Better Password Scheme

At this point, we have a generic login page that will work if you want to use a single name and password for entry. However, most Web sites, even simple Web sites, will require better protection than a single name and password, which means that we have to create a better login checking method.

You'll need to change two files in order to create a better password scheme. The first file is the Login Page itself. Right now, it validates the user name and password against a single static entry, which isn't secure enough for most applications. The second file is the WEB.CONFIG that we discussed in the "Using the Config Page" section. In order to make the new authentication work, you must provide a list of names and passwords that the application can use for validation purposes. Form-based authentication doesn't rely on Windows authentication. It's a separate authentication method, which actually makes it more secure, in some respects, because you can specify Web-based application user names and passwords that are separate from those used generally by the Windows users on your LAN.

TIP *This chapter provides an overview of many complex technologies. The process of authentication relies on a provider, so knowing about the provider can help you understand the authentication itself better. You can get the details on the Forms Authentication Provider at* http://msdn.microsoft.com/library/en-us/cpguide/html/cpconthecookieauthenticationprovider.asp. *Information on the WindowsAuthenticationModule Provider appears at* http://msdn.microsoft.com/library/en-us/cpguide/html/cpconthewindowsauthenticationprovider.asp. *Make sure you read about both technologies before you make a security decision.*

The change needed in the Login Page is relatively simple. Listing 4-3 shows the modifications you'll have to make to the code.

Listing 4-3. The Modified Login Page Code

```
void LoginBtn_Click(Object sender, EventArgs e)
{

    if (Page.IsValid)
    {
        if (FormsAuthentication.Authenticate(UserName.Text, UserPass.Text))
        {
            FormsAuthentication.RedirectFromLoginPage(UserName.Text, true);
        }
        else
        {
            Msg.Text = "Invalid Credentials: Please try again";
        }
    }
}
```

As you can see, the only thing that's changed is the method used for validation. In this case, we pass the user name and password to the FormsAuthentication.Authenticate() method. This method looks through the list of names in the WEB.CONFIG file and determines if they're valid. The method returns true whenever it can validate the user's identity.

CAUTION *The example application uses the clear password format for example purposes. It's safer and more secure to use one of the other password formats that ASP.NET supports. These other formats enable you to encrypt the password before sending it to the server, making it less likely that prying eyes will discover how to access your server. You can learn more about the password formats at* http://msdn.microsoft.com/ library/en-us/cpguide/html/ cpconformsauthenticationcredentials.asp.

The change to the WEB.CONFIG file is a little more extensive. Listing 4-4 shows the code that we're using now.

Listing 4-4. The Updated Version of the WEB.CONFIG File

```
<?xml version="1.0" encoding="UTF-8" ?>

<configuration>

    <system.web>

        <customErrors mode="Off"/>

        <authentication mode="Forms">
            <forms name=".ASPXAUTH" loginUrl="Login.aspx">
                <credentials passwordFormat="Clear">
                    <user name="John" password="Hello" />
                    <user name="Bill" password="Goodbye" />
                </credentials>
            </forms>
        </authentication>

        <authorization>
            <deny users="?" />
        </authorization>

    </system.web>

</configuration>
```

The biggest change to the WEB.CONFIG is the addition of a credentials element. This element contains an attribute that specifies the password format. The siblings of this element contain the user names and passwords for this application. You can create separate files for each of the applications on your system, making each application unique from a security perspective. Figure 4-8 shows the XML Notepad view of the WEB.CONFIG file. This view shows you the nesting of the various elements in better detail.

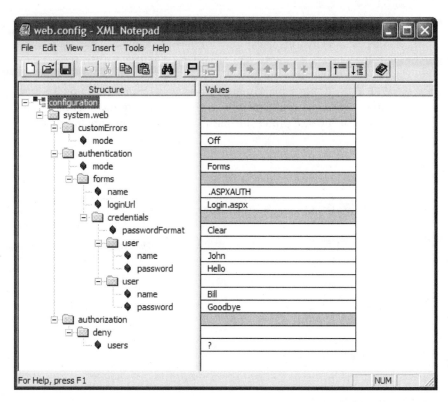

Figure 4-8. Use XML Notepad to validate the nesting of your WEB.CONFIG file when necessary.

···

How Safe Is This Solution?

At this point, you might wonder about the actual security of this method of using passwords. After all, even if you secure everything in the application and make sure you use a secure method of user name and password transfer, the WEB.CONFIG file is still going to appear on the hard drive in plain text. The use of plain text password storage would seem an open invitation to some cracker who wants to learn your company's innermost secrets.

The user of your application can't access the WEB.CONFIG directly. Any attempt to access this file directly will display an error message similar to the one shown in the following illustration. As you can see, this type of page isn't served—the user can't even view it, at least not directly. Theoretically, no one can casually access a WEB.CONFIG file using a browser or other external connection. IIS and ASP.NET simply won't allow the access, even if you have administrator rights on the target server. If you also protect the file at other levels, the work to access it increases.

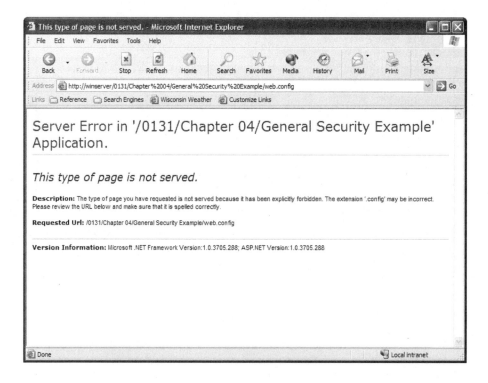

You can also enhance the security of the WEB.CONFIG solution by using alternative data stores. For example, you could store the names and passwords in SQL Server or within an XML file. The SQL Server solution is the more secure of the two solutions because it comes with its own security. However, the XML file option has the advantage of costing less.

Of course, crackers can always find a way around your security measures. Yes, the WEB.CONFIG file is less secure than storing your password in an encrypted storage media or using one-time passwords. However, building a bigger barrier only slows the cracker down. You still have to exercise diligence in maintaining system security. Maintaining security includes enforcing strong passwords and making sure that users change their passwords regularly. The main reason to use WEB.CONFIG is ease of application maintenance and guarding the LAN passwords—keeping your LAN environment separate from your Web environment. Using the WEB.CONFIG file represents a good tradeoff when viewed from this perspective.

A General Security Example

It's time to put the pieces of the application together. It's important to see how the original example works so you can determine if it will work for a simple login. This example puts the pieces together so that you can see how the general security pages provided by Web Matrix work. We'll use the slightly augmented version of the Login Page discussed in the "Devising a Better Password Scheme" section of the chapter, so you can use your standard user name and password to log in to your test Web site.

CAUTION   *The general security example makes no effort at all to encrypt your user name and password—it passes this information between the client and server in clear text that anyone with a network sniffer can read. Normally, you'd set the server up to use an HTTPS (secure) connection to pass the password, as well as using a secure password format. The goal of this example is to demonstrate Web Matrix project functionality, so some safeguards aren't in place for this application. If you use this example on a production Web site, make sure you secure the login page and its associated elements so that the application will encrypt the user name and password.*

You'll actually need four files for this application including the Login Page, the Logout Page, the Config File page, and some content. The content page should contain a link that the user can use to log out of the system. For this example, we'll use a modified version of the ASP.NET example from Chapter 3. This file is now called DEFAULT.ASPX to ensure you'll actually see it, even if you simply type the name of the directory containing the application. Figure 4-9 shows the simple change to this page.

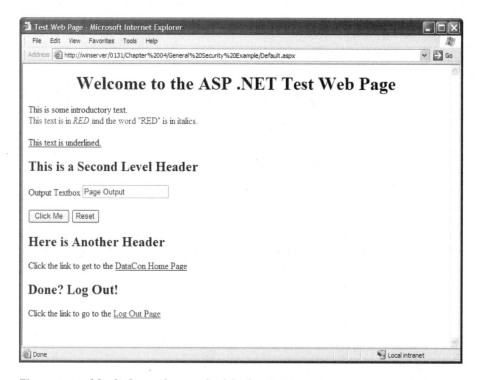

Figure 4-9. Add a link or other method for logging out of your content pages.

One of the configuration issues for this application is that you have to create an IIS application to support the security feature. If you place this example in a standard folder and try to execute it, you'll see an error message similar to the one shown in Figure 4-10. The error message description doesn't really tell you what you need to know. However, if you look at the second sentence for the Parser Error Message, you'll notice that not configuring the directory as an application in IIS can cause this problem. That's the key, in this case, because we haven't created the application yet.

NOTE *No matter what you do, you won't get the error message in Figure 4-10 to print out using a remote connection. This is one of the few situations where you must create a localhost connection to see the error message. If you don't create a localhost connection, you'll see the usual nebulous error message from IIS. This is the message that doesn't tell you anything about the problem, but will tell you about the WEB.CONFIG entries that you need to make in order to see the message. Needless to say, this error message is a bit confusing if you've already made the required entries.*

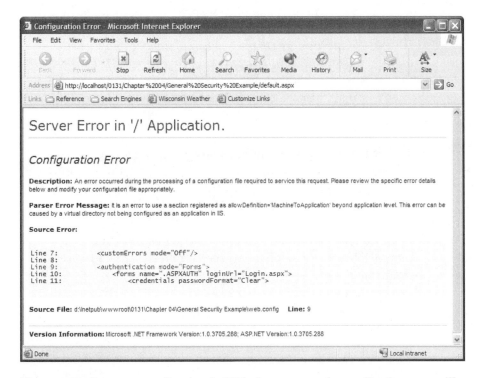

Figure 4-10. Create an application in IIS before you test the application, or you'll see this error screen.

Creating an application in IIS is easy. The following steps will guide you through the process.

1. Open the Internet Services Manager. You'll find this Microsoft Management Console (MMC) in the Administrative Tools folder found in either the Control Panel or the Start menu.

 NOTE *You can't access the Cassini Web server that ships with Web Matrix from the Internet Services Manager MMC snap-in. In general, all you need to do is press F5 to display the Start Web Application dialog box, select the Use ASP.NET Web Matrix Server option, and then click Start. The application will start, and you'll see a browser window open with the application loaded. You'll also see the server icon in the Notification Area of the Taskbar. To stop the server when you're finished running the application, right-click the server icon in the Notification Area and choose Stop from the context menu. Stopping the server will save resources*

2. Connect to your Web server (if necessary) by right-clicking the root node (marked Internet Information Services) and selecting Connect from the context menu. Type the name of your server in the Computer Name field of the Connect to Computer dialog box, and then click OK.

3. Locate the folder containing the four files for this application. Figure 4-11 shows the setup for my server. Your server setup will look similar, but not precisely the same as mine.

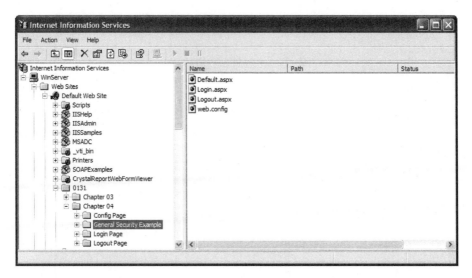

Figure 4-11. Locate your application on the host server.

4. Right-click the folder containing the application and choose Properties from the context menu. You'll see a properties dialog box similar to the one shown in Figure 4-12. This is the dialog box you use to configure your application.

5. Click Create on the Directory tab of the properties dialog box. IIS will create an application for you. Notice that the application has the same name as the directory that holds the application.

Figure 4-12. Use this dialog box to configure your IIS application.

NOTE *This procedure is only looking at the essential configuration issues. You might find that you need to perform other configuration steps to meet specific requirements for your application. For example, you might want to disable directory browsing or perform other security setups. You can find out more about IIS configuration at* http://msdn.microsoft.com/library/ en-us/iisref60/htm/cl_as_manageconfig.asp.

6. Click OK. The icon for the directory containing the application will change, as shown in Figure 4-13. Make sure you look for this change. Theoretically, you're done. However, I found that I had to restart IIS to get the application change to take on some occasions. These last few steps (7 and 8) are optional, and you don't have to do them in order to get a working application in most cases.

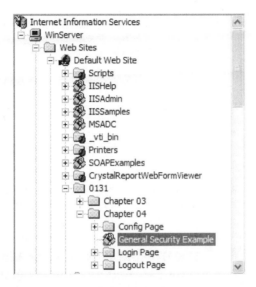

Figure 4-13. Look for the change in the application icon to ensure that IIS has accepted the change in folder status.

7. Right-click the server folder (WinServer in Figure 4-13). Choose All Tasks ➤ Restart IIS from the context menu. You'll see the Stop/Start/Reboot dialog box shown in Figure 4-14.

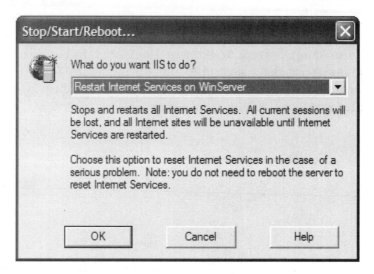

Figure 4-14. Choose an action from the Stop/Start/Reboot dialog box.

8. Select the restart option for your server (should be the default option), and then click OK. IIS will shut down and then restart.

At this point, you should have a working application. You can verify that it works by attempting to open the DEFAULT.ASPX file on the Web server. Instead of seeing this file, you should see the login page first. After you enter a correct user name and password, the requested resource should appear. Click the logout link, and you'll see the logout page. It should contain the name that you used for logging in to the system. Click Log Off, and the display should tell you that you're no longer authenticated. It should also contain a link to the application home page.

Windows-Validated Security

The example in this chapter has demonstrated the capabilities of Web Matrix. It hasn't demonstrated everything that either ASP.NET or IIS provide in the way of security because many of these features require additional programming or a few configuration changes. The following sections point out a few of the configuration changes you can make to IIS so that you don't need the special pages that Web Matrix provides. More importantly, it points out a feature that most (if not all) Web servers have—the ability to provide security without additional programming. We'll also look at a few ASP.NET security changes you can make to use Windows security going that route.

Why Use Windows-Validated Security?

Of course, the most important question is why Windows-validated security is so great. It might seem odd to show the security projects included with Web Matrix and then say that you can also use something else that isn't Web Matrix specific—especially in a book about Web Matrix. There aren't any perfect security solutions out there—just those that work in a given situation. The Web Matrix solution presented in this chapter works fine for most small applications and even a few medium-sized applications, but let's face it, creating a list of names to include in the WEB.CONFIG file is just too much work for a large application. Consequently, as the size of the application increases, the Windows validation method becomes more attractive.

The Windows validation method also solves a problem with ASP.NET security. The ASP.NET runtime only provides protection for files that it processes. This means that the ASPX files in your application are secure, but the HTM, ZIP, EXE, GIF, JPG, and other support files aren't secured.

Many users are also concerned about cookies today because of the bad press they have received in the media. Windows authentication doesn't require the use of cookies—the authentication is made without adding this file to the user's machine. On the other hand, form-based security does require a cookie, so it might not work if the user has cookies disabled.

You also need to consider the security of the file. See the "How Safe Is This Solution?" sidebar for more details on this issue. In sum, using Windows security is marginally more secure, in some areas, but could leave your LAN passwords open to prying eyes unless you implement a combination of a Virtual Private Network (VPN) SSL solution—a time-consuming and error-prone process. Therefore, you need to consider how much security you gain by using Windows security and determine how much you lose when a user passes their LAN user name and password over a nonsecure wire. Someday, someone will come up with a perfect solution to the security issues of today, but that solution isn't even a glimmer in someone's eye right now.

A final consideration is the user. Trying to get some users to remember one password without writing it down is akin to asking them to recite the history of the entire world while standing on one foot. Just imagine the fun you'll have trying to get these users to remember two passwords without writing them down. Let's just say that a two-password system might present some difficulties. Of course, you could always use a solution such as smart cards, but this solution also has problems.

Using the Web Server Security Approach

One of the easiest ways to add security to any Web server is to tell the server that you want to secure the directory. The steps required to do this vary by server, so you'll need to spend some time with the vendor documentation for your particular setup. In fact, the steps even vary for different *versions* of IIS. This section looks at the latest version of IIS for Windows 2000 and Windows XP.

The first rule that many administrators forget about Web server security is that a Web server always provides two methods for obtaining access to any given resource: the LAN and the Web. A number of crackers have used techniques that rely on breaking the Web portion of the server to gain access to the LAN. They then use the open door that most administrators forget to lock to access the resource using the LAN connection. In short, make sure you set the security for your application directory from a LAN perspective, as well as a Web perspective.

Setting the LAN security is easy in Windows. Simply locate the directory that holds your application on the Web server. For example, I placed the example for this chapter in the D:\Inetpub\wwwroot\0131\Chapter 04\General Security Example folder of my Web server. Right-click this folder and choose Properties from the context menu. Select the Security tab and look at your settings. If you see Everyone as one of the groups (see Figure 4-15), you might as well hang an "Open for Business" sign on your Web server. This is unfortunately the default setting for many Windows setups, and many administrators don't know to change it.

Figure 4-15. Verify that you've set the LAN security for your Web application correctly.

The second part of the security setting appears in the Internet Services Manager console. Right-click the application folder and choose Properties from the context menu. Select the Directory Security entry, and you'll see a properties dialog box similar to the one shown in Figure 4-16.

Figure 4-16. Use the Directory Security tab of the properties dialog box to change the Internet security for your Web application.

Notice the three sections included on this dialog box. The first section helps you secure the application directory by modifying the requirements to access it. We'll look at this option in detail in a few seconds. The second section sets access restrictions for the application—it detects who's trying to access the application and determines if their IP address falls within the required range. The third section secures client and server communication using certificates. These three sections together provide a lot more security than the simple solution we created in this chapter, but it also requires a lot more work to implement.

However, let's look at how you can secure the application using Windows security to provide a level of security that's slightly better than the one in this chapter. Click Edit in the Anonymous access and authentication control section, and you'll see the Authentication Methods dialog box shown in Figure 4-17. Setting this option to Anonymous access, as shown in the figure, allows anyone to access the Web site without logging in unless you implement a solution similar to the one demonstrated in this chapter. To use Windows security, you must clear the Anonymous access option and check one or more of the other three options.

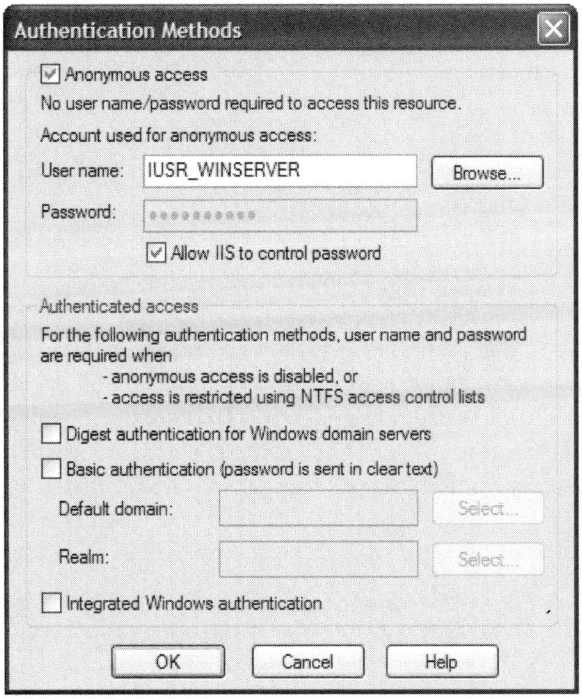

Figure 4-17. Using the Anonymous access option means that you must implement security outside of the IIS environment.

Using the WEB.CONFIG Security Approach

If you don't want to rely on an administrator somewhere to configure your application correctly or you simply want to make your application more secure, you can use the other WEB.CONFIG options. Web Matrix doesn't care how you set up your WEB.CONFIG file, it merely suggests a particular course of action, which happens to be form authentication. If you want to use Windows security, then you'd configure WEB.CONFIG, as shown in Listing 4-5.

Listing 4-5. A Windows Security Version of WEB.CONFIG

```
<?xml version="1.0" encoding="UTF-8" ?>


<configuration>

  <system.web>
```

```
<authentication mode="Windows" />

<authorization>
  <deny users="?" />
</authorization>

</system.web>

</configuration>
```

As you can see, this version is similar to the forms version—the only difference is that the authentication mode is set to Windows. You can also use the digest form of security, which relies on Active Directory, with a domain controller. You can learn more about these options at http://msdn.microsoft.com/library/default.asp?url=/library/en-us/dnbda/html/authaspdotnet.asp.

 TIP *You can include a copy of WEB.CONFIG in each folder of an application. Using this technique provides localized security for that folder, rather than relying on a single WEB.CONFIG file to provide global security. ASP.NET allows the developer to set security at the machine, application, and subapplication levels.*

Notice that Listing 4-5 contains both an `<authentication>` element and an `<authorization>` element. Both elements are needed because authentication is different from authorization. *Authentication* is the process of discovering the identity of a requestor using some type of credential. For example, when the user provides a name and password, Windows can authentication them. *Authorization* determines if the requestor is allowed to access or use a resource. The authorization steps always occurs after authentication because you must first know who the requestor is before you can determine their level of access.

While this chapter doesn't provide a complete documentary on every aspect of the WEB.CONFIG file, you do need to know about an important element that isn't included as part of the default template. The `<location>` element provides control over the security in a particular location. For example, you can use this element to say that one location has a high trust level, while another location has a low trust level. However, the most important feature of the `<location>` element is that it gives you the ability to lock down security to a specific level—you can say that a user can't override security by using a local WEB.CONFIG file. Here is an example of the `<location>` element.

```
<location path="http://mysite/somepage/" allowOverride="false">
  <trust level="high" />
</location>
```

In this case, the `<location>` element states that the `http://mysite/somepage/` URL has a high trust level. The `allowOverride` property states that the user of that site can't override the current security setting. You can learn more about the `<location>` element methods and properties at `http://msdn.microsoft.com/library/en-us/cpgenref/html/gnconlocationmembers.asp`. Look at the article entitled "Locking Configuration Settings" (`http://msdn.microsoft.com/library/en-us/cpguide/html/cpconlockingconfigurationsettings.asp`) for some ideas on how to use the <location> element in your next application.

Summary

This chapter has helped you explore the issue of security and demonstrated how Web Matrix can help you achieve it. We've discussed the types of pages that Web Matrix provides to answer the security question, and you've learned a little more about configuration. This chapter also presented some information about IIS configuration, and we built a secure application. In short, I've shown you everything regarding security in a Web Matrix example in one short chapter.

The problem is that crackers are always inventing new ways to break into your Web site, errors in configuration and development provide opportunity, and known gaps in environment security provide the key. The bottom line is that a cracker is going to break into your Web site sometime during your career. Your best defense is knowing that a break-in will occur so that you can guard against it by exercising some measure of vigilance. While the application we created provides some safeguards, you still need to monitor your Web site for potential problems.

Chapter 5 will present one of the most commonly used applications—the database. We'll explore everything Web Matrix has to offer from simple form views to grid views, to reports and beyond. You'll learn how to make connections, manage your database, and even create some new resources. While this chapter won't show you how to design the next accounting system for your credit card company, it will assist you with basic database applications such as contact management systems that will help users on the road.

CHAPTER 5

Web Matrix Database Development

In This Chapter

- Learn How to Configure MSDE Using MSDE Query

- Learn How to Use the Code Builders

- Build Your Own SQL Scripts

- Create an Application Using a Simple Stored Procedure

- Create an Application Using the DataList and Repeater Controls

- Develop a Simple Data Display Application

- Discover How to Use Data Grids

- Discover How to Use Data Reporting

- Develop a Complete Database Application

- Learn About the Limitations of the Web Matrix Approach

Databases represent the one commonality in all businesses—no matter how large or small. The database acts as the company memory. This complex application stores all of the data a company produces, and most employees in a company are unaware of just how much data their employer's database contains. Companies jealously guard their databases and go to great lengths to protect them. Database users manipulate, manage, and mine the data contained within a database. Great theorists have developed rules for working with databases, only to have other theorists develop other, contrasting, rules. Some developers work with nothing but databases. If any application represented the concept of "knowledge is power," the database is it.

Given the extreme importance of databases, it's no wonder that Web Matrix provides some functionality for working with them. In fact, you can build some reasonably complex applications using Web Matrix alone. However, Web Matrix isn't (and doesn't pretend to be) a "top-of-the-line" tool—it lacks many features for creating complex applications. We'll see later that you don't have access to Visual Studio .NET features such as Server Explorer, and that I found it impossible to connect to anything but SQL Server or MSDE. You also have to consider the benefits of automation for tools such as those Visual Studio .NET provides. A small business could probably use Web Matrix for a serious development tool. Consultants will probably find Web Matrix useful for looking at a client's data quickly. Some developers will want to keep this tool handy for quick edits. In a few cases, you might even want to use it as a tool for experimentation.

Before we go any further, I wanted to tell you what to expect from this chapter. This chapter was extremely difficult to write because I'm trying to create the same material that most authors write in 500 or 600 pages in a mere 40 pages. Let's just say I had to get creative. I looked at the resources in the Web Matrix Project Guide Tour (http://www.asp.net/webmatrix/tour/getstarted/intro.aspx) and *Inside ASP.NET Web Matrix* (http://www.asp.net/webmatrix/web%20matrix_doc.pdf) and decided to avoid duplicating these free resources. Consequently, my grid view example is absurdly short because these two resources already demonstrate the grid view, and you also have access to a template for that purpose with Web Matrix. Some other database elements also fall into the "already demonstrated" category, so you won't see them here, but I will tell you where to find them.

Given that you have some free information available, I had to decide what to address in this chapter. I looked through the various newsgroup posts and learned that many of you would like to know more about form view presentations. In addition, I also looked at features I haven't discussed in other areas of the book, such as the Code Builders. Finally, I felt that you should know about a third-party product, MSDE Query, which I used to create the test database and other database elements using scripts instead of direct entry as shown in the example on the Web Matrix site (http://www.asp.net/webmatrix/default.aspx). The result of my research is the chapter you see before you.

This chapter shows you the database functionality Web Matrix provides. Most of you will be surprised at just how much you can do with Web Matrix. For example, you can create a data grid using standard drag-and-drop techniques. You'll learn that a form view is quite doable but requires more work. Although Web Matrix doesn't include support for advanced data reporting tools, you can use it to create simple reports based on the projects provided. You'll even find that Web Matrix provides access to several specialized database controls including the DataList and Repeater controls. We'll explore all of these issues in the sections that follow.

NOTE   *Web Matrix doesn't include a database engine. You can easily connect to SQL Server or use the Microsoft Database Engine (MSDE). (It's theoretically possible to connect to other Database Management Systems (DBMSs), but not without a lot of complex coding. Given that Web Matrix lacks a debugger, you won't want to use it for other DBMSs.) We discussed MSDE installation in the "Installing the MSDE" section of Chapter 2. Make sure you install all patches and updates for both SQL Server and MSDE. The current SQL Server update as of this writing is Service Pack 2* (http://www.microsoft.com/sql/downloads/2000/sp2.asp). *You also want to install the SQL Server security patch described at* http://www.microsoft.com/technet/treeview/ default.asp?url=/technet/security/prodtech/ dbsql/default.asp.

You'll also learn about MSDE Query in this chapter. This tool can make your Web Matrix experience a lot more complete, especially if you don't have a copy of SQL Server to use for development purposes. Like all of the other tools discussed in this book, MSDE Query is easy to download from the Internet (http://www.msde.biz/download.htm).

NOTE   *If you're using a full copy of SQL Server for this book and don't want to work with MSDE Query, you can use Query Analyzer (which ships with SQL Server 7 and higher) to create and populate the test database. The MovieGuide2.SQL file in the \Chapter 05\Data folder of the source code (available at* http://www.apress.com/book/download.html) *is designed to work with Query Analyzer. Simply load the file and execute it. You can then populate the database by importing the content of the MovieGuideData.TXT file using the DTS Import/Export Wizard. These two files won't work with MSDE. Use the information in the "Configuring MSDE Using MSDE Query" section to work with MSDE.*

Configuring MSDE Using MSDE Query

If you've worked with MSDE at all, you might have noticed that it's not exactly easy to configure. Microsoft never meant MSDE to provide full SQL Server functionality—it's a tool to help developers create applications that rely on SQL Server as a data source without actually having to purchase a copy of SQL Server. Even so, it would be nice to have some means for interacting with MSDE using a query application like the Query Analyzer utility provided with SQL Server 2000. Fortunately, you can get Query Analyzer–like functionality out of a third-party product called MSDE Query (`http://www.msde.biz/download.htm`).

NOTE *Nothing you do will make MSDE into SQL Server. If you need full database support to develop a project, then you'll need to obtain a copy of SQL Server. For example, there isn't any substitute for Enterprise Manager that you can use with Web Matrix. Consequently, the features that Enterprise Manager provides, such as Database Diagrams, are unavailable to Web Matrix users.*

After you download MSDE Query, extract the files to a temporary directory on your system. Double-click SETUP.EXE to start the installation process. Follow the few prompts to install the product. When you're finished, you can open MSDE Query to interact with the copy of MSDE installed on your machine. Figure 5-1 shows a typical view of MSDE Query. In this case, I've made a query against the movie database that we'll use for the examples in this chapter.

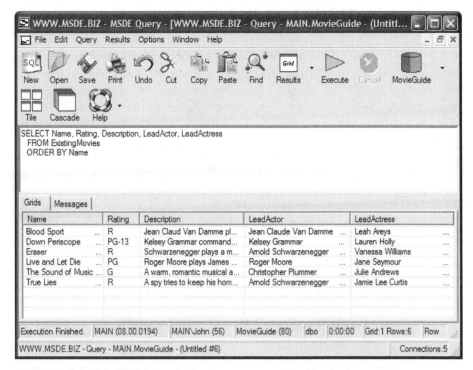

Figure 5-1. Using MSDE Query helps you get more out of the database features provided by MSDE.

Now that you've got the big picture for MSDE Query, let's look at this product in a little more detail. The following sections show you how to perform a few basic tasks with MSDE Query. If you have experience using Query Analyzer, the features that this tool provides should look familiar. We'll discuss enough of the basics so that even if you haven't used Query Analyzer, you'll be able to perform some basic tasks.

TIP *There's a good chance that by the time you read this the same person who created MSDE Query will have an MSDE version of Enterprise Manager available. The product is currently under development, so I was unable to test it in time for the book. This utility will enable a Web Matrix developer to work with a variety of database entities using a GUI similar to the one used by SQL Server owners.*

Opening a Database

Before you can do anything with MSDE Query, you need to create some connections. The first is to the DBMS itself. The second is to a particular database managed by the DBMS. Once you have these two connections in place, you can begin creating queries that request data in specific tables or execute stored procedures.

> **NOTE** *This section assumes that you have MSDE installed and that it's started. To determine if MSDE is running (it normally starts when you boot the system), hover the mouse over the SQL Server Service Manager icon in the Notification Area of the Taskbar. The balloon help will tell you if the service is running. If it isn't running, right-click the icon and choose Open SQL Server Service Manager from the context menu. Select SQL Server in the Services field and click Start/Continue. After a few moments the indicator will change from a red square stop indicator to a green triangle running indicator.*

To create the DBMS connection, click New Query (the button that looks like a page with the letters SQL on it). You'll see a Connect to SQL Server dialog box like the one shown in Figure 5-2. Notice that this dialog box contains options for creating both local and remote connections.

Figure 5-2. Create a DBMS connection using the Connect to SQL Server dialog box.

You'll need to supply the connection information and the authentication method. If you're accessing a local copy of MSDE, leave the settings as shown in Figure 5-2, and click OK. A local copy of MSDE will always use Windows NT Authentication. The only time you need to consider SQL Server Authentication is if you want to make a connection to an actual copy of SQL Server.

Once you have a DBMS connection made, MSDE Query will enable all of the buttons on the toolbar. It assumes that you want to use the master database. However, you can select any database managed by the DBMS using the drop-down list shown in Figure 5-3. You must select the database for a query before you create and execute it.

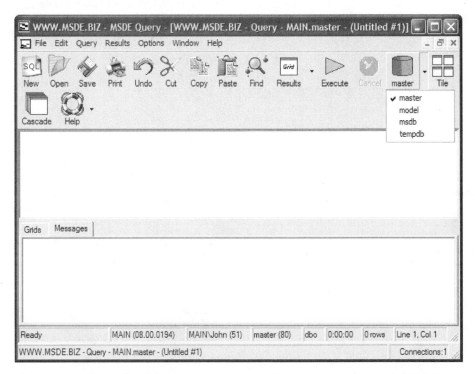

Figure 5-3. Select a database to query once you have a connection to the DBMS.

Formatting and Executing a Query

Working with MSDE Query means executing SQL statements. You can write your own queries or use queries generated by someone else. This chapter doesn't show you how to write SQL—that's a topic for another book. However, let's assume that you've installed the MovieGuide database and want to make a query on the ExistingMovies table. A simple query might look like this.

```
SELECT * FROM ExistingMovies
```

Right now your local MSDE DBMS doesn't contain the MovieGuide database, but let's try it anyway. Type this query into the top of half of MSDE Query. Click Execute and you'll see that the DBMS doesn't return any records, as shown in Figure 5-4—not totally unexpected. In fact, MSDE Query tells you that the database engine experienced an error because the requested object doesn't exist. We'll fix this problem in the sections that follow. For now, all you need to know is that executing a query means typing a command, and then clicking Execute.

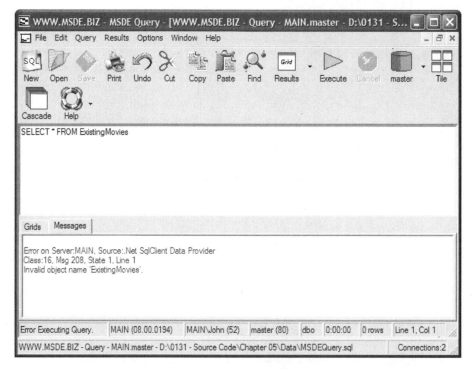

Figure 5-4. Making a query on a nonexistent database won't return any records.

Saving Queries to Disk

You can save any query that you can write and test to disk. If you execute the same query (or queries) on a regular basis, saving them to disk can save time and effort. Saving queries to disk also allows you to send a design to someone else. In general, saving queries is a good idea if you plan to work with the same database for a while.

Before you save a query to disk, make sure it's complete and that you've tested it. Click Save to display the Save SQL Query dialog box. Use the hierarchical display to find a location to store the file, type a name, and then click OK.

That's all there is to it. MSDE Query will create a SQL file containing your query. The interesting thing about these queries is that they're in plain text and you can view them in any text editor (including Web Matrix).

Let's save the query that we created in the previous section (see Figure 5-4 for details). Click Save. You'll see the Save SQL Query dialog box. Type **MSDEQuery**, and then click Save. That's all there is to it.

Using Saved Queries

The database we'll use in this example is stored in two files in the \Chapter 05\Data folder of the source code, available from the Downloads section on the Apress Web site (`http://www.apress.com/book/download.html`). The first file, MovieGuide.SQL, contains the queries (the script) required to re-create the MovieGuide database on your machine. Without the instructions in this script, you'd have to re-create the database and associated tables by hand. Because of some limited functionality in MSDE Query, we'll still need to perform some steps by hand.

 CAUTION *MSDE Query doesn't appear to support all of the script features supported by Query Analyzer. For example, you'll find that the GO command (used by SQL Server's Transact-SQL to separate T-SQL commands or batches of commands) is unsupported, which means that some scripts you create with SQL Server need to be divided into sections to work with MSDE Query. In some cases, attempts to use a standard script within MSDE Query cause the application to fail. The script might perform some, but not all of the steps, in the script. In general, you'll want to use files saved with MSDE Query and not files created by SQL Server.*

Although MSDE Query doesn't quite support all of the features that Query Analyzer supports, it's still a great tool for making queries and fills a large hole in database support for Web Matrix. Of course, before we can do anything with the database, we'll have to create it. We'll perform this step using a manual query. Begin by opening a connection to MSDE as we did in the "Opening a Database" section if you don't have a connection already established. Type the information shown in Listing 5-1 in the query window (you'll also find this query in the CreateMovieGuide.SQL file). Make sure you substitute a data path that you can actually use for your system.

Listing 5-1. SQL Query for Sample Database

```
CREATE DATABASE [MovieGuide]
   ON (NAME = N'MovieGuide',
       FILENAME = N'E:\MyData\MovieGuide.mdf' ,
       SIZE = 1,
       FILEGROWTH = 10%)
   LOG ON (NAME = N'MovieGuide_log',
           FILENAME = N'E:\MyData\MovieGuide_log.LDF' ,
           FILEGROWTH = 10%)
```

Notice that this command has several sections. First, it tells MSDE to create a database named MovieGuide. The database file is also named MovieGuide, and this database resides in a specific location on disk. We'll start with a 1 MB file and allow a file growth of 10 percent as data requirements demand. This file also has a log associated with it as expressed by the LOG ON entry. The log file also has a specific file location and a file growth allotment.

When you finish typing this information, click Execute. MSDE Query will pause for a few moments. The results pane will display a message saying that 0 rows were returned from the query (the expected result). You'll also notice that MSDE shows a new local database, as shown in Figure 5-5. Make sure you select this database before we proceed.

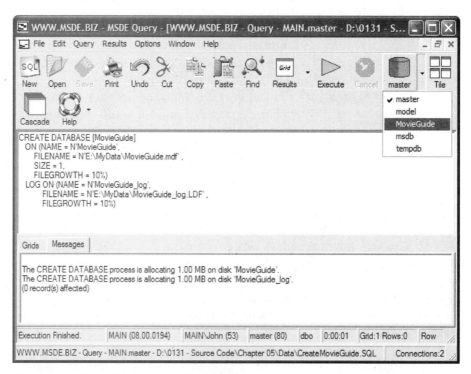

Figure 5-5. Create the MovieGuide database and then check the results.

Now that we have a database to use, we'll need to set options, create a table, and generally make it useful. The following steps will show you how to re-create the MovieGuide database content. In the process, you'll learn how to use saved queries in MSDE Query.

1. Click Open. You'll see an Open a SQL Query dialog box.

2. Locate the MovieGuide.SQL file on your system. Highlight this file and click Open. MSDE Query will load the file, as shown in Figure 5-6.

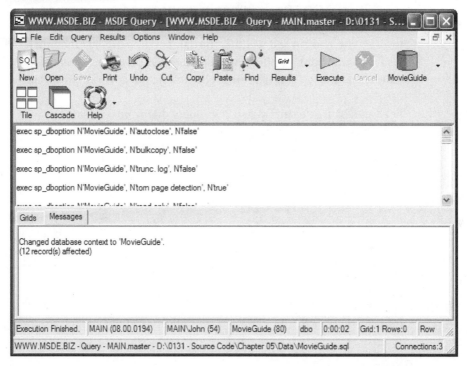

Figure 5-6. Load the MovieGuide.SQL file so you can create the database on your machine.

3. Click Execute. MSDE Query will appear to pause for a few seconds. You should hear some hard drive activity as it configures the database for use. When the query (script) is complete, you'll see a "(12 row(s) returned)" result value. At this point, you have a table to fill with data, so let's do just that.

4. Click New Query to create a new query. Make sure MovieGuide is selected in the Database list box. Creating a new query ensures you don't end up with any results from the previous query.

5. Type the following text in the query window.

```
BULK INSERT MovieGuide..ExistingMovies
    FROM 'E:\MyData\MovieGuideData.DAT'
    WITH (FORMATFILE = 'E:\MyData\MovieGuideData.FMT')
```

This command will insert all of the predefined records in the MovieGuideData.DAT file. Make sure you change the path to match the actual location of this file on your hard drive.

6. Click Execute. MSDE Query will insert the requested data into the database. The Messages tab will show that the change affected 12 records. At this point, we need to test whether the database is actually functional. This is an important step before we begin to rely on the database in the sections that follow. This next step relies on the query we saved earlier.

7. Click Open. You'll see an Open a SQL Query dialog box. Select the MSDEQuery.SQL file we created earlier and then click Open. You'll see the query on screen. Click Execute. Figure 5-7 shows the results of all our work. You can now see the data that the database contains.

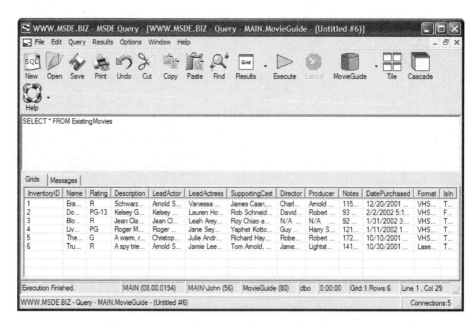

Figure 5-7. The final output of all the work with MSDE Query shows that you have full control over MSDE when using this product.

Using the Web Matrix Code Builders

Up to this point in the book, I've emphasized that Web Matrix contains little, if anything, in the automation department. However, what I've failed to mention until now is that you don't necessarily have to live with this situation. Sure, it's nearly impossible to add any automation to your application templates, but other forms of automation are available. In this case, the automation comes as a Code Builder. Essentially, a *Code Builder* is a wizard for creating specific types of code.

The Code Builders become available (visible) on the Toolbox when you choose the Code tab in the editor window. Figure 5-8 shows the list of five Code Builders that come with Web Matrix. As you can see, four of these Code Builders provide you with some type of database functionality—which is why the Code Builders appear in this chapter, rather than somewhere else.

Figure 5-8. Rely on the Code Builders to help you create consistent code for your applications.

The following sections show how you can use these Code Builders to create better applications more quickly than you could using hand-coding techniques. While these Code Builders might not provide all of the features of a product such as Visual Studio .NET, they do help. There's also the possibility that you could build your own Code Builders to automate "in-house" tasks.

NOTE *At the time of this writing, some of the resource material on the Web Matrix Web site indicates that you can create your own Code Builders and add-ins. Unfortunately, the Web Matrix development staff is still working on this aspect of the product. Make sure you check the Web Matrix Web site from time to time for the promised detailed instructions.*

Using the Send Email Code Builder

One of the most common pieces of code on any Web page is the e-mail contact link. It doesn't matter what type of site you look at, who created it, or its intended purpose, most Web sites include some type of e-mail response technology. Consequently, it makes sense that a Code Builder designed to create an e-mail response is the first one we look at.

We'll begin this example by creating a button in the Design window. I gave my button a caption of Send A Message and called it btnSendMessage. Double-click the button to create the btnSendMessage_Click() event handler. Now we're ready to work with the Send Email Code Builder.

Using a Code Builder is as simple as using a control in the Design window. All you need to do is drag the Code Builder you want to use to the editing area. In this case, drag it to the area between the starting and ending brace for the btnSendMessage_Click() event handler. The Send Email Code Builder displays a dialog box similar to the one shown in Figure 5-9. Notice that this dialog box offers fields for the To and From address, a Subject, the e-mail type, and the location of the Simple Mail Transfer Protocol (SMTP) Server. Obviously, the entries are generic, but they do allow for customization of all of the normal e-mail entries that you might need. In fact, using this setup, you could create an entire page of e-mail contacts similar to the pages found on many corporate Web sites.

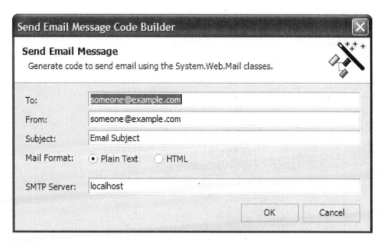

Figure 5-9. Create an e-mail contact using this Code Builder.

NOTE *The example in this section won't run unless you have SMTP support enabled for your server. Fortunately, although the mini-server included with Web Matrix doesn't provide the required support, you can use Internet Information Server (IIS) to test this example. If the example won't run, verify that the test server has the required SMTP support installed. As an alternative strategy, provide the name of the SMTP server for your personal e-mail, supply your e-mail address on that server, and make sure you have a live connection from which to run the test application. You'll have to download your e-mail as normal to verify the results of any tests.*

Once you fill in the required information, click OK. The Code Builder will create most of the code required to implement your e-mail response. Listing 5-2 shows a typical example of code created using some standard values—in this case, I used my own personal e-mail address and a typical e-mail subject.

Listing 5-2. Typical E-Mail Response Code

```
void btnSendMessage_Click(Object sender, EventArgs e)
{
    //  Build a MailMessage
    System.Web.Mail.MailMessage mailMessage =
        new System.Web.Mail.MailMessage();
    mailMessage.From = "YourEmailAddress@example.com";
    mailMessage.To = "JMueller@mwt.net";
    mailMessage.Subject = "Web Site Comments";
    mailMessage.BodyFormat = System.Web.Mail.MailFormat.Text;

    //  TODO: Set the mailMessage.Body property

    System.Web.Mail.SmtpMail.SmtpServer = "localhost";
    System.Web.Mail.SmtpMail.Send(mailMessage);
}
```

Notice that the Code Builder creates all of the typical code for you and even leaves a TODO in place for code that it doesn't handle. In this case, it doesn't provide a message body, which only makes sense because the Web Matrix designers have no idea of what you'd like to say in the message. One area of specialization would be to create special e-mail response Code Builders that also provide a body for you.

At this point, the example will send an e-mail message that lacks a body and has a string From field value. To complete the example, you'd add a From field to the form and a field in which the user could type a message for the body. Depending on the type of message, you could also provide access to the Subject field. The btnSendMessage_Click() event handler would have to substitute these values for the current values in Listing 5-2. The example merely provides some values you could use for testing purposes.

Using the Database Code Builders

You might wonder why Web Matrix would include a set of database Code Builders when you can simply move the table you want to use from the Database window to the Design window. Performing this simple step creates a grid and database connection, so it seems that everything you need is right there. The problem is that this technique only works well if you want to create a grid or summary display of your data. What if you want to see the data one record at a time or you need to perform some type of special data handling? That's where these database Code Builders come into play.

NOTE *The following sections use the database-related Code Builders to create a form-based application using the MovieGuide database we created earlier in the chapter. You'll find this example in the \Chapter 05\ViewForm folder of the source code (available at* http://www.apress.com/book/download.html).

Using the SELECT Data Method Code Builder

The first task that most database applications perform is to select some data for display on screen. You'll use the SELECT Data Method Code Builder to perform this task. Unlike the other methods we'll create in this example, this method normally appears in the Page_Load() event handler. Generally, you want the user to see data when they first start the application, so placing this method in the Page_Load() event handler makes sense.

When you drag and drop the SELECT Data Method Code Builder onto the form, you'll see a Connect to SQL or MSDE Database dialog box similar to the one shown in Figure 5-10. You'll need to choose the host you want to use. When using Web Matrix, the local host is normally MSDE unless you've installed SQL Server locally. You'll also need to choose an authentication method and the database you want to use. The dialog box includes an option for creating a new database, if desired. The example will use the MovieGuide database that we created earlier in the chapter.

Figure 5-10. Choosing a database is the first step in using the SELECT Data Method Code Builder.

When you click OK to make the connection, Web Matrix will present the Query Builder shown in Figure 5-11. The Tables pane contains a list of tables in the current database. Selecting a particular table will display its fields in the Columns list. Select the * column if you want to include all of the columns in the query. You can also click Select All, which selects the entries individually. The WHERE clause pane contains a list of conditions that an entry must fulfill in order to appear as part of the query output. (Curious why I capitalized WHERE? SQL "keywords" by convention are typically all uppercase.)

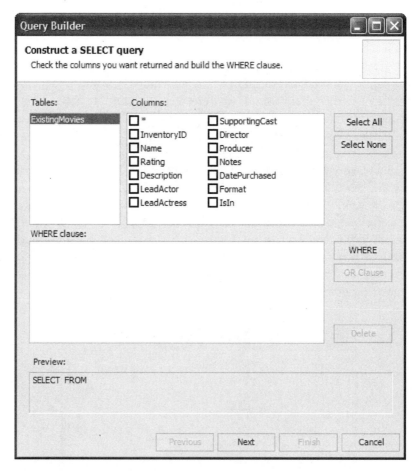

Figure 5-11. Use the Query Builder to reduce the work required to create a query.

 TIP *If the Query Builder doesn't provide quite enough help, you can copy the text from the Preview pane and paste it into MSDE Query. Execute the query to determine what results it will return in your application. Using this technique helps you refine your database connections as you build them.*

The example will use all of the columns in the database and won't require a WHERE clause. Click Select All and then click Next. You'll see a Preview Query dialog box. This dialog box helps you determine if you created the correct query. Click Test Query. You'll see output similar to that shown in Figure 5-12. If your output doesn't match the output in Figure 5-12, click Previous and try again. In a normal application design scenario, you could click Next and Previous as often as needed to get the query correct.

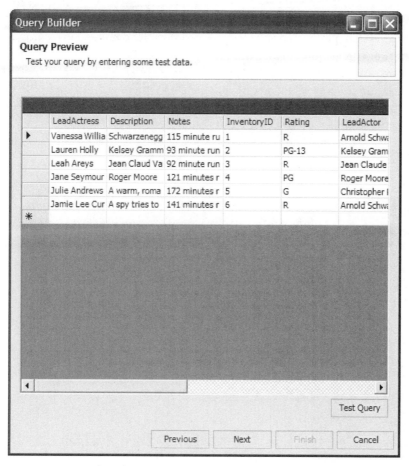

Figure 5-12. Test your query using the Test Query button located in this dialog box.

At some point, the query will produce the results you want. Click Next in the Query Preview dialog box shown in Figure 5-12, and you'll see the Enter a Caption for this Wizard Panel dialog box. The top of this form contains a field where you can type the name of the query. Always use something descriptive. For this example, use ExistingMoviesSelect.

You'll also see an option to choose between a DataSet and a DataReader. Unfortunately, the dialog box doesn't explain this option. In most cases, a DataSet works best because it downloads all of the required rows at one time. You don't need the connection to the database manager after that time because all of the required data appears on the client machine. Of course, this technique could also consume a great deal of network bandwidth and local resources if you don't create your query carefully.

The DataReader has an advantage in that it creates a read-only, forward-only live connection to the database. The client only requires enough memory to hold one record at a time. Consequently, this technique is very efficient and can increase system performance. The user won't download unneeded records, saving network bandwidth. In fact, this technique might be your only option when working with a device such as a PDA. However, there's the little problem of requiring a live connection. If you think the client might want to work with the data in a disconnected application scenario, then this method isn't an option. The example application will use a DataSet, because I'm assuming you're working on a desktop machine with lots of resources and the data set isn't that large.

TIP *This section provides a very quick overview of the DataReader and DataSet objects. You can find more comparison information online. One of the best articles on the topic discusses the differences between ADO and ADO.NET. You'll find it at* http://msdn.microsoft.com/library/ en-us/vbcon/html/vbconADOPreviousVersionsOfADO.asp. *The second article, at* http://msdn.microsoft.com/library/ en-us/dnadonet/html/adonetbest.asp, *describes the best practices for using ADO.NET.*

After you make these final selections, click Finish. The SELECT Data Method Code Builder will create the required code for you.

Demonstrating the SELECT Data Method Code Builder

At this point, you should have a fancy new method in your application named ExistingMoviesSelect() along with a Page_Load() method. It's time to create an application to go with this code. We'll begin with the layout of the data entry form. Figure 5-13 shows the basic layout for this example. As you can see, this example makes use of the Absolute Position feature of Web Matrix. The control names appear as part of the code that follows.

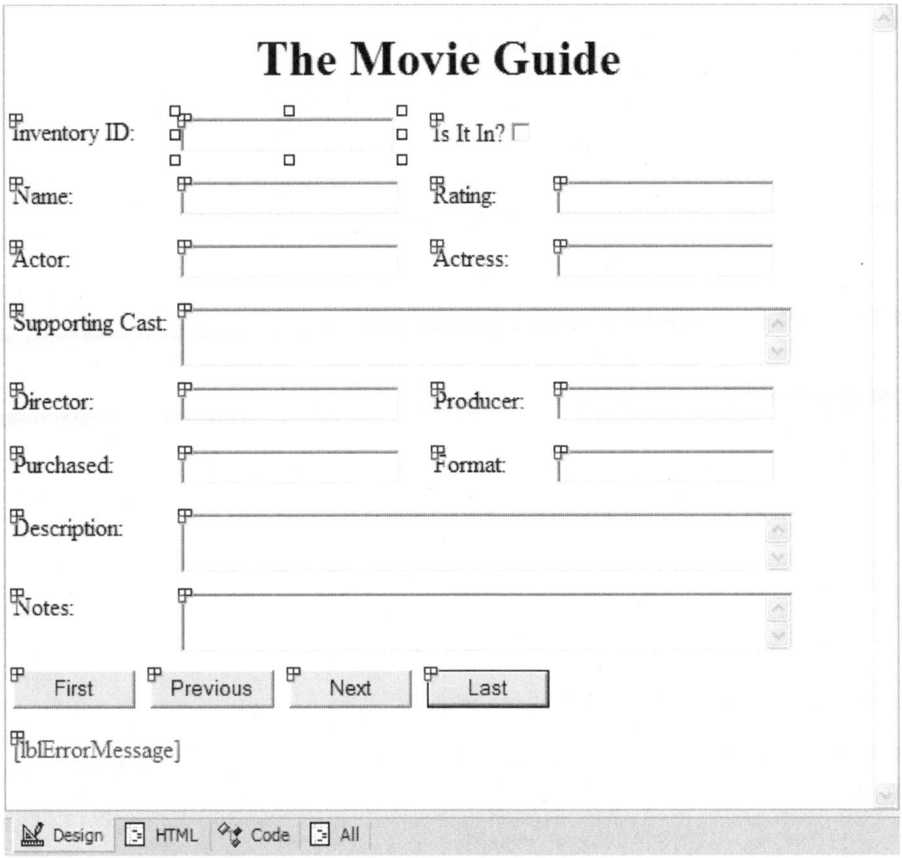

Figure 5-13. Begin this example by creating a form.

As you can see, the form includes fields for each of the columns in the table, four positioning buttons, and a label for error messages. The positioning buttons make it possible to move to any record in the database. They also make it possible to view the records one at a time. Listing 5-3 shows the code you'll need to make this example work.

Listing 5-3. Typical Record Selection and Display Code

```
// Global variable to hold the dataset.
System.Data.DataSet DS;

// Global variable to track the current record.
static int RecordNumber;
```

```csharp
// Perform the required startup tasks.
void Page_Load(Object sender, EventArgs e)
{
    // Fill the dataset.
    DS = ExistingMoviesSelect();

    // Display the data found in the dataset.
    DisplayData();
}


// This function displays the data.
void DisplayData()
{
    // Create a local DataRow to make the code shorter
    // and easier to read.
    System.Data.DataRow DR;

    // Initialize the DataRow.
    DR = DS.Tables[0].Rows[RecordNumber];

    // Fill each of the text boxes with data.
    txtInventoryID.Text = DR["InventoryID"].ToString();
    txtName.Text = DR["Name"].ToString();
    txtRating.Text = DR["Rating"].ToString();
    if (DR["IsIn"].ToString() == "True")
        cbIsItIn.Checked = true;
    else
        cbIsItIn.Checked = false;
    txtActor.Text = DR["LeadActor"].ToString();
    txtActress.Text = DR["LeadActress"].ToString();
    txtCast.Text = DR["SupportingCast"].ToString();
    txtDirector.Text = DR["Director"].ToString();
    txtProducer.Text = DR["Producer"].ToString();
    txtPurchased.Text = DR["DatePurchased"].ToString();
    txtFormat.Text = DR["Format"].ToString();
    txtDescription.Text = DR["Description"].ToString();
    txtNotes.Text = DR["Notes"].ToString();
}
```

```
void btnNext_Click(Object sender, EventArgs e)
{
    // Determine if this is the last record.
    if (RecordNumber < DS.Tables[0].Rows.Count - 1)
    {
        // Advance the record number, clear any error
        // message and display the data.
        RecordNumber++;
        lblErrorMessage.Text = null;
        DisplayData();
    }
    else
    {
        // Display an error message.
        lblErrorMessage.Text = "Already at last record!";
        DisplayData();
    }
}

void btnFirst_Click(Object sender, EventArgs e)
{
    // Select the first record.
    RecordNumber = 0;

    // Clear the error message.
    lblErrorMessage.Text = null;

    // Display the information.
    DisplayData();
}

void btnPrevious_Click(Object sender, EventArgs e)
{
    // Determine if this is the first record.
    if (RecordNumber == 0)
    {
        // Display an error message.
        lblErrorMessage.Text = "Already at first record!";
        DisplayData();
    }
```

```
    else
    {
        // Move back one record, clear any error message
        // and display the data.
        RecordNumber--;
        lblErrorMessage.Text = null;
        DisplayData();
    }
}

void btnLast_Click(Object sender, EventArgs e)
{
    // Move to the last record.
    RecordNumber = DS.Tables[0].Rows.Count - 1;

    // Clear the error message.
    lblErrorMessage.Text = null;

    // Display the data.
    DisplayData();
}
```

As you can see, the example begins by declaring some variables. The data set, DS, is re-created every time the page loads, so there's no need to do anything but make it global. Notice, though, that RecordNumber is static. Making it static allows RecordNumber to maintain state between calls. Normally, you'd use a cookie to maintain the state information—the code uses this technique for the sake of simplicity.

NOTE *You also have the choice of using a page-only ViewState or application session state for storing session information. The ViewState is the least memory intensive, but can slow the application down if you store a lot of information in it. Neither the ViewState nor the session state techniques require the use of cookies, but many developers aren't familiar with their use, and you might find them difficult to debug using Web Matrix (since there is no debugger).*

The Page_Load() method creates DS, and then calls DisplayData(). The DisplayData() method provides centralized display code. It begins by extracting the current data row, DR, using RecordNumber as an index. The code uses DR to fill each of the textboxes in turn. Notice that the field name is used as an index into DR. Also notice the method used to handle the cbIsItIn checkbox. The code could have also included a cast or some other method to determine the cbIsItIn checked state, but this technique works fine for this example.

Moving from record to record is accomplished by changing the RecordNumber value and then displaying the data again using DisplayData(). Because the First and Last buttons position RecordNumber at an absolute position, all they need to do is change the value of RecordNumber, clear any error messages, and display the data. However, the Next and Previous buttons could cause error conditions if the user tried to position RecordNumber beyond the beginning or end of the table. Consequently, the event handlers for these buttons check for the error condition first, and then take the appropriate action. In some cases, this means displaying an error message instead of changing the value of RecordNumber. Figure 5-14 shows the output of this portion of the application.

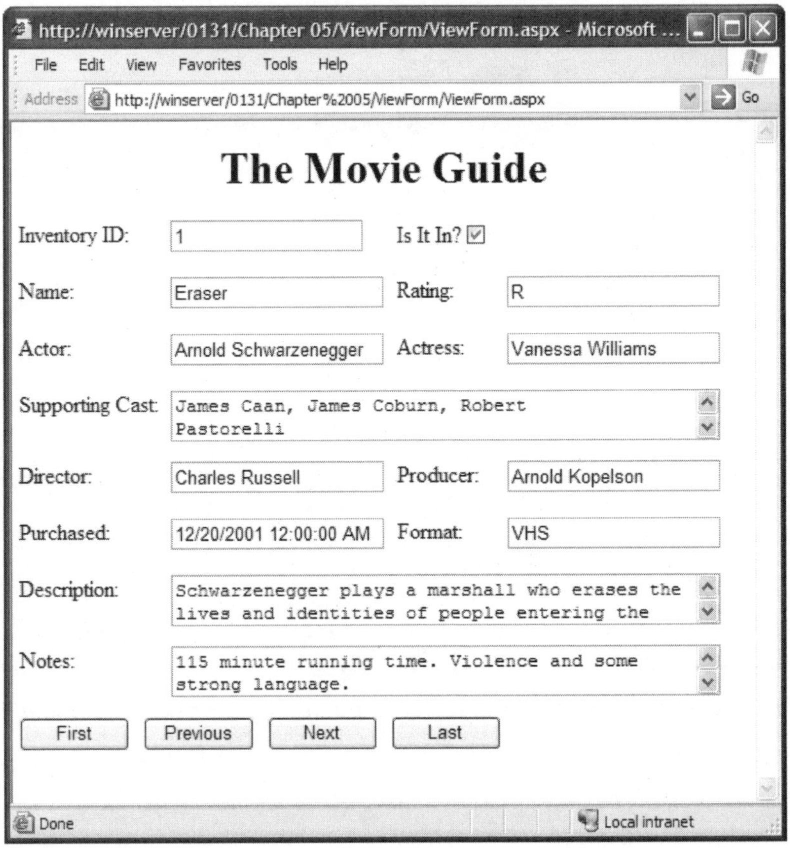

Figure 5-14. Displaying records on a form is relatively easy when using the Code Builders.

Using the UPDATE Data Method, INSERT Data Method, and DELETE Data Method Code Builders

The procedure for using these Code Builders is essentially the same as using the SELECT Data Method Code Builder. However, there are small differences between them. For example, the UPDATE Data Method Code Builder uses a slightly different Query Builder, as shown in Figure 5-15. As you can see, the differences aren't that great. In this case, you have to select the fields you want to update separately. However, the general appearance of the dialog box is the same. Notice that I've already filled the Query Builder dialog box out.

Figure 5-15. Building an update query means selecting the fields individually.

TIP *Make sure you set security properly within SQL Server. The user requires permission to update, insert, and delete records. For that matter, the user can't even view the data without the proper permissions.*

The reason you have to select the fields separately in the UPDATE Data Method Code Builder is that you have to provide a name for each of the fields you want to update using the Set Value dialog box. In this case, we don't want the user to update the InventoryID field because that value is automatically assigned by the database. In fact, you'll notice that txtInventoryID is set to read-only for this very reason.

You do need to consider one other difference. Notice that the WHERE pane has an entry in this case. The selection operation works with multiple records. Typically, you'll update, delete, or add a single record, which means that you have to tell the database which record to use. The InventoryID field is unique. The purpose of this field is to make selecting a single record easy, so we'll use it as the WHERE clause of the SQL query.

The Query Builder dialog box for the INSERT Data Method Code Builder shown in Figure 5-16 knows that you're creating a new record, so all it asks for are default values for the fields. The figure shows the default state of the Query Builder dialog box for the example database. The SQL Server database we created defines default values for some fields, so these fields are filled in automatically. You must allow a default value for the InventoryID field because the user isn't allowed to change that value—the DBMS generates it automatically.

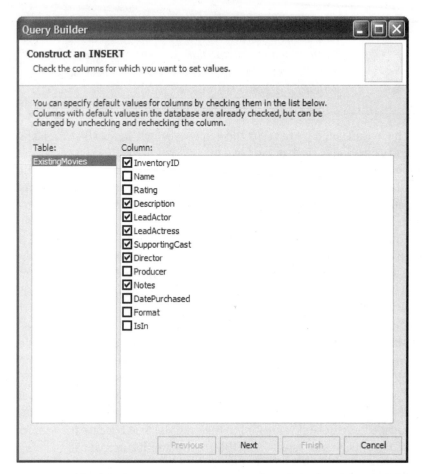

Figure 5-16. Building an insert query means providing default values for fields as needed.

The Query Builder dialog box for the DELETE Data Method Code Builder is the easiest of all to understand. As shown in Figure 5-17, all you need to provide is a WHERE clause. The Code Builder knows that the entire record will be deleted, so there's no need to include any field names.

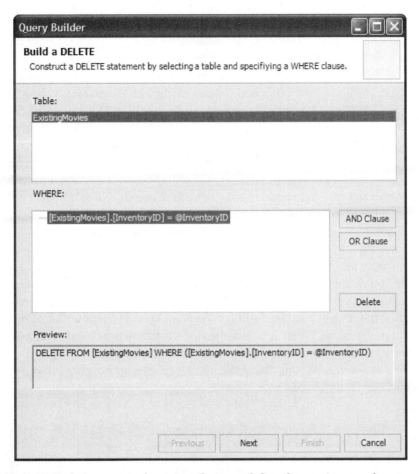

Figure 5-17. Deleting a record requires that you define the precise record you want to delete, but nothing else.

The remaining steps are essentially the same as for the SELECT Data Method Code Builder. You'll see a Query Preview dialog box where you can test the query, and then an Enter a Caption for this Wizard Panel dialog box. Note that when you test the query, you should see a Preview dialog box that asks you to enter a specific InventoryID value. This is your assurance that you created the query correctly. The three queries you'll need to build using the three Code Builders have names of ExistingMoviesUpdate, ExistingMoviesInsert, and ExistingMoviesDelete.

Demonstrating the UPDATE Data Method, INSERT Data Method, and DELETE Data Method Code Builders

We have three new pieces of code for the database, so we'll add three new buttons to the form (Update, New, and Delete), along with the associated code for the event handlers. Let's begin with the code for the UPDATE Data Method Code Builder. The Update button exercises the `ExistingMoviesUpdate()` method code. Normally, I'd add the update code to the record positioning event handler. However, for the sake of simplicity, this form has an Update button. Given that this application requires a round trip to the server for every update, it probably isn't such a bad idea to include a separate Update button, but some users will find it inconvenient because they're not used to seeing one.

Before you go any further, we do need to discuss a special issue for this demonstration. When setting up a form for updates, deletes, and inserts, make sure you also set the form controls properly. Every control that you want to use for the update should have the AutoPostBack property set to true if you use server-side processing. Although this first setting isn't mandatory, it does help. In addition, the control must be bound to the page. Use the (DataBindings) property for this purpose. When you click the ellipses next to the (DataBindings) property, you'll see a DataBindings dialog box similar to the one shown in Figure 5-18. Notice that this dialog box already has the appropriate changes for the txtName control in place.

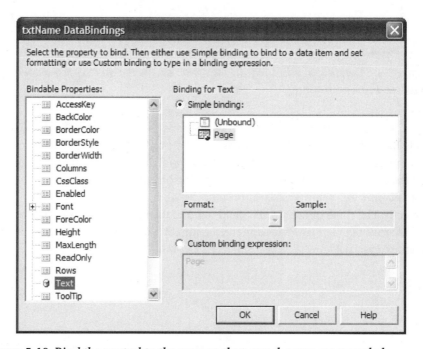

Figure 5-18. Bind the control to the page so that any changes are recorded.

In this case, we're working with the Text property. The icon for the Text property has changed to a database symbol. You can bind any number of properties to the page using this textbox. Of course, you'll only want to bind the properties that you actually use in the application. There are always exceptions to the rule. The cbIsItIn control relies on the Checked property to transfer data values. You don't have to bind this property to the page in order to make this control work property. Interestingly enough, if you try to bind the Checked property to the page, you'll receive an error message.

Now that you have some idea of what we'll do in this section, let's look at the code you'll need to add to the example. Listing 5-4 shows the code required to update, insert, and delete records in the example database. At this point, the application can perform the majority of tasks that someone would ask of an online form-based database application.

Listing 5-4. Typical Code for Updating, Inserting, and Deleting Records

```
void btnUpdate_Click(Object sender, EventArgs e)
{
    int Rows = 0;    // Rows affected by command.

    // Update the record.
    Rows = ExistingMoviesUpdate(Int32.Parse(txtInventoryID.Text),
                                txtName.Text,
                                txtRating.Text,
                                txtDescription.Text,
                                txtActor.Text,
                                txtActress.Text,
                                txtCast.Text,
                                txtDirector.Text,
                                txtProducer.Text,
                                txtNotes.Text,
                                System.DateTime.Parse(txtPurchased.Text),
                                txtFormat.Text,
                                cbIsItIn.Checked);

    // Verify the changes actually happened.
    if (Rows == 0)
        lblErrorMessage.Text = "Update error! Please check data entries.";

    // Reset the dataset so we get an accurate record display.
    DS = ExistingMoviesSelect();
```

```
        // Display the data.
        DisplayData();
    }


    void btnNew_Click(Object sender, EventArgs e)
    {
        int Rows = 0;    // Rows affected by command.

        // Insert a new record.
        Rows = ExistingMoviesInsert("Movie Name",
                                    "PG",
                                    "Movie Producer",
                                    System.DateTime.Now,
                                    "DVD",
                                    true);

        // Display an error message if the record isn't added.
        if (Rows == 0)
            lblErrorMessage.Text = "Couldn't Add Record!";

        // Otherwise, make sure the reader knows to update the record.
        else
            lblErrorMessage.Text = "Click Update when finished.";

        // Reset the dataset so we get an accurate record display.
        DS = ExistingMoviesSelect();

        // Move to the last record.
        RecordNumber = DS.Tables[0].Rows.Count - 1;

        // Display the data.
        DisplayData();
    }

    void btnDelete_Click(Object sender, EventArgs e)
    {
        int Rows = 0;    // Rows affected by the command.

        // Delete the current record.
        Rows = ExistingMoviesDelete(Int32.Parse(txtInventoryID.Text));

        // Display an error message if the record isn't deleted.
        if (Rows == 0)
            lblErrorMessage.Text = "Couldn't Delete Record!";
```

```
    // Reset the dataset so we get an accurate record display.
    DS = ExistingMoviesSelect();

    // Move to the previous record.
    RecordNumber-;

    // Display the data.
    DisplayData();
}
```

All of these methods have some common elements. Notice that all of the methods create a Rows variable. If this Rows variable returns from the call with 0, it means that call failed. Theoretically, you should be able to check for a value of 1 because all of these commands only affect one record. If the Rows count is incorrect, the method displays an error message and redisplays the data.

One of the important features common to these methods is that they all update the data set. Remember that the data set is disconnected from the database. If you don't update it, then the results you see will reflect the old content of the database, not the update that you just performed in the method. This is also the reason why you need to update the display afterward. Otherwise, the on-screen presentation could contain incorrect data.

The call to the ExistingMoviesUpdate() method in btnUpdate_Click() is relatively straightforward. Notice that all of the strings use a straight transfer. The txtPurchased.Text value requires conversion to an actual DataTime object. You do this using the Parse() method as shown. The Parse() method also comes in handy for converting the txtInventoryID.Text value to a number. Unlike the other values obtained from the form, you'll use the cbIsItIn.Checked value directly—it provides a bool output.

Notice that the call to ExistingMoviesInsert() in the btnNew_Click() method only requires default values for the elements we didn't check in the Query Builder (see Figure 5-16). In short, you can save yourself some coding time by defining default values for all fields during the query building process if possible. The example used the default settings, so we need to supply default values for the missing fields. Also notice that adding a record doesn't mean that the database contains a record with complete information. All the insertion process does is create a blank record. The user still has to click Update, in this case, to make the new data values stick.

Using the ExistingMoviesDelete() call in the btnDelete_Click() method is the easiest of all. The code only needs the current InventoryID value to delete a record. The only trick here is to ensure RecordNumber isn't pointing to a nonexistent record. That's why the code decrements the value by 1 for each deletion. Figure 5-19 shows the final version of the form-based database application.

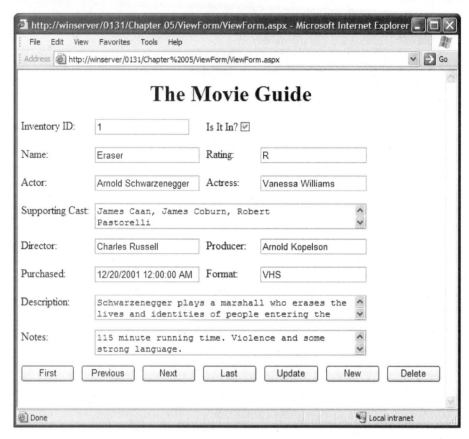

Figure 5-19. The final application can display, update, insert, and delete records as needed.

Using the SQL Script Page

We've already discussed SQL Scripts as part of the "Using Saved Queries" section of the chapter. However, it's important to know that you can create SQL scripts using Web Matrix as well. You'll find the SQL Script template in the (General) template category of the Add New File dialog box. The default template contains a comment, but not much else. SQL Scripts are just text files written in SQL, or, more accurately, SQL Server and MSDE's dialect of SQL called T-SQL.

Using the Simple Stored Procedure

The Simple Stored Procedure template is the first template that we'll use in the Data Pages category of the Add New File dialog box shown in Figure 5-20. This template isn't an actual stored procedure. Instead, it's a Web page that shows how to access a SQL Server stored procedure. You can learn more about stored procedures and how to use them at http://msdn.microsoft.com/library/en-us/architec/8_ar_da_0nxv.asp.

Figure 5-20. Use the Data Pages category templates to create database elements for your application.

NOTE *If you want to skip past the stored procedure part, you can use the GetRecord.SQL file located in the \Chapter 05\Stored Procedure folder to create the stored procedure. Simply load the SQL script into MSDE Query and execute it on the MovieGuide database. The stored procedure will appear in the Stored Procedures folder for the MovieGuide connection in the Data tab of Web Matrix.*

To use this page, we'll need to create a stored procedure. The following steps will take you through the process of creating the stored procedure. You'll also create the connection required for the rest of the example.

1. Click the Connect button on the Data tab in Web Matrix. You'll see a Connect to Database dialog box.

2. Select MovieGuide in the Database field and click OK. The MovieGuide database will appear in the Data tab. This entry will include the Tables and Stored Procedures folders.

3. Highlight the Stored Procedures folder and click New Item. You'll see the Create Stored Procedure dialog box shown in Figure 5-21. The figure shows the simple code you'll need to type for this stored procedure.

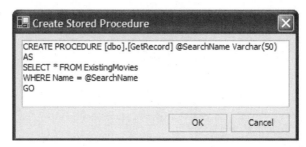

Figure 5-21. Create a new stored procedure using the features provided by Web Matrix.

4. Type the following code into the Create Stored Procedure dialog box.

```
CREATE PROCEDURE [dbo].[GetRecord]
    (
    @SearchName Varchar(50)
    )
AS
SELECT * FROM ExistingMovies
WHERE Name = @SearchName
GO
```

5. Click OK. Web Matrix will create the new stored procedure for you. Figure 5-22 shows how the Data tab should appear at this point.

Figure 5-22. Check the Data tab to ensure the stored procedure is displayed correctly.

At this point, we have all of the resources needed to complete the example. Now it's time to rework the template code for our purposes. Listing 5-5 shows the modified version of the code that we'll use.

Listing 5-5. The Modified Stored Procedure Code

```
void Page_Load(object sender, EventArgs e)
{

    // The connection string for the database.
    string ConnectionString =
        "server=(local);database=MovieGuide;trusted_connection=true";

    // Create the command string for the stored procedure.
    string CommandText = "GetRecord";

    // Create the connection and command.
    SqlConnection myConnection = new SqlConnection(ConnectionString);
    SqlCommand myCommand = new SqlCommand(CommandText, myConnection);

    // Set the command type.
    myCommand.CommandType = CommandType.StoredProcedure;

    // Add the single parameter for this application.
    myCommand.Parameters.Add("@SearchName", SqlDbType.VarChar).Value =
        "The Sound of Music";

    // Open the connection.
    myConnection.Open();
```

```
// Execute the command.
DataGrid1.DataSource =
    myCommand.ExecuteReader(CommandBehavior.CloseConnection);
DataGrid1.DataBind();
}
```

This code takes you through the process of creating a connection, executing a command, and binding the results to a data grid. The connection string is very simple, in this case—it includes just the server and the database name, along with the connection type. The command string contains the name of the stored procedure. Notice that we don't provide the parameters at this point.

The code creates the connection and then the command. The template also includes a SqlParameter, but we don't need it for this example. Make sure you remove this entry if you don't need it in your code.

At this point, the code sets the command type to a stored procedure and adds the parameters to it. It's important that you set the parameter to the correct type using the SqlDbType enumeration. The example looks for "The Sound of Music" entry in the database. You could easily turn this example into a search procedure if desired.

Once all of the setup is complete, the code opens the connection and executes the command. The result is bound to DataGrid1. Figure 5-23 shows the output of this example.

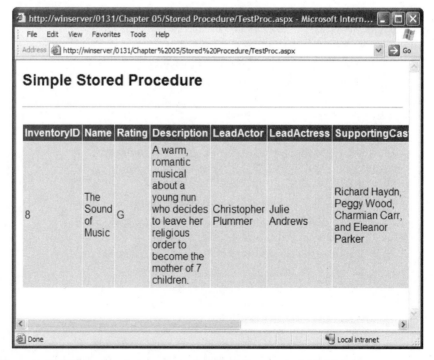

Figure 5-23. Using stored procedures is relatively easy in Web Matrix.

Using the DataList and Repeater Controls

The DataList and Repeater controls provide an interesting means for displaying information on screen. Both controls can display repetitive data. They're also free form—meaning you can define a template for displaying the information. You can use these controls to create specialized form views or reports. A user could display the report on screen and then print it out on a local printer if desired. In short, these two controls provide a flexible method of displaying information.

Both the DataList and the Repeater rely on the concept of a template. So, the first step in working with these controls is to construct a template around a data source. This requirement brings the third control into the picture—the SqlDataSourceControl. If you want to use the DataList or the Repeater, you need to provide a data source. You can do that using the programmatic method shown in Listing 5-5, but this method is far easier for this type of application.

NOTE   *One of the essential differences between a DataList and a Repeater is that the DataList relies on a GUI to create the template, while the Repeater uses a pure code environment. The DataList has a speed advantage because you can create the template faster. The Repeater has a flexibility advantage because you can perform tasks such as splitting a tag across template element boundaries. Both controls use the same template elements and are therefore interchangeable to an extent.*

When you first start an ASP.NET Page project that includes a DataList or a Repeater and a SqlDataSourceControl, you'll see what amounts to two gray squares, as shown in Figure 5-24. The SqlDataSourceControl will remain blank. However, the DataList or Repeater will eventually display the contents of the template you create.

Figure 5-24. Starting with a blank template, you'll see two gray squares on screen.

Let's begin by setting the SQL data source. Because I'm only using one data source and I don't want to have to type *War and Peace* to create an application, I gave the example SqlDataSourceControl an ID of DS (for data source). You'll need to add a connection string like the one shown here.

```
server=(local);database=MovieGuide;trusted_connection=true
```

The minimum command setup you can use is the entry in the SelectCommand property. We'll use the code shown here to create this single command.

```
SELECT InventoryID, Name, Description FROM ExistingMovies
```

You can also use other commands. As with the form view application later, the SqlDataSourceControl also supports commands to update, insert, and delete records. The control also makes it possible to automatically generate these commands. Make sure you only use this feature when working with simple tables. Multiple table setups tend to confuse the automatic generation process.

Now that we have a data source, we need to tell the DataList or Repeater about it. The way you do that is to select DS in the DataSource property. If we were using a DataSet control, you'd also need to select a specific table using the DataMember property. The SqlDataSourceControl control only offers access to a single data source, so you don't need to perform this step, but it's an important piece of information to put away for later.

The DataList also supports a DataKeyField property that you can use to designate the key data field. The example sets this property to InventoryID since that's the key field. However, you don't need to perform this step in most cases.

A final configuration step is to give the DataList or Repeater control an ID—the example uses EMDisplay.

It's time to create the template. We'll use the DataList control in this section because it provides a GUI that shows the various template elements and makes the process easier to understand. The Repeater control requires the same input. The only difference is that you need to duplicate the information in code. The following steps will help you create your first template.

1. Right-click the DataList control and choose Edit Templates from the context menu. You'll see the Edit EMDisplay Templates dialog box shown in Figure 5-25. I've already filled out the header in this case. The figure also shows the types of templates you can use: header, footer, item, and separator. Not shown in the list are the various versions of the ItemTemplate. We'll see these alternatives in the steps that follow.

Figure 5-25. Create a header for your control using the HeaderTemplate.

2. Select the ItemTemplate option. The setup for this example is very easy. All you need is some descriptive text and three labels to display the data. Figure 5-26 shows the setup you'll start with. Notice also that this figure shows the types of ItemTemplate that you can create using the GUI. The only configuration you need to perform is to give the label an ID you can use for access later (if necessary) and perform the data configuration. We'll perform this step next.

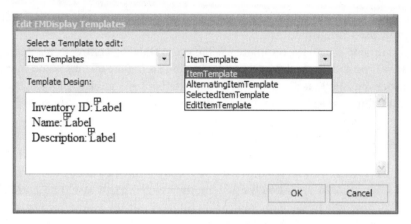

Figure 5-26. Design an ItemTemplate to display the data.

3. Click the ellipses next to the (DataBindings) property. You'll see
    a DataBindings dialog box similar to the one shown in Figure 5-27. We
    have to create a custom entry, in this case, because you want to bind
    each control to the field that will fill it with data. Notice the code that
    appears in Figure 5-27. It uses the `DataBinder.Eval()` method to perform
    an evaluation of the container's `DataItem` property. Repeat it for all three
    controls, using the field associated with that entry.

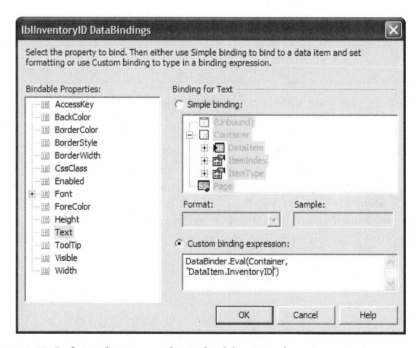

Figure 5-27. Define a data source for each of the controls.

4. Select the SeparatorTemplate option. All we'll use, in this case, is a simple horizontal rule. That's right, you can mix HTML and ASP.NET controls in the template without any problems. Add the Horizontal Rule entry.

5. Click OK. Figure 5-28 shows the output of the template at this point. Notice that it includes entries for each of the ItemTemplate options, even though we only defined the standard ItemTemplate.

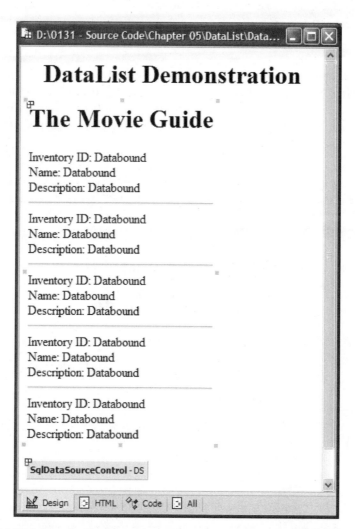

Figure 5-28. Web Matrix displays the template appearance after you define it.

At this point, the example is almost finished. That's right—using the DataList or Repeater controls is mainly a matter of creating connections. You do need to add the `Page_Load()` method to the application. Listing 5-6 shows the code you'll need to add to it.

Listing 5-6. Binding the Data to the DataList or Repeater Controls

```
void Page_Load(Object sender, EventArgs e)
{
    // Bind the data source to the DataList.
    EMDisplay.DataBind();
}
```

The simple act of calling the `DataBind()` method of the control in question is enough to fill the page with data. Figure 5-29 shows the output of this application. Notice that it's perfect for a report or as a simple overview of the information. With a little additional work, you could also make this into an editing screen.

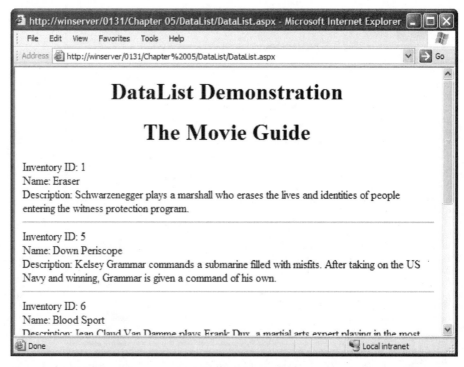

Figure 5-29. Viewing the output of the application shows a ready-to-use report.

Creating a Data Grid

There are several ways to create a data grid view of your data using Web Matrix. One of the easiest methods is to select one of the two data grid pages and modify it to meet your needs. However, you can also use the same technique that we used in the "Using the DataList and Repeater Controls" section of the chapter. The only big difference if you employ this technique is that you'll use one of the DataGrid controls in place of the DataList or Repeater controls used in that section.

Essentially, we've already done all of the work required to create a data grid display as part of the form view example in the beginning of the chapter. You need to create commands to update, insert, and delete records, just as we did for that example. The only difference is that the user will access these features in a grid, rather than on a single view form. You'll find a simple version of the data grid view in the \Chapter 05\ViewGrid of the source code (available at http://www.apress.com/book/download.html).

Data Reporting

Web Matrix provides a number of report templates. Each report builds on its predecessors to add features and functionality. This section discusses the most complex of those reports, the Data Report with Paging and Sorting template. Actually, all of the reports require the same modifications, so this report is representative of all of them.

Open a new project using the Data Report with Paging and Sorting template as usual. The example appears in the \Chapter 05\Report folder of the source code (available at http://www.apress.com/book/download.html). It has a name of Report.ASPX. You'll need to make two changes to the BindGrid() method of this report, as shown in Listing 5-7. Notice that these changes are very similar to the changes we've made for other predefined projects.

Listing 5-7. Modifications Required for a Data Report

```
// Create the connection.
string ConnectionString
    = "server=(local);database=MovieGuide;trusted_connection=true";
string CommandText;

// Define the command text.
if (SortField == String.Empty)
    CommandText = "select * from ExistingMovies order by InventoryID";
else
    CommandText = "select * from ExistingMovies order by " + SortField;
```

As you can see, the changes involve creating a new connection string and defining the command text. However, this command text can use one of two forms. The first form provides a default sorting scheme based on the natural order of the database. The second provides a sort value based on a string named SortField.

The SortField is actually a protected property that ASP.NET saves automatically between calls. It relies on the special ViewState property to retrieve the information stored between calls. This technique has a number of uses that could relieve some of the problems of using cookies in your application.

So, where does the original value of SortField come from? Whenever the user clicks one of the sort fields, the DataGrid_Sort() method is called. This method receives the user's sort expression as part of the e.SortExpression value passed in by ASP.NET. Now that you understand the basic mechanism of this example, let's look at the output. Figure 5-30 shows a typical display.

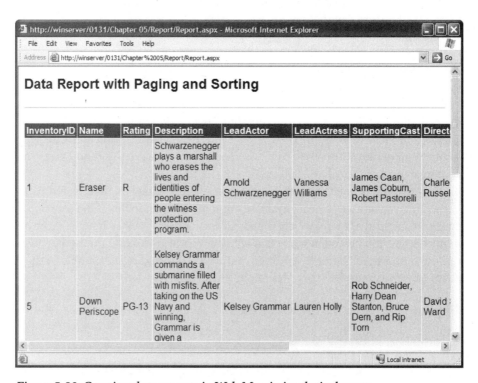

Figure 5-30. Creating data reports in Web Matrix is relatively easy.

Putting It All Together

At this point, you've seen every type of database development that Web Matrix can perform in its default configuration. You've seen grid and form views. The chapter has also shown you how to create a number of report pages, and that using stored procedures isn't only possible, but mandatory, for certain types of projects such as search pages.

What you need to do now is decide which of these elements best meets your needs and then combine them. I've provided a building block approach in this chapter. The examples show various methods of creating modules that you can simply hook together using event handlers. For example, you can connect a grid view to a form view using an ItemCommand event handler that reacts to a double-click on one of the grid records.

Use cookies to provide data communication between modules. You set a cookie using the ASP.NET Response object. Here's a piece of code that would send the information in the txtName control using a cookie named Name.

```
Response.SetCookie( new HttpCookie("Name", txtName.Text));
```

Normally, ASP.NET sends cookies to the post-back of the current page. (When working with Visual Studio .NET, the default method is to use the ViewState—something which is difficult to troubleshoot with Web Matrix because there is no debugger.) You can change that behavior using the Response object. Redirection is essential if you want to send data from the current page to another page (such as from a grid view to a detail view). Here's an example of redirection code.

```
Response.Redirect("MyDetailView.ASPX");
```

Finally, when the new page starts, you need to retrieve the cookies. Normally, you'll use the Page_Load()method for this task. Instead of using the Response object, you'll use the Request object in this case. Here's an example of the technique you'd use to retrieve a cookie.

```
TxtName.Text = Request.Cookies["Name"].Value;
```

Cookies provide the most efficient and cleanest method for passing data between forms (You can learn more about ASP.NET state management techniques at http://msdn.microsoft.com/library/en-us/cpguide/html/cpconaspstatemanagement.asp.) However, you can also use the tried-and-true method of adding data to the command line or even rely on special headers to perform the task. The idea is that you create a data package for the new page type, activate the page, and then rely on the new page to retrieve the data you sent. This communication cycle forms the glue between the modules you create and helps you design a complete application using the modules we designed in this chapter.

Limitations of the Web Matrix Approach

This chapter has focused on all of the interesting database-related tasks you can perform with Web Matrix. However, Web Matrix isn't the end-all of development platforms in this area, and you need to know that it can't do some types of tasks. Sure, you can use it to access tables and stored procedures in your application. But there are many missing features that will hinder your efforts in a large application—Web Matrix simply isn't designed to answer that need. If you want to create large, complex database applications, then you need a development environment capable of supporting that kind of work, such as Visual Studio .NET.

> **NOTE** *Don't get the idea that I'm saying that Web Matrix isn't a great product or that the development staff didn't do a good job. Given what you can do with this product, Web Matrix is actually quite capable, and the development staff did a phenomenal job. In fact, given that this is a free product, it really shines. However, it's also useful to examine a product to determine where you can use it successfully—that's the purpose of this section.*

I found that Web Matrix works well if you want to start your application with a summary view. Dragging and dropping a table creates the required grid for you automatically. Once you have the summary view created, designing a form view to go with it is relatively easy, but not as easy as it could be. You still have to perform a lot of hand coding to get the job done. The missing feature, in this case, is the ability to access individual fields within a table using the Data tab of the Workspace window. When working with Visual Studio .NET, you gain access to a number of SQL Server features from Server Explorer (pictured in Figure 5-31). As you can see, Server Explorer provides access to a broader range of server data, including the individual fields in a table.

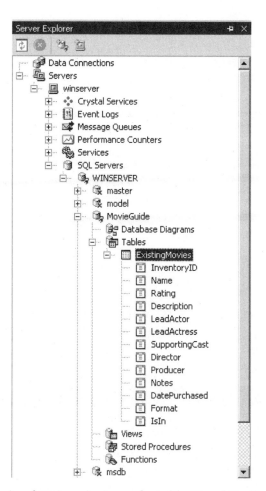

Figure 5-31. Accessing data is easier in products like Visual Studio .NET than it is in Web Matrix.

One of the more interesting Web Matrix limitations is the selection of DBMS it will work with. The only connection you can create is to SQL Server (or the MSDE alternative)—Visual Studio .NET provides a broad range of connection types. This is an interesting limitation because Microsoft also produces Access, which might actually provide better database support for the type of application that Web Matrix can produce. If you don't want to develop a database application with SQL Server, then Web Matrix won't work at all for your development needs. Again, this is another area where Visual Studio .NET provides access to a broader range of features.

TIP   *If you're still looking for a low-cost solution to create Web pages online and would like something other than Web Matrix, you can try SQLControl's Web Site Builder. This product doesn't use code to create Web sites at all—it relies on the content provided in a database to create the site dynamically. The use of "skins" helps you define the appearance of your Web site, and you can use more than one skin per Web site. Web Site Builder includes an HTML editor and an administrative interface. You can use this product with either Microsoft Access or SQL Server. Learn more about this product at* http://www.data-centrum.com/sqlcontrol/default.asp?pi=1.

Many developers have complained about the lack of the various forms of help in Web Matrix that Visual Basic developers take for granted. For example, you can't list the members of a class or view the parameters for a call by right-clicking the target code and selecting an option from the context menu. I didn't really notice the loss of this functionality while building most of the applications in this book. Yes, it was time consuming to look parameters up online, but it wasn't that time consuming. However, you're going to notice this lack of functionality when creating database applications. Look again at the complexity of some calls and you'll see why. The nesting of classes, methods, and properties can become quite deep. You can partially overcome this problem by using intermediate variables as I did in Listing 5-3, but the loss of help is still very noticeable.

Most of you will eventually see other limitations with the Web Matrix approach to database development. However, as you can see from the examples in this chapter, creating great-looking database applications isn't only possible, it's relatively easy, as long as you keep the purpose of Web Matrix in mind. This application can provide a gateway to learning various Web technologies, including database development. It can also create a variety of simple database applications for any business. However, you can't use it to create the complex applications that many businesses are trying to introduce to the Internet today. For that task, you'll need a high-end product such as Visual Studio .NET. In sum, make sure you use the right tool for the job at hand.

Summary

This chapter has shown you how to create basic database applications using Web Matrix. We've discussed the various forms that Web Matrix provides for creating database applications, and you've seen how to create an application with all the normal features. We've also discussed the limitations of Web Matrix when it comes to database application development. In most cases, it won't work well for large application development because it simply doesn't provide all of the functionality you'd need for such a project.

Web Matrix is capable of creating a vast array of simple database projects—everything from a simple contact manager to data entry forms for a small business. It's in this area that you should try experimenting first. Check out the example code and use it as a basis for determining if Web Matrix will work for your application needs. You'll also want to consider the various alternatives provided in the chapter.

Chapter 6 discusses how to use and create custom controls and components. Most developers have a whole toolbox full of controls and components or know where to find them online. This chapter tells you how these application building blocks work with Web Matrix and shows how you can overcome any problems. Fortunately, it's extremely easy to build and test components and controls with Web Matrix, so you can start building a managed component and control toolbox that will also work with Visual Studio .NET.

CHAPTER 6

Applications with Custom Components and Controls

In This Chapter

- Learn to Use the Component and Control Tools Provided with the .NET Framework

- Develop Applications Using Existing Components

- Customize the Toolbox Tabs in Web Matrix to Meet Your Needs

- Develop Applications Using Existing Controls

- Learn to Use the Class Page

- Create an Application That Implements a Component

- Learn to Use the ASP.NET User Control

- Create an Application That Uses an ASP.NET User Control

Until now, we've used the controls that Web Matrix provides, along with the components of the .NET Framework, to create applications. These objects provide most of what you need to create any application that Web Matrix is capable of handling. We've already discussed the issue of Web Matrix orientation—its intended audience—so I won't cover that ground again. However, given the Web Matrix audience, the control and component coverage is great.

Unfortunately, developers are component and control junkies—they live for their next new widget fix in the hope that it does something, anything, exciting. Some developers scour the programmer's catalogs and developer magazines with the same expression of avarice that shows in the face of a child scanning the

Christmas catalog. In some cases, developers even go further and develop their own widgets—sharing the code with others like trading cards. The only problem is that Web Matrix appears to make most forms of unmanaged component and control sharing impossible. (Using managed components and controls—those created using the .NET Framework—is just as easy with Web Matrix as it is with Visual Studio .NET.) Of course, this problem dashes any hope the developer might have of standing apart from the crowd with the creation of a new application based on the super widget.

This chapter won't make you the next widget guru, and I'm not going to provide you with the gory details of creating advanced controls and components. Visual Studio .NET is the tool of choice if you want to create complex managed or unmanaged components or controls. However, we'll look at ways of overcoming the problem of custom component and control withdrawal in Web Matrix. This tool can help you create simple components and controls to use within your Web Matrix applications, and this chapter will show you how to create them. You'll learn how to perform the following tasks.

- Import existing managed components into your application.

- Import existing unmanaged components into your application.

- Import existing managed controls into your application.

- Import existing unmanaged controls into your application.

- Use the Class project to create your own managed components.

- Use the ASP.NET User Control project to create your own managed controls.

We'll use simple examples in this chapter. The emphasis is on making these components and controls work with Web Matrix. You'll find that the process is completely different from using components and controls in Visual Studio .NET, so even experienced developers will need to spend time with this chapter. For example, Web Matrix doesn't provide a build option—you need to build your components at the command line. In addition, this chapter uses the .NET Framework SDK as a resource because, like Web Matrix, it's free for the price of a download.

NOTE *We've performed many tasks in the book using the functionality provided by Web Matrix and the .NET Framework. However, this chapter requires that you have an external compiler for the component and control examples because Web Matrix lacks support for this feature. You can obtain a compiler by downloading the .NET Framework SDK (*`http://msdn.microsoft.com/downloads/sample.asp?url=/msdn-files/027/000/976/msdncompositedoc.xml`*) or by using Visual Studio .NET. This download is immense at 131 MB, so you might consider ordering the CD instead. The download page has instructions on ordering the .NET Framework SDK. You can learn more about the .NET Framework SDK at* `http://msdn.microsoft.com/nhp/Default.asp?contentid=28000451`*.*

Working with the .NET Framework Tools

The .NET Framework SDK provides you with some new tools that you don't get with Web Matrix alone. These tools help you do more with the .NET environment and make it practical to use existing components in your applications. In fact, the .NET Framework SDK contains more tools than we need to use Web Matrix, but they all perform useful tasks that you might want to know about. You'll find an overview of all of the .NET Framework tools in the help topic at `ms-help://MS.VSCC/MS.MSDNVS/cptools/html/cpconnetframeworktools.htm`.

TIP *You have access to the full .NET Framework help file in the Programs\Microsoft .NET Framework SDK folder of the Start menu. I'll provide .NET Framework SDK help topic URLs wherever appropriate throughout the remainder of the book. You can type these URLs directly into your browser and go straight to the topic without opening the help file. In addition, you can type this URL into the address field of the .NET Framework help file to access topics and see the associated location in the help table of contents.*

The following sections describe the .NET Framework tools that we'll use specifically in this chapter to work with components and controls. Knowing about these tools is essential because you need to use them to perform tasks such as building wrappers for existing COM controls or making a component or control generally accessible on your machine. All of these controls work at the command prompt, so I'll also provide some tips on making them easier to access anywhere on your machine.

Making Your Tools Accessible

It didn't take a very long time for me to realize that Windows has become a GUI operating system with little to offer someone working at the command prompt. However, just a few small changes to your computing environment can turn a hassle into an easy setting in which to work. One of the first changes I made was to add a special entry to the content menu for Explorer that opens a command prompt wherever I need it. This feature makes it possible to open a command prompt in your current project and work with the files without having to change directories. The following steps show how to make your command prompt just a little easier to access. (You can also cheat and double-click the CommandPromptHere.REG file found in the Chapter 6 source code, available from the Downloads section on the Apress site at http://www.apress.com/book/download.html.)

1. Use the Windows Explorer Tools ➤ Folder options command to open the Folder Options dialog box.

2. Select the File Types tab and highlight the Folder file type, as shown in Figure 6-1 (not the File Folder type right above it).

3. Click Advanced to display the Edit File Type dialog box. This dialog box helps you add new actions for a specific type of file.

4. Click New to display the New Action dialog box.

5. Type **Command Prompt Here** in the Action field and **cmd.exe /k "cd %1"** in the Application Used to Perform Action field.

6. Click OK three times to close the dialog boxes.

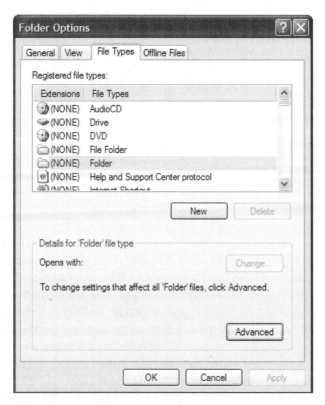

Figure 6-1. Modify the Folder file type, not the File Folder file type.

Now, you can right-click any folder in Windows Explorer and you'll see a new Command Prompt Here entry on the context menu. Select this option, and Windows will open a command prompt at the current location.

Unfortunately, you still can't access your tools because Windows doesn't supply a path to them. Adding a path enables you to access the tools from the command prompt without typing the full path information. Use the following steps to add a new path entry to your system.

1. Right-click My Computer and choose Properties from the context menu. You'll see the System Properties dialog box.

2. Select the Advanced tab of the System Properties dialog box.

3. Click Environment Variables and you'll see the Environment Variables dialog box.

4. Highlight the Path entry in the System Variables list. Click Edit to display the Edit System Variable dialog box.

5. Add a semicolon and then the path to the .NET Framework SDK Bin folder (normally \Program Files\Microsoft Visual Studio .NET\FrameworkSDK\Bin) on your system.

6. Click OK three times to make the change permanent.

At this point, your system is ready to use. You have access to all of the required command line tools.

Using TLbImp

The TLbImp (type library import) utility wraps a COM component type library in an assembly so that you can access it from your managed application. The type library normally appears as part of the OCX or DLL that contains the component, but you'll also find separate TLB files that have the same name as their associated component. The resulting assembly will contain the interoperability features required to access the component objects. This access includes the methods, properties, and events that the type library supports. However, the assembly won't include any separate functions that the library file might contain. To access these functions, you need to use PInvoke.

The Runtime Callable Wrapper (RCW) assembly created by TLbImp doesn't actually contain the component code. You still need to register the component as you normally would using RegSvr32. When your managed application makes a call to the component, the Common Language Runtime (CLR) transfers the request through the RCW to COM, which instantiates a copy of the control. Of course, this is a quick take on a complex process, but it gives you the idea.

The TLbImp requires that you supply the name of a component file as a minimum. You can also provide a resource identifier as part of the command line by separating it from the component filename with a slash like this.

```
TLbImp MyLibrary.DLL/1
```

In this case, the RCW assembly would only contain the code required to access the component with a resource identifier of 1. This utility also accepts a number of command line switches, all of which are optional. Table 6-1 tells you about each option.

Table 6-1. TLbImp Command Line Switches

SWITCH	DESCRIPTION
? or help	Display a help screen containing helpful information about the utility.
asmversion:Version	Assigns a version number to the assembly. If you don't provide this value, TLbImp usually tries to use the version number of the component file. Otherwise, the utility assigns a version number of 1.0.0.0 to the assembly.
delaysign	This option enables you to register an assembly in the Global Assembly Cache (GAC) without giving it a strong name first. Use this option for testing only. You should always sign the assembly before sending it to someone else.
keycontainer:FileName	Defines the name of the key container that holds the key pair used to sign the assembly. Use this option to give the assembly a strong name for placement in the GAC.
keyfile:FileName	Defines the name of a file that contains the key pair used to sign the assembly. Use this option to give the assembly a strong name for placement in the GAC.
namespace:Namespace	Use this option to place the classes contained within the assembly into a particular namespace. Using this option ensures that the component is in an easily identifiable namespace that doesn't cause conflicts with other components.
nologo	Tells the utility not to display its logo.
out:FileName	Defines the name of the output file. Normally, you'll use a DLL extension and a derived form of the filename.
primary	Creates a primary assembly—one in which you're the publisher of the component. This option requires that you create a strong name for the assembly.
publickey:FileName	Defines the name of a file that contains a public key used to sign the assembly. Use this option to support test keys and delay signing scenarios. Normally, you won't use this option for a production release of the assembly.
reference:FileName	Defines the name of a file that contains reference information for the current assembly. Whenever TLbImp finds an external reference in the assembly, it attempts to resolve the reference using the supplied filename first. If the reference assembly doesn't contain the required reference, TLbImp will continue looking for the reference using the local assemblies and those found in the GAC.
silent	Tells TLbImp not to display any success messages while creating the RCW.

(continued)

Table 6-1. TLbImp Command Line Switches (continued)

SWITCH	DESCRIPTION
strictref	Tells TLbImp not to create a wrapper assembly if it can't resolve all references using the current assembly or the assemblies provided as part of the /reference switch.
sysarray	Ensures that TLbImp converts COM SAFEARRAY references to System.Array references.
unsafe	Produces interface references that work without the normal .NET security checks. Avoid using this option if you don't understand the ramifications of unsafe code. Generally, components will work fine without this option.
verbose	Tells TLbImp to display extended messages while creating the assembly. These additional messages help you understand the conversion process and could alert you to potential problems in the conversion.

Using AXImp

The AXImp utility serves a purpose similar to the TLbImp utility. However, you'll use this utility to create a wrapper for controls instead of components. AXImp supports many of the same command line options used with TLbImp. Read the "Using TLbImp" section for details on the command line options. We'll use this utility several times in the chapter, so you'll get to see it in action.

Using TLbExp

We won't actually use the TLbExp (type library export) utility in this chapter, but I wanted to include this entry for the sake of completeness. You use this utility when you want to create an RCW for an assembly. The RCW enables an unmanaged application to see the assembly as a COM component or control. The utility works about the same as the TLbImp utility. Of course, you're supplying an assembly and getting a DLL as output in this case.

After you create the RCW, you need to register it using RegSvr32, just as you would for any COM component or control. The RCW manages the interaction between the unmanaged environment and the assembly. The assembly thinks that an application is calling on it through CLR, just as normal, and the unmanaged application sees a COM component. All required data marshalling takes place behind the scenes.

Using SN

The SN (strong name) utility helps you create an individualized assembly. The only way that we'll use this utility in this book is to generate key pairs. The key-pair file is used as input to several of the utilities in order to sign the assemblies that we use. Adding the key-pair file signs the assembly—giving it a strong name, one that's associated with a specific cryptographic entry. You can find complete information about the SN utility at ms-help://MS.VSCC/MS.MSDNVS/cptools/html/cpgrfstrongnameutilitysnexe.htm. Make sure you completely understand all of the implications of using a particular command line switch, especially when working with an existing assembly. This utility can affect the usability of a public component by modifying its signature.

You must sign an assembly before adding it to the GAC. The GAC is actually a series of folders under the \Windows\Assembly folder. As you can see in Figure 6-2, the act of signing the assembly gives it a public token value that's displayed in Windows Explorer when you look at the GAC. The public token uniquely identifies the originator of the assembly, just as the version number uniquely identifies a particular release of the assembly. When added together, the public token and the version number provide unique identification for any assembly.

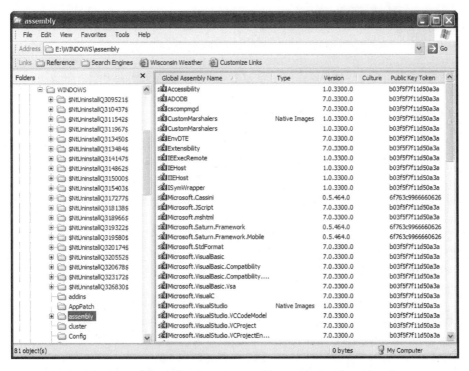

Figure 6-2. Adding a public token to an assembly uniquely identifies the originator.

Signing an assembly has another purpose—it ensures the integrity of the assembly. If someone else tries to modify the assembly, CLR will identify the modification during the loading process and refuse to continue loading the assembly. In short, this measure ensures that a virus can't modify the file and then hide its tracks. The modification is apparent and prevents damage to the affected system.

Creating a key file is easy. All you need to do is type the following command at the command prompt:

```
SN -k <Key Filename>
```

where <Key Filename> is the name of the file you want to generate. The resulting file contains a public and a private key pair. Once you create a key file for your organization, you should protect it so that no one else can sign an assembly using your identity. In addition, it's a good idea to use the same key file to sign all of your production assemblies so that it's easy to identify the assemblies associated with your company.

Using GACUtil

The two main reasons to use GACUtil are to install (using the –i switch) and uninstall (using the –u switch) assemblies that you want available for system-wide use. You can make an assembly available to an application in one of two ways. First, you can simply place the assembly in the same folder as the executable. CLR will look for the referenced assembly first in this folder, so this is the most direct way to couple an application and support assembly. Second, you can place the assembly in the GAC. This step makes the assembly accessible from any application on the current machine.

To install an assembly in the GAC, you must give it a strong name. This means creating a key pair with the SN utility and then adding the key-pair file as input to the assembly creation process. Normally, you'd add this information as part of the command line switches for either the TLbImp or AXImp utilities. The key pair normally appears as a special entry in the AssemblyInfo file for a managed component or control, but you can also add it to the command line when compiling the application at the command prompt. In addition, nothing stops you from adding the key-file entry to any part of the source code for a managed component or control.

You can also use GACUtil to list the GAC contents using the –l switch. The utility has a number of other switches, but the three described in this section are the ones that you'll use most often. For example, you can use the –if switch to force GACUtil to overwrite any existing copies of an assembly during the installation process. Generally, this is a bad idea because you want to maintain the older versions of the assembly for compatibility purposes. However, using the –if switch can come in handy during testing.

Developing with Existing Components

You'll have a wealth of components to use from projects that you created in the past. These components have value in that you've purchased them, know how to use them, and they appear in other applications you've created. Existing components feel like a worn-out shoe—they're comfortable. Working with existing .NET components is easy because they don't require any type of wrapper or special handling. You can also work with existing unmanaged components (such as those created with COM), but they require some type of wrapping to ensure the .NET environment handles them correctly by performing tasks such as marshaling the variables you use.

 NOTE *I've run into a few developers who use the terms com-ponent and control interchangeably. I don't want to get into a debate with anyone over the meanings of these two terms, but it's important for you to know how I'm using them throughout the book. The term* component *will always refer to object code that works in the background without benefit of a user interface. The term* control *will always refer to object code that works in the foreground and includes a user interface element of some type (such as a pushbutton).*

The following sections discuss how to work with both managed and unmanaged components in Web Matrix. No, it's not quite the same as performing the identical task using Visual Studio .NET. Remember that you won't have any automation at your disposal, so you'll need to perform many tasks manually. On the other hand, Web Matrix actually provides better control over how you import components because you get to see all of the details. The control-over-productivity tradeoff is a constant theme today—some developers value one over the other and vice versa in a given circumstance.

Development with a Managed Component

Using a managed component in Web Matrix is relatively easy. You have a few choices in how you actually access the component, but using it is relatively easy. I'm not going to show the component code for this example, but you'll find it in the download directory for the Chapter 6 source code (available at `http://www.apress.com/book/download.html`). The only task that the component performs is to accept a string as input, reverse the characters, and return the reversed string. It's a fun component to test.

The first decision you need to make is whether to use a local component or a global component. Generally, if you plan to use a component regularly, you should load it into the GAC and make it globally available. Using this technique means that you'll run into fewer problems using the component in multiple applications. For example, multiple copies of a component could lead to a problem in which you've updated the component for one application, but not another—leaving the application open to possible problems.

On the other hand, when you use a local component, you don't need to worry as much about compatibility issues. The component that you used to construct your application is the same component the application will use for normal operation. However, you do need to consider the tradeoffs.

Setting up the application is relatively easy. The first step is to create your Web page. We'll use a simple Web page, in this case, that consists of some text, a textbox, a label, and a pushbutton, as shown in Figure 6-3. Listing 6-1 shows the simple code used to access the component and change the input text.

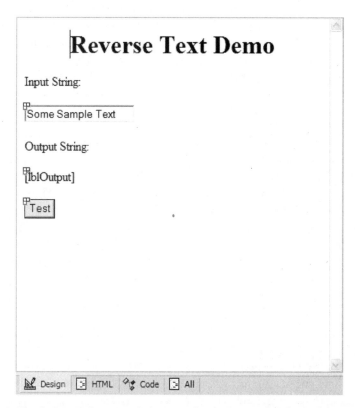

Figure 6-3. The form used to test the external component is relatively simple.

Listing 6-1. Accessing a Managed Component

```
void btnTest_Click(Object sender, EventArgs e)
{
    // Reverse the text in the input textbox and display
    // it in the label.
    lblOutput.Text =
        ManagedComponent.ReverseIt.DoReverse(txtInput.Text);
}
```

Notice that the code doesn't rely on a using statement to access the external component. This functionality won't work. You must use the fully qualified name every time you want to access the external component from your code. The component function is static, so you don't need to create an instance of the class in order to reverse the text. This technique is a convenience for the developer. It means that you have one less step to worry about when using custom components in your application.

In order to make this application work properly, you must configure it as an application in IIS. We already discussed that technique in the "A General Security Example" section of Chapter 4. If you don't perform the IIS setup, ASP.NET will look in the wrong place for the component. The component must appear in a \bin folder beneath the main application folder.

The application also requires some connectivity between the ASP.NET page and the underlying component. You perform this step by modifying the WEB.CONFIG file. The WEB.CONFIG file supplied with the downloadable source code (available at http://www.apress.com/book/download.html) also includes the debugging entry we've used in the past. Listing 6-2 shows the essential code for this application. Note that this code appears within the Configuration/System.Web folder of the hierarchy, as shown in Figure 6-4.

Listing 6-2. Modifications Required to WEB.CONFIG

```
<!--
    This entry enables us to use an existing managed component
    as part of this application.
-->
<compilation>
    <assemblies>
        <add assembly="ManagedComponent" />
    </assemblies>
</compilation>
```

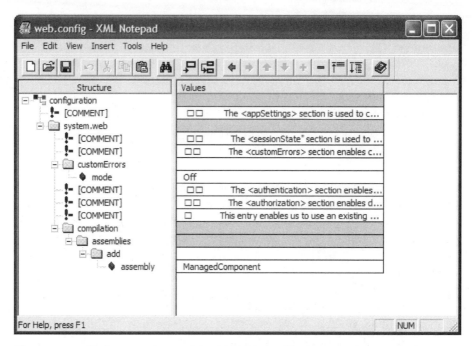

Figure 6-4. Add these entries to WEB.CONFIG to tell ASP.NET where to find your component.

Listing 6-2 shows the simplest entry you can make in WEB.CONFIG and still get the application to work. The <Add> element can contain a number of attributes in addition to the assembly attribute shown. For example, you can choose to load an assembly based on the version number or the culture. You can read more about this element at ms-help://MS.VSCC/MS.MSDNVS/cpgenref/html/gngrfaddelementforassemblies.htm.

Now that you have the ASPX and WEB.CONFIG files put together, the \bin folder containing the component, and the correct IIS configuration, you can test the application. These four steps define every use of a local component. Figure 6-5 shows the output of the example application.

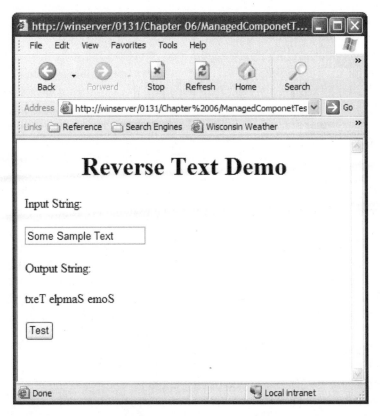

Figure 6-5. Putting all of the pieces together enables you to use custom managed components.

Development with an Unmanaged Component

Many developers wonder how they can use the vast selection of COM components at their disposal in an ASP.NET application. The investment in COM is huge at most businesses, and it would be hard to give this investment up. In addition, many developers grow attached to their components after spending months honing code so that it's bug free and performs well. The following sections will guide you through the process of installing and using a typical unmanaged component with Web Matrix.

An Overview of the Issues

First the good news. You can use all of your COM components with your ASP.NET applications. It's not possible to use them directly, but I'll show you how to wrap a component in an assembly so that it becomes accessible from your ASP.NET application. In sum, your current investment is intact.

Unfortunately, the conversion process isn't all good news. You have to consider that the data transfer between the application and the COM component undergoes several additional levels of transition—it's not a straight transfer. The additional transitions take their toll on performance—you won't see the same performance level because the data stream is doing more work. We'll discuss ways around this performance issue in the "Unmanaged Component and Control Performance Facts and Tips" section of Chapter 10.

In some cases, you'll also find that the data types that you're used to working with in ASP.NET don't marshal directly to a data type for your COM component. For example, BSTR values require special handling in some cases. You might also have to allocate local memory for variables and perform other tricks to make the component work as anticipated. Generally, these issues are the exception to the rule when working with COM, although they're a common occurrence when accessing the Win32 API.

Now that we have some of the preliminaries out of the way, just how do you use your COM component in an ASP.NET application when using Web Matrix? It turns out that this process is a lot less automatic than when you work with Visual Studio .NET. When you work with Visual Studio .NET, all you need to do is add a reference, and the IDE does the rest of the work for you. In Web Matrix, you need to perform the conversion manually. As with the managed component example, you'll find the source code for the unmanaged component example in the downloadable code for Chapter 6 (available at `http://www.apress.com/book/download.html`). We'll concentrate on the actual conversion process.

Working with the Managed Component

For this example, I created an unmanaged component using Visual C++ that obtains the computer name based on the `GetComputerNameEx()` Win32 API function call found at `ms-help://MS.VSCC/MS.MSDNVS/sysinfo/sysinfo_8k6w.htm`. The `GetCompName()` method requires that the caller provide a name type, such as ComputerNameNetBIOS, as input. It outputs a BSTR containing that version of the computer name. A second method, `GetAllNames()`, returns all of the names associated with a computer based on the `GetComputerNameEx()` function.

Before we do anything else, you need to register the component on the server using the `RegSvr32 CompName.DLL` command at the command prompt. When you issue this command, you'll see a success message similar to the one shown in Figure 6-6. In most cases, I place the component in the same \bin folder used to store the assembly wrapper so that all of the pieces stay together. Make sure you place the component in the folder that you want it to use before you register it—the registry entries will look for the component in a specific location.

Figure 6-6. Use the RegSvr32 command to register the COM component on the server.

After you finish working with the component, unregister it using the `RegSvr32 -u CompName.DLL` command. Failure to unregister the component won't result in anything terrible, but doing so does tend to clog your registry with component entries that you don't need any longer. In some cases, if you accumulate enough dead entries, you could actually see the performance of your system suffer. In short, make sure you unregister any COM components you use in this chapter.

Creating the Assembly Wrapper

It's important to remember that we're working with a component and not a control in this example. This fact means that we'll use the TLbImp utility to create the assembly wrapper. You also need to decide on a name for your component. Generally, it pays to add "interop" to the current component name. This naming scheme shows that the assembly provides interoperability for a component with a specific name. You can also use the default behavior of adding "Lib" to the end of the component name. Either naming scheme works well.

With this issue out of the way, type **TLbImp CompName.DLL** in the same folder that you used for CompName.DLL storage. The TLbImp utility will create a CompNameLib.DLL file. This isn't a strongly named assembly, so you can't place it in the GAC. However, we don't need to place it in the GAC to use it for this example. All you need to do is ensure that you place the assembly in the \bin folder below the application folder.

Creating the Web Matrix Application

The form we're creating is a little more complex this time. We need to create a DropDownList control that contains the computer name selections. This example will also look at a feature that's always turned on in Visual Studio .NET, but that you get to actually select in Web Matrix—Absolute Position feature. So far, the controls have appeared where we placed them in accordance to the rules that HTML uses. This example will show you how to break that rule and create a layout that looks a little more like a desktop application.

> **CAUTION** *Most of the properties you'll use with the DropDownList control are the same as any other control. Noticeably missing is the ToolTip property. The lack of this feature could cause problems for your Web site if you need to meet Web Accessibility Initiative (WAI) or Section 508 accessibility requirements.*

Let's begin with the DropDownList control. We need to add a list of names to this control so the user can select from one of several choices. In addition, you want to make sure that one of the items is the default, so the form has an item selected when you start the application. You can add these items using the List Item Collection Editor dialog box shown in Figure 6-7. Access this dialog box by clicking the ellipses next to the Items property entry in the Properties window.

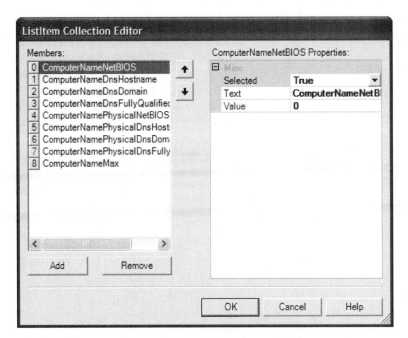

Figure 6-7. Access the List Items Collection Editor to add items to the DropDownList control.

Some developers actually prefer to code this control in the HTML window, rather than use the GUI. In this case, they're probably right in saying that using the GUI is slower and that you can code the DropDownList control items faster by hand. Listing 6-3 shows the code you'll need to type for this control.

Listing 6-3. Populating the DropDownList Control Item List

```
<asp:DropDownList id="comboName" accessKey="N" runat="server" Width="500px">
    <asp:ListItem Value="0" Selected="True">ComputerNameNetBIOS</asp:ListItem>
    <asp:ListItem Value="1">ComputerNameDnsHostname</asp:ListItem>
    <asp:ListItem Value="2">ComputerNameDnsDomain</asp:ListItem>
    <asp:ListItem Value="3">ComputerNameDnsFullyQualified</asp:ListItem>
    <asp:ListItem Value="4">ComputerNamePhysicalNetBIOS</asp:ListItem>
    <asp:ListItem Value="5">ComputerNamePhysicalDnsHostname</asp:ListItem>
    <asp:ListItem Value="6">ComputerNamePhysicalDnsDomain</asp:ListItem>
    <asp:ListItem Value="7">ComputerNamePhysicalDnsFullyQualified</asp:ListItem>
    <asp:ListItem Value="8">ComputerNameMax</asp:ListItem>
</asp:DropDownList>
```

It's time to turn on absolute positioning. This feature assigns positioning information to each of the controls on screen, which helps you control the appearance of the display with more accuracy. To turn on absolute positioning, select all of the controls, and then select the Layout ➤ Absolute Position command. Figure 6-8 shows the layout of the window for this example.

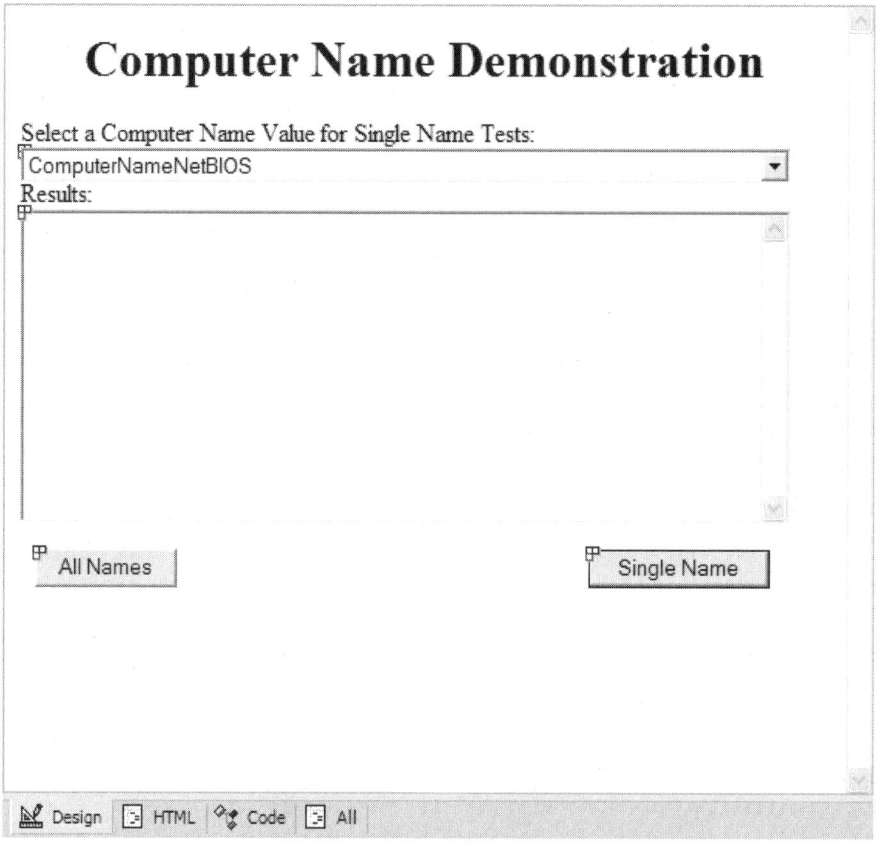

Figure 6-8. Access the List Items Collection Editor to add items to the DropDownList control.

The application has two command buttons. The first accesses the component and obtains all of the names for the computer, while the second accesses the component and retrieves just one name. Listing 6-4 shows the code for this portion of the example.

Listing 6-4. Methods for Interacting with the Component

```
void btnSingle_Click(Object sender, EventArgs e)
{
    CompNameLib.NameValuesClass    Values;       // CompName Object
    int                            Selected;    // Selected value.

    // Initialize the values.
    Values = new CompNameLib.NameValuesClass();
    Selected = Int32.Parse(comboName.SelectedItem.Value);

    // Get the single value.
    txtResults.Text =
    Values.GetCompName((CompNameLib.MYCOMPUTER_NAME_FORMAT)Selected);
}

void btnAll_Click(Object sender, EventArgs e)
{
    CompNameLib.NameValuesClass    Values;   // CompName Object

    // Initialize the object.
    Values = new CompNameLib.NameValuesClass();

    // Get all of the values.
    txtResults.Text = Values.GetAllNames();
}
```

Both click event handlers work in the same way. The application instantiates
a copy of the component, and then uses it to gain access to the appropriate
function call. The btnSingle_Click() method also needs to convert the item
selected in the DropDownList control, comboName, into an integer, which is then
used to select one of the options in the CompNameLib.MYCOMPUTER_NAME_FORMAT
enumeration. This value is the input required by the GetCompName() method.

As with the managed component example, you must configure the folder
hosting this example as an application. In addition, the example requires
a WEB.CONFIG file with the elements shown in Listing 6-5 as a minimum. This
code creates the linkage between the application and the component.

Listing 6-5. Linkage Code for the CompNameLib Assembly

```
<compilation>
    <assemblies>
        <add assembly="CompNameLib" />
    </assemblies>
</compilation>
```

At this point, the application is ready to run. Figure 6-9 shows the application output. Of course, the goal of this application is to show you that Web Matrix can work with managed or unmanaged components with equal ease. You might experience a little loss in performance, but otherwise the component will work just as before.

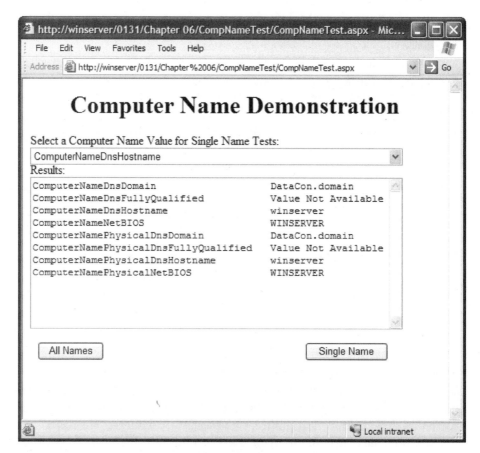

Figure 6-9. Seeing the output of this application demonstrates that Web Matrix works with managed and unmanaged components with equal ease.

This example does have one other lesson to demonstrate. The reason I don't normally use absolute positioning is the problems that it can cause. Figure 6-9 shows the application using medium-sized text. Although this text is just fine for anyone with good eyes, it can be hard for someone with vision problems to see. Unfortunately, absolute positioning hinders the use of larger fonts because you're telling the application precisely where to place the various screen elements. Look at what happens to the display in Figure 6-10 when you select an extra large font.

Figure 6-10. Using absolute positioning may make your display look nice, but it can cause visual problems as well.

As you can see, the buttons end up in the textbox. This is only a minor example of the effects of absolute positioning—they get much worse. In fact, your application can become completely unusable for someone who needs a high-contrast, large-character display. Absolute positioning might make your display look nice, but you should consider the cost to your users of using it .

Developing with Existing Controls

Components are relatively easy to move to Web Matrix because they don't involve any user interface elements. Controls, on the other hand, do have a user interface and are therefore harder to move. The problem isn't one of using the code—using the code is easy, as we saw with the component examples. The issue is finding a means for displaying the control's user interface on screen. Unless ASP.NET provides the means for performing the task, you'll find your work cut out for you.

Unlike components, not all controls will work in ASP.NET. In some cases, you can get around the problems using HTML coding such as the <OBJECT> tag, but this method won't always work and might not work at all with some browsers. In short, you know that the controls that come with Web Matrix will work, but beyond that, you need to perform extensive testing to ensure that the control will perform the desired task. With this in mind, the following sections provide you with some ideas on how to get your existing controls to work with Web Matrix.

TIP *Many developers have worked with third-party controls in the past. Vendors recognize the need to move these controls to the managed environment provided by the .NET Framework, and some have already made the move. If you have a favorite third-party control that you'd like to use with Web Matrix, check with the vendor to see if it has become available. For example, Chart FX from Software FX is a third-party control that helps you create dazzling charts and graphs for your Web Matrix application. Interestingly enough, they have a trial version you can download for experimentation purposes. You can learn more about this product at* https://www.softwarefx.com/SFXNetProducts/CfxWebMatrix/.

Importing Managed Controls

Managed controls are the easiest to use with your Web application because they don't require any form of wrapper. However, there are limits on what Web Matrix will import into the IDE. The first limitation is that you won't see individual controls, as you will when working with Visual Studio .NET. The IDE only provides access to entire assemblies. The second limitation is that the assembly must provide Web controls—you can't import some types of controls because Web Matrix lacks the automation required to make them work.

The following sections look at two types of managed control support (in addition to the online support we discussed in the "Connecting to the Online Component Gallery" section of Chapter 2). You'll commonly use local support for custom controls created specifically for an application or an application type. The GAC support comes in handy for custom controls that will see use in a majority of applications.

Creating Your Own Toolbox Tab

You may have noticed the Toolbox tabs provided in Web Matrix are somewhat limited, and you can't add new ones directly. Yes, there are enough tabs to get started, but not really enough if you want to expand this utility to meet specialized needs. Fortunately, the Web Matrix development team was sharp enough to make the Toolbox settings accessible so you can perform some customization. In fact, you can actually customize this Toolbox better than the one in Visual Studio .NET because you can associate tabs with specific project types—you won't see your custom tabs unless the project calls for them.

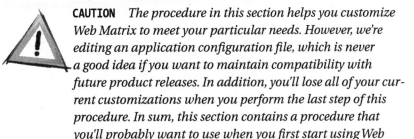

> **CAUTION**   *The procedure in this section helps you customize Web Matrix to meet your particular needs. However, we're editing an application configuration file, which is never a good idea if you want to maintain compatibility with future product releases. In addition, you'll lose all of your current customizations when you perform the last step of this procedure. In sum, this section contains a procedure that you'll probably want to use when you first start using Web Matrix.*

Just in case I haven't worn down your resistance to using XML Notepad (or a suitable alternative) yet, we'll use it again in this section. In the \Program Files\Microsoft ASP.NET Web Matrix\v0.5.464 folder, you'll find the WebMatrix.EXE.CONFIG file. This file is yet another one of those that rely on XML, but don't have an XML extension. Mind you, modifying this file in the wrong way could make Web Matrix unusable, so the smart developer always makes a copy before fiddling with it.

Open the microsoft.Saturn\toolbox\ element, and you'll see a group of toolboxSection entries like the ones shown in Figure 6-11. Each of these toolboxSection elements contains the name of a tab on the toolbar in Web Matrix. The name attribute controls the name of the tab, while the type attribute controls when the tab appears. The name attribute is the one that you'll customize to create a new tab—the type attribute must match an existing tab. For example, if you're creating a new tab just for custom controls, then create a copy of the Custom Controls tab entry. On the hand, the My Snippets tab is a good choice if you want to sort your snippets by type, and the HTML tab is a good choice if you want to create something generic.

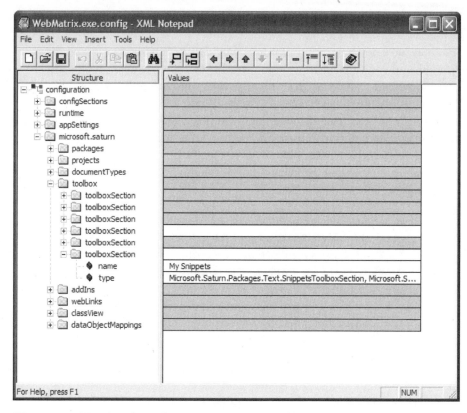

Figure 6-11. Viewing the WebMatrix.EXE.CONFIG file tells you a lot about Web Matrix configuration.

You can't actually add the entry using XML Notepad because it will complain that the configuration file isn't well formed. You do want to use this tool to check your changes. I used a plain text editor (Notepad is a good choice) to add the new entry. Don't make the changes using Web Matrix because you need to keep the IDE closed during the editing process. I decided to add a special tab for local controls (in contrast to those found in the GAC). Here's the entry I added directly below the Custom Controls entry in the WebMatrix.EXE.CONFIG file. (Note that all of this text appears on one line in the file, although it appears on multiple lines in the book.)

```
<toolboxSection name="Local Controls" type="Microsoft.Saturn.Packages.Web.
WebForms.CustomControlsToolboxSection,Microsoft.Saturn.Packages.Web"/>
```

At this point, you need to save any code snippets that you've created using the procedures we discussed in the "Understanding Code Snippets" section of Chapter 3. The next task is to reset the Toolbox so that the new Toolbox tab appears. After you save your code snippets, right-click the Toolbox and choose

Reset Toolbox from the context menu. You'll see a confirmation dialog box like the one shown in Figure 6-12.

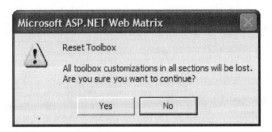

Figure 6-12. Make sure you actually want to lose your customizations before you click Yes.

This is your last opportunity to keep any customizations that you might have created. If you want to see the new tab, however, click Yes. Figure 6-13 shows the results of my customization. The Local Controls tab is completely separate from the Custom Controls tab. It enables me to store local controls separately from those found in the GAC.

Figure 6-13. Set up a local controls tab in Web Matrix if you want to keep local controls separate from those in the GAC.

Using Local Controls

The control we'll use for this example is available as part of the source code download for Chapter 6, available at `http://www.apress.com/book/download.html`. This control performs a basic task: It provides support for a specialized header that you can use on a Web page. As with the component examples, we'll concentrate on adding the control to Web Matrix and using it within that environment.

You can approach this problem in a number of ways. However, the first thing that I do for a local control is to create a \bin folder for the application—if it doesn't have one already. Place the control you want to use in the \bin folder so that it's readily available to the target application. The reason you must perform this step is that the control doesn't appear in the GAC. Placing the control in the \bin folder makes it accessible to the application. The following steps will help you install the control in Web Matrix.

1. Select the Custom Controls tab in the Toolbox. It's a good idea to place all of the controls that don't appear in Web Matrix by default in a separate area. (You can also use a Local Controls tab that you create using the procedure in the "Creating Your Own Toolbox Tab" section.)

2. Right-click the Toolbox and choose Add Local Toolbox Components from the context menu. You'll see the Select Assemblies dialog box shown in Figure 6-14. This dialog box lists the assemblies found in the GAC.

3. Click Browse. You'll see a Select Assembly dialog box that looks like a standard File Open dialog box. This dialog box enables you to choose a local assembly.

4. Locate the assembly that you want to add to the Toolbox. Click Open. You'll see the assembly added to the Selected Assemblies list of the Select Assemblies dialog box.

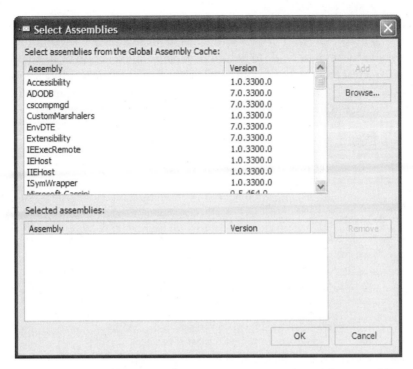

Figure 6-14. The Select Assemblies dialog box contains a list of the assemblies found in the GAC.

5. Click OK. You'll see a dialog box like the one shown in Figure 6-15 that asks if you want to install the assembly in the GAC.

6. Click No. Web Matrix will display a dialog box that tells you that it added the Web control to the Toolbox. This dialog box also provides instructions for using the assembly in a local configuration. You'll also see the new control in the Toolbox tab you selected.

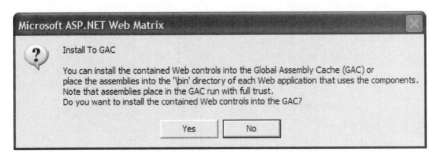

Figure 6-15. Install assemblies in the GAC when you want to use them globally.

At this point, you'll have access to a new control. The example control creates a header label on screen. You have full access to the header level at runtime. The control also makes it possible to output either absolute position or standard HTML. The test page includes controls for changing both the heading level and the label centering. A Command button submits the requested changes to the server. Listing 6-6 shows the code required to make the form functional.

Listing 6-6. Form Modification Code

```
void btnSubmit_Click(Object sender, EventArgs e)
{
    // Set the common settings.
    SpecialHeader1.Centered = cbCentered.Checked;
    SpecialHeader1.HeaderLevel = Int32.Parse(comboSize.SelectedItem.Value);
    SpecialHeader1.Width = Int32.Parse(txtDisplayWidth.Text);
    SpecialHeader1.BorderStyle = (BorderStyle)comboBorder.SelectedIndex;
    SpecialHeader1.BorderWidth = Int32.Parse(txtWidth.Text);

    // Set the absolute positioning settings.
    SpecialHeader1.AbsolutePosition = cbAbsolute.Checked;
    SpecialHeader1.Top = Int32.Parse(txtTop.Text);
    SpecialHeader1.Left = Int32.Parse(txtLeft.Text);
    SpecialHeader1.HeaderSubstitute = cbHeaderSubst.Checked;

    // Determine how to set the display for the header level.
    if (cbAbsolute.Checked)
    switch (comboSize.SelectedIndex)
    {
        case 0:
            SpecialHeader1.Font.Size = FontUnit.XLarge;
            break;
        case 1:
            SpecialHeader1.Font.Size = FontUnit.Large;
            break;
        case 2:
            SpecialHeader1.Font.Size = FontUnit.Medium;
            break;
        case 3:
            SpecialHeader1.Font.Size = FontUnit.Small;
            break;
        case 4:
            SpecialHeader1.Font.Size = FontUnit.XSmall;
            break;
    }
}
```

One of the biggest advantages of this control is that you can tell it programmatically to switch gears between HTML and absolute positioning output. A user could make a choice as part of their input to your site, or you could simply detect the capabilities of their browser and adjust accordingly. The example control also provides support for borders and an interesting feature called HeaderSubstitute. This particular feature comes in handy when you want to create a fancy header, but display the rest of the page in pure HTML. The control automatically outputs a "fake" HTML header that keeps the rest of the HTML entries in line. You can test this feature out with the example application.

The example application shown in Figure 6-16 demonstrates the various features of the control. The control actually supports a number of other features such as font changes, but this application demonstrates the most interesting features. You'll find the test application in the \Chapter 06\ManagedControlTest folder of the source code (available at http://www.apress.com/book/download.html).

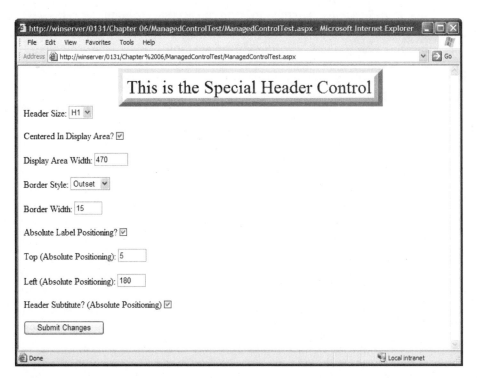

Figure 6-16. Use the special header control in this example when you need to control the appearance of the header on screen.

When you copy the control to the server, you'll need to reference it in WEB.CONFIG, just as we did the component examples. The control must appear in the \bin folder (it should already be there during local testing), and you'll need to create an application in IIS for the example. In short, the display aspects of the managed control make it special, but many other elements for a local control are the same as for a component.

Using Controls in the GAC

The GAC makes using a control a lot easier because you have access to it wherever needed on the local machine. However, before you can place a control in the GAC, it must have a strong name. This means creating a key-pair file using the SN utility (see the "Using SN" section earlier for details), adding the key pair to the control during compilation, and, finally, adding the control to the GAC using the GACUtil application.

Once you add a control to the GAC, you can access it from the Select Assemblies dialog box shown in Figure 6-14. However, remember that you're selecting the assembly, not the control. If an assembly contains more than one control, Web Matrix will load all of them when you load the assembly. You remove the controls that you don't want in the Toolbox by right-clicking the control and selecting Remove from the context menu.

A Method for Using COM Controls

We're finally to the hardest nut to crack—the unmanaged COM control. You do have a number of options at your disposal for dealing with this type of control, but most of them aren't going to work very well. The problem is the user interface element that a COM control provides. In general, you'll find that your best option is to avoid creating an assembly out of the unmanaged COM control and using the tried and true <OBJECT> tag instead. The following sections show you the easiest way to create an <OBJECT> tag and incorporate it into Web Matrix. You'll end up with a mixed mode ASP.NET page that can use a combination of unmanaged controls, Web controls, and standard HTML to create an on-screen presentation.

Understanding the Need for the <OBJECT> Tag

Interestingly enough, the <OBJECT> tag is part of the HTML 4.0 specification (see http://www.w3.org/TR/REC-html40/ for details). Developers have used the <OBJECT> tag with good success for quite some time now. Of course, some users turn this functionality off, which means you have to provide an alternative means of seeing information in that case. You can read the complete documentation for this tag at `ms-help://MS.VSCC/MS.MSDNVS/DHTML/workshop/author/dhtml/reference/objects/OBJECT.htm`.

The example control, in this case, is a simple pushbutton written in Visual C++. You'll find the code for it in the Chapter 6 folder of the source code (available at `http://www.apress.com/book/download.html`). The unmanaged control provides a special feature whereby setting the OnOff property to true turns the pushbutton into a two-state setup. In one state, the button is on, and in the other it's off. The ModalResult property records the current state. You can also set the button to provide predefined captions and modal results. Finally, the button can act as a standard command button, but you really wouldn't want to use it in this mode in a Web-based application because you can get the same functionality using other methods.

The `<OBJECT>` tag provides several essentials that we need to work with unmanaged COM controls. The first is providing the user with access to the control. Unlike the managed Web controls we've used in this chapter, a COM control must appear on the user's machine. That requirement means that you have to provide some means for the user to download and install the control on the user machine, and the `<OBJECT>` tag provides this functionality. The second essential is access to the control properties. The `<OBJECT>` tag includes parameters that help you manage the configuration of the control. The `<OBJECT>` tag also provides other functionality, such as a means to access control events (for scripting) and placement of the control on screen.

Making the Job Easier With ActiveX Control Pad

Unfortunately, using an unmanaged COM control means writing the `<OBJECT>` tag by hand or using a tool that can make the job easier. Microsoft provides the ActiveX Control Pad as a means for writing the `<OBJECT>` tag with some level of automation. You can download it at `http://msdn.microsoft.com/downloads/sample.asp?url=/msdn-files/027/000/228/msdncompositedoc.xml`. I even use this tool when working with Visual Studio .NET because it actually provides better control-handling capabilities and access to control features.

ActiveX Control Pad is a perfect companion for Web Matrix because it helps you create the `<OBJECT>` tag and can aid with the scripting required to use the control. That's right—you'll need to use scripts to interact with the control, rather than use the techniques we've employed so far in the book. This means the control will work equally well on an ASP.NET or a standard HTML page. Let's begin by creating the `<OBJECT>` tag.

When you start the ActiveX Control Pad, you'll see an editor window similar to the one shown in Figure 6-17. Essentially, the designers created this tool to work with HTML pages. It doesn't provide many features, but ActiveX Control Pad does provide exceptional handling of COM controls. You'll also like the Script Wizard functionality that this application provides.

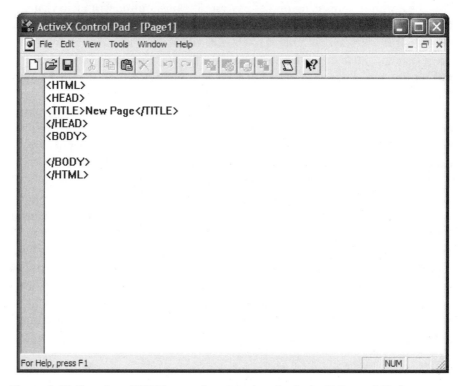

Figure 6-17. Creating `<OBJECT>` *tags is easy using the ActiveX Control Pad.*

As you can see, the page already includes all of the required HTML tags, and you can use the output for quick tests before you add the `<OBJECT>` tag to your Web Matrix project. The following steps show how to create the `<OBJECT>` tag and the associated script for this example.

1. Use the Edit ➢ Insert ActiveX Control command to display the Insert ActiveX Control dialog box. Locate the control you want to use. The PButton1.OCX control used in this example appears in the ActiveX Control dialog box as the On/Off Pushbutton Control (MFC), as shown in Figure 6-18.

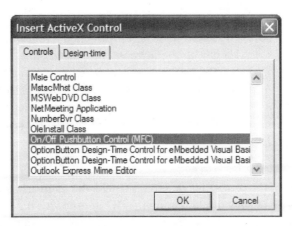

Figure 6-18. Use the special header control in this example when you need to control the appearance of the header on screen.

2. Highlight the control you want to use and then click OK. ActiveX Control Pad will display a copy of the control and a Properties dialog box, as shown in Figure 6-19. These two windows show you how the control will look and enable you to configure it properly for use, even if the control doesn't provide the full range of settings on a property page.

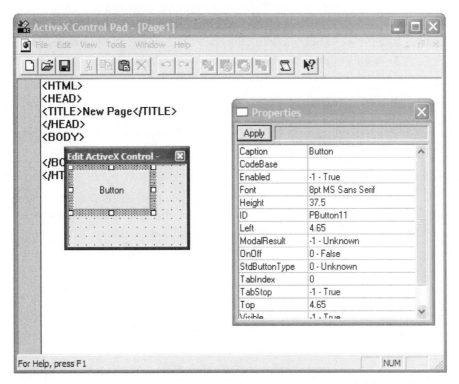

Figure 6-19. Use the special header control in this example when you need to control the appearance of the header on screen.

227

NOTE *If you want the user to download an unmanaged control used in your application, you must define the CodeBase property. The CodeBase property defines the download location for the control. If the user's browser detects that the control isn't available on the user's machine, it will look for the control on the Web server and prompt the user to download it.*

3. Set all of the properties required to make the control functional. The three that the example sets are the OnOff property, the ID, and the CodeBase property. Set the OnOff property to True so that the control works as anticipated for the example. Set the CodeBase property to a location for downloading the control from your server. Set the ID property to btnTest.

TIP *If you click the button in the window provided, you can see it work at this point. With each click you'll see the caption on the button alternate between On and Off.*

4. Close the window containing the control. The ActiveX Control Page will create the required <OBJECT> tag for you. You'll see a button on the left side of the <OBJECT> tag entry that you can click if you want to change any of the settings.

5. Create an output textbox for the control by typing **<INPUT TYPE=Text NAME="txtOutput" />**. Make sure you assign a name to the textbox or it won't show up in the Script Wizard.

6. Click the Script Wizard button. You'll see a Script Wizard dialog box similar to the one shown in Figure 6-20. Notice that I've already opened the list of events for the btnTest control in the Select an Event pane. This control only supplies one event—Click. I've also selected the txtOutput entry in the Insert Actions pane.

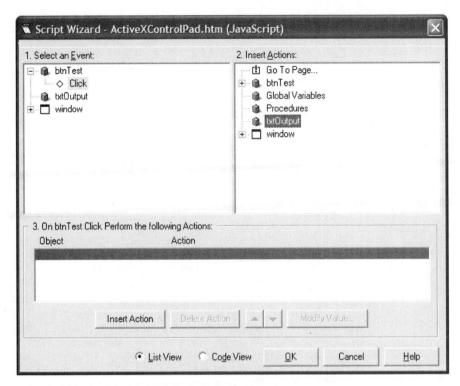

Figure 6-20. Use the Script Wizard to create scripts.

7. Click Code View. The lower pane will change so that you see the Click event prototype. Type **txtOutput.value = btnTest.Caption**. This action will assign the current value in the control's Caption property to the txtOutput.value property.

8. Click OK. The Script Wizard will create the script for you. If you need to change the script, just click the script button on the left side of the display next to the <SCRIPT> tag. Your ActiveX Control Pad should look similar to the one shown in Figure 6-21 at this point.

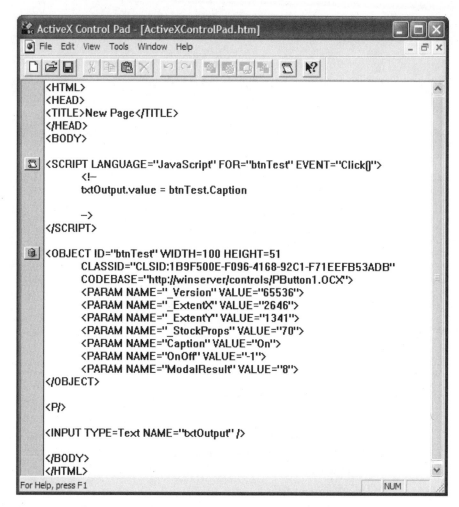

Figure 6-21. The ActiveX Control Pad made creating this page relatively simple.

Designing the Web Matrix Page

At this point, you have an <OBJECT> tag and a script for using the output of the control. To use this ActiveX Control Pad output in your Web Matrix project, just copy the text from the ActiveX Control Pad display and paste it into the HTML view of the Web Matrix editor.

To the elements created by ActiveX Control Pad, I added a header as a title and a few pieces of text. Listing 6-7 shows the final code for this example.

Listing 6-7. A Simple Web Page That Uses an <OBJECT> Tag

```
<html>
<head>
<SCRIPT LANGUAGE="JavaScript" FOR="btnTest" EVENT="Click()">
    <!--
    txtOutput.value = btnTest.Caption


    -->
</SCRIPT>
<Title>Unmanaged Control Test</Title>
</head>
<body>
    <form id="MyForm" title="Unmanaged Control Test" runat="server">
        <h1 align="center">Unmanaged Control Test
        </h1>
        <p align="left">
            Click the button to see the output in the textbox:
        </p>
        <p>
            <object id="btnTest"
                codebase="http://winserver/controls/PButton1.OCX"
                height="51" width="100"
                classid="CLSID:1B9F500E-F096-4168-92C1-F71EEFB53ADB">
                <param name="_Version" value="65536" />
                <param name="_ExtentX" value="2646" />
                <param name="_ExtentY" value="1349" />
                <param name="_StockProps" value="70" />
                <param name="Caption" value="On" />
                <param name="Enabled" value="1" />
                <param name="OnOff" value="-1" />
                <param name="ModalResult" value="8" />
                <param name="StdButtonType" value="8" />
            </object>
        </p>
        <p>
            Output:
            <input type="text" name="txtOutput" />
        </p>
    </form>
</body>
</html>
```

As you can see, the <OBJECT> tag contains all of the parameter entries for the control. It also includes a class ID value that uniquely identifies the control. To test this page completely, you need to unregister the control locally using the RegSvr32 -u PButton1.OCX command. When you access the page, your browser should offer to download the control for you. Because this control is unsigned, you should also see a security warning. The control will download, and you'll see an ActiveX interaction warning (if your browser is set up to detect this potential security issue). Click OK, and you'll see the test page shown in Figure 6-22. Clicking the On/Off button should change both the button caption and the text in the textbox.

Figure 6-22. The output of this example shows that your old COM controls are still usable.

Using the Class Page

We've used several prebuilt components in this chapter so far. Web Matrix can also help you create new components. However, I have to emphasize that this isn't a forte of the product because it lacks a build capability. If you plan to build very many components, then getting Visual Studio .NET is probably the best idea. Web Matrix provides only a marginal experimental capability in this case.

The following sections show you how to build a very simple component. We'll use the Class page to start. At some point, we'll switch to the command line to build the component, and then I'll show you how to install it in the GAC so you can access it from anywhere on the same machine.

Creating a Simple Component

This section shows how to build a component using Web Matrix. We'll begin by creating a Class page named MyComponent. You'll need to specify a class name and a namespace—you don't have an option, in this case, because the compiler uses the namespace and class as part of the component description. The class name for the example is MathFunctions. I used my company name for the namespace—DataCon. It's important to use a namespace that makes sense for your organization, so that you can begin all components at the same top-level namespace. You can also create a namespace hierarchy by separating the namespace elements with dots.

The project creates a file that contains the namespace and class definition, along with the constructor. You don't have to add any code to the constructor (unless it's needed for the component). This example contains two methods. The first will calculate the length of the hypotenuse given the length of two sides. The second will calculate the length of a side, given the length of one side and the hypotenuse. Listing 6-8 shows the code for this example.

Listing 6-8. Component Code for Triangles

```
// These assembly level attributes help with identification
// and other assembly issues.
using System.Reflection;
using System.Runtime.CompilerServices;
using System.Web.UI;
[assembly: AssemblyTitle("Class Page Demonstration")]
[assembly: AssemblyDescription("Shows how to use the Class page.")]
[assembly: AssemblyCompany("DataCon Services")]
[assembly: AssemblyVersion("1.0.0.0")]
[assembly: AssemblyKeyFile("MyKey")]

namespace DataCon {
    using System;
```

```csharp
/// <summary>
/// This class contains some math functions for working with
/// triangles.
/// </summary>
public class MathFunctions
{

    /// <summary>
    /// Creates a new instance of MathFunctions
    /// </summary>
    public MathFunctions()
    {
    }

    public static double Hypotenuse(double Side1, double Side2)
    {
        // Calculate the length of the hypotenuse.
        return Math.Sqrt(
            Math.Pow(Side1, 2) + Math.Pow(Side2, 2));
    }

    public static double Side(double Hypotenuse, double Side1)
    {
        // Calculate the length of the side.
        return Math.Sqrt(
            Math.Pow(Hypotenuse, 2) - Math.Pow(Side1, 2));
    }
}
}
```

The code begins with some assembly identification information. This information is helpful if someone finds your component installed somewhere and wonders which vendor created it and wants to know what it does. A Visual Studio .NET project normally includes this information in a separate file, but for this small project, placing it in the main file isn't a problem.

The namespace and class descriptions come next, followed by the constructor. These three entries appear in every Class Page project you create. The two methods used for this example appear next. The math calculations they contain rely on the Math class found in the System namespace. The example uses static methods so the user can access the methods without having to instantiate an object based on the class first. It helps to use static methods, whenever possible, because they tend to reduce development effort and improve application performance by reducing memory requirements.

Compiling and Registering the Component

You've created a C# file that contains some code you want to use in a component. At this point, you need to open a copy of the command line in the directory containing the source code. We'll need to perform two tasks to create the component. The first task is to create a key pair using the SN utility. Remember that we have this line of code at the beginning of the file:

```
[assembly: AssemblyKeyFile("MyKey")]
```

This code tells the compiler to add a strong name to the component based on the key pair found in a file named MyKey. Of course, the directory doesn't have such file yet, so you need to create it. To create the key pair, type

```
SN -k MyKey
```

at the command line. The file will appear as soon as the SN utility generates it.

It's time to compile the component. All you need to do is type

```
CSC /Target:library MyComponent.cs
```

at the command line. The C# Compiler (CSC) will create a component (DLL) that you can use in an application. The CSC compiler comes with the .NET Framework, so you can use it as needed to experiment with various types of .NET application programming. The compiler can produce modules and executable files, as well as DLLs. It also has a variety of command line switches you can use to add specific features to an assembly, such as icons.

We have a new component with a strong name. That means you can add it to the GAC if desired. To register the component, type

```
GACUtil -i MyComponent.DLL
```

at the command line. GACUtil will install the component in the GAC. Now you can access it from within Web Matrix with relative ease.

NOTE *Make sure you also register the assembly on the server to perform a two-machine test. Installing the component on the local machine isn't enough to ensure that it will also work on the server.*

Using the Component in Web Matrix

Using this component is much the same as the other components we've used. The only significant difference is that we've registered the component in the GAC. The test application includes three text boxes to hold the values of the two sides and the hypotenuse. It also has two pushbuttons. The first calls the component to calculate the value of the hypotenuse based on the value of the two sides. The second button calls the component to calculate the value of the second side based on the value of the first side and the hypotenuse. Listing 6-9 shows the code required to make this portion of the example work.

Listing 6-9. Command Button Code

```
void btnHypotenuse_Click(Object sender, EventArgs e)
{
    double   Temp; // Temporary data storage.

    // Determine the hypotenuse value.
    Temp = DataCon.MathFunctions.Hypotenuse(
        Double.Parse(txtSide1.Text),
        Double.Parse(txtSide2.Text));

    // Modify the hypotenuse text value.
    txtHypotenuse.Text = Temp.ToString();
}


void btnSide_Click(Object sender, EventArgs e)
{
    double   Temp; // Temporary data storage.

    // Determine the side value.
    Temp = DataCon.MathFunctions.Side(
        Double.Parse(txtHypotenuse.Text),
        Double.Parse(txtSide1.Text));

    // Modify the Side2 text value.
    txtSide2.Text = Temp.ToString();
}
```

As you can see, we need to perform some data conversions to use the control. You need to decide how to handle such situations. In some cases, it's actually better to accept a string and perform the conversion within the component. However, I chose this method because it ensures that the component will at least receive a value it can use—making error handling a lot easier. Figure 6-23 shows the output of this application.

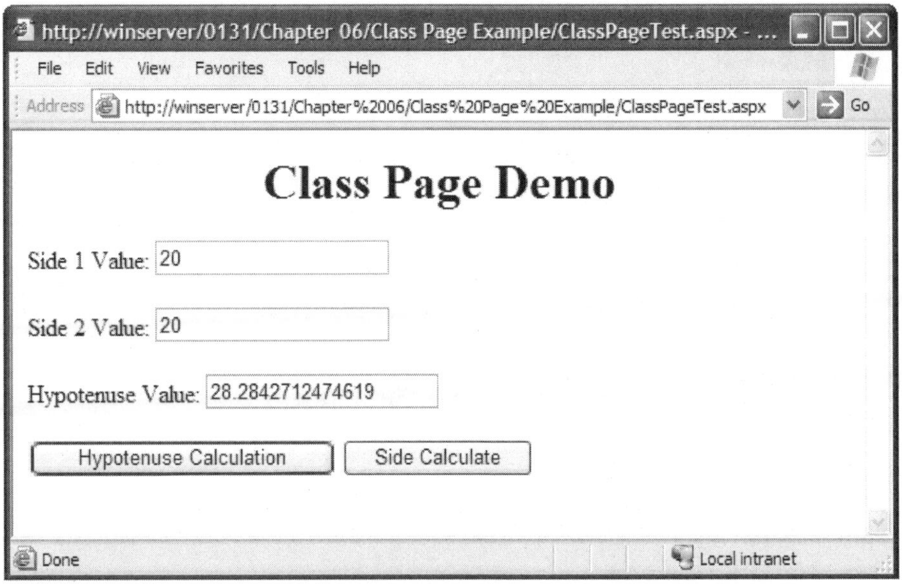

Figure 6-23. Calculating the hypotenuse or side of a triangle is easy with this application.

Using an ASP.NET User Control

A user control is a special type of control that you create using standard ASP.NET components and controls, HTML elements, and even standard text if you want. A user control enables you to create packaged code that you can use in an application later, much like server-side includes in the past, but more powerful. Some developers use the ASP.NET user control to package common page elements so that other developers can simply place them on screen. Of course, you can add properties for configuration, methods for interaction, and events to learn when something happens.

Let's begin with the User Control page. You create it as you would an ASP.NET page. The only real difference is that it has an ASCX file extension. The example has two labels on the page. The first is a header, while the second is a label. I've added two properties to the example to show how to control the Text properties of both labels. Listing 6-10 shows the full source code for the example user control.

Listing 6-10. A Simple User Control

```
<script runat="server">

    public String HeaderText
    {
        get { return lblHeader.Text; }
```

```
        set { lblHeader.Text = value; }
    }

    public String GreetingText
    {
        get { return lblGreeting.Text; }
        set { lblGreeting.Text = value; }
    }

</script>
<h1 align="center">
    <asp:Label id="lblHeader" runat="server">This is the Header</asp:Label>
</h1>
<p align="left">
    <asp:Label id="lblGreeting" runat="server">This is the Greeting</asp:Label>
</p>
```

The code in this example looks much like a portion of the code for any control and it works the same way. When you provide both a get() and a set() method, as shown in the example, the user can read and write the property. Using get() alone allows property reading and using set() alone allows property writing.

The only tricky part about creating a user control is setting the linkage between the Web page and the control. To set the linkage, you must add a special entry on the All tab of the editor. This tab shows a few entries that don't appear on the other tabs. In this case, you need to add the following tag immediately below the <@ Page Language> tag.

```
<%@ Register TagPrefix="Standard" TagName="Info" Src="MyControl.ascx" %>
```

Adding this tag creates the required link. The example adds the control using the code shown in Listing 6-11. This listing also shows the additional text string used by the example to indicate where the control ends and where the Web page begins.

Listing 6-11. The User Control Test Page

```
<script runat="server">

    void Page_Load(Object sender, EventArgs e)
    {
        Control1.HeaderText = "This is a Test Page";
        Control1.GreetingText = "Welcome to the Text Page";
    }
```

```
</script>
<html>
<head>
</head>
<body>
    <form runat="server">
        <p>
            <STANDARD:INFO id="Control1" runat="server"></STANDARD:INFO>
        </p>
        <p>
            This is some additional text--it isn't part of the user control.
        </p>
    </form>
</body>
</html>
```

The Page_Load() method sets the property values for the control. This is the only additional code you need to use this particular example. As you can see, adding the control to the page means using a special tag composed of the TagPrefix and TagName values used for registering the control. Figure 6-24 shows the output of this example.

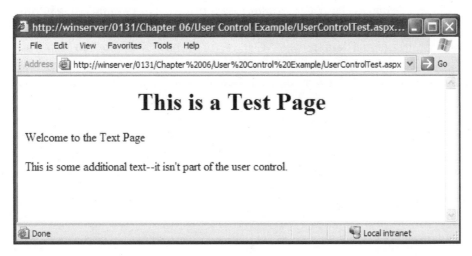

Figure 6-24. Creating user controls can greatly decrease your development burden.

Summary

This chapter has shown you techniques for using various types of components and controls in Web Matrix. Now that you've completed this chapter, you should be able to move your existing components and controls to the Web Matrix environment, and create new components and controls as needed. Of course, you'll need the rather large .NET Framework SDK download to do it, but at least it doesn't cost you anything to download it. If you do plan to create a number of complex components or controls, you really should consider using Visual Studio .NET—Web Matrix answers the needs of simple component and control development only.

Of course, now that you know how to work with Web Matrix, it's time to work with some of your own components and controls. The trick is to build up to those complex components and controls slowly because Web Matrix doesn't automate a lot of the functionality you need in the same way that Visual Studio .NET does. Make sure you learn about the various tools that the .NET Framework provides for working with components and controls too. These tools help you create the interoperability files that Web Matrix needs to work with unmanaged components and controls, as well as make your managed components and controls easier to use.

Chapter 7 explores the use of eXtensible Markup Language (XML) with Web Matrix. The XML technology actually covers a broad range of Web application support methodologies such as SOAP—one the technologies that we'll discuss for Web application data transfer. In addition, XML is used in a number of data storage technologies. Many Database Management Systems (DBMSs) now allow use of XML for external data storage. We've seen in the past that even Web Matrix uses XML for data storage in the form of code snippet exports. In short, knowing how you can use Web Matrix with XML to create Web applications is essential.

CHAPTER 7

Web Matrix and XML

In This Chapter

- Use the XML Support That Web Matrix Provides

- Use Microsoft XML Notepad to View XML-Formatted Files

- Create Applications with the XMLEditGrid Control

- Create Applications with the XML File Page

- Create Applications with the XSL Transform Page

- Create Applications with the XML Schema Page

- Design an XML Data Display Application

Everyone's learning to use eXtensible Markup Language (XML) today and employ it in a variety of formats. You'll find XML just about everywhere. Developers use XML to transfer data from one place to another and as part of specifications designed to perform special types of data transfers. It also appears as part of other specifications, such as the Simple Object Access Protocol (SOAP)—see Chapter 8 for details. Some Web sites use XML as a means for displaying data. Many developers have created unique uses for the eXtensible Stylesheet Language (XSL) Transformation (XSLT) in performing data manipulation. A few applications I've seen use XML as an alternative to centralized storage for application settings. You'll even find XML in Database Management Systems (DBMSs). In short, XML is the latest nonplatform, non–language-specific means for storing information.

The fact that you can use XML anywhere and even use it to bridge gaps between computer systems makes it a perfect match for Web Matrix—a tool that I'm convinced will also help you bridge platform gaps. The fact that Web Matrix is lightweight and doesn't perform a lot of interpretation for you means that this product is perfect for working on XML on any platform you choose. The ability to create an FTP connection to manipulate content remotely only makes things better.

This chapter discusses the XML support provided by Web Matrix. As with the material in Chapter 3, this material is decidedly open for anyone to use. You don't have to work on a Microsoft platform or use other Microsoft products to create something with XML. An XML-formatted Web page using XSLT works equally well on an Apache server as it does on Internet Information Server (IIS). You'll find that XML schemas are pretty much universal as well.

We'll discuss two Microsoft-specific topics in this chapter. The first is XMLEditGridControl. This special control helps you create impressive data displays quickly. We'll use this control in the XML data display example application in this chapter. This example provides practical advice on how to implement XML solutions using the XML features of Web Matrix. It also presents you with a specific application of XML that you can use as a source of ideas for your next Web development project.

Understanding XML Support in Web Matrix

The introduction to this chapter says a lot. XML is a text-based data storage technology that relies on tags to separate the various data elements. The formatting required for the tags is relatively straightforward and free form, but the specification includes precise rules you have to follow. For example, every opening tag requires a closing tag, or the document isn't well formed. Web Matrix helps you follow the rules required by the XML specifications, yet simplifies the task of reading and manipulating the data by making the XML classes of the .NET Framework available. (You'll find an overview of the XML classes at http://msdn.microsoft.com/library/en-us/cpref/html/frlrfSystemXml.asp.)

This section of the chapter provides an overview of the XML support provided by the .NET Framework, and as a result, by Web Matrix. Microsoft groups the System.Xml namespace with other data-oriented namespaces such as System.OleDb. Essentially, the System.Xml namespace provides classes oriented toward the management and control of data. Many developers think that they'll only use XML for data transfer because of the placement of the System.Xml namespace in the hierarchy, and because of articles that they've read in the trade press and magazines. However, the System.Xml assembly has a lot more to offer than simple data import and export functionality.

XML has a basic structure that lends itself to distributed application development because every computer out there can interpret text. XML relies on a formal use of tags to delineate data elements and format them in a way that two machines can understand. Formatting requires the use of attributes that define the type, scope, and use of the data in question. An XML file usually contains a header that shows the version of XML in use. In some cases, XML also requires special constructs such as the CDATA section to ensure that the recipient interprets the XML-formatted code directly. It's also possible to add comments to an

XML file to help document the content (although the use of comments is relatively uncommon except as a means of identifying the data source). Finally, you need some way to read and write XML to a data stream (be it a file or an Internet connection).

Now that you have some idea of what an XML namespace would have to include, let's look at some class specifics. The following list doesn't tell you about every class within System.Xml, but it does tell you about the classes you'll use most often. We'll use several of these classes in the examples in this chapter.

XmlAttribute and XmlAttributeCollection: Defines one or more data features such as type. Attributes normally appear as part of a database schema or within a Document Type Definition (DTD). Applications need attribute data to convert the text representation of information such as numbers to their locally supported type.

XmlCDataSection: Prevents the XmlReader from interpreting the associated text as tag input. An application could use a CDATA section for a number of purposes, including the transfer of HTML or other tag-based code. CDATA sections are also used with escaped or binary data.

XmlComment: Represents a comment within the XML document. Generally, vendors use comments to include data source information or standards adherence guidelines. However, comments can also document XML data or serve any other human readable text need the developer might have.

XmlDataDocument, XmlDocument, and XmlDocumentFragment: Contains all or part of an XML document. The XmlDataDocument class enables the developer to work with data found in a data set. Data stored using an XmlDataDocument can be retrieved, stored, and manipulated using the same features provided by a data set. Use the XmlDocument to represent the World Wide Web Consortium (W3C) Document Object Model (DOM) that relies on the typical tree representation of hierarchical data. An XmlDocumentFragment represents just a part of an XML document. Developers normally use an object of this class for data insertions into an existing tree structure.

XmlDeclaration: Contains the XML declaration node. The declaration node includes information such as the XML version, encoding level, read-only status, and namespace. An XML document usually contains a single declaration node, but it's possible to use multiple declaration nodes to provide multiple layers of data support.

XmlNode: Represents a single leaf of the XML data hierarchy. An XmlNode usually consists of a single tag pair with associated data (contained within an XmlText object). The XmlNode is the Root object for many other classes in the System.Xml namespace. For example, the XmlDocument and XmlDocumentFragment container classes are derived from XmlNode. At the lower end of the scale, XmlAttribute and XmlEntity are both leaf nodes based on XmlNode. In some cases, developers will use XmlNode directly to parse an XML document.

XmlNodeReader, XmlReader, XmlTextReader, and XmlValidatingReader: Performs a read of XML data from a document, stream, or other source. The XmlReader is the base class for all other readers. This reader provides fast, forward-only access to XML data of any type. The XmlNodeReader reads XML data from XmlNodes only—it doesn't work with schema or DTD data. The XmlTextReader doesn't perform as quickly as other readers, but it does work with DTD and schema data. This reader checks the document and nodes for well-formed XML, but doesn't perform any validation in the interest of speed. Use the XmlValidatingReader when the validity of the data is more important than application speed. This reader does perform DTD, XML-Data Reduced (XDR) schema, and XML Schema Definition (XSD) language schema validation. If either the XmlTextReader or XmlValidatingReader detect an error in the XML, both classes will raise an XmlException.

TIP *Using the correct reader is the most important way to improve application reliability and performance. Using the slow XmlValidatingReader on simple node data ensures your application will perform poorly (much to the consternation of the user). On the other hand, using the XmlNodeReader on mission critical data could result in data loss and unreliable application operation. In fact, due to the need to resend missing or incorrectly resolved data, application performance could suffer as well.*

XmlResolver and XmlUriResolver: Resolves external XML resources pointed to by a Uniform Resource Identifier (URI). For example, many common data types appear as definitions in external, standards-maintained resources. In addition, external resources on your company's Web site, such as a DTD or schema, will also appear in this list. Most developers will use the default resolution capabilities provided by XmlUriResolver. However, you can also create your own resolver using the XmlResolver class as a basis.

XmlTextWriter and XmlWriter: Performs a write of XML data to a data stream, file, or other output. The XmlWriter provides a means of manually controlling the output stream—a requirement in some cases. For example, the XmlWriter provides control over the start and stop of each data element and enables you to declare namespaces manually. However, the XmlTextWriter greatly simplifies the task of outputting data by performing some tasks automatically and making assumptions based on the current application environment.

Working with Microsoft XML Notepad

XML is almost, but not quite, readable by the average human. Reading simple files is almost trivial, but once the data gets nested a few layers deep, reading it can become tiresome. That's why you should have a tool for reading XML in your developer toolkit. The only problem is that some of these tools cost quite a bit for the occasional user. Microsoft has remedied this problem a little with the introduction of XML Notepad (`http://msdn.microsoft.com/library/default.asp?url=/library/en-us/dnxml/html/xmlpaddownload.asp`). This utility is free for the price of a download and does a reasonable job of reading most XML files. The current version, 1.5, is in beta as of this writing. In addition, although the Web site doesn't mention it, this version works fine with both Windows 2000 and Windows XP. The following sections provide a brief overview of this tool. We'll use this tool in several sections of the book to read XML data, so you'll want to download a copy.

Opening XML Files

When you start XML Notepad, you'll see a blank project. Use the File ➤ Open command to display an Open dialog box that allows you to open XML files from a local drive or from a Web site. All you need is a filename (and path) or a URL to get started.

 TIP *Not all XML files have an XML file extension. We've already seen one case in the book where a CONFIG file was actually an XML file in disguise. Often, you'll find that the file extension matches the customized use of the file, rather than the actual content. When in doubt, try to open a file that looks like it contains XML data to see if XML Notepad will make it easier to understand.*

Figure 7-1 shows the content of a movie database example I created by exporting the MovieGuide database ExistingMovies table to the Movie.XML file. (You'll find several XML files to view in the \Chapter 07\Sample XML Data folder of the source code, available from the Downloads section on the Apress site at `http://www.apress.com/book/download.html`.) Notice that the name of the elements matches the name of the table for the movie database (found in the Movie.XML file). Likewise, each of the child elements matches the name of one of the fields within the table. The right pane shows the data contained within each one of the child elements.

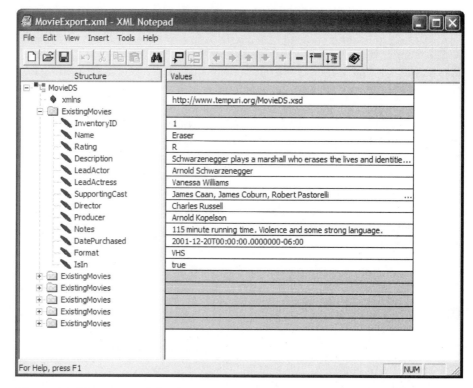

Figure 7-1. The names of the elements are important when working with exported data in XML format.

TIP *If you want to use XML from your SQL Server 2000 installation, then you'll want to download the XML feature packs found at* `http://msdn.microsoft.com/downloads/sample.asp?url=/MSDN-FILES/027/001/824/msdncompositedoc.xml`. *These feature packs add to the capabilities already found in SQL Server 2000. In addition, they help you keep your setup current by ensuring that your SQL Server 2000 installation always meets the specification requirements.*

Modifying Existing Data and Creating New Data

You can use XML Notepad for more than just viewing data. Creating new data for testing purposes is relatively painless once you see the exported data from an existing database. In fact, we'll create some sample data in this section for use in an application later. The following steps will get you started.

1. Create a blank project using the File ➤ New command.

2. Type the name of the data set in the Root object. The example uses SampleData as a name, but you'll want to select something a little more descriptive for a production application.

3. Rename the first element to reflect the new table. The example application uses NewDataElement as the name. DBMSs normally use the database name for the Root object and the table name for the first element. (See Figure 7-1 for an example of actual database output.)

4. Add a new child element using the options on the Insert menu. You'll notice that the first element changes into a folder. Type the name of the first data column in this element. The example uses Data1 for the first child element. However, a database would use the name of the first field in the selected table (see Figure 7-1).

5. Add additional columns as needed until you complete one record's worth of entries. The example uses Data2 and Data3 as entries to complete one record in the sample database, but you should also look at Figure 7-1 as another example of what you could do.

6. Type values for each of the child elements. Now that you have one complete record, you can use the Duplicate command to create copies of it. Each copy will become one record within the XML database.

7. Right-click the NewDataElement folder and choose Duplicate from the context menu. The example provides three records for the sample, but you can include any number you wish. Figure 7-2 shows the structure and contents of the SampleData.XML file. It also shows the content we'll use for the example.

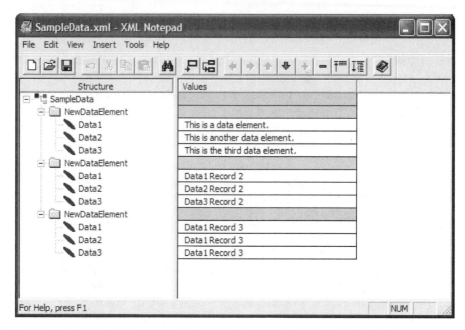

Figure 7-2. Creating an XML database using XML Notepad is relatively easy as long as you follow a few rules.

Now that you've seen what XML Notepad can do, you need to realize that other vendors do provide other alternatives. XML Notepad doesn't have some of the bells and whistles of high-end products such as XML Spy (http://www.xmlspy.com/). However, XML Notepad is a good alternative if you only use an XML editor occasionally and don't want to spend any money. The important consideration is that you have an XML editor that you can use to view the output from your applications.

Using the XmlEditGrid Control

Just in case you've forgotten, the XmlEditGrid control isn't part of the usual assortment of Web Matrix controls. This control is the one we downloaded from the Online Component Gallery in the "Connecting to the Online Component Gallery" section of Chapter 2. If you haven't downloaded this control already, you'll want to download it using the instructions in Chapter 2 before you begin working with this section of the chapter.

TIP *Don't get the idea that the Online Component Gallery is the only place to get new controls for your Web Matrix setup. The online community has worked hard to put together an impressive list of controls that you can use with Web Matrix. In some cases, the controls aren't well documented, but they're normally based on existing (documented) controls and consequently easy to figure out. See the Control Gallery at* `http://www.asp.net/Default.aspx?tabindex=2&tabid=30` *for details.*

The XmlEditGrid control is unique in that it treats correctly formatted XML files as database input. Of course, the key phrase is "correctly formatted"—the XML file must use a format that lends itself to display within a grid. The SampleData.XML file we discussed earlier does have the proper format for display in the XmlEditGrid, so we'll use it in this example. Other files in the Sample XML Data folder will also work, but this file is particularly easy to understand.

You can use the XmlDataGrid as you would any other grid for database work. The XmlDataGrid includes features that help you edit, delete, and add records to the XML file using an interface that looks just like a standard database grid. Figure 7-3 shows an example of the XmlDataGrid loaded with the movie database (found in Movie.XML) we looked at earlier in the chapter.

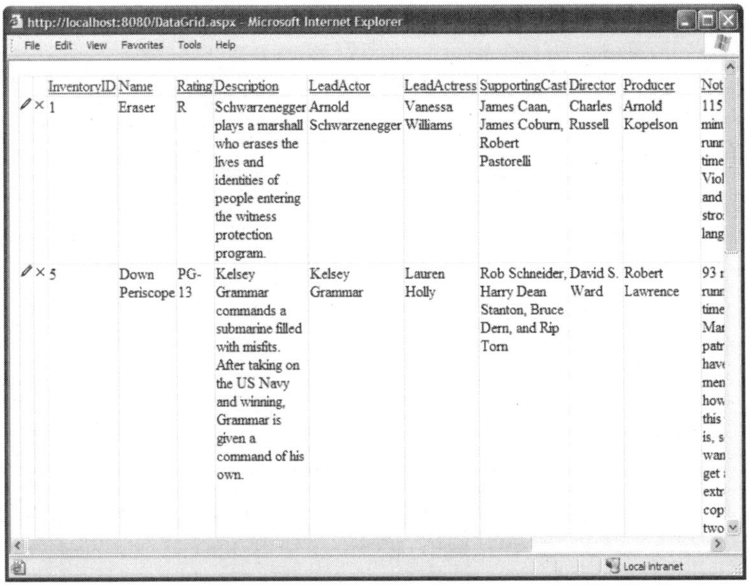

Figure 7-3. Use the XmlDataGrid to view XML files as you would any database file.

Setting the XmlEditGrid up for use is easy. Begin by adding the control to the form. If you want to use this control for XML files, you must supply the name of a file in the XmlFile property. The XmlEditGrid can also use a data source employing techniques similar to the ones we examined in Chapter 5. In short, the XmlEditGrid is a data grid with some extra features.

I found that some configuration tasks are easier if you open the properties dialog box shown in Figure 7-4 by clicking the Property Pages icon in the Properties window. The dialog box groups some task elements, such as formatting, in an easy to understand manner. You can still use the Properties windows, but the dialog box presents fewer problems. The default setup for this control uses almost no formatting at all, making it difficult to see some features, such as the currently selected record, so you'll definitely want to perform some configuration.

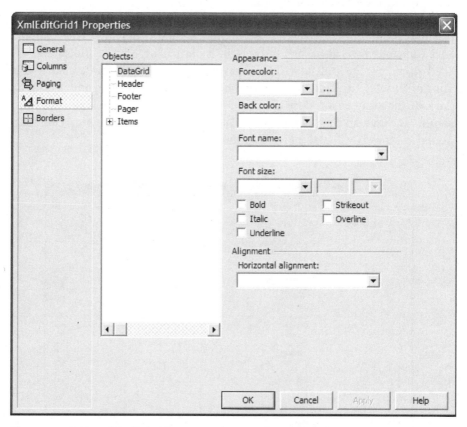

Figure 7-4. Using this dialog box to perform tasks such as formatting makes the job easier.

Depending on how you configure the XmlEditGrid, it will automatically provide basic editing functionality for XML files (I didn't test the database capability because we have other controls to use for that purpose). You can edit, delete, and add records to your XML file database. The XmlEditGrid provides an edit icon in the leftmost column (looks like a pencil). Click this icon the first time, and the XmlEditGrid will select the row for editing—click it the second time, and the changes appear in the file and the control deselects the record. Immediately to the right of this icon is the delete icon (looks like an X). The control doesn't provide any warning about deleting a record—it simply performs the act on the selected row when clicked. The add feature appears as the Add new item link at the bottom of the grid. You can override most of the default actions performed by the XmlEditGrid by creating event handlers for them.

You'll find that there are a couple of idiosyncrasies with this control. The first is that when you install the control from the Web, it will usually register itself in the GAC on your local machine. (If you don't register it in the GAC, make sure you create a \bin folder for each application and place the control there.) Unfortunately, when you move the application to your server for testing, it will fail. You'll find the control located in the \Program Files\Microsoft ASP.NET Web Matrix\v0.5.464\Components folder of your machine. Copy the control to the server and use GACUtil to register it. The control location doesn't matter, as long as you properly register the control—CLR will find it.

The second problem is a little harder to figure out. Figure 7-5 shows the display you'll see when you get the application running the first time. Notice that all of the icons are missing. This problem doesn't prevent the application from working, but it's an annoying problem from an appearance perspective.

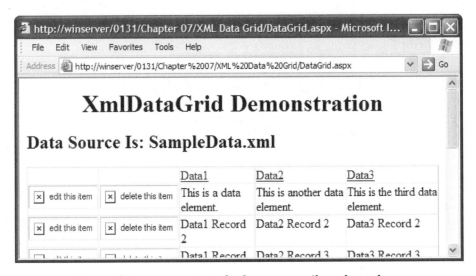

Figure 7-5. Fixing this error can prove bothersome until you know how.

The way to fix this problem is to use the View ➤ Source command in Internet Explorer to view the source code that the control creates. You'll notice that every entry has this bit of code.

```
<img src='/aspnet_client/Swarren_XmlEditGrid/1_0_0_0/edit.gif'
```

The only problem is that you don't have the required folder on your server, nor did the control tell you where to find the image on your local machine. You can find the errant icons in the \Program Files\ASP.NET\Client Files\Swarren_XmlEditGrid\1_0_0_0 folder of your local hard drive.

It seems that the installation program assumes that you'll use the local Web server for all testing. Simply create an \aspnet_client\Swarren_XmlEditGrid\1_0_0_0 folder in the root directory of your IIS installation, and copy the GIF files to it. The icons will mysteriously reappear in your application. Of course, this opens the door for customization. If you don't particularly like the icons that the XmlEditGrid uses, replace the GIF files in this folder with icons that you do like—just make sure you use the correct names.

The XmlEditGrid control performs a lot of the work for you right out of the package. Even so, I needed to add two pieces of code to the example. The first displays the name of the XML file, while the second allows for sorting. The one feature that doesn't appear to work correctly right out of the box is sorting. Listing 7-1 shows how to add both features to your application.

Listing 7-1. Code for Sorting Grid and Display Filename

```
void Page_Load(Object sender, EventArgs e)
{
    // Display the name of the XML file.
    Label1.Text = "Data Source Is: " + XmlEditGrid1.XmlFile;
}


void XmlEditGrid1_SortCommand(Object source, DataGridSortCommandEventArgs e)
{
    // Define a sort order for the XmlEditGrid.
    Response.SetCookie(new HttpCookie("SortOrder", e.SortExpression));

    // Tell the user about the sort order.
    Label2.Text = "The sort order is: " + e.SortExpression;
}
```

As you can see, the application adds the filename during the page loading process, which means you could allow editing of more than one XML file using the same page without losing the user. The XmlEditGrid1_SortCommand() uses the same technique the DataGrid control uses for sorting—you send a cookie back to the server with the required sort order. This method also adds text to a second label that shows the sort order to the user. The XmlEditGrid is unsorted when you first display the data. Figure 7-6 shows the final output of this example using the SampleData.XML file.

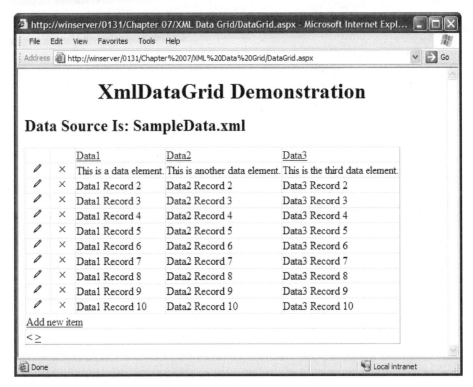

Figure 7-6. Creating output with any XML file that contains data in the correct format is easy with XmlEditGrid.

Removing Custom Controls from Your Project

There's a small, but important, change that occurs when you add a custom control to your project—one that you downloaded from the Internet or otherwise added to your toolbox. Web Matrix automatically adds a `<%@ Register>` tag to your code. As we saw in Chapter 6, this tag registers the control for you and makes it possible for ASP.NET to load it. Consequently, adding the tag is a good service for Web Matrix to provide.

Unfortunately, as shown in the following illustration, this tag is only visible when you view the All tab of the editing window. For example, I added the XmlDataGrid control to this project. You can see the `<%@ Register>` tag immediately below the `<%@ Page>` tag.

```
1  <%@ Page Language="C#" %>
2  <%@ Register TagPrefix="xedit" Namespace="Swarren.XmlEditGrid"
3  <script runat="server">
4
5      // Insert page code here
6      //
7
8  </script>
9  <html>
10 <head>
11 </head>
12 <body>
13     <form runat="server">
14         <!-- Insert content here -->
15     </form>
16 </body>
17 </html>
```

Design | HTML | Code | All

When you remove a custom control from the Design tab, the `<%@ Register>` tag remains in place. Unless you happen to look at the All tab, you won't see the tag and could try to deploy your application with the `<%@ Register>` tag in place. If you don't include the requisite DLL with your application, it won't run even if the code is correct. Removing the tag will fix the problem.

Using the XML File

Let me begin by reiterating that using Web Matrix isn't the best way to create an XML file unless you like to do a lot of typing and don't want to see what your data actually looks like. That said, the ability to create XML files is important. When you use the XML File page template, you get a basic tag that starts you on your way. All you need to do is begin typing the elements and attributes for your XML file.

 TIP *Web Matrix provides a text editor for the XML files. This might seem problematic at first, but I've found it's quite useful. Most XML editors on the market, including XML Notepad, operate on the premise that the XML file you want to edit has "well-formed" XML. Some XML files won't meet this requirement in certain situations, such as some CONFIG files I've viewed. The fact that Web Matrix provides text-editing functionality means you can view the errant XML file and fix it if required. The point is that Web Matrix provides you with another alternative—another tool for your toolkit.*

This section looks at a relatively simple example. Learning to type XML by hand is actually a good idea because it helps you see problems in automatically generated XML later. Some of the elusive issues behind a relatively simple packaging technique begin to make sense as you spend more time working with XML. With this in mind, consider the XML code in Listing 7-2.

Listing 7-2. A Simple XML File

```xml
<?xml version="1.0" encoding="utf-8" standalone="yes" ?>
<PhoneMessages>
    <Date Day="09/16/02">
        <Message Name="George">
            "Hello, Sorry I missed you!"
        </Message>
        <Message Name="Sam">
            "Are you gone again?"
        </Message>
    </Date>
    <Date Day="09/17/02">
        <Message Name="Ann">
            "Want to go fishing Thursday?"
        </Message>
    </Date>
```

```
<Date Day="09/18/02">
    <Message Name="Jerry">
        "Hope to see you tomorrow!"
    </Message>
    <Message Name="Samantha">
        "Call the office ASAP!"
    </Message>
    <Message Name="Jan">
        "Give me a call at work!"
    </Message>
</Date>
</PhoneMessages>
```

This XML is well formed because it includes a header, and each of the elements has an opening and closing tag. Each element contains either another element or at least one attribute. The attributes take two different forms. You give the attribute a name and place it within the tag, or your can place it between an opening and closing tag. The specification doesn't require indenting. However, most developers find it useful for reading the XML in this format. Figure 7-7 shows how this XML file looks in XML Notepad.

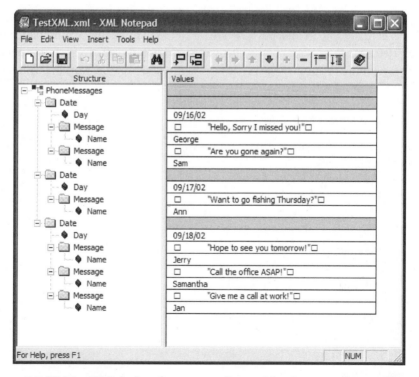

Figure 7-7. Writing XML by hand can reward you with a better understanding of how this data storage format works.

Using the XSL Transform

Defining methods for reading XML must occupy more than a few passing thoughts for some developers because the developer community has created a number of ways to present XML in a readable format. The XSL Transform page provides another text-oriented method for working with what appears as XML. However, XSLT files can contain more than just XML, and browsers don't use them for direct display. An XSLT file contains formatting information—a means for displaying the content of an XML file in a form that the average human can read. In addition, the combination of an XML and an XSLT file can create a presentation in a standard browser.

The XML file provides content, while the XSLT file provides format. You can take the same content and present it in a number of ways by changing XSLT files. This feature makes it possible for some Web sites to provide a standard and printer friendly view of the same data. The data hasn't changed—only the XSLT file content has changed.

Let's begin with the one and only change you have to make to the XML file. To use an XSLT file, you need to add a tag to the beginning of the XML file. This tag tells the browser which XSLT file to use to format the data contained within the XML file. If the browser doesn't find the XSLT file, it will still display the data using whatever method it normally uses for displaying XML files, which isn't very readable by the average user.

```
<?xml-stylesheet type="text/xsl" href="PFormat.XSLT"?>
```

As you can see, the tag simply says that this XML file uses a stylesheet. The type of information in the stylesheet file is a combination of text and XSL. Finally, the name of the XSLT file is PFormat.XSLT. These three entries are all you need to change the way the browser displays the XML file.

Creating an XSLT file is a little more complicated. Listing 7-3 shows one of two XSLT files we'll discuss in this section.

Listing 7-3. A Simple XSLT File

```
<?xml version='1.0'?>
<xsl:stylesheet version='1.0'
xmlns:xsl='http://www.w3.org/1999/XSL/Transform'>
<xsl:output method="xml" indent="yes" />
<xsl:template match="/">

<!-- Create the HTML Code for this stylesheet. -->
<HTML>
```

```
<HEAD>
    <TITLE>Remote Performance Monitor</TITLE>
</HEAD>

<BODY>
<CENTER><H3>Performance Monitor Results</H3></CENTER>

<TABLE BORDER="2">
    <TR>
        <TH>Time</TH>
        <TH>Percent User Time Value</TH>
    </TR>
        <xsl:apply-templates select="//Item"/>
</TABLE>

</BODY>
</HTML>
</xsl:template>

<!-- XSL template section that describes table content. -->

<xsl:template match="Item">
    <TR>
        <TD>
            <xsl:value-of select="Time"/>
        </TD>
        <TD>
            <xsl:value-of select="Data"/>
        </TD>
    </TR>
</xsl:template>

</xsl:stylesheet>
```

The code begins with a heading. Always include the XML heading because this is essentially a form of XML. The next tag defines this file as a stylesheet, while the third tag defines the method of output. The fourth tag is especially important because it defines which tags this stylesheet matches in the source XML file. In this case, the stylesheet matches (or imports) all of the tags.

The next bit of code begins defining the HTML output for this example. The code is purposely simple in this case—it won't even pass the W3C test because it lacks features such as the <DOCTYPE> tag. However, the HTML output will display a result in a browser, which is all we need now. Nothing prevents you from creating relatively complex HTML using an XSLT file.

After the code defines a header, it begins defining the body of the page. In this case, we'll use a table. However, now you need to understand something about the XML file we're using. The target XML file contains entries in this format.

```
<Item>
  <Time>6:25:57 PM</Time>
  <Data>0</Data>
</Item>
```

The file places each entry within an <Item> element. The subelements, <Time> and <Data>, include the information we want to display. Look at the code and you'll see an <xsl:apply-templates select="//Item"/> entry. This entry tells the browser to display each entry in the XML file according to the definitions provided in the XSL template that matches the <Item> element. The template begins after the code completes the HTML portion of the information with the <xsl:template match="Item"> tag. At this point, we select the values contained in each of the subelements and display them on screen using standard HTML. Figure 7-8 shows the output of the XML file and XSLT file combination.

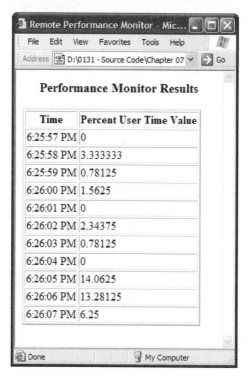

Figure 7-8. Reading this output is easier than viewing straight XML.

Let's look at a more complex XSLT file. Remember that the data hasn't changed—only the content of the template has changed. In this case, the view will add a counter, so we know which entry we're looking at, and use a two-column format in place of the single-column format shown in Figure 7-8. Listing 7-4 shows the code we'll use in this case.

Listing 7-4. A Better XSLT File

```
<?xml version='1.0'?>
<xsl:stylesheet version='1.0'
xmlns:xsl='http://www.w3.org/1999/XSL/Transform'>
<xsl:output method="xml" indent="yes" />
<xsl:template match="/">

<!-- Create the HTML Code for this stylesheet. -->
<HTML>
<HEAD>
    <TITLE>Another Performance Monitor View</TITLE>
</HEAD>

<BODY>
<H3 ALIGN="Center">Performance Monitor Results</H3>
<P ALIGN="Center">Version 2</P>

<TABLE BORDER="2">
    <TR bgcolor="#C0C0FF">
        <TH>Entry</TH>
        <TH>Time</TH>
        <TH>Percent User Time Value</TH>
        <TH>Entry</TH>
        <TH>Time</TH>
        <TH>Percent User Time Value</TH>
    </TR>
    <xsl:apply-templates select="//Item"/>
</TABLE>

</BODY>
</HTML>
</xsl:template>

<!-- XSL template section that describes table content. -->
```

```
<xsl:template match="Item">
    <xsl:if test="position() mod 2 = 1">
        <xsl:text disable-output-escaping = "yes">
            &lt;TR&gt;
        </xsl:text>
    </xsl:if>
        <TD>
            <xsl:value-of select="position()"/>
        </TD>
        <TD>
            <xsl:value-of select="Time"/>
        </TD>
        <TD>
            <xsl:value-of select="Data"/>
        </TD>
    <xsl:if test="position() mod 2 = 0">
        <xsl:text disable-output-escaping = "yes">
            &lt;/TR&gt;
        </xsl:text>
    </xsl:if>
</xsl:template>

</xsl:stylesheet>
```

A lot of this code is the same as before—at least the layout of the code is the same. We still have an HTML section and a template section that interprets the data. As you can see, the HTML section includes a new header and then doubles the headers so we can see two rows. I added a little color to the table header for this example—it's a nice touch to differentiate between the two areas.

TIP   *XSLT code might look a little intimidating at first, but it's relatively straightforward once you work with it for a while. You'll find an excellent XSLT reference and examples at* http://www.zvon.org/xxl/XSLTreference/Output/ index.html. *The examples are a little abstract—they aren't HTML specific, but that's actually a good feature because you can use XSLT for more tasks than we are doing here. Developers use XSLT for a number of translation tasks.*

The template uses a few more XSLT features. The first <xsl:if> tag performs a test on the current position within the file. If the entry is an odd value, then it executes the code that follows. Otherwise, execution continues with the next step, which is to display one of the entries. The code that this first <xsl:if> tag executes is to print out some text using the <xsl:text disable-output-escaping = "yes"> tag. Using this tag permits you to output a <TR> tag to the browser. However, the tag only appears on screen when the template is processing an odd entry.

This version of the template will output an item number. You still use the <xsl:value-of> tag. However, instead of selecting the output of an entry in the XML file, this tag selects the output of the position() function. The position() function comes in very handy in processing XML files because it tells you where you are—it's the equivalent of the record number for a database table.

The final change for this XSLT file is to add another <xsl:if> tag. Instead of checking for odd entries, this one checks for even entries. As with the first <xsl:if> tag, this one outputs text in the form of the closing </TR> tag. Because of the arrangement of <xsl:if> tags, the display will show two XML file entries in each row. Figure 7-9 shows the output of this example.

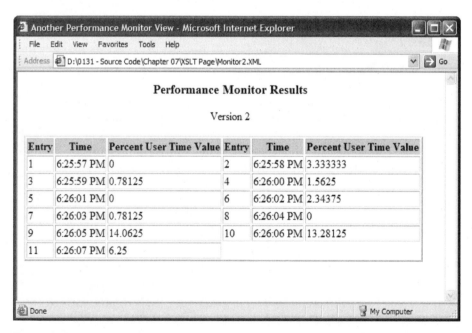

Figure 7-9. Creating a different look means changing the XSLT file, not the XML data.

Using the XML Schema

Databases require a schema to define their content. The tables within the database have columns that contain specific types of data. Each entry has a name, such as LastName, for the last name entry in a contact management database. The entry has a data type such as text, a length, and other characteristics that define that entry. An application relies on these entries to interact with the database. For example, the entry will tell the application whether an edited entry is too long or of the wrong type. All of this information helps create a reliable flow of information between the database and the application.

TIP   *Most DBMSs will create XSD files for you. However, if you find that you have to create such a file by hand, make sure you use the standards-recognized method. One of the best places to learn about the XSD file format is the XML Schema page on the W3C site at* `http://www.w3.org/XML/Schema`. *You can find a few coding examples on the Got Dot Net site at* `http://samples.gotdotnet.com/quickstart/howto/doc/Xml/XmlReadWriteSchema.aspx` *that will help you understand how XSD works.*

In order for XML applications to provide the same level of support that their desktop counterparts do, they need some form of schema to use with the XML data they receive from a remote location. The XSD file contains the information that a desktop application would normally obtain using the database schema. As with everything else in this chapter, the data appears in XML format. In fact, many of the XML editors on the market also provide direct support for XSD files. Figure 7-10 shows an example of an XSD file that I created for the Movie.XML file mentioned elsewhere in this chapter. (You'll probably want to open a copy of this file in XML Notepad as well.)

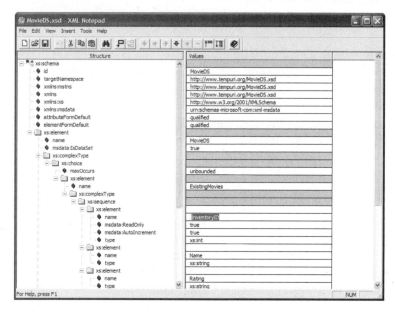

Figure 7-10. Create an XSD file such as this one to describe the format of any table you produce.

We won't look at the source code for this file because it's relatively large. However, you should notice a few things in the XML Notepad display. For example, you'll find a number of namespace entries at the top of the file. Each <xlmns> tag defines a particular namespace used within the file or by applications. In a few cases, the application will ignore the namespace for now, but might use it in the future.

Immediately below the headers, we begin creating the data set. The first element is the data set name, MovieDS. The file contains some settings for the data set and then names the first (and only) table, ExistingMovies. Beneath the table entry are some more settings and, finally, the field names, each with their settings. In short, this is a complete description of a data set used to access the ExistingMovies table in a database.

Now that you've seen a schema for a data set, let's concentrate on something a little simpler. As previously mentioned, creating an XML Schema page will generate an XSD file with the opening and close tags, along with a few namespace entries. You have to generate all of the other code required to define the schema you want to create. Listing 7-5 shows a simple XSD file that defines a schema for a contact entry database.

Listing 7-5. A Simple XSD File

```xml
<?xml version="1.0" encoding="utf-8" ?>
<xsd:schema targetNamespace="http://tempuri.org/Simple.xsd"
  xmlns="http://tempuri.org/Simple.xsd"
  xmlns:xsd="http://www.w3.org/2001/XMLSchema">

<xsd:annotation>
    <xsd:documentation xml:lang="en">
        A simple XSD file used to demonstrate schemas.
        This is a contact management database.
    </xsd:documentation>
</xsd:annotation>

<xsd:element name="ADatabase">
    <xsd:complexType>
        <xsd:element name="MyContacts">
            <xsd:complexType>
                <xsd:sequence>
                    <xsd:element name="name"      type="xsd:string"/>
                    <xsd:element name="street"    type="xsd:string"/>
                    <xsd:element name="city"      type="xsd:string"/>
                    <xsd:element name="state"     type="xsd:string"/>
                    <xsd:element name="zip"       type="xsd:string"/>
                    <xsd:element name="telephone" type="xsd:string"/>
                </xsd:sequence>
            </xsd:complexType>
        </xsd:element>
    </xsd:complexType>
</xsd:element>

</xsd:schema>
```

This example is simplified, but it demonstrates essential features a schema would require. You need to define the relevant namespaces to begin. Adding some annotation helps anyone who uses the schema you create. Finally, the main section of this schema describes the database. The database name is ADatabase. It contains a single table called MyContacts. The MyContracts table includes a number of text fields that describe the contacts for this person. Figure 7-11 shows how this schema appears in XML Notepad.

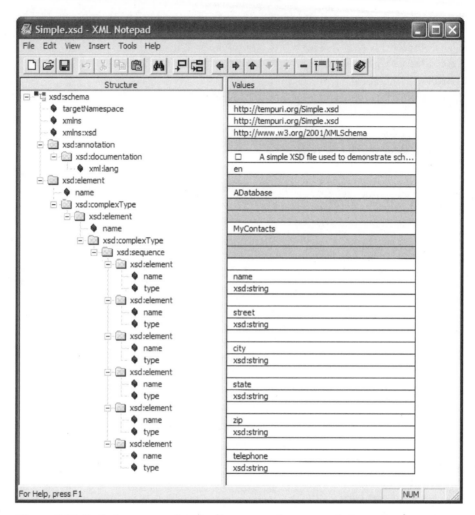

Figure 7-11. Defining even a simple schema can become code intensive.

Summary

This chapter has shown you how to work with the XML features that Web Matrix provides. More importantly, you've learned one more way in which Web Matrix helps you bridge the gap between platforms and diverse technologies. Of course, you also learned about two Microsoft-specific XML implementations, the XMLEditGrid control and a technique for using it to display XML-formatted data.

Now it's time to work with some XML data of your own. Look at the various ways that you can use Web Matrix to bridge gaps in your own organization. You'll also want to download XML Notepad to work with the data files created by Web

Matrix and other XML applications. We only touched on some of the more important features that XML Notepad provides in this chapter. I think you'll find this utility is an essential part of any toolkit designed to work with XML and its derivatives.

Chapter 8 is almost a continuation of this chapter. However, we move beyond mere XML into the world of Web services—a special means of sharing code and data with other companies. Web service applications have a lot of potential that's unrealized now because vendors still have some problems to work out with it (such as a secure method for transferring requests). This chapter will contain a few surprises for many of you because recent developments have made Web services a viable way to work with distributed applications.

CHAPTER 8

Web Matrix and Web Services

In This Chapter

- Understand How Web Services Affect You

- Develop Applications Using XML Web Services

- Learn to Use the Simple Page

- Learn to Use the SOAP Headers Page

- Explore Techniques for Developing Custom Web Service Pages

- Create a Simple Web Service Application

- Learn to Use the Custom Class

- Create a Custom Class

- Learn to Use Output Caching

- Design with Enhanced Performance in Mind

For some developers, learning to use the eXtensible Markup Language (XML) involves a "What's next?" conclusion. The simplicity of XML makes it a perfect mechanism for data exchange. It doesn't take a lot of code to decipher the pure text of XML. However, the very simplicity that XML provides can hide its usefulness in a broad range of applications.

This chapter discusses just one of many uses for XML—Web services. A *Web service* is a type of application exchange. One company advertises services that it can provide to another company through a data connection. For example, a travel agent might rely on a Web service to contact an airline about flight information, and then make a reservation for a client. The two systems don't share a real link—not in the same way as two applications can over a Local Area Network (LAN) connection. Instead, the information travels through the Internet using a temporary connection.

We'll discuss how Web Matrix can help you develop simple Web service applications—mostly from the client side of picture. You'll learn about the Simple Object Access Protocol (SOAP), which is the main data packaging protocol employed by Web service applications. (Developers have created a wealth of XML-based data transfer methods that we won't discuss in this chapter.)

As the chapter continues, you'll learn a bit about how to create classes and use them in applications. Just like many components and controls, you'll find that the lack of a build feature and full debugging functionality will limit the depth of classes you can create with Web Matrix. Then again, you might be surprised at just how much you can do as long as you understand how Web services work. We'll discuss some simple examples, along with what you can expect from Web Matrix in the way of support.

The final section of the chapter helps you understand the performance problems that you'll experience when using Web Services. The use of XML, which is essentially formatted text, means that an application can't pack the data tightly. In addition, Internet data transfers are relatively slow when compared to a LAN. Consequently, you'll see some performance degradation, and this last section will help you overcome it.

An Introduction to Web Services

It's hard to open a trade magazine, go to a trade show, visit a computer store, read a newspaper, or even watch television without running into some mention of Web services. One of the biggest problems with Web services today is that so many people have defined this term in so many ways. A simple definition is that a Web service is a convenience you provide to a client using an Internet or intranet connection. As previously stated, a Web service involves discovering and then using application code located on another machine. However, the big difference between Web services and other code-sharing technologies is that you don't necessarily need to know much about the remote connection—all you need to know is that the connection exists.

The following sections will provide an overview of Web services that defines them as shared application code. This view won't always agree with other sources you read because the term *Web service* is nebulous. The uses, technologies, and issues of Web services create a specific definition in the minds of some people based on experience, while others base their definition on the sources they've read. Many of the protocols used for Web services are also evolving, which means the definitions provided by those protocols (after all, a protocol is a set of rules) are changing as well. In sum, the following sections aren't only an overview of Web services, but an overview based on a particular viewpoint.

Web Service Uses

When I first started looking at Web service technologies, there were many plans, but very limited implementation. The ethereal quality of these plans made the continuation of Web services more the stuff of myth than reality. Although many developers talked about Web services, most of the discussion centered on how to resolve negative issues—not the least of which was problematic security and issues of intellectual property.

Today, Web services are finally seeing some use. In fact, you can discover the Web services provided by two large online companies: Google and Amazon. These two companies exemplify one type of Web service—one in which a company benefits by your use of the Web service, even if the company doesn't know your identity. In this case, you can use their database to search for something you need. Both Google and Amazon provide extensive databases coupled to speedy search engines, so allowing access to this search engine is a natural Web service for both companies.

TIP   *Web Matrix doesn't provide the level of Web service discovery found in Visual Studio .NET, so many forms of automation provided in that product are unavailable to you. However, you can still use the Web services provided online by both Google and Amazon. You can learn about the Google Web service at* `http://www.google.com/apis/`*, and the Amazon Web service at* `http://soap.amazon.com/`*. Another interesting place to look for Web services to try is the Web Service page on the CapeScience site at* `http://www.capescience.com/webservices/index.shtml`*.*

The natural use of a Web service is for its intended purpose. For example, *InfoWorld* currently relies on the Google search engine to provide search services for its Web site, and it's almost certain that other companies have followed suit. (The preceding tip provides details on how you can become a user of these services as well.) Many developers have discussed using the Amazon search engine. The CapeScience site has also garnered attention—I actually learned about it through the application of another developer.

Public release of a Web service often provides developers with ideas that turn into other Web services, which rely on the original service for some functionality. For example, after Google released its API, some developers turned the Google search engine into components of their own applications. For example, the Googlematic service (`http://www.interconnected.org/googlematic/`) enables you to search Google using Instant Messaging. Send an Instant Message with your request, and you'll receive a reply with the top search responses. If all you have available is e-mail, then you can use `google@capeclear.com` to query Google and `amazon@capeclear.com` to query Amazon. One person felt that Amazon's search engine was too complicated, so we now have the Amazon Light search engine at `http://www.kokogiak.com/amazon/`.

In some cases, a Web service launches a related, value-added, service. For example, consider the TouchGraph site at `http://www.touchgraph.com/TGGoogleBrowser.html`. In this case, the developer has added relationship data to the picture. A search consists of finding and graphing sites similar to a target site. The search often creates a revealing graph that helps the user understand the relationships between one site and those around it. The best sites to check are those that have a large following—a personal site often lacks a large enough following to produce a significant graph.

Web services will actually see the greatest amount of use for "private" applications due to security concerns and because developers are still experimenting with the technology. One company might want to make a catalog or other database information available to partner companies using a Web service. In fact, once the standards committees solve the security issues around Web services, database access is probably the place where Web services will take off because database applications are the most common application in use right now. From the previous paragraphs, you know that this isn't the only use of Web services, but it will become a major use.

Security companies are already providing access to another kind of information through Web services. A number of companies now offer information about your home security system, appliances, and other systems through an Internet connection. More often than not, this connection accesses a Web service that helps you monitor your home and family using a browser.

A final category of usage is the "utility" Web service. The first use of a Web service that I saw was a utility for performing some math calculations—performing one of the four standard calculator functions on two numbers, in this case. Send the utility some numbers, and it would spit out an answer. Other early applications performed data conversions. For example, not all of us keep an inches-to-centimeter calculator in our back pocket (or brain), so having a Web service utility to perform this type of conversion is convenient. Generally, this is going to be the experiment or small Web site contribution to the Web service community, but it's a valuable contribution nonetheless.

Web Service Technologies

XML is the best known of the Web service technologies, and a few developers assume that XML is all there is. However, XML by itself is just a language specification, so it suffers from a lack of built-in functionality. It doesn't have the formatted message that other technologies do, and therefore it's harder to create a communication path using XML. Consequently, many developers end up creating a custom technology based on XML or using one of the public XML derivatives.

Of course, there are many XML derivatives from which to choose. XML has found its way into a number of technologies including some of these interesting choices.

- **Math Modeling Language (MathML):** `http://www.w3.org/Math/`

- **Synchronized Multimedia Integration Language (SMIL):** `http://www.w3.org/AudioVideo/`

- **Scalable Vector Graphics (SVG):** `http://www.w3.org/Graphics/SVG/Overview.htm8`

- **eXtensible HyperText Markup Language (XHTML):** `http://www.w3.org/TR/2002/WD-xhtml2-20020805/`

- **Speech Application Language Tags (SALT):** `http://www.saltforum.org/`

Of all the public derivatives based on XML, SOAP is probably the best known. XML provides the means to format the content of the message, while SOAP provides a means to package the formatted content. Using SOAP helps two applications communicate because they have a common framework to perform the communication.

NOTE   *Don't assume that SOAP is always the best choice for a given application. Yes, SOAP does have a huge following and it's an easy-to-understand protocol. Recent developments have also fixed some of the problems with SOAP. However, articles such as the one from XML.com about SOAP interaction with Google (`http://www.xml.com/lpt/a/2002/04/24/google.html`) make it apparent that SOAP isn't always the best choice. Make sure you research the Web service technology you want to use before you begin the design process. I suspect many of you will want to use SOAP, though, so I've included a sample later in the chapter.*

You must couple SOAP with other technologies to create applications that can actually do what they think they will. For example, you need some method for describing your service—a common approach is using Web Services Description Language (WSDL).

If you provide a public Web service, the application will also need some method of public discovery. Many developers turn to Universal Discovery, Description, and Interrogation (UDDI) for this purpose; however, you'll also use technologies such as Discovery of Web Services (DISCO) and Web Services Inspection Language (WS-Inspection). (You can find an excellent article on the differences between UDDI and DISCO at http://msdn.microsoft.com/msdnmag/issues/02/02/xml/xml0202.asp— a short discussion of how UDDI and WS-Inspection differ appears at http://jmvidal.cse.sc.edu/talks/uddi/.)

Private communication means securing the message, so you'll need a technology such as Web Services Security (WS-Security). As you can see, a Web service isn't created by using one standardized technology in most cases—it requires several. The following list contains some Web sites you should consider as sources for this alphabet soup of standards.

- **XML:** http://www.w3.org/XML/

- **SOAP:** http://www.w3.org/TR/SOAP/

- **WSDL:** http://www.w3.org/TR/wsdl

- **UDDI:** http://www.uddi.org/

- **DISCO:** http://msdn.microsoft.com/library/en-us/cpguide/html/
  cpconwebservicediscovery.asp,
  http://www.devx.com/javaSR/articles/smith2/smith2-1.asp,
  http://www.perfectxml.com/WebSvc3.asp, and
  http://msdn.microsoft.com/library/en-us/cpguide/html/
  cpcondiscoveringwebservices.asp

- **WS-Inspection:** http://msdn.microsoft.com/library/
  en-us/dnglobspec/html/wsinspecspecindex.asp and
  http://www-106.ibm.com/developerworks/webservices/library/
  ws-wsiluddi.html

- **WS-Security:** http://www.oasis-open.org/committees/wss/

It's important to note that we haven't discussed a transport methodology for Web services yet. A transport protocol determines how the package created by SOAP or some other technology moves from one machine to another. The assumption that most developers make is that any useful application will rely on the HyperText Transfer Protocol (HTTP). However, none of the standards shows that using HTTP is a requirement. In fact, you'll find that many mention the use of the Simple Mail Transfer Protocol (SMTP) as one of several alternatives. Using SMTP creates an asynchronous communication environment that's quite useful for some types of Web service applications. The point I'm trying to make is that you need to choose each of the protocols carefully and not assume that one protocol is necessarily dependent on another unless the specification includes a secondary protocol as a requirement.

NOTE *You'll find situations when one protocol does depend on another. For example, the SOAP specification specifically states that the message relies on XML as its formatting protocol. Derived protocols often use the base protocol specification as a starting point and merely discuss the details of base protocol extensions.*

Potential Problems with Web Services

Any assumption that you might have that there's a perfect technology out there somewhere is probably not well founded. Most technologies today represent tradeoffs from older technologies. Consequently, you'll find that a new technology often creates new problems while solving problems left behind by an existing technology. The reason that a particular new technology is successful is that it solves more critical problems than it creates. (I know more than a few of you disagree with this perspective. However, look at how many problems computers have today, and then try to find a reason that we still have problems if every new technology only improves the computing environment.)

CAUTION   *Some companies assume that because something isn't documented the developer won't bother to use it. Microsoft has made this assumption for years and found that writers are all too willing to write books exposing the hidden features in their products. The same principle applies to a Web service, only more so. For example, some developer at Google probably left a few undocumented back doors to make life easier. However, sites such as Research Buzz* (http://www.researchbuzz.com/articles/2002/ googledate0422.html) *have documented these previously undocumented features. The moral of the story is that undocumented simply means other developers will take longer to discover a site feature. If you want to keep something secret, then don't make it part of your Web service.*

The following sections discuss some of the more important problems you'll have to consider when working with Web services. In some cases, you can resolve an issue through careful planning, design, implementation, and deployment. Unfortunately, some problems are simply inherent in Web services, and you won't find an easy answer for them (assuming that such an answer exists).

Speed

Every user starts work on a single machine and finds it incredibly fast. Moving to a network does involve a small loss of speed, but the user hardly notices it. In addition, the small loss of speed is more than compensated by the increased capabilities that a LAN can provide. Moving to a Wide Area Network (WAN) or a Metropolitan Area Network (MAN) usually involves another decrease in speed, but again, it's quite small. However, moving to a Web service application usually results in a dramatic decrease in speed from the user perspective. In addition, many Web service applications provide a browser front end, making them less visually appealing than their desktop counterparts. From the user perspective, Web services provide less capability in a much slower package. When working in a company that hasn't used Web services before, the user is often the most difficult part of the equation to solve because they have little or no reason to accept the change in environment. On the contrary, a Web service application is often pure loss from the user perspective.

Users have a comfort problem with the speed of Web service applications—waiting up to 30 seconds for an answer is uncomfortable. The company itself has a problem with the productivity of Web service applications. It's hard to demonstrate that a Web service application makes employees more productive if every answer requires a long wait. The information has a higher availability, which does improve performance, but the wait tends to mitigate part of that gain.

NOTE *This section describes raw performance problems. You can overcome some of these problems by using robust programming techniques. For example, you can overcome the user wait problem by working with the Web service asynchronously in the background. Asynchronous data transfer means anticipating user needs and gaining access to information before the user actual needs it so that the perception is nearly instantaneous access to resources. In addition, these issues aren't unique to Web services. Any networked application will experience performance problems of this nature. The trade-off you must consider is the need to access remotely located information, and the delay due to accessing that information.*

Administrators also have a problem with Web service application speed. These applications tend to use more system resources, and the delays they cause tie up resources for longer time intervals. When economic conditions dictate making due with the current system hardware, anything that uses more resources for longer intervals tends to cause problems that the administrator is unlikely to appreciate.

As a developer, you have three groups that are hostile toward Web services, and one group that's marginally accepting because it represents a new toy to play with. Solving the speed problem is one of the most pressing issues that you have. Every time I consult for a company, speed is a higher precedence than security because of the perception that Web services is a losing proposition. This book won't solve your speed problems, but here are a few suggestions you can try. (Make sure to read Chapter 10 for ideas as well.)

- Use Web services only when some other solution won't work.

- Keep resource requirements low by keeping requests short.

- Always make complete requests, rather than using several transactions.

- Cache commonly used information locally and update it periodically when the system isn't busy.

- Call Web services asynchronously to eliminate UI wait times.

- Maintain realistic performance objectives for Web service applications.

Intellectual Property

Knowledge is power—at least according to some sage. However, knowledge is also money—just check the copyright and patent offices if you have any doubt. The problem with Web service applications is that they tend to break down the walls that keep intellectual property (or knowledge) safe. Every time you give someone access to a piece of code, a database, a utility, or some other piece of functionality, they're using the knowledge the access provides. Some people fear that Web services will expose the knowledge they've carefully protected to someone who will disregard any safety measures a developer may have put in place to protect that knowledge. In short, the perception (or fear, if you prefer to use that term) is that Web service applications will make your knowledge someone else's property.

Unfortunately, knowledge is one of the most fleeting resources that a company owns because someone will always acquire it, with or without Web services. The effects of new technology often amplify this age-old problem, but they don't cause the problem. Unfortunately, there never has been, nor will there ever be, a solution for this problem. If you give someone access to your data, you also give them access to your intellectual property (usually abbreviated IP). The best way to keep a secret is not to tell anyone, and that little bit of wisdom applies here more than anywhere else. If you don't want someone to steal your intellectual property, then don't give them access to it.

The perception that Web services will make your knowledge someone else's property is incorrect. Web services merely provide you with the capability to exchange data more easily. What you do with that capability is up to you. If you decide that it's good for your business to expose some data from behind your firewall to a trusted partner (or to the public), that's completely up to you. Web services don't require you to expose any data that you don't want to expose. In sum, the potential for losing control of your intellectual property is always there; Web services can make the problem worse if you let it, but the choice is for you to make.

Security

If the headlines regarding security haven't grabbed your attention over the last few years, you must be a hermit. My mailbox is packed with security-related messages, the trade press is covered in them, all of my electronic newsletters resound with them, and I even see security-related issues presented on television. In short, a developer would have to try very hard to avoid seeing security messages of some type.

Now consider that Web services rely on XML—a text-based protocol that lacks any security. SOAP, likewise, lacks even a hint of security. Given the less-than-stellar reports on security for the computing community as a whole, using a text-based data transferal mechanism that everyone can read seems hardly appropriate. The standards community is developing solutions. For example, I previously mentioned the WS-Security effort. You can read a story about this solution at `http://www.infoworld.com/articles/hn/xml/02/07/23/020723hnoasisws.xml`. This article mentions a host of other standards that are under discussion, but haven't seen the light of day yet. A good overview of this technology appears at `http://msdn.microsoft.com/library/en-us/dnwssecur/html/securitywhitepaper.asp`.

NOTE *You'll want to check Microsoft's Global XML Web Services Architecture (GXA) Web site at* `http://msdn.microsoft.com/webservices/understanding/gxa/`. *GXA promises to offer support for security features such as WS-Security. In fact, this page has a wealth of links you'll want to visit as Microsoft updates them.*

The World Wide Web Consortium (W3C) and Internet Engineering Task Force (IETF) released the XML Signature specification (`http://www.w3.org/Signature/`) as an industry standard recently as well. Using an XML Signature means that the recipient can validate the sender of XML data and verify that the data is unmodified. Look for third-party vendors to offer products that add XML Signature support for a variety of products including Visual Studio .NET (which may mean it will be available in the form of an assembly for Web Matrix as well). You can read about this standard at `http://www.w3.org/TR/2002/REC-xmldsig-core-20020212/`. The W3C and IETF are still working on two other XML security standards: XML Encryption (`http://www.w3.org/TR/xmlenc-core/`) and XML Key Management (`http://www.w3.org/TR/xkms/`).

The use of biometrics is also becoming an important part of local application security. Biometrics make it difficult for a third party to steal passwords because the password is based on a body feature such as fingerprints, facial components, voiceprints, or the construction of the iris. Previous biometric encoding techniques relied on binary technology, which doesn't work well with XML—a text-based technology designed to overcome the limits of binary data transfer. The XML Common Biometric Format (XCBF) is a new standard designed to make biometrics accessible to XML communication. You can see overviews of this technology at `http://www.eweek.com/article/0,3658,s=1884&a=23693,00.asp`, `http://www.infoworld.com/articles/hn/xml/02/03/07/020307hnoasis.xml?0308fram`, and `http://www.internetnews.com/dev-news/article/0,,10_987001,00.html`. You can find a more comprehensive discussion of this topic at `http://www.oasis-open.org/committees/xcbf/`.

Using the XML Web Service Page

The XML Web Service page helps you create a Web service. When you select the project in the Add New File dialog box, you'll see that you have to provide both a class name and a namespace, as shown in Figure 8-1. The example uses a class name of MathFunctions and my company name, DataCon, as the namespace.

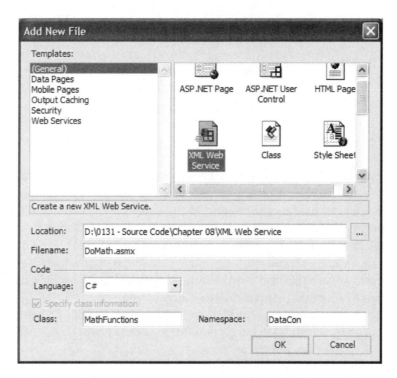

Figure 8-1. Always add a class name and namespace to the XML Web Service page.

Interestingly enough, the project automatically inserts a math function—adding two numbers. The file also includes a number of .NET Framework namespace declarations and an important attribute, [WebMethod]. Using the [WebMethod] attribute alone is enough to make your method usable from a Web application. However, you'll find that you need some of its additional properties at times. We'll use the [WebMethod] attribute in the example in this section of the chapter. You can also learn more about this attribute at http://msdn.microsoft.com/library/en-us/cpref/html/frlrfSystemWebServicesWebMethodAttributeClassTopic.asp and http://msdn.microsoft.com/library/en-us/vbcon/html/vbtskUsingWebMethodAttribute.asp.

At a minimum, you should include the Description property in your code because it tells other developers what task the method performs. A short sentence or two usually provides enough information for the developer using the Web service, although you might want to provide more information such as the calling syntax.

Another good addition, especially if you provide multiple overrides of the same method, is the MessageName property. This property tells SOAP what to use for a message name when sending the data from the client to the server. Using a MessageName tends to avoid confusion when working with numbers. XML transfers numeric information as text. When it arrives at the destination, the listener converts the text back into a number—you can see how the conversion process might lead to problems.

We'll see during the example demonstration that the XML Web Service page relies on SOAP to perform the required data transfer work, but it performs this task in the background—you don't have to worry about working with SOAP directly. However, you can choose to work with SOAP directly using the SOAP Headers page discussed in the "Using the SOAP Headers Page" section of the chapter. You'll want to review "A Quick Overview of SOAP" if you plan to work with SOAP directly. For now, let's look at the code we'll use for this example. Listing 8-1 contains a short XML Web Service page example.

Listing 8-1. A Simple XML Web Service Page

```
<%@ WebService language="C#" class="MathFunctions" %>

using System;
using System.Web.Services;
using System.Xml.Serialization;

[WebService(Namespace="http://winserver/0131/WebService/")]
public class MathFunctions
{
```

```
[WebMethod (Description = "This method reverses text.",
            MessageName = "ReverseText")]
public string ReverseIt(string Input)
{
    String   Temp; // Temporary data holder.

    // Initialize Temp.
    Temp = "";

    // Reverse the string.
    for (int Counter = Input.Length - 1; Counter >= 0; Counter-)
        Temp = Temp + Input[Counter];

    // Return the reversed string.
    return Temp;
}

[WebMethod (Description = "This method reverses integers.",
            MessageName = "ReverseInteger")]
public int ReverseIt(int Input)
{
    String   Temp;   // Temporary data holder.
    String   DataIn; // Data to convert.

    // Initialize DataIn.
    DataIn = Input.ToString();

    // Initialize Temp.
    Temp = "";

    // Reverse the string.
    for (int Counter = DataIn.Length - 1; Counter >= 0; Counter-)
        Temp = Temp + DataIn[Counter];

    // Return the reversed string.
    return Int32.Parse(Temp);
}
}
```

As you can see, the two functions perform the same task—they reverse the input you provide and return it. In the first case, the input is a string. The second function reverses an integer. Functions with multiple overrides are relatively common in the world of .NET, so this is a good example of how to work in such an environment. It's also important to note the use of attributes in this example. You must provide a [WebService] attribute to tell the application where to locate the namespace information. The two [WebMethod] attributes describe the individual methods.

You might think that you have to do some additional work, at this point, but the Web service is ready to use. All you have to do is save the code and place the file on your Web server. When you access the ASMX file directly, you'll see a display similar to the one shown in Figure 8-2.

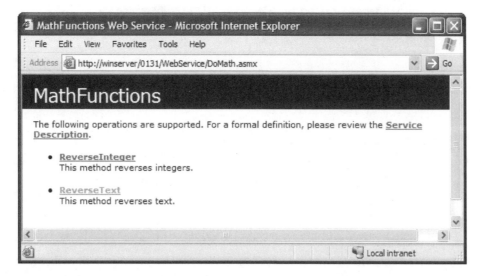

Figure 8-2. Access the ASMX file directly, and you'll see a Web page similar to this one.

Click the Service Description link, and you'll see a display similar to the one shown in Figure 8-3. This display shows the WSDL file that ASP .NET automatically generates based on the content of the ASMX file that we created. The WSDL describes the Web service to applications that need this information to determine how to call the Web service. Notice that the Address field contains the address for this information. All an application need do is request the ASMX and make a request for the WSDL file output as shown.

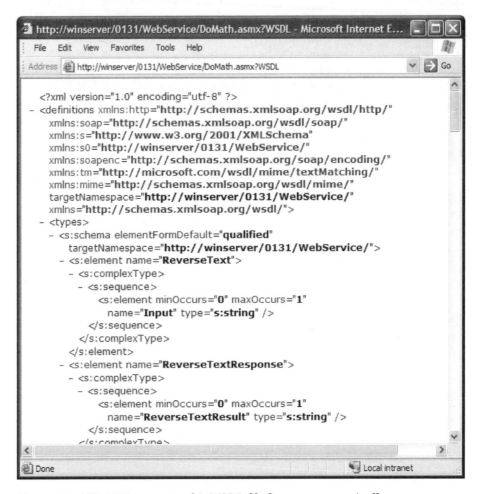

```
http://winserver/0131/WebService/DoMath.asmx?WSDL - Microsoft Internet E...

File   Edit   View   Favorites   Tools   Help

Address   http://winserver/0131/WebService/DoMath.asmx?WSDL              Go

  <?xml version="1.0" encoding="utf-8" ?>
- <definitions xmlns:http="http://schemas.xmlsoap.org/wsdl/http/"
    xmlns:soap="http://schemas.xmlsoap.org/wsdl/soap/"
    xmlns:s="http://www.w3.org/2001/XMLSchema"
    xmlns:s0="http://winserver/0131/WebService/"
    xmlns:soapenc="http://schemas.xmlsoap.org/soap/encoding/"
    xmlns:tm="http://microsoft.com/wsdl/mime/textMatching/"
    xmlns:mime="http://schemas.xmlsoap.org/wsdl/mime/"
    targetNamespace="http://winserver/0131/WebService/"
    xmlns="http://schemas.xmlsoap.org/wsdl/">
  - <types>
    - <s:schema elementFormDefault="qualified"
        targetNamespace="http://winserver/0131/WebService/">
      - <s:element name="ReverseText">
        - <s:complexType>
          - <s:sequence>
              <s:element minOccurs="0" maxOccurs="1"
                name="Input" type="s:string" />
            </s:sequence>
          </s:complexType>
        </s:element>
      - <s:element name="ReverseTextResponse">
        - <s:complexType>
          - <s:sequence>
              <s:element minOccurs="0" maxOccurs="1"
                name="ReverseTextResult" type="s:string" />
            </s:sequence>
          </s:complexType>

Done                                          Local intranet
```

Figure 8-3. ASP .NET generates this WSDL file for you automatically on request.

Back on the initial page shown in Figure 8-2, you'll notice that the names of the two services match the MessageName property value for each of the methods in Listing 8-1. At this point, one of the reasons to use the MessageName property is obvious—using this feature makes the purpose of each method clear, even though the methods provide two overrides of the same function, ReverseIt().

Click either of the links, and you'll see a display similar to the one in Figure 8-4. This display serves multiple purposes. First, you'll see the SOAP code needed to access this method. Actually, the code listings extend further than shown in the figure. They also include the request/response syntax used for this method. In short, if you were to generate the SOAP statement required to access the method by hand, this display would provide all of the input you'd need.

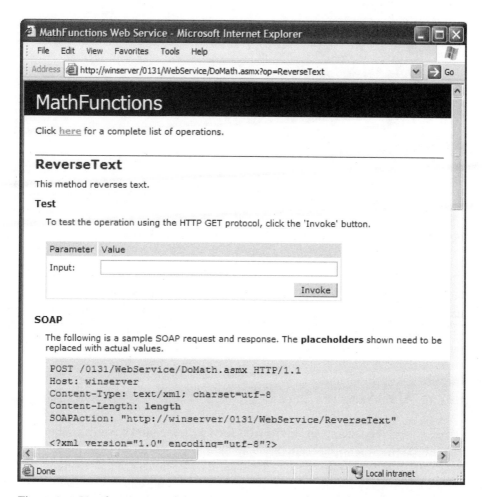

Figure 8-4. Use the content of this page to test your application and help create the requisite SOAP statements.

Second, you can use the information in Figure 8-4 to test your code without actually creating an application to do it. Simply add the requested information to the Input field and click Invoke. The Input field doesn't provide any error handling, so you'll need to verify the input before you send it. Figure 8-5 shows typical output from the ReverseText() method using "Hello World" as input.

Figure 8-5. View the output of a method using this simple display.

Notice that the browser's Address field contains the URL used to create this page. The page itself is a simple XML statement. It includes the Web service namespace, the answer data type, and the answer. Using the output of the page as an example, you could easily create an application that relies on HTML for output and never worry about the SOAP used to transfer the data.

Using the Simple Page

Although this project appears in the Web Services folder and it has a different name from the other projects in this chapter, it has the same features as the XML Web Service page that we discussed earlier. Please refer to the "Using the XML Web Service Page" section earlier for details on using this project.

Using the SOAP Headers Page

The SOAP Headers page is a bit like the Simple page, but it has a little kick added. This project adds a SOAP header to the project, which is essentially a global variable or other global resource required by the Web service as a whole. For example, you could use a SOAP header to pass authentication information or a session identifier. When your application calls on the Web service, it must provide any required SOAP headers and can optionally provide any nonrequired headers.

Using the SOAP Headers page requires a lot more information than needed to use the other templates we've discussed in the book. Consequently, a few of you might find the material in the upcoming sections a little complex. It's important to realize that you don't have to use SOAP to work with Web services in Web Matrix. This is an option for those who want a little more control over the communication process. If you aren't well versed in the protocols used by the Internet, then you might want to skip this section for a while until you've learned more about Web Matrix and what it can do for you.

TIP *Microsoft provides several tools that you can use to make working with Web services easier. The first is the WSDL tool used to create a file that describes your Web service. You can find this tool at* http://msdn.microsoft.com/library/en-us/cptools/html/ cpgrfwebservicesdescriptionlanguagetoolwsdlexe.asp. *The second is the DISCO tool used to advertise your server. Download this tool at* http://msdn.microsoft.com/library/en-us/cptools/ html/cpgrfwebservicesdiscoverytooldiscoexe.asp. *These tools come as part of the .NET Framework tools described at* http://msdn.microsoft.com/library/en-us/cptools/html/ cpconnetframeworktools.asp.

This section helps you understand the basic layout of a SOAP message. I'm not going to show every element that you'll run across, but we will discuss the common elements because you need to know about them in order to use Web Matrix effectively. This section will also show how to use SOAP headers to make your application easier to code, examining both required and optional headers. You'll also learn how the various elements can augment a common method.

TIP *You can gain additional information about SOAP by looking at the various SOAP implementations. You can learn about these implementations at* http://www.xmethods.net/ve2/ViewImplementations.po.

A Quick Overview of SOAP

You can divide SOAP messages into two basic categories: requests and responses. The client sends a request to the server. If the server can fulfill the request, then it sends a data message back to the client. Otherwise, the server sends an error message indicating why it couldn't send a response back to the client. In most cases, the problem is one of security, access, equipment failures, or an inability to find the requested object or data.

SOAP messages don't exist within a vacuum. If you send just a SOAP message, it will never reach its destination. SOAP is a wire protocol—it relies on another protocol such as HTTP or SMTP for transport. This is the same technique used by other wire protocols, so there's nothing strange about SOAP when it comes to data transfer needs. The most common transport protocol in use today is HTTP, so that's what we'll look at in this section. Keep in mind, however, that SOAP can theoretically use any of a number of transport protocols and probably will in the future.

SOAP messages look and act like XML messages. Therefore, in addition to the HTTP wrapper, a SOAP message requires an XML wrapper. All that the XML wrapper does, in this case, is tell the data receiver that this is an XML-formatted message. The SOAP part of the message contains all of the data; however, SOAP uses XML-like tags to format the data.

Figure 8-6 shows a common SOAP message configuration. This isn't the only configuration that you'll see, but it is the most common configuration in use as of this writing. Notice the SOAP message formatting. This isn't the only way to wrap a SOAP message in other protocols, but it's the most common method in use today.

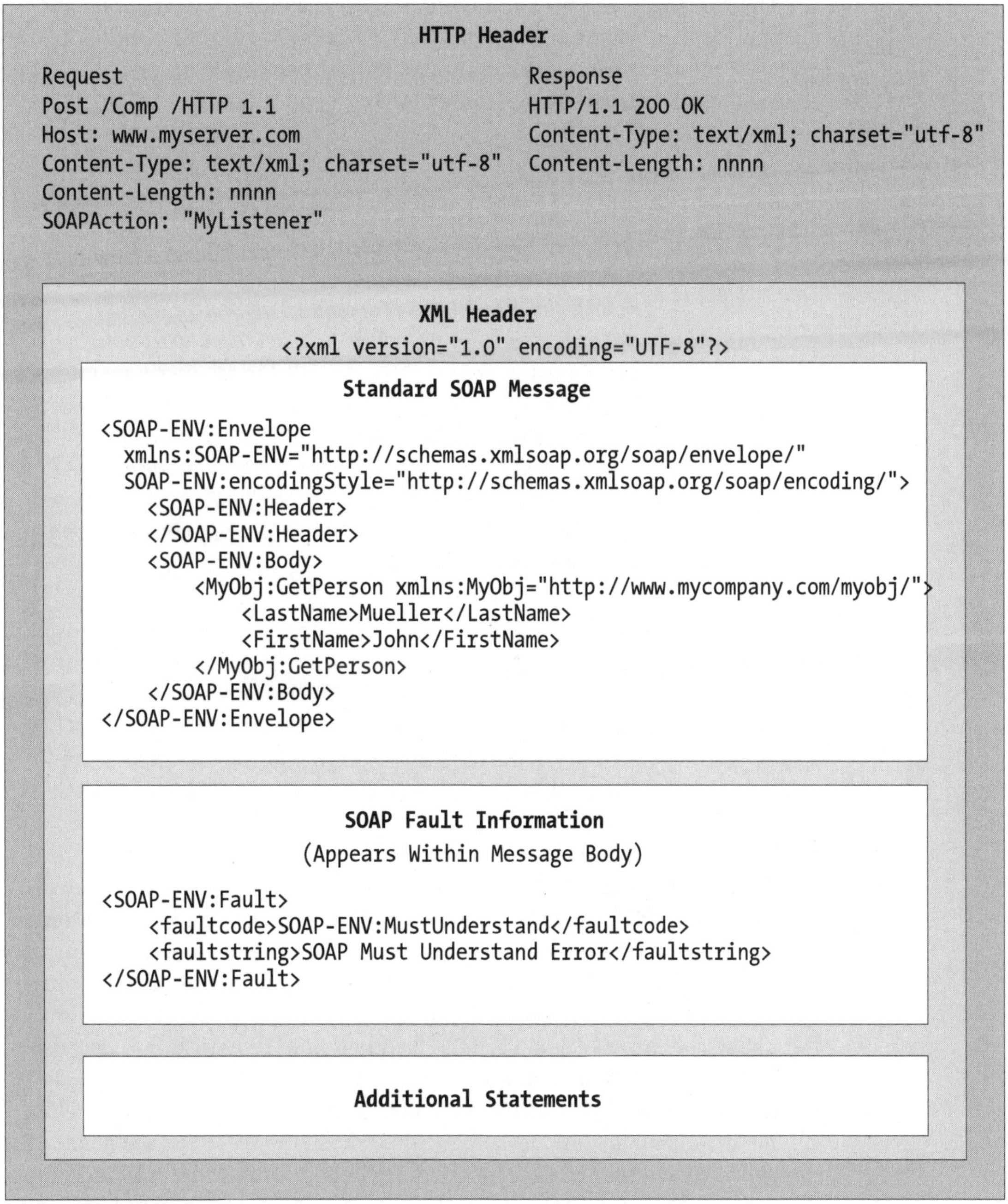

```
                              HTTP Header

Request                              Response
Post /Comp /HTTP 1.1                 HTTP/1.1 200 OK
Host: www.myserver.com               Content-Type: text/xml; charset="utf-8"
Content-Type: text/xml; charset="utf-8"  Content-Length: nnnn
Content-Length: nnnn
SOAPAction: "MyListener"


                              XML Header
                <?xml version="1.0" encoding="UTF-8"?>

                         Standard SOAP Message

<SOAP-ENV:Envelope
   xmlns:SOAP-ENV="http://schemas.xmlsoap.org/soap/envelope/"
   SOAP-ENV:encodingStyle="http://schemas.xmlsoap.org/soap/encoding/">
     <SOAP-ENV:Header>
     </SOAP-ENV:Header>
     <SOAP-ENV:Body>
         <MyObj:GetPerson xmlns:MyObj="http://www.mycompany.com/myobj/">
             <LastName>Mueller</LastName>
             <FirstName>John</FirstName>
         </MyObj:GetPerson>
     </SOAP-ENV:Body>
</SOAP-ENV:Envelope>


                       SOAP Fault Information
                   (Appears Within Message Body)

<SOAP-ENV:Fault>
     <faultcode>SOAP-ENV:MustUnderstand</faultcode>
     <faultstring>SOAP Must Understand Error</faultstring>
</SOAP-ENV:Fault>


                       Additional Statements
```

Figure 8-6. An illustration of how SOAP a message is commonly encased within other protocols.

The next three sections tell you how a SOAP message appears during transmission. We'll use Figure 8-6 as an aid for discussion. It's the only time we'll explore a complete request or response in the book since you only need to worry about the SOAP message in most cases.

TIP   *Working with the new capabilities provided by technologies like XML and SOAP means dealing with dynamically created Web pages. While it's nice that we can modify the content of a Web page as needed for an individual user, it can also be a problem if you need to troubleshoot the Web page. That's where a handy little script comes into play. Type **javascript: '<xmp>'+document.all(0).outerHTML+'</xmp>'** in the Address field of Internet Explorer for any dynamically created Web page, and you'll see the actual HTML for that page. This includes the results of using scripts and other page construction techniques.*

Viewing the HTTP Portion of SOAP

The HTTP portion of a SOAP message looks much the same as any other HTTP header you may have seen in the past. In fact, if you don't look carefully, you might pass it by without paying any attention. As with any HTTP transmission, there are two types of headers—one for requests and another for responses. Figure 8-6 shows examples of both types.

As with any request header, the HTTP portion of a SOAP message will contain an action (POST, in most cases), the HTTP version, a host name, and some content length information. The POST action portion of the header will contain the path for the SOAP listener, which is either an ASP script or an ISAPI component. Also located within a request header is a Content-Type entry of text/xml and a charset entry of UTF-8. The UTF-8 entry is important right now because many SOAP toolkits don't support UTF-16 and many other character sets. The SOAP specification also uses UTF-8 for all of its examples.

You'll also find the unique SOAPAction entry in the HTTP request header. It contains the Uniform Resource Identifier (URI) of the ASP script or ISAPI component used to parse the SOAP request. If the SOAPAction entry is "", then the server will use the HTTP Request-URI entry to locate a listener instead. This is the only SOAP-specific entry in the HTTP header—everything else we've discussed could appear in any HTTP-formatted message.

TIP *UTF stands for Unicode Transformation Format. UTF represents a one-way standard method for encoding character. One of the better places to learn about UTF-8 is* http://www.utf8.org/. *You can find a good discussion of various encoding techniques at* http://www.czyborra.com/utf/. *This Web site presents the information in tutorial format. The fact remains that you need to use the UTF-8 character set when working with SOAP.*

The response header portion of the HTTP wrapper for a SOAP message contains all of the essentials as well. You'll find the HTTP version, status, and content length as usual. Like the request header, the response header has a Content-Type entry of text/xml and a charset entry of UTF-8.

There are two common status indicators for a response header: 200 OK or 500 Internal Server Error. While the SOAP specification allows leeway in the positive response status number (any value in the 200 series), a server must return a status value of 500 for SOAP errors to indicate a server error.

Whenever a SOAP response header contains an error status, the SOAP message must include a SOAP fault section. We'll talk about SOAP faults later in this chapter. All you need to know now is that the HTTP header provides the first indication of a SOAP fault that will require additional processing.

A message can contain other applicable status error codes in the response header. For example, if the client sends a standard HTTP header, and the server wants to use the HTTP Extension Framework, it can respond with a status error value of 510 Not Extended. The 510 error isn't necessarily fatal—a client can make the request again using the mandatory HTTP Extension Framework declaration. In this case, an error message serves to alert the client to a special server requirement.

Viewing the XML Portion of SOAP

All SOAP messages are encoded using XML. SOAP follows the XML specification and can be considered a true superset of XML. In other words, it adds to the functionality already in place within XML. Anyone familiar with XML will feel comfortable with SOAP at the outset—all you really need to know is the SOAP nuances.

Although the examples in the SOAP specification don't show an XML connection (other than the formatting of the SOAP message), most real-world examples will contain at least one line of XML specific information. Here's one example of an XML entry:

```
<?xml version="1.0" encoding="UTF-8" standalone="no"?>
```

As you can see, the tag is quite simple. The only bits of information that it includes are the XML version number, the character set (encoding), and whether the message is standalone. As with the HTTP header, the XML portion relies on the UTF-8 character set for now. The version number will change as new versions of XML appear on the scene. The standalone attribute determines if external markup declarations could affect the manner in which this XML document is processed. A value of no means external documents could affect the processing of this document.

TIP *We won't discuss all of the XML tag attributes (declarations) in this chapter. You can find a complete listing of these attributes at* `http://www.w3.org/TR/REC-xml`. *For those of you who don't read specifications very well (or prefer not to), look at Tim Bray's annotated XML specification Web site at* `http://www.xml.com/axml/testaxml.htm`. *Another good place to look is the XML.com Web site at* `http://www.xml.com/`. *Finally, if you want to see the tools and other resources available for XML, look at* `http://www.projectcool.com/developer/xmlz/xmlref/examples.html`.

Some developers don't include all of the XML tag attributes in their SOAP messages. So far, I haven't seen any problems with leaving the encoding and standalone attributes out of the picture. You should, however, always include the XML version number—if for no other reason than the need to document your code and ensure there are no compatibility problems with future SOAP implementations.

Working with the SOAP Message

A simple SOAP message consists of an envelope that contains both a header and a body. The header can contain information that isn't associated with the data itself. For example, the header commonly contains a transaction ID when the application needs one to identify a particular SOAP message. The body contains the data in XML format. If an error occurs, the body will contain fault information, rather than data.

Now that you have a summary of the SOAP message content, let's look at some particulars you'll need when working with SOAP. The following sections will fill you in on some technical details needed to understand the SOAP message fully.

HTTP and the SOAP Transfer

SOAP is essentially a one-way data transfer protocol. While SOAP messages often follow a request/response pattern, the messages themselves are individual entities. They aren't linked in any way. This means that a SOAP message is stand-alone—it doesn't rely on the immediate presence of a server, nor is a response expected when a request message contains all of the required information. For example, some types of data entry may not require a response since the user is inputting information and may not care about a response.

The envelope in which a SOAP message travels, however, may provide more than just a one-way transfer path. For example, when a developer encases a SOAP message within an HTTP envelope, the request and response both use the same connection. The connection is created and maintained by HTTP, not by SOAP. Consequently, the connection follows the HTTP way of performing data transfer—using the same techniques as a browser uses to request Web pages for display.

SOAP Fault Messages

Sometimes a SOAP request will generate a fault message instead of the anticipated reply. The server may not have the means to answer your request, the request you generated may be incomplete, or bad communication may prevent your message from arriving in the same state as you sent it. There are many reasons that you may receive a SOAP fault message. However, you can categorize them into four general areas, as shown in the following list.

Client: The client generated a request that the server couldn't process for some reason. The most common problem is that the XML format of the SOAP message is incorrect (malformed). Another common problem is the server can't find the requested component, or the client doesn't provide all of the information the server needs to process the message. If the client receives an error message of this type, it must re-create the message and fix the problems of the original. The server usually provides amplifying information if it can determine how the request is malformed or otherwise in error.

mustUnderstand: This error only occurs when you set the SOAP message mustUnderstand attribute to 1. The error occurs when the client sends a request that the server can't understand or obey for some reason. The server may not understand a request when the client relies on capabilities of a version of SOAP that the server's listener doesn't provide. A server may not obey a client request due to security or other concerns.

Server: The server couldn't process the message even though the request is valid. A server error can occur for a number of reasons. For example, the server could run out of resources for initializing the requested component. In a complex application environment, the server may rely on the processing of another server that's offline or otherwise inaccessible. The server usually provides amplifying information if it can determine the precise server-side error that occurred.

VersionMismatch: SOAP doesn't have a versioning system. It does rely on the namespaces that you define to perform useful work. This error message occurs when the SOAP envelope namespace is either incorrect or missing.

When a server returns a fault message, it doesn't return any data. Look at Figure 8-7 and you'll see a typical client fault message. Notice the message contains only fault information. With this in mind, the client-side components you create must be prepared to parse SOAP fault messages and return the information to the calling application in such a way that the user will understand the meaning of the fault.

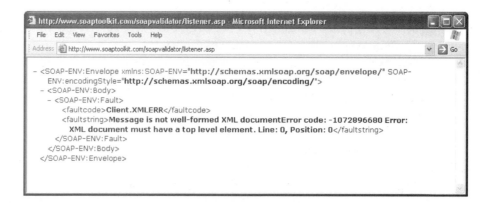

Figure 8-7. Viewing an error message tells you what went wrong with a SOAP data transfer.

Figure 8-7 shows the standard presentation of a SOAP fault message. Notice that the fault envelope resides within the body of the SOAP message. A fault envelope will generally contain a faultcode and faultstring element that tells you which error occurred. All of the other SOAP fault message elements are optional. The following list tells you how they're used.

faultcode: The faultcode contains the name of the error that occurred. It can use a dot syntax to define a more precise error code. The faultcode will always begin with a classification. For example, the faultcode in Figure 8-7 consists of a Client error code followed by an XMLERR subcode. This error tells you that the request message is malformed because the XML formatting is incorrect. Since it's possible to create a list of standard SOAP faultcodes, you can use them directly for processing purposes.

faultstring: This is a human readable form of the error specified by the faultcode entry. This string should follow the same format as HTTP error strings. You can learn more about HTTP error strings by reading the HTTP specification at `http://www.normos.org/ietf/rfc/rfc2616.txt`. A good general rule to follow is to make the faultstring entry short and easy to understand.

faultactor: This element points to the source of a fault in a SOAP transaction. It contains a URI similar to the one used for determining the destination of the header entry. According to the specification, you must include this element if the application that generates the fault message isn't the ultimate destination for the SOAP message.

detail: You'll use this element to hold detailed information about a fault when available. For example, this is the element that you'd use to hold server-side component return values. This element is SOAP message body specific, which means you can't use it to detail errors that occur in other areas like the SOAP message header. A detail entry acts as an envelope for storing detail subelements. Each subelement includes a tag containing namespace information and a string containing error message information.

Creating the SOAP Headers Page

Now that you know a little more about SOAP and understand how it works, it's time to look at the SOAP Headers page included with Web Matrix. As previously mentioned, a SOAP header commonly provides access to a global resource. The application provides this global resource to all of the methods in a Web service that require its use. The use of SOAP headers comes with the same possibilities and problems that using global variables in any environment brings. You need to consider the effects of a resource that every method can access, such as the potential for data corruption. Consequently, use the SOAP headers when needed, but only when needed.

> **TIP** *Although Web Matrix does provide some good tools for working with SOAP, you might want to look at some of the free add-on products available on the Internet. For example, the CapeScience site provides a number of Web service related tools, including a good WSDL editor, at* `http://www.capescience.com/downloads/index.shtml`.

Adding a SOAP header to the Web service requires two steps. First, you need to define a class based on the `SoapHeader` class. This class contains the resource templates for the resources that you want to pass. For example, if you want to pass a string to the Web service using a SOAP header, then you need to define a string resource in the class. Second, you need to include the `[SoapHeader]` attribute before each method that will use a particular SOAP header. The attribute tells how to use the SOAP header within the affected method. Not every method needs to use the attribute in the same way. Listing 8-2 shows an example of a Web service that relies on a SOAP header.

Listing 8-2. A Web Service That Uses a SOAP Header

```
<%@ WebService language="C#" class="SOAPSample" %>

using System;
using System.Web.Services;
using System.Xml.Serialization;
using System.Web.Services.Protocols;

// A class containing the SOAP header information.
public class SimpleHeader : SoapHeader
{
    // The single value passed by the header.
    public String Value;
}
```

```csharp
// This class contains all of the methods that will use
// the SOAP header.
[WebService(Namespace="http://winserver/0131/WebService/")]
public class SOAPSample
{
    // Create an instance of the SimpleHeader class so we
    // retrieve the data.
    public SimpleHeader        soapHeader;
    // This class contains a list of headers that the client
    // doesn't understand.
    public SoapUnknownHeader[] unknownHeaders;

    [WebMethod (Description="Displays the SOAP header type received")]
    [SoapHeader("soapHeader", Required=false)]
    [SoapHeader("unknownHeaders", Required=false)]
    public string GetValueOfSoapHeader()
    {
        // If the client sends the custom header, then print
        // out its value.
        if (soapHeader != null)
            return soapHeader.Value;
        else
            // If the client sends unknown headers, it means
            // that it doesn't understand something about the
            // SOAP contract.
            if (unknownHeaders != null)
                return "SOAP Header Type is Unknown!";
            else
                // A client doesn't have to send a SOAP header
                // at all.
                return "SOAP Header is Empty!";
    }

    [WebMethod (Description = "This method reverses text.")]
    [SoapHeader("soapHeader", Required=false)]
    public string ReverseIt(string Input)
    {
        String  Temp;   // Temporary data holder.
        String  Data;   //The data we'll convert.

        // Initialize Temp.
        Temp = "";
```

```
        // Initialize Data.
        if (soapHeader != null)
            Data = soapHeader.Value;
        else
            Data = Input;

        // Reverse the string.
        for (int Counter = Data.Length - 1; Counter >= 0; Counter-)
            Temp = Temp + Input[Counter];

        // Return the reversed string.
        return Temp;
    }

    [WebMethod (Description = "This method requires the SOAP header.")]
    [SoapHeader ("soapHeader", Required=true)]
    public string RequiredSoapHeader()
    {
        if (soapHeader == null)
            return "Error! No SOAP Header Supplied!";
        else
            return soapHeader.Value;
    }
}
```

Notice that the listing begins with a declaration of the soapHeader class. This class derives from the SoapHeader class. It includes a single string value as the SOAP header package. You can treat this class as you do any other class. The SOAP header could contain any resource.

As you can see, the example includes three methods. Each method tests a different aspect of using SOAP headers. The GetValueOfSoapHeader() method tests for the type of header received. In this case, all of the headers are optional. The ReverseIt() method shows the effects of using a SOAP header on the functionality of the method that we tested earlier. If the global string is available, then ReverseIt() will ignore the local Input string. In short, the string you see on output depends on what type of information you provide to the method. The RequiredSoapHeader() method is the only one that actually relies on the soapHeader entry. If you don't supply the header, then the method registers an error.

The SOAP header requirement in the RequiredSoapHeader() method has an odd effect on the testing methodology we used earlier. Figure 8-8 shows what happens when you require a SOAP header for input. As you can see, there isn't any way to invoke the method. The automatically generated page no longer allows testing of the method because it can't generate the required header. When you use required SOAP headers in your application, you give up the easy testing method that ASP.NET provides. (In other words, you give up the automatic Web page generation that we used for testing the Web services in the past.)

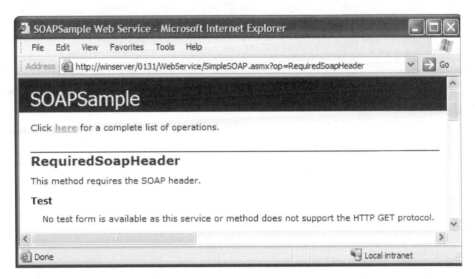

Figure 8-8. Using SOAP headers means you must rely on custom test code for your Web service.

Testing Your Code Using the SOAP Validator

You've been seeing a lot of SOAP header information floating around in the various figures in this chapter. SOAP is a form of XML, but it has to have certain features to make it correct. This fact makes the testing of SOAP messages important when you don't have the automation provided by Visual Studio.NET to perform the testing for you. Microsoft maintains two Web sites to check your SOAP messages. The first accepts SOAP messages, parses them, and provides a check of their validity. You'll find it at http://www.soaptoolkit.com/soapvalidator/. Figure 8-9 shows what this Web site looks like. (You'll find this message as the Test.XML file in the \Chapter 8 folder of the source code, available from the Downloads section on the Apress site at http://www.apress.com/book/download.html.)

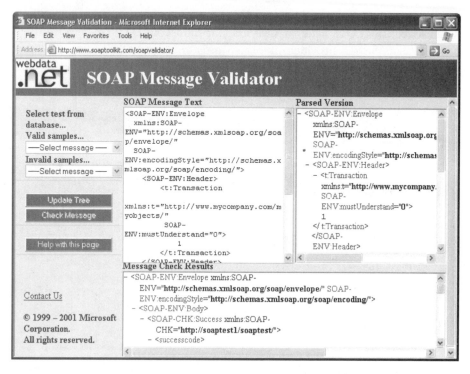

Figure 8-9. The SOAP Message Validation site tests your SOAP knowledge.

As you can see, there are three panes in this display. The SOAP Message Text window contains the message you want to verify. You can also choose one of the valid or invalid samples from the drop-down list boxes. These samples can teach you quite a bit about SOAP by showing what you can and can't do within a message and the results that you'll get when performing certain actions. You don't need to include the HTTP or XML headers in the SOAP Message Text window, just the SOAP message.

The Parsed Version window shows what the message looks like after the SOAP listener parses it. This window doesn't tell you about the validity of the message, but it does help you understand the XML formatting better. You can use this window to determine if the message is well formed. The use of text coloring also helps you to distinguish between specific text elements.

The Message Check Results window will show the results of diagnostics the site performs on your SOAP message. You'll see error messages in places where the SOAP message doesn't contain required entries or the entry format is incorrect. When all of the error messages are gone, the SOAP message is ready for use. Of course, the Web site doesn't check the validity of the data within the SOAP message. You can create a perfect SOAP message that still doesn't work because the server-side component is expecting the data in a different format or even requires other arguments.

The second Web site is a generic SOAP listener. You can send a SOAP message to it using an application. The site will test the message much like the Message Check Results window of the SOAP Message Validation site. You'll find this Web site at http://www.soaptoolkit.com/soapvalidator/listener.asp. Figure 8-8 shows an error output from this site. This is also an example of the SOAP fault message that we'll discuss in the next section of the chapter.

Using the Custom Class Page

You create the Custom Class page using the same process as many of the other pages so far in this chapter. Like all of the other pages, you must supply a class name and a namespace to create the project. The page itself contains a quantity of code obtained from the IBuySpy.COM Web site (http://ibuyspy.com/), as shown in Figure 8-10. Unlike some of the other pages we've discussed, this is purely example code, and you won't find the remainder of the example code for IBuySpy.COM anywhere in the Web Matrix folders.

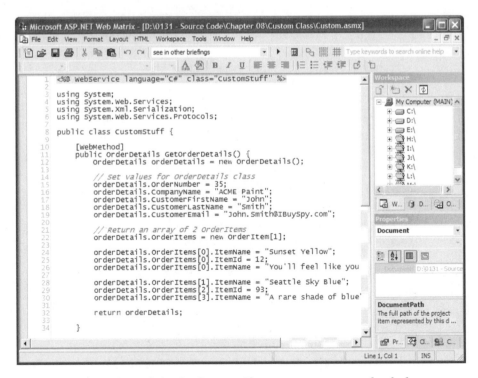

Figure 8-10. View the code in the Custom Class page as an example of what you can do, not as a template.

The code you receive with the project does demonstrate some of what you can do with the Custom Class page, so you'll want to spend some time studying it. However, at some point, you'll want to create an example of your own. Listing 8-3 shows the code we'll use for this example.

Listing 8-3. A Simple Interest Custom Class

```csharp
<%@ WebService language="C#" class="CustomStuff" %>

using System;
using System.Web.Services;
using System.Xml.Serialization;
using System.Web.Services.Protocols;

[WebService(Namespace="http://winserver/0131/WebService/")]
public class CustomStuff
{

    [WebMethod (Description="Perform a simple interest calculation.")]
    public InterestCalc CalculateInterest(double BeginningAmount,
                                          int NumberOfIntervals,
                                          double InterestRate,
                                          int Interval)
    {
        // Create a return structure of the correct size.
        InterestCalc    TheCalc = new InterestCalc();

        // Create the array contained within the return structure.
        TheCalc.TheDetails = new InterestDetails[NumberOfIntervals];

        // Calculate the interest per month.
        double          TheRate = InterestRate / Interval;

        // A temporary value holder.
        double          TempValue = BeginningAmount;

        // Perform the calculation.
        for (int Counter = 0; Counter < NumberOfIntervals; Counter++)
        {
            // Create a temporary variable to hold a single
            // InterestDetails object.
            InterestDetails TempDetail = new InterestDetails();
```

```
            // Fill the temporary detail object with data.
            TempDetail.MonthNumber = Counter + 1;
            TempDetail.DollarAmount = TempValue;

            // Transfer the data to the return structure array.
            TheCalc.TheDetails[Counter] = TempDetail;

            // Update the temporary money value.
            TempValue = TempValue + TempValue * TheRate;
        }

        // Return the array of calculations.
        return TheCalc;
    }
}


public class InterestCalc
{
    // An array of calculation details.
    [XmlArray(ElementName="InterestItemDetail",
                  Namespace="http://winserver/0131/WebService/")]
    public InterestDetails[]    TheDetails;
}

public class InterestDetails
{
    // The current month.
    public int MonthNumber;
    // The value of the account for the current month.
    public double DollarAmount;
}
```

This class has a few interesting details that you won't want to ignore when creating your own custom class. Although it isn't nearly as complex as the IBuySpy.COM example, you'll find that it provides a few details you'll probably need. The most important detail is that you can't pass an array back to the caller for whatever reason. As shown in the code, you need to encase the array in another class. In this case, the InterestCalc class acts as a container for the InterestDetails class array.

The CalculateInterest() method is the focus of this example. It accepts four values as input and outputs a list of simple interest calculation values based on the input the client provides. The calculation relies on determining a rate per interest period, and then applying that to the current principle amount. The number of array elements matches the number of interest periods requested. Consequently, if the user inputs an Interval value of 12 and a NumberOfIntervals value of 12, then the array elements would reflect individual months and the method would return enough entries for a year.

Notice the technique used to create values in the for loop. Each loop will create a new TempDetail object. This object contains the values of the array elements. The code makes the individual TheDetails array element equal to the TempDetail object. This is another problem area that you could run into. You must create the array object and apply it to the array. Direct access of the array elements doesn't work. For example, you couldn't include a line such as this in the code:

```
TheCalc.TheDetails[Counter].MonthNumber = Counter + 1;
```

Although it seems as if this line of code should work, it won't. However, it will compile, so the output from the application is a message saying that the page isn't accessible.

Fortunately, you can test this page without creating a custom Web page. All you need to do is access the ASMX file as we did previously. You'll see a test page with four fields that correspond to the four input values and an Invoke button. The output of this application is in XML format, as shown in Figure 8-11.

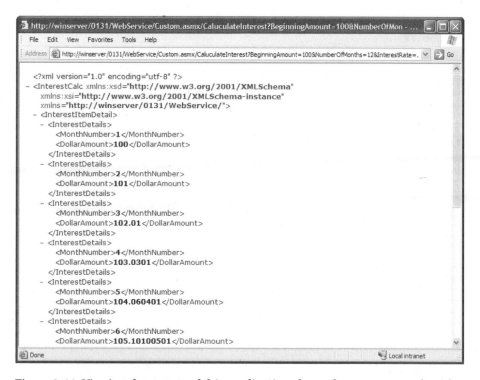

Figure 8-11. Viewing the output of this application shows that you can work with custom structures and arrays as needed.

TIP *You'll find a lot of interesting XSLT information and code examples at* `http://www.tanguay.info/category.aspx?s=WEB&c=xslt` *on the Tanguay.info Web site. The reason this site is so valuable is that the author constantly adds new content. In addition, the content provided is well rounded—you'll learn about a variety of new techniques, rather than focus on just one or two.*

Using the Output Caching Page

The Output Caching page demonstrates one of the performance enhancements you can make to your Web applications. *Caching* is the act of placing some resources in memory where the application can access them more quickly. Some developers feel that caching is a sure way to increase performance because books and magazine cite it so often. Few things in the development world are sure—the cache performance enhancement only works if your server meet these three criteria.

- The server has enough memory to support cached components.

- The application uses the same resources often enough to make caching worthwhile.

- The developer codes the page in such a way that it uses caching effectively.

You'll create this example page the same way that you've created others in this section. The ASMX page requires both a class name and a namespace. When you create this example, you'll see some code that shows the effects of caching. It displays the time that the information was cached. The difference, in this case, is the `CacheDuration=30` property. This property tells ASP .NET how long to cache the method in seconds. You can set the property differently for each method in a Web service, so the level of performance is customized. If you want to be sure that ASP.NET won't cache a method, use the `CacheDuration=0` property value.

TIP *The other main performance-related property is the* `BufferResponse` *property. In most cases, ASP.NET assumes that you want* `BufferResponse` *set to true, so that any response is buffered at the server until the buffer is full or the server reaches the end of the data return value. Set this property to false if you want to see the response as it's serialized. You'll find a* `BufferResponse` *example in the Chapter 8 folder of the source code (available at* http://www.apress.com/book/download.html*). Normally, you'll want to keep* `BufferResponse` *set to true for small return values and false for large return values. Using a buffer tends to reduce network bandwidth requirements, while eliminating the buffer tends to reduce server memory requirements.*

Listing 8-4 shows a modified version of the code that I used for testing. Notice that I've included two methods: one with a cache and one without. You can use the two methods to determine the effects of caching on your system.

Listing 8-4. A Demonstration of Caching Effects

```
<%@ WebService language="C#" class="TestCache" %>

using System;
using System.Web.Services;
using System.Xml.Serialization;
using System.Reflection;

[WebService(Namespace="http://winserver/0131/WebService/")]
public class TestCache
{

    [WebMethod(CacheDuration=120,
              Description="Shows the effects of output caching.")]
    public string TimeStampForOutputCache()
    {
        object[]            Attr;   // Array of attributes.
        MethodInfo          MI;     // Information about this method.
        WebMethodAttribute  WMA;    // WebMethod attribute information.
        string              RetVal; // Return value.

        // Get the method information for this method.
        MI = typeof(TestCache).GetMethod("TimeStampForOutputCache");

        // Use the method information to obtain a list of attributes.
        Attr = MI.GetCustomAttributes(typeof(WebMethodAttribute), false);

        // Obtain the WebMethodAttribute information.
        WMA = (WebMethodAttribute)Attr[0];

        // Return the CacheDuration property value to the user.
        RetVal = "CacheDuration Value: " + WMA.CacheDuration.ToString();

        // Return the current time.
        RetVal = RetVal + " - Output Cached at: "
                        + DateTime.Now.ToString("r");
```

```
            // Return the data.
            return RetVal;
      }


      [WebMethod(CacheDuration=0,
                 Description="No output caching for this method.")]
      public string TimeStampForNoOutputCache()
      {
            object[]            Attr;   // Array of attributes.
            MethodInfo          MI;     // Information about this method.
            WebMethodAttribute  WMA;    // WebMethod attribute information.
            string              RetVal; // Return value.

            // Get the method information for this method.
            MI = typeof(TestCache).GetMethod("TimeStampForNoOutputCache");

            // Use the method information to obtain a list of attributes.
            Attr = MI.GetCustomAttributes(typeof(WebMethodAttribute), false);

            // Obtain the WebMethodAttribute information.
            WMA = (WebMethodAttribute)Attr[0];

            // Return the CacheDuration property value to the user.
            RetVal = "CacheDuration Value: " + WMA.CacheDuration.ToString();

            // Return the current time.
            RetVal = RetVal + " - Output Cached at: "
                             + DateTime.Now.ToString("r");

            // Return the data.
            return RetVal;
      }
}
```

The code begins by determining the state of the CacheDuration property of the [WebMethod] attribute. To perform this task, you need to use the reflection capability build into the .NET Framework. The example obtains the information for the current method, and then uses that object to obtain a list of [WebMethod] attributes attached to the method. Because you can only use one of these attributes at a time, the method doesn't use a for loop to check each attribute value—there's only one. You must convert the output into a WebMethodAttribute type, and then use the resulting object to retrieve the CacheDuration property value. This technique works for any attribute. Figure 8-12 shows the output of this example.

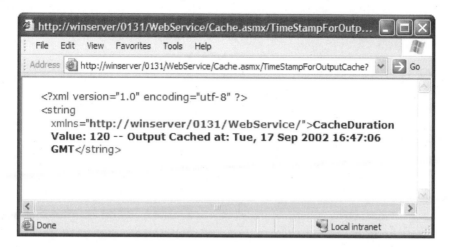

Figure 8-12. The output of this example shows the value of the CacheDuration *property, as well as the current time.*

Summary

This chapter has helped you understand Web services and see how Web Matrix can help you implement them. We haven't really scratched the surface of what Web services can do for an organization, but you know enough now that you could build a simple application and begin to learn how Web services can help your organization. You've also learned how to build simple classes. Finally, we discussed some performance issues that you'll face, no matter how simple your application.

The next steps are to see where Web services can take your organization. Some small companies will never need the functionality that Web services can provide, so it's important to experiment. Learn just what the limitations are before you leap into a major project. It's also important to learn about security—an issue we haven't covered in this chapter at all. A good Web service application requires just as much, if not more research than a LAN application.

Chapter 9 takes you into another distributed application arena, the mobile application. If you can believe the trade press, mobile applications are the next major area of development for most companies. Developers will need to learn how to work with devices as small as a cellular telephone. Although the device is tiny, users will still expect robust applications that are easy to use—it's a big step for even the most advanced developer.

CHAPTER 9

Web Matrix Mobile Applications

In This Chapter

- Create a Mobile Device Emulation Environment

- Learn to Design with Mobile Support in Mind

- Create an Application with the Simple Mobile Page

- Design a Simple Mobile Solution

- Create an Application with the Simple Mobile User Control

- Design a Mobile Solution with User Controls

- Design a Secure Mobile Application

- Learn to Create Applications for a Specific Device

Some developers are still working exclusively with desktop applications, but those days are almost gone, as are the days of exclusive LAN or WAN development. Today, most developers need to know about the desktop, the LAN, the Internet, and the air around them. That's right—if you aren't working with wireless applications today, it's likely that you'll work with them tomorrow. The world has become a mobile place, frantic and constantly moving. Some developers are frantic, too—they're trying to keep up with users who seem to move at the speed of light.

The key to most mobile applications today is creating a Web-based application that "sizes" appropriately. An application that works equally well on the desktop, a tablet, a Personal Digital Assistant (PDA), and a cellular telephone is worth its weight in gold. Of course, there are many problems to overcome when creating a mobile application. For example, you have to consider the size of the display. This book won't help you with all of the problems you'll run across, but it will point you in the right direction when it doesn't. The focus of this chapter is showing how Web Matrix can make the task of creating mobile applications easier.

Part of the challenge of working with mobile devices is figuring out how to test your application. The problem is that mobile devices come in so many "form factors" that you could end up pulling your hair out long before you buy them all. The first section of the chapter discusses emulators—software that helps you test your application without using a physical device. Of course, you'll still want to test your application on "real" physical devices too—you just won't have to use as many as you normally would require to test an application completely.

NOTE *You'll see a number of references to size and form factor in this chapter. Unlike desktop machines, mobile devices are typically small. They have display screens and input areas that can cause size and functionality problems. For example, how do you input characters using the numeric keypad of a cellular telephone? This kind of question plagues developers who create mobile applications. The combination of all device features is called a* form factor. *The form factor includes all of the physical and operating system characteristics that the developer will need to consider, including elements such as memory and processor speed.*

The chapter progresses by telling you how Web Matrix supports mobile devices. We'll discuss a simple example after that, so you can see the usual "Hello, World" application before we delve into something a little meatier. You'll learn about the various forms that Web Matrix provides for creating mobile applications, and we'll delve into some of the interesting features, such as mobile components and controls.

A final consideration for this section is learning how to adapt your applications to fit onto various mobile devices. Creating a mobile application means considering screen size, input capabilities, processor speed, memory, and other factors. Sure, you can test for compatibility using emulators and see where you need to tweak a form, but it's still important to handle all devices with equal ease. This final section isn't the end-all guide to customization, but I think you'll learn enough to get around the most common problems.

Installing Mobile Device Emulation Support

One of the problems that developers must solve when working with mobile devices is testing for multiple models. Unlike desktop systems, it's not always easy to determine if an application will provide the correct presentation on a mobile setup. Each mobile device has different capabilities, installed software, and a host of other problem areas for the developer to consider.

Most developers turn to emulation software to help test their mobile applications. An emulator provides the equivalent environment of the mobile device that it's supposed to model. I stress the word equivalent, because most of these emulators don't provide a complete picture of the mobile device environment. You can rely on an emulator to tell you whether the application fits within the screen area that the mobile device provides, but you can't rely on it to tell you about memory issues or whether a particular device has a piece of support software you need. These other issues require testing on an actual machine—something you should do for at least a subset of the mobile devices you want to support.

NOTE *You might find that you need other emulators to provide the kind of support required for your application. The emulators discussed in the following sections provide support for popular devices, but they don't emulate every device on the market today. In general, if you choose an emulator, make sure you test it against the real device so that you know how the emulator compares. Some emulators are less useful than others are because the level of emulation varies.*

The following sections help you install three emulation software options. I chose these options because they provide a broad range of support, and you can download at least evaluation units of all three emulators. Here are the download locations so that you can get your copies of the products before you begin this section. The following sections assume that you've downloaded the software required for the installation.

- **Microsoft eMbedded Visual Tools (304 MB):**
  http://www.microsoft.com/mobile/downloads/emvt30.asp

- **Openwave version 5.1 SDK (15.9 MB):**
  http://developer.Openwave.com/download/

- **SmartPhone (9.5 MB):** http://www.yospace.com/spewe.html

NOTE   *The SmartPhone download can be a little confusing. The download provides you with a 5-day free trial, not the 10-day free trial listed on the initial Web page. You'll need to create a user name and password to access the download area. This is your site user name and password that you'll use for subsequent visits to the Yospace Web site. After you download the product, check your inbox for an e-mail message from Yospace. This message contains a user name and password that you must use to initialize the product.*

Microsoft eMbedded Visual Tools

The Microsoft eMbedded Visual Tools option is free. All you need to do is download the product and unpack it in an installation directory. When you double-click the downloaded file, it will suggest an installation directory of Mobile Development Tools. The extraction tool will create two subfolders: Disk1 and Disk2. The Disk1 folder contains the desktop application development tools.

The Disk2 folder contains the three emulators, and you can install them individually if desired by using the Setup program found in the individual emulation product folder. For example, if you want to install just the Pocket PC emulator, you can double-click the Setup program in the \Mobile Development Tools\DISK2\PPC12SDK folder. However, because Web Matrix doesn't provide any means for creating mobile client applications (those that operate within the mobile device, rather than relying on the Web), you might find that you want to install the compiler as well. With this in mind, the following steps show how to create a full installation.

1. Double-click the Setup application found in the \Mobile Development Tools\DISK1 folder. This Setup program will have the special eMVT icon in lime green letters. You'll see the eMbedded Visual Tools dialog box.

2. Click Next. You'll see the End User License Agreement dialog box.

NOTE   *If you don't agree with the licensing terms, select the "I Don't Accept the Agreement" option, and then click Exit. The installation will end at this point. Of course, you won't have access to the eMbedded Visual Tools product either and will have difficulty using the examples in this chapter.*

3. Read the agreement, select the "I Accept the Agreement" option, and then click Next. You'll see the Product Number and User ID dialog box shown in Figure 9-1. The Microsoft Web site provides a user ID that you can enter in this dialog box. You'll also find the user ID in the CDKey.TXT file found in the \Mobile Development Tools folder. The current key also appears in the figure.

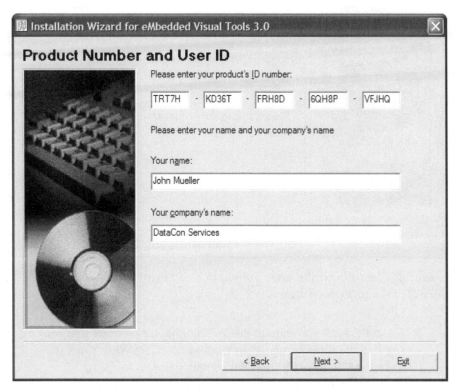

Figure 9-1. Enter the Microsoft-supplied user ID in this dialog box.

4. Type the key code, and then click Next. You'll see the Install eMbedded Visual Tools dialog box shown in Figure 9-2. The only tools that we'll use in this chapter are the three platform SDK options. These options provide you with access to the three device emulators. However, it's a good idea to install the eMbedded Visual Tools 3.0 option, as well, because the compilers it provides help you build any desktop applications you might need.

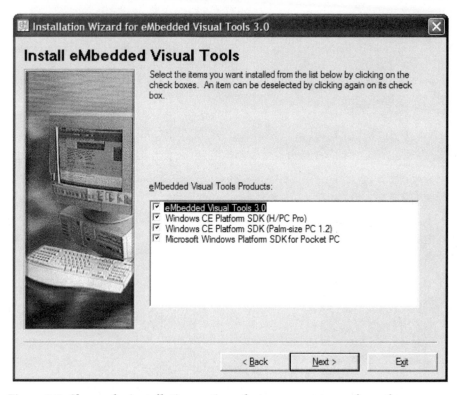

Figure 9-2. Choose the installation options that you want to use from the eMbedded Visual Tools package.

5. Select the tools you want to install. This chapter assumes that you've selected the three emulators as a minimum. Click Next. You'll see a Choose Windows CE Tools Folder dialog box.

6. Type or choose a destination for the tools if you don't want to use the default folder. Click Next. The eMbedded Visual Tools setup will begin at this point, if you chose to install this feature. Otherwise, skip to Step 9 where we'll begin the first emulator setup. You'll see an initial warning screen telling you to close all applications for a good install.

7. Click Continue. Click OK when you see the product identification dialog box. Setup will search for installed components and then display the eMbedded Visual Tools Setup dialog box shown in Figure 9-3.

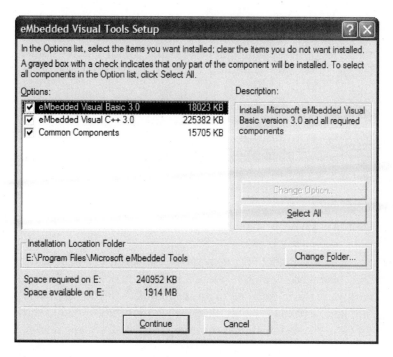

Figure 9-3. Select one or both of the development languages.

NOTE *You must install the common components. However, you can install either or both the eMbedded Visual Basic and the eMbedded Visual C++ compiler. Note that these compilers are specially designed for embedded application work and won't provide the means to create desktop applications. If you choose the eMbedded Visual C++ option, you can also choose which processors to support with your application (a feature that makes it more attractive than eMbedded Visual Basic, which is limited to platforms that can support the runtime).*

8. Select the installation options you want to use, and then click Continue. Setup will check for the required disk space, and then begin copying the files to the installation directory. After the installation completes, the Handheld PC setup will begin. You'll see the Welcome dialog box.

9. Click Next. You'll see the Software License Agreement dialog box.

10. Read the licensing terms and click Yes if you agree with them. (If you click No, the installation will end.) You'll see a User Information dialog box.

11. Type your user information, and then click Next. You'll see the Choose Destination Location dialog box.

12. Select an installation location, and then click Next. You'll see the Setup Type dialog box. It pays to choose the Custom option so that you can customize the installation to meet your needs. In addition, the Typical option doesn't always copy all of the features the emulation software can provide. If you choose the Custom option, you'll see an additional dialog box like the one shown in Figure 9-4 that contains a list of the features you can install.

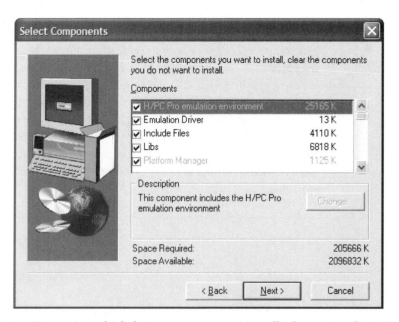

Figure 9-4. Determine which features you want to install when using the Custom setup option.

13. Select the setup options you want to use, and then click Next. You'll see a Select Program Folder dialog box.

14. Choose a location for the program entries in the Start menu, and then click Next. You'll see a Start Copying Files dialog box.

15. Examine the installation options. Use the Back button to return to previous setup screens if you need to change an option. When you're happy with the setup options, click Next. Setup will begin copying the files to the hard drive. After some time, the installation program will complete and you'll see some installation notes. You can read the notes now or simply minimize the browser window to complete the installation process. After you finish looking at the installation notes, you'll see the Setup Complete dialog box.

16. Click Finish. The next installation procedure will start unless you've installed all of the emulators.

17. Repeat Steps 9 through 16 for the Palm-size PC and Pocket PC emulators.

When you finish installing everything, it's important to test each of the emulators to ensure you received a good installation. If one of the emulators fails to work, you can always uninstall just that emulator using the appropriate entry in the Add/Remove Programs applet. Reinstall the emulator using the Setup program in the appropriate emulator folder in the setup folder mentioned at the beginning of this section.

Figure 9-5 shows a typical example of the Handheld PC. One oddity of this particular emulator is that it will sit in the upper-left corner of your display and not move. However, it does provide a good environment in which to test your mobile application.

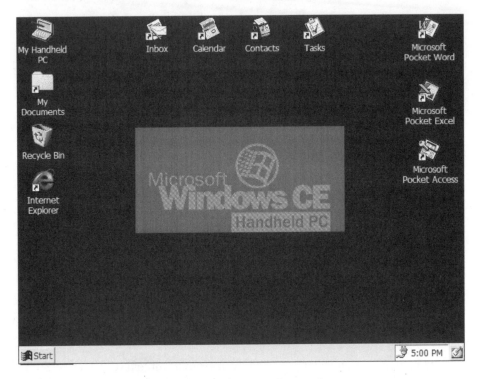

Figure 9-5. Test each of the emulators to ensure they work.

Another potential problem with these three emulators is that you can only run one of them at a time. Make sure you close an existing emulator before you start a new one. Generally, the new emulator will check for this problem and tell you to close the existing emulator. We'll discuss other emulator issues as the chapter progresses.

Openwave 5.1 SDK

The Openwave SDK is also a free download, but the Openwave Web site offers plenty of opportunity to purchase products for sale as well. The Openwave file you download is an executable, so double-clicking it starts the installation process. The following steps assume that you've already started the installation program and can see the Welcome dialog box.

NOTE *The different versions of the Openwave 5.1 SDK will work fine with MMIT 1.0. However, if you decide to use the Openwave 6.1 SDK, then you'll need to install MMIT Device Update 2. This update will become available on Microsoft Developer Network (MSDN). Neither Openwave 6.1 nor the MMIT Device Update 2 are available as of this writing, so I can't provide you with specific URLs.*

1. Click Next to get past the Welcome dialog box. You'll see the License Agreement dialog box.

2. Read the licensing agreement, and then click Yes if you agree to it. You'll see a Screenshots and Image Use Agreement dialog box. Again, you'll need to click Yes to accept the terms of this agreement. After this, you'll see a Safe Country Verification dialog box—yet more legal material. Click Yes if you live in a safe country. At some point, you'll finally get through all of the legal material and arrive at the Choose Destination Location dialog box. Note that choosing No at any of these legal screens will cause the installation to stop.

3. Select a destination for your emulator, and then click Next. You'll see a Setup Type dialog box. The Custom option provides the best flexibility for installing this product. If you choose this option, you'll see a Select Components dialog box similar to the one shown in Figure 9-6 when you click Next. It's important to note that this SDK supports a number of emulators—each of which has different features. You can also obtain different "skins" for the emulators to make them look like specific phones.

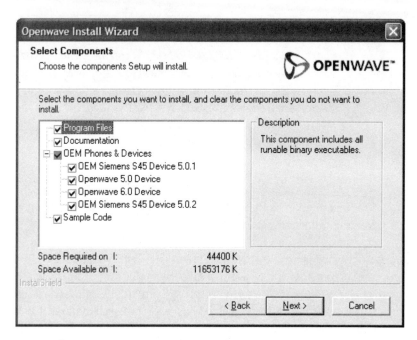

Figure 9-6. Select custom options as needed for your emulator setup.

4. Select a setup type and associated options as needed. Click Next. You'll see a Select Program Folder dialog box.

5. Choose a location for the emulator shortcuts, and then click Next. Setup will begin copying files to the installation folder. At some point, the installation will complete, and you'll see the InstallShield Wizard Complete dialog box.

6. Select a restart option, and then click Finish. According to Setup, you must restart your machine to use the product.

Once you get Openwave installed and have restarted your machine, you'll want to test this product out. Unlike some of the other emulators you'll use, this one is actually part of an IDE. The Openwave SDK 5.1 entry in the Start menu or the Desktop shortcut will open an IDE similar to other IDEs you may have used in the past. However, for this book, the important feature is the emulator that appears in the right-side pane. To use this feature, you'll need to use the Simulator ➤ Go to Address command, enter an URL in the Go To Address dialog box, and then click OK. Figure 9-7 shows a typical example of the Openwave emulator.

Figure 9-7. Using the Openwave emulator means starting the associated IDE and entering an URL using a menu command. (Image courtesy Openwave Systems Inc.)

SmartPhone

The SmartPhone emulator is one of the timed usage options you can try. After you download the product, you can try it for 5 days free, at which time your license will expire and the product will cease working. The SmartPhone emulator is in a ZIP file that you download and unpack to a temporary folder. The following steps show how to install the product.

1. Double-click the setup application that appears in the ZIP file (the actual name varies by SmartPhone version number). You'll see a License Agreement dialog box.

2. Read the license agreement and select Yes if you agree with it. Click Next. You'll see a Choose Install Folder dialog box.

3. Type an installation location and click Install. The setup program will begin installing the files. When the installation is complete, you'll see an Install Complete dialog box.

4. Click Done. The emulator is ready to test.

Now that you have the product installed, you can test it out to see if it works. The first time you start this product, you'll see a dialog box that requests your licensing details. This dialog box accepts your name and licensing term, e-mail address, and the key that you were sent in the e-mail message from Yospace. Make sure you use the information from the e-mail because this step is quite picky.

You also have a choice of starting the product in Development or Display mode. The Development mode opens an IDE you can use to create applications. This mode also shows multiple forms of the emulation, as shown in Figure 9-8. These aren't the only emulators available. I was surprised by the number of emulation options provided, all of which are available on the Workspace ➤ Add Emulator menu. This product also uses the concept of an emulator group. Figure 9-8 shows the default emulator group. A single test sends the same input to all of the emulators in a group—greatly reducing the time required for testing.

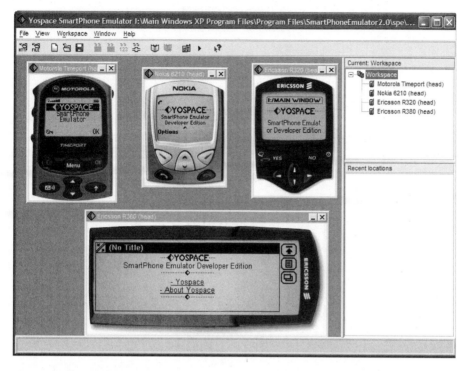

Figure 9-8. Create a complex emulator environment using the SmartPhone Development mode.

Display mode opens a single emulator, as shown in Figure 9-9. Use this option when you want to fine-tune the display details of your application. Most of the emulators have a full view and several zoomed views. Figure 9-9 shows a full view. We'll use several of the zoomed views as the chapter progresses.

Figure 9-9. Fine-tune display details and perform final testing using the SmartPhone Display mode.

Understanding Mobile Support

At this point, it may seem as if we've installed an entire world of development software for Web Matrix. After all, in Chapter 2 we installed Web Matrix and the Microsoft Mobile Internet Toolkit (MMIT). This chapter has seen the installation of three additional products—all of which include their own IDEs. However, at this point, you now have the tools to develop most types of Web applications for mobile devices and a variety of desktop applications, should you choose to do so. All of these tools help make you an effective mobile application developer. The best part of all is that you haven't invested a cent yet to gain all of this functionality.

NOTE   *Microsoft is changing the name of MMIT to ASP.NET Mobile Controls. The MMIT moniker still appears on all of the Microsoft Web sites as of this writing, and you'll also find it on many other Web sites. Given the number of places where MMIT appears, I'll continue to use this term for the book. However, you should be aware of the name change so that you can find new resources that Microsoft creates using the new name. Interestingly enough, because Visual Studio .NET also requires MMIT to provide mobile support, you have many of the same capabilities as a Visual Studio .NET developer. The difference is that you don't have the same level of automation at your disposal. The IDE also doesn't provide as much protection—it doesn't help you create applications that will run without a lot of work. In short, you can develop the same types of projects, but it will take you longer to do so because you have to create all the required code manually, and this code is more prone to error.*

TIP   *For those of you who are wondering just how much support you'll get from Microsoft with your mobile application development needs, Microsoft is constantly introducing new products and new tools to help. One of the latest offerings is the Microsoft Enterprise Location Server. This new server product helps developers build applications that rely on a user's location to provide output. For example, you could use this server to send maps for the user's current location as part of an application data package. The information works the other way as well—the local application could send location-specific data such as client information for clients in the area or application updates to meet local needs. You'll find a good overview of this product at* `http://www.infoworld.com/articles/hn/xml/ 02/09/18/020918hnmsdemo.xml?0918weam.`

Once you install MMIT, you'll notice a Mobile Pages folder added to the Add New File dialog box, as shown in Figure 9-10. The two projects in this folder help you create display pages and specialized controls for mobile applications. ASP.NET adds to this support by providing support for various device types. For example, it automatically adjusts the screen size as needed for devices with smaller displays. Of course, this support depends on the devices that ASP.NET can recognize. As new devices come out, Microsoft adds them to the list. That's why we needed to install the various updates to MMIT as part of the installation process in Chapter 2.

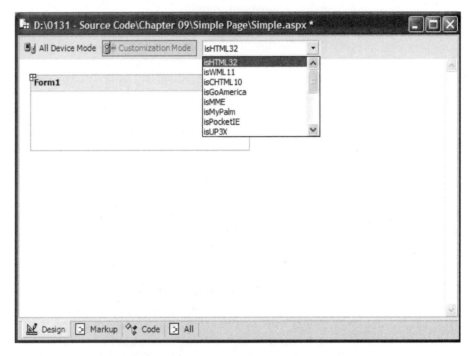

Figure 9-10. Including MMIT support in your Web Matrix installation adds mobile projects that you didn't have with a default installation.

TIP *MMIT provides a number of features that we won't even discuss in this chapter. It's actually a complex product that gives the developer a lot of flexibility in working with a broad range of mobile devices. You can learn more about MMIT at* http://msdn.microsoft.com/msdnmag/issues/ 02/11/MMIT/default.aspx.

The way in which MMIT adds support for certain devices brings up an interesting point. You can't assume that your application will run on every system out there, even if the system provides Web browser capability and follows the standards. Some developers have the impression that Web applications run anywhere, and this simply isn't true in the world of mobile devices. In fact, you need to consider a wealth of potential problems when working with mobile devices that you'd never need to consider when working with a desktop system. (Fortunately, MMIT allows the developer to add new devices, and some devices simply use support for similar devices already found in MMIT.) Here's a list of the factors that most developers should consider when it comes to mobile device support.

- Form factor

- Screen size

- Color capability

- Processing capability

- Memory

- Button availability

- Transmission speed

- Browser capability

- Browser adherence to standards

- Object support

- Scripting capability

Most of these items are self-explanatory. For example, the form factor affects the user's ability to interact with the device, while the screen size determines the amount of information the application can display. Button availability affects how your application reacts to the user. Some devices will supply the equivalent of an Enter key, but your application might have to react to the pound (#) key as well. The transmission speed is important because you can't expect the user to wait an indeterminate amount of time for a page to download. If anything, mobile device users are even less patient than those who use desktop machines are. The last two requirements, object support and scripting capability, often determine what you can expect the client to do. For example, some mobile devices can use SOAP, but require a third-party library to do so. Likewise, support for scripting means fewer round trips to the server and better response times.

Even if you consider all of these factors, you'll still run into problems when working with mobile devices. For example, you don't know the user's ability. Perhaps the user has never worked with a computer system before. It's for this reason mobile applications require simple interfaces—some developers even use the phrase "light switch simple" to define them. Some developers are beginning to change their assumption of user ability as users become more knowledgeable, but the limitations of a mobile device will still reduce the amount of data you can transfer and the complexity of the application. In sum, even if MMIT provides all of the support you could ever want for a particular mobile device, you still may find that you can't create the application of your dreams due to other support issues.

To this end, this section describes a situation where a developer has to have a level of flexibility that exceeds the problems of the mobile environment. A one-language, one-environment developer isn't going to go very far in the world of mobile devices today. In some cases, Web Matrix, or even Web applications as a whole, won't provide a viable solution to an application need. Sometimes, you'll need to provide a solution based on the same skills that you've used for desktop programming, which means using one of those other IDEs that we downloaded.

Obtaining Cellular Telephone Support Information

As a mobile device developer, you'll run into a wealth of new acronyms for specifications that you might not know about. This is especially true when working with cellular telephones because they represent one of the newest areas of application development. Sometimes it's tough to know which acronyms to pursue, much less where to find information about them.

Two of the most important acronyms for Web Matrix developers are Wireless Markup Language (WML) and Compact HyperText Markup Language (cHTML). These two acronyms describe the technique used to communicate with the cellular telephone and therefore describe what you'll use to write applications for them. Remember that the Microsoft Mobile Internet Toolkit provides support for these two access methods, so you need to install this product before you do anything else (see the "Microsoft Mobile Internet Toolkit Installation" section of Chapter 2 for details).

You can obtain a wealth of specification information for WML (and other mobile technologies) at http://www.wapforum.org/what/technical.htm. I was a little surprised at just how many WML specifications are already available online—make sure you select the most current version of the specification when you do download it (version 2.0 at the time of this writing). A good overview of the technology appears at http://www.oasis-open.org/cover/wap-wml.html. Finally, the Wireless Developer Network has a tutorial on using WML at http://www.wirelessdevnet.com/channels/wap/training/wml.html.

One of the first places to look for cHTML information is at http://www.w3.org/TR/1998/NOTE-compactHTML-19980209/ on the World Wide Web Consortium (W3C) site. This discussion document helps explain some of the issues in using cHTML. A good introduction to iMode and cHTML appears at http://www.devx.com/wireless/articles/i-Mode/i-ModeIntro.asp. You can find an interesting article that explains how cHTML works, including example code, at http://www.webreview.com/1998/08_21/webauthors/08_21_98_1.shtml. And you can find a listing of HTML 4.0 tags and elements that work with cHTML at http://www.webreview.com/1998/08_21/webauthors/08_21_98_2.shtml.

Note that the world of online development is in a constant state of flux. For example, the article at http://www.mcommercetimes.com/Technology/82 has XHTML Basic replacing both WML and cHTML. Many developers dispute this viewpoint, but you still need to consider your development options carefully.

Using the Simple Mobile Page

This might be the first mobile application that many of you have created, even if you've worked with Web sites for some time. Mobile technology is new, some-what difficult due to a number of factors, and represents the latest way to work with data for many people. In a few years this type of development will seem like old hat, but today it's new and decidedly different from anything developers have done in the past.

With these factors in mind, the following sections introduce mobile develop-ment in two stages. First, we'll look at the environment that Web Matrix provides. Interestingly, it's very capable of creating robust mobile applications of the cal-iber that you might normally require Visual Studio .NET to create. Second, we'll discuss a simple project. I chose not to engulf you in a database project immedi-ately. It's more important to understand the mechanics behind mobile page development before you decide to take on major corporate projects.

Updating Your Server

Your local machine is only one part of the picture for mobile development. Before any of the examples in this chapter will work, you must install Web Matrix on the server. As an alternative, you can move and register the Microsoft.Saturn.Framework and Microsoft.Saturn.Framework.Mobile assemblies in the server's GAC. These two assemblies provide the support that Web Matrix applications require.

In addition, you must install the Microsoft Mobile Internet Toolkit on the server. You can also install the required System.Web.Mobile assembly in the server's GAC. This assembly provides the MMIT support that the Web Matrix assemblies reference.

If these assemblies aren't installed, the application will fail. Fortunately, the error message that results will tell you about the missing assemblies so that you have a good starting point.

After you install the required support, you might find that the Web server doesn't reply to requests. Restart Internet Information Server (IIS) by right-clicking the server entry in the Internet Information Services MMC snap-in and choosing the Restart IIS or the All Tasks ➣ Restart IIS command from the context menu. The following illustration shows the Internet Information Services snap-in menu.

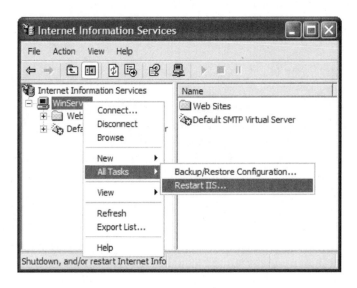

An Overview of the Environment

Starting the Simple Mobile Page is about the same as starting any other project we've discussed so far in the book. You need to provide a location for the project and a project name. In addition, you can specify a class name and a namespace, but these entries are optional in this case. However, once you create the project, you'll see a page that looks nothing like the other projects. Figure 9-11 shows that you'll see some additional features that you didn't see in other projects.

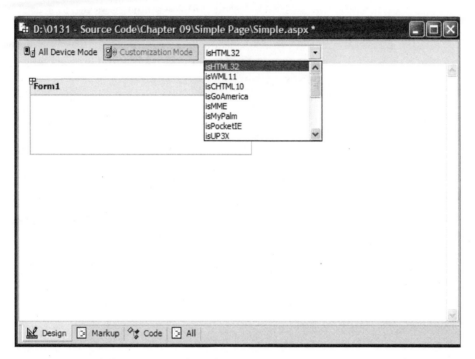

Figure 9-11. Mobile projects include features that other projects we've discussed don't include.

Notice that this page includes four tabs—the same number as the ASP.NET Page project provides. However, instead of an HTML tab, you now have a Markup tab. The difference is that mobile device pages don't use strict HTML—they use WML instead because the page has to fit within the confines of a mobile device screen. Mobile devices use the concept of individual screen-sized pages instead of relying on one long page that the user has to scroll down. (A PDA can often use screen-sized pages or one long page, making the PDA more flexible than a cellular telephone or a pager.)

The screen-sized page orientation of mobile devices brings us to the form shown on screen. A form outlines a single page of content. You can add multiple forms to one project page. The mobile device will simply inform the user of the additional pages of information in most cases.

Near the top of the page you'll see two options: All Device Mode and Customization Mode. When you select All Device Mode, the IDE creates a page that will work on all the devices that MMIT supports. On the other hand, if you select Customization Mode, the IDE configures itself to match the requirements of the specific device that you select. It's interesting to see the changes in the Properties window as you make configuration choices. Of course, the important changes happen under the covers where you can't see them unless you look at the code.

Customization Mode is interesting because it offers options such as supportsCookies and supportsJavaScript. I couldn't find a method for selecting both these options at once—there is one, but it's not apparent.

During my testing, I found Customization Mode can also lead to some interesting problems if you don't look at the Markup tab. For example, try this little experiment. Place a Label and a Command control on the form with the isHTML32 option selected. Type **Output** in the Text property of Label1 and **Click Me** in the Text property of Command1. Now, select the isPocketIE Customization Mode option. You'll notice three changes. First, the Command control becomes wider, which is expected since a PDA has a relatively large screen compared to some mobile options. The other two changes are that the text for Command1 and Label1 change back to their original settings. Type **Output** in the Label1 Text property again and **Click Me** in the Command1 Text property a second time. Now, look at the Markup tab and you'll see the code shown in Listing 9-1.

Listing 9-1. Customization Mode Coding Example

```
<mobile:Form id="Form1" runat="server">
    <Mobile:Label id="Label1" runat="server">
        <DeviceSpecific>
            <Choice filter="isPocketIE" text="Output"></Choice>
            <Choice filter="isHTML32" text="Output"></Choice>
        </DeviceSpecific>
Label</Mobile:Label>
    <Mobile:Command id="Command1" runat="server">
        <DeviceSpecific>
            <Choice filter="isPocketIE" text="Click Me"></Choice>
            <Choice filter="isHTML32" text="Click Me"></Choice>
        </DeviceSpecific>
Command</Mobile:Command>
</mobile:Form>
```

Once you look at this code, the method for supporting multiple devices without supporting all of the devices becomes obvious. Notice the use of the `filter` attribute in this code. The code itself is about the same, but the `filter` is different. Obviously, this is a simple example. What happens when two machines can't support the same complex setup? That's when you use separate coding for each device. The filter determines which devices use specific controls. Consequently, even though the concept of creating mobile pages using the Design window is the same as working with an ASP.NET page, the actual process is different. You need to make different design decisions than when working with a desktop machine.

 TIP *Use All Device Mode for simple pages where the use of the same controls for all devices is unlikely to cause usage problems. The advantage of using All Device Mode is that you can design pages quickly and without regard for individual device requirements. Always use All Device Mode to create your initial design and assign ID values to the controls. Use Customization Mode for complex pages where each device will require a separate configuration. The advantage of using Customization Mode is that you can compensate for individual device needs.*

The Mobile Controls tab of the Toolbox also differs from the Web Controls tab used for ASP.NET projects, as shown in Figure 9-12. The reason is simple—most mobile devices don't provide the resources to create some of the complex controls used on desktop machines. Even if a mobile device could display the complex control, it probably wouldn't have the local computing resources to make the control functional. Using all server-side resources is out of the question because mobile devices don't provide the data transmission speed of a desktop machine. In short, it's easier to limit controls to a subset that will work than create a situation in which you have to pick controls based on platform functionality.

Figure 9-12. Web Matrix provides a subset of the controls used for ASP.NET Page projects when working with mobile devices.

Designing Your First Page

The concepts behind designing a page for mobile use is about the same as those for designing a page for desktop use except you need to provide convenient breaks in the output for a mobile page. That's why a mobile development effort creates problems for some developers—they don't know how to break the content up into little pieces that a mobile device can display, and yet allow that content to come together as a whole document as well. A mobile application has to provide flexibility that allows the mobile device to display one, two, three, or more of the forms within a page as a set. Figure 9-13 shows one example of a single page broken up into three forms for easy display on a number of device types.

Figure 9-13. Use forms to break your page into smaller, easier-to-display pieces for mobile devices.

TIP *Setting the BreakAfter property value on controls is important. Web Matrix assumes that every control you add to a form will appear on a separate line. However, if you set the BreakAfter property to false, two small controls can appear on the same line and conserve precious screen space. The problem with this approach is that not all screens can support multiple controls on a single line, so be sure you perform a lot of testing if you use this approach. In some cases, you might want to provide customized settings to ensure you maximize screen usage on devices that can support more controls per line.*

Notice that the content in Figure 9-13 would normally fill one page for a desktop application. Actually, I wouldn't go so far as to say it's even one page of content, but let's use that number for the sake of argument. You could display the content in Figure 9-13 on a phone one form at a time and still see something understandable. The forms will display in order, so the context of moving from one form to the next isn't lost. Likewise, a PDA could display the first two forms as one page and the third form as a second page without losing context. The page flows from one form to the next as anticipated.

Unfortunately, there's a problem with our page. It displays the same set of three forms no matter which device you use. We'll discuss how to fix this problem in the "Enhancing the Simple Mobile Solution Example" section of the chapter. The page shown in Figure 9-13 is a good starting point, however, so let's add some code to the two pushbuttons. Listing 9-2 shows the code we'll use in this case.

Listing 9-2. Pushbutton Code for the Simple Mobile Example

```
void btnTest1_Click(Object sender, EventArgs e)
{
    // Only work with the control on the first form.
    lblOutput1.Text = "This is the first control form.";
}

void btnTest2_Click(Object sender, EventArgs e)
{
    // Only work with the control on the second form.
    txtOutput2.Text = "This is the second control form.";
}
```

As you can see, the buttons only change the value of the label or textbox text. The purpose of this code is to show how the buttons interact with the label and textbox using the various test emulations.

You should notice one other feature in the forms shown in Figure 9-13. Each form has a link in it. This link enables the user to move from form to form within the page. The absence of these links would mean the first form would show—the others won't. Web Matrix makes it easy to configure these links. It provides a drop-down list box for the NavigateUrl property of the Link control, as shown in Figure 9-14.

Figure 9-14. Adding a local destination for the NavigateUrl property is easy using this drop-down list box.

At this point, you can test the simple page using any of the emulators we've installed. Figure 9-15 shows the emulation of this application using the SmartPhone Siemens C35 emulator. Notice that the form contents precisely fills the display. If we'd made this form any bigger, it wouldn't have fit. The user can scroll down if needed, but you want to keep scrolling to a minimum on such a small device. Of course, this form will barely fill even a small portion of some of the other displays that we'll work with.

Figure 9-15. Use small forms as needed for mobile applications.

WEB.CONFIG Considerations for Mobile Applications

You'll remember from past examples that we've had to work with the WEB.CONFIG file in order to meet certain application requirements. For example, the source code for almost every example in the book includes an `<customErrors mode="Off"/>` entry in the WEB.CONFIG file to facilitate application debugging.

In some cases, you need to make changes to the WEB.CONFIG file for mobile applications as well. The first of these settings is the standard `<sessionState>` element shown in Listing 9-3.

Listing 9-3. A Typical <sessionState> Element

```
<sessionState mode="InProc"
    stateConnectionString="tcpip=127.0.0.1:42424"
    sqlConnectionString="data source=127.0.0.1;trusted_connection=true"
    cookieless="false"
    timeout="20" />
```

Normally, Web Matrix leaves this element commented out. In most cases, you can leave it commented out as well. However, notice the timeout attribute of this element. In some cases, the transmission speed of a mobile device makes this value too small. When this happens, you'll receive an error message similar to the one shown in Figure 9-16 (displayed in a standard browser to make it easier to see).

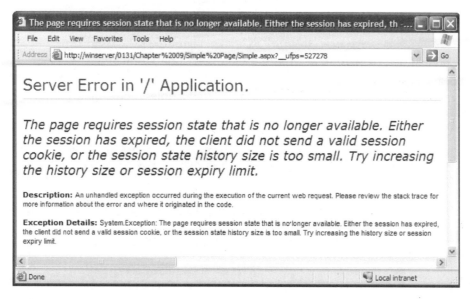

Figure 9-16. Changing the WEB.CONFIG file settings can help prevent this error.

The `<sessionState>` timeout value of 20 minutes is usually long enough, so you'll also want to check the `<mobileControls>` element. The WEB.CONFIG file doesn't contain this element by default, so you'll have to add it in manually. You can learn all the details about this element in the Mobile Internet Toolkit help file at `ms-help://MS.VSCC/ms.MobileInternetToolkit/mwsdk/html/mwlrfmobileControls.htm` or online at `http://msdn.microsoft.com/library/en-us/mwsdk/html/mwlrfmobileControls.asp`. The attribute you want to change to correct this error is `sessionStateHistorySize`. A typical `<mobileControls>` element appears in Listing 9-4.

Listing 9-4. A Typical <mobileControls> Element

```
<mobileControls
    allowCustomAttributes="true"
    sessionStateHistorySize="40"
    cookielessDataDictionaryType="">
</mobileControls>
```

You'd include this code as a subelement of the `<system.web>` element—the same location as the `<sessionState>` element. Figure 9-17 shows an XML Notepad view of this entry. Listing 9-4 shows a standard form of the `<mobileControls>` element. Normally, you won't need to provide the other elements supported by the `<mobileControls>` element unless your application has special needs.

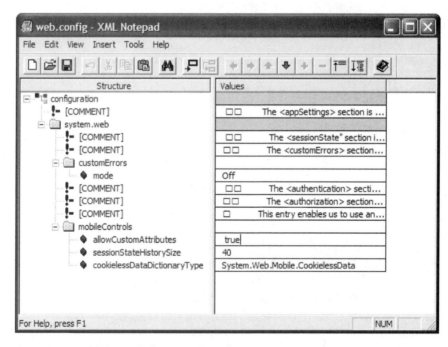

Figure 9-17. Add the <mobileControls> element as a <system.web> subelement.

A Weblog Project You Might Enjoy Doing

I'm sure most of you are at least aware of what a Weblog is, but for those who aren't, I want to provide a bit of background information. A relatively new Web trend is the creation of public diaries, generically referred to as *Blogs*. The term originated from "WeB log." This technology was originally promoted by pyra.com (http://pyra.com/) as a Blog at its BLOGGER site (http://www.blogger.com/). People who "Blog" are called Bloggers, and right now there are thousands of Blogs on the Net. The sites just mentioned allow Bloggers to use their software to easily produce their own individual Blog on the Internet.

A Weblog isn't only an easy way to publish to the Web but a way to organize all your published product over time so that friends, associates, and customers can easily find and interact with it. The Weblog software places your most recent posts at the top of your home page along with everything else you published that day. An integrated calendar keeps track of your daily posts and allows site users to quickly access archived posts.

A quick search of Blog, Blogging, or Weblog on Google (http://www.google.com/) will produce more links than you could ever imagine. Many people and even businesses are using Blogs to communicate. For example, a business could use a Blog to provide updates on a project, such as the release for a new product. People generally use Blogs to chronicle their daily lives or special events, such as a trip.

I thought it would be an interesting project for you to design your own Blog using Web Matrix and the Blog User Control control that's available for download at the Control Gallery site (http://www.asp.net/ControlGallery/default.aspx?Category=34&tabindex=2). Download BLOG.ZIP and you'll find that it contains 27 files, including a README.TXT file that will explain, in detail, everything you'll need to do to use the control. The control also includes a nice calendar that will save you many hours of development time if you had to code one on your own.

This project is incredibly easy to use. All you need to do is copy the appropriate files to your project directory, create the SQL Server database using the supplied script, make a few changes to the code, and then create some content. Note that this is another project that will benefit from the MSDE Query product we discussed in the "Configuring MSDE Using MSDE Query" section of Chapter 5. You can use MSDE Query to create the initial database and also to monitor the entries as you create them.

It requires little effort on your part to turn this control into a nice application to produce your own Blog using Web Matrix. The control is free for the price of the download and requires little time to download since the file is just over 50 KB. I hope you'll try this project since it involves using Web Matrix, a downloaded control from the Control Gallery and a database. I would enjoy hearing your comments about this project should you decide to give it a try.

(Sidebar by Russ Mullen)

Enhancing the Simple Mobile Solution Example

Our previous example proved a little disappointing because it displays the same way no matter what device you use to display it. When developers create a Web page as part of a desktop application, consistent appearance is something that they try to achieve, but let's face the fact that mobile development is different. Just because your friend decides that squinting at the decidedly small text on a cellular telephone is just fine doesn't mean you should live with the same limitation.

For the sake of argument, let's say you'll use the same application to display information on a desktop browser, a PDA, and a cellular telephone. This section shows how you to modify the example from the "Designing Your First Page" section of this chapter. We'll begin by modifying the three forms to look like the ones in Figure 9-18. Note that some of these controls are only visible to the full browser and some only to the full browser and Pocket PC. You'll see how this functionality is controlled in the source code.

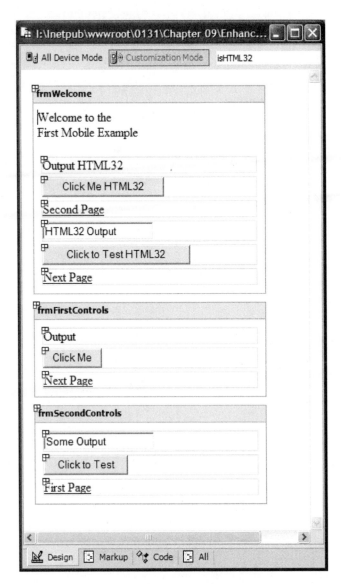

Figure 9-18. Create new forms that better reflect the three target platforms.

Interestingly enough, you can set up the basic elements of this form in
Design view, but then you have to switch to Markup view to make some of the
adjustments. Listing 9-5 shows the markup for the first page of this example—
the first page is the key to making the example work properly. Notice that we
aren't using any new event handlers for this example, but that we are using the
<DeviceSpecific> tag entries.

Listing 9-5. The Enhanced Display Markup

```
<Mobile:Form id="frmWelcome" Paginate="True" runat="server">
<p>
    Welcome to the<br />
    First Mobile Example
</p>
<p>
    <Mobile:Label id="lblOutput3" runat="server" Visible="False">
        <DeviceSpecific>
            <Choice filter="isPocketIE"
                    visible="True"
                    text="Pocket PC Output"></Choice>
            <Choice filter="isHTML32"
                    visible="True"
                    text="Output HTML32"></Choice>
        </DeviceSpecific>
    Label</Mobile:Label>
    <Mobile:Command id="btnTest3"
                    onclick="btnTest1_Click"
                    runat="server" Visible="False">
        <DeviceSpecific>
            <Choice filter="isPocketIE"
                    visible="True"
                    text="Click Me"></Choice>
            <Choice filter="isHTML32"
                    visible="True"
                    text="Click Me HTML32"></Choice>
        </DeviceSpecific>
    Command</Mobile:Command>
    <Mobile:Link id="Link1"
                 runat="server"
                 NavigateUrl="#frmSecondControls" Visible="False">
        <DeviceSpecific>
            <Choice filter="isPocketIE" visible="True"></Choice>
            <Choice filter="isHTML32" visible="False"></Choice>
```

```
                </DeviceSpecific>
        Second Page</Mobile:Link>
        <Mobile:TextBox id="txtOutput4" runat="server" Visible="False">
            <DeviceSpecific>
                <Choice filter="isPocketIE
                        visible="False"
                        text="Some Output"></Choice>
                <Choice filter="isHTML32"
                        visible="True"
                        text="HTML32 Output"></Choice>
            </DeviceSpecific>
        </Mobile:TextBox>
        <Mobile:Command id="btnTest4"
                        onclick="btnTest2_Click"
                        runat="server"
                        visible="False">
            <DeviceSpecific>
                <Choice filter="isPocketIE"
                        visible="False"
                        text="Click to Test"></Choice>
                <Choice filter="isHTML32"
                        visible="True"
                        text="Click to Test HTML32"></Choice>
            </DeviceSpecific>
        Command</Mobile:Command>
        <Mobile:Link id="Link2" runat="server" NavigateUrl="#frmFirstControls">
            <DeviceSpecific>
                <Choice filter="isPocketIE" visible="False"></Choice>
                <Choice filter="isHTML32" visible="False"></Choice>
            </DeviceSpecific>
        Next Page</Mobile:Link>
</p>
</Mobile:Form>
```

Let's begin with a few generalizations about this code. You'll notice that
all of the <Choice filter="isPocketIE"> entries appear before the
<Choice filter="isHTML32"> entries. An odd thing happens if you try to reverse
the order—your Pocket PC is apt to use the isHTML32 settings instead of the
isPocketIE settings. This is the only interaction I ran into during testing, but
there may be others that you should consider. If something on screen doesn't
look as anticipated, the order of your tags might be the problem.

Look at all of the controls in this example. Except for the introductory text
and the final link, all of them have the visible=false property in place. This

means that the example assumes that any device not specifically handled by the page can't display the controls on a single page. Using this technique ensures that any browser that visits your site can use it, even if such use is limited to the lowest common denominator.

Of course, if the control is invisible, you have to make it visible in some way. A look at the filter entries shows another series of visible=true or visible=false settings. The controls are displayed or not displayed based on the specific device support required. It can be difficult to keep all of these entries straight even in the Design view because you can't see what's happening. Consequently, I normally check the results of changes using the emulators to ensure that what I think is displayed on a particular device is what the user will actually see.

Sometimes you have to duplicate functionality across multiple forms. The only problem is that you can give two controls the same name. You can, however, use the same handler for more than one control. Unless you need to assign different functions to a button with the same function on two different areas of the form, using the same handler makes sense because it's easier to maintain the functional portion of the code. All you really need to do is ensure each of the affected controls uses the same handler as do the pushbuttons in Listing 9-5. The handler code must include output for every affected output control. Listing 9-6 shows the updated handlers for this example.

Listing 9-6. Updated Event Handler Code

```
void btnTest1_Click(Object sender, EventArgs e)
{
    // Only work with the control on the first form.
    lblOutput1.Text = "This is the first control form.";
    lblOutput3.Text = "This is the first output control.";
}


void btnTest2_Click(Object sender, EventArgs e)
{
    // Only work with the control on the second form.
    txtOutput2.Text = "This is the second control form.";
    txtOutput4.Text = "This is the second output control.";
}
```

As you can see from Listing 9-6, the essential logic of the event handler need not change. The only change you must make is to ensure that each of the output controls receives the information produced by the event handler. Figures 9-19 through 9-21 show the three output levels from this one ASPX page. As you can see, the browser outputs all of the information, the PDA outputs the information from the first two forms, and the cellular telephone outputs just one form at a time.

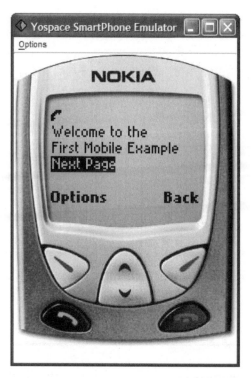

Figure 9-19. Users can view just one form using a cellular telephone.

Figure 9-20. Accessing the site with a PDA allows viewing of two forms.

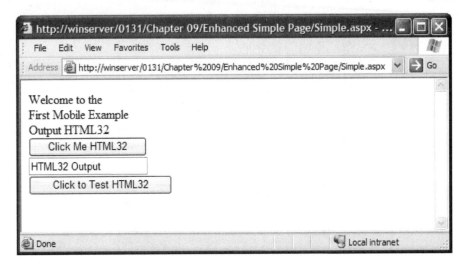

Figure 9-21. Using a browser to access the site allows viewing of all three forms at once.

Using the Simple Mobile User Control

Creating a mobile control is similar to creating any other Web control, except you have to consider the same things that you do for a Web page. For example, you need to determine if the device can actually display the control that you want to create. Like the Simple Mobile Page, the Simple Mobile UserControl provides functionality that helps you change the output of the control to match a specific platform. You'll find the same All Device Mode and Customization Mode options as you did when working with the Web page.

The example control will display the date when a Web page first displays it. Clicking the control will change the date to the current time. Consequently, this control relies on a command button as a starting point. The example shows the Format property set to Link for easier viewing. It's a simple control that demonstrates how to create a mobile user control. Listing 9-7 shows the code for the control portion of the example.

Listing 9-7. A Mobile User Control for Telling Date and Time

```
// Keep track of the date status.
bool _IsDate;

void btnTimeDate_Load(Object sender, EventArgs e)
{
    // Display the current date.
```

```
    btnTimeDate.Text = DateTime.Now.ToLongDateString();

    // Set the date status.
    _IsDate = true;
}


void btnTimeDate_Click(Object sender, EventArgs e)
{
    // Determine the date status. Set the date or time
    // as appropriate, along with the state.
    if (_IsDate)
    {
        btnTimeDate.Text = DateTime.Now.ToLongTimeString();
        _IsDate = false;
    }
    else
    {
        btnTimeDate.Text = DateTime.Now.ToLongDateString();
        _IsDate = true;
    }
}


// Provide a property for getting and setting the date state.
bool IsDateSet
{
    get { return _IsDate; }
    set { _IsDate = value; }
}
```

As you can see, the control's initial state is set by the btnTimeDate_Load()
method. This method uses a simple call to DateTime.Now.ToLongDateString() to
retrieve the current date in long format as a string and place it in the pushbutton's caption. The string will appear as a link, as shown in Figure 9-22. The
btnTimeDate_Load() method also sets a local variable, _IsDate, that indicates the
current date or time display on the pushbutton.

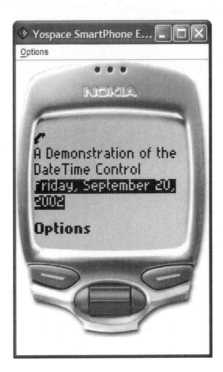

Figure 9-22. View the current date and time using this example.

When the user clicks the link, the display changes to either the date or the time depending on the current setting of _IsDate. The control acts as a toggle between the date and time. The control also includes a property, IsDateSet, that enables a developer to check the control status from within the mobile application. This could come in handy if the developer decides that the display should automatically return to the date or time after a certain time.

Making Your Mobile Secure Application

The software mechanics of creating a secure environment for your mobile application are similar to those used for desktop applications. In Chapter 4 you learned about various security features that Web Matrix provides. We also discussed some IIS and ASP.NET specific methods you can use to implement security. Generally, these techniques work well for mobile applications too, but you need to consider the screen size and input capabilities of the device. In some cases, a numeric password entry is about the best you can hope to achieve. Using a custom page for password entry might prove difficult, as well, since the screen size of many mobile devices is so small.

You need to consider a wealth of other security issues with mobile devices—most of which are well outside the scope of this book. For example, you need to plan around the natural problems caused by using a wireless connection. Securing the hardware can become extremely difficult. Mobile devices tend to eschew a physical connection to the network for the obvious reason—a user with a wire hanging off the end of their device isn't very mobile.

Wireless connections are far from safe and the methods used to secure them far from reliable. The hardware and software connections for wireless communication tend to have security holes that anyone can crack. In short, you might want to consider how much sensitive data to allow a mobile application to see. Working in Customization Mode can help in this regard because you can create pages that simply don't allow sensitive information to leave the server if the client is a mobile device.

Nothing in the .NET Framework will make a mobile application completely secure today. Even with the addition of third-party products, you'll find it nearly impossible to prevent someone from breaking your security. Consequently, any application that could transmit data through a wireless connection isn't a good candidate to handle your company's innermost secrets. Use the mobile application capabilities provided by any tool with caution and with an eye toward limiting damage during the inevitable attack on your system security.

Summary

The chapter has shown you how Web Matrix can help you create mobile applications. We haven't necessarily looked at everything you'll ever do to get a mobile application to work, but you do know how Web Matrix can help you perform the task with less effort than ever before. As part of this discussion, we've considered various testing techniques, including the use of emulators. You've also learned how to customize your application to work with a specific device.

You actually have a lot of work to do now. For example, you'll want to download, configure, and test the various emulators we've discussed in this chapter. You might also want to look at other emulators online. Other developers are running into the same problems that you are, so it's important to realize there are other solutions that you can use to create better mobile applications.

Chapter 10 will help complete your Web Matrix skills. We'll look at an important part of most applications today—performance. Although most developers don't worry about low-level bit twiddling anymore, performance is an important issue because the environment in which most applications operate isn't helpful.

Consider that many Web-based applications have to operate over dial-up connections. Even when you have a T1 or cable modem connection, the telephone company seldom guarantees any specific level of support unless you're willing to pay for it (something you won't find in a motel). Fortunately, Web Matrix has a few tricks up its sleeve that makes it easier to create robust applications that are also fast.

CHAPTER 10

Improving Performance with Web Matrix

In This Chapter

- Learn Methods to Improve Unmanaged Component Performance

- Discover Downloadable Controls That Improve User Performance

- Learn How to Use Output Caching

- Learn How to Work with the Performance Console

- Create a Vary By None Page

- Create a Vary Cache By Browser Page

- Create a Vary Cache By Headers Page

- Create a Vary Cache By Parameters Page

At this point in the book, we've worked with Web Matrix to create a variety of applications and perform a variety of application maintenance tasks. We've discussed everything from database management to security to creating controls. However, there's one topic we haven't really discussed, and that's performance. We live in a world where every second is considered precious, and people are constantly trying to squeeze yet one more thing out of the 24 allotted hours in a day. Our society is filled with examples of speed.

The point of working with Web applications, mobile devices, and computers with extremely fast chips is to get current information fast. *Anyone* can create a static Web page filled with yesterday's news and make it run fast. Perhaps not as fast as getting the same information locally from the company's LAN, and definitely not as fast as a local hard drive access, but fast enough that the user won't care. Unfortunately, getting Web applications that provide up-to-the-minute information about the latest events to run in "real time" is nigh on to impossible.

This chapter helps you improve the performance of your Web Matrix–based applications in three ways. First, we discuss some of the methods you can use to make the software run faster. However, fast software doesn't always guarantee fast results. The second issue is really a usability issue: how to "speed up" the user by making the application easy and intuitive to use. Finally, we discuss the important problem of performance monitoring. An application can provide fast response times only so long as the environment in which it runs is also optimized. You can build a fast application, but the only way that you'll know whether it's fast enough is to keep tabs on its performance. In short, monitoring is an essential task for anyone building applications.

Unmanaged Component and Control Performance Facts and Tips

Most developers, even new developers, have access to a wealth of COM-based components and controls. These components and controls fall into the unmanaged category because they don't rely on a memory manager to help maintain a safe memory environment. These older bits of code rely on the programmer to allocate and release memory, and to work with pointers in a way that's safe. Unfortunately, a lot of these older components and controls break the rules and cause a variety of resource leaks. However, the point of this section isn't to convince you to toss those older pieces of code—I know that *my* projects will continue to benefit from COM for quite some time.

The point of this section is to discuss some of the issues surrounding the use of unmanaged code with Web Matrix. After all, Web Matrix is a managed environment because it relies on ASP.NET, which, in turn, relies on the Common Language Runtime (CLR) and the .NET Framework. The implication is that the managed environment is different from the unmanaged environment you might have used in the past. In general, you can use unmanaged code safely with Web Matrix, but you need to be aware of what this usage means.

The biggest consideration for the purposes of this chapter is the connection between the managed and unmanaged environment. Every time managed code calls unmanaged code, a transition takes place. Generally, this transition takes place automatically within a wrapper. You learned how to create the wrapper in the "Development with an Unmanaged Component" section of Chapter 6. In some situations, the developer must still manage memory and data translations manually. You do this using the members of the Marshal class (learn more about this class at http://msdn.microsoft.com/library/en-us/cpref/html/frlrfSystemRuntimeInteropServicesMarshalClassTopic.asp). In some cases, it's also important to know how to use the [DllImport] attribute when working with unmanaged code (learn more about this attribute at http://msdn.microsoft.com/library/en-us/cpref/html/frlrfSystemRuntimeInteropServicesDllImportAttributeClassTopic.asp).

TIP *You can gain a detailed view of working with unmanaged code in my book,* .NET Framework Solutions: In Search of the Lost Win32 API *(ISBN: 0-78214-134-X). This book includes examples of both standard Win32 API calls and COM component and control use.*

Every time the application has to make a call to unmanaged code, work with unmanaged memory, or perform some level of marshaling, it incurs a performance penalty. The fact that some level of translation occurs means there's some type of translation code using resources. These resources aren't used for your application; they're used to perform data translation and other marshaling tasks. The performance penalty depends upon the amount and type of marshaling taking place, but there's *always* some penalty. A number of developers have suggested that the best way around this problem is to make all of the calls that you plan to make at one time and to keep the number of calls to a minimum.

TIP *You'll find an overview of the various interoperability topics (including drawings) at* http://msdn.microsoft.com/ library/en-us/cpguide/html/ cpconinteroperatingwithunmanagedcode.asp. *You can see an overview of how Platform Invoke (P/Invoke) works at* http://msdn.microsoft.com/library/en-us/cpguide/html/ cpconacloserlookatplatforminvoke.asp. *An overview of how COM interoperability works appears at* http://msdn.microsoft.com/library/ en-us/cpguide/html/cpconruntimecallablewrapper.asp.

Some developers are under the impression that they can never have a resource leak in a .NET application because it uses a garbage collector. (As the name implies, the garbage collector looks for unused objects and other resources and deallocates the memory they use after performing any required finalization.) While it's true that the garbage collector does a great job with resources that it knows about, it doesn't know about your unmanaged resources. This means that a .NET application can still have a resource leak when using unmanaged resources. Any resource leak your application creates will rob the application of performance. More importantly, it will cause problems with the server as a whole. Eventually the server will run out of resources. When working with unmanaged components and controls, it pays to allocate and deallocate memory only as needed. Make sure you deallocate any memory used by an object before you set the object to null for garbage collection. Also use performance monitoring to check your application. For example, you can use various memory counters to help you understand the memory usage patterns of your application. (See the counters in the Performance console loaded in the Administrative Tools folder of the Control Panel for details—we'll also discuss this topic in the "Working with the Performance Console" section of the chapter.)

In some cases, you'll find that the COM wrapper automatically generated by the tools discussed in Chapter 6 doesn't provide access to the entire DLL. Some COM DLLs also contain embedded functions that you must access using the [DllImport] attribute. In general, you'll find that working with DLLs that contain embedded functions is extremely difficult in Web Matrix, so you should avoid using them. Even with the advanced features provided by Visual Studio .NET, working with these DLLs is difficult.

In some cases, you should consider moving the functionality provided by an unmanaged component or control over to a .NET equivalent. For example, a component or control that provides some simple functionality such as a math calculation or keeping track of an application's status is a good candidate for moving to the managed environment. The time required to rewrite these types of components and controls will be small compared to the performance and maintenance benefits you'll receive.

Downloadable Controls That Improve User Performance

The user is often the largest impediment to good application performance, especially if the user's in a hurry. Data entry errors, buttons that are clicked accidentally, and controls that are hard to find all contribute to user-related performance problems. Every time your application determines that a user entry is incorrect, it must not only reverse the error, but also convince the user there's a problem, show how to correct the error, and check the new input. Consequently, anything you can do to improve user performance greatly improves application performance as well.

We discussed how to download controls from the Online Component Gallery in the "Connecting to the Online Component Gallery" section of Chapter 2. The "Using the XMLEditGrid Control" section of Chapter 7 shows you how to use one of the controls from this gallery to make your XML applications better. The following sections show you how to use two more controls from the gallery that not only make your application development faster, but also improve the user experience—making the user more efficient. (Make sure you also look at the other controls at http://www.asp.net/ControlGallery/.)

Using the AssociatedLabel Control

Giving users access to controls on screen is important. If you have a number of controls on a screen, pressing Alt-A to access the one named Address is definitely easier than pressing Tab multiple times. All of the ASP.NET controls have an Access property, but a good number of controls created by other vendors don't provide this feature. Let's look at a simple example. Figure 10-1 shows a simple Web page containing the AssociatedLabel control. The AssociatedControlID property of the AssociatedLabel control is set for txtOutput. In addition, the AccessKey property is set to B (the first letter of the label prompt). I've added other property changes to the example, but you can view them as part of the source code in the \Chapter 10 folder (available from the Downloads section on the Apress site at http://www.apress.com/book/download.html).

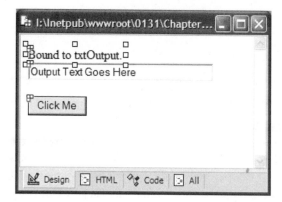

Figure 10-1. Add an AssociatedLabel control to your application to provide accessibility for older controls.

View the output of this example when you run it on a Web server. Figure 10-2 shows an example of the output. (Some elements of your output, such as the cookie, will differ from mine.) The highlighted text in the figure is the most important because it shows how this label differs from the standard label.

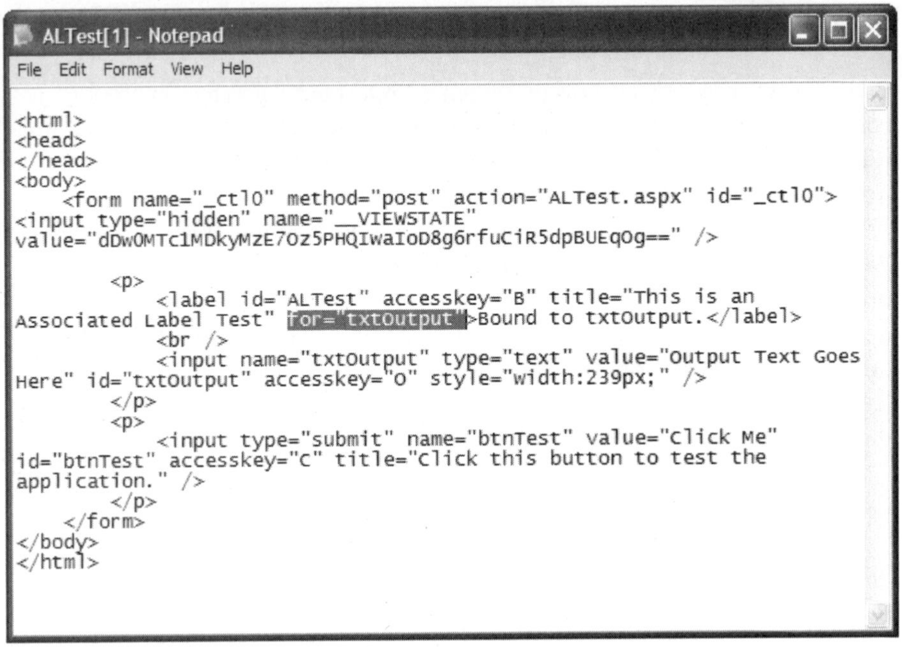

ALTest[1] - Notepad

File Edit Format View Help

```
<html>
<head>
</head>
<body>
    <form name="_ctl0" method="post" action="ALTest.aspx" id="_ctl0">
<input type="hidden" name="__VIEWSTATE"
value="dDwOMTc1MDkyMzE7Oz5PHQIwaIoD8g6rfuCiR5dpBUEqOg==" />

        <p>
            <label id="ALTest" accesskey="B" title="This is an
Associated Label Test" for="txtOutput">Bound to txtOutput.</label>
            <br />
            <input name="txtOutput" type="text" value="Output Text Goes
Here" id="txtOutput" accesskey="O" style="width:239px;" />
        </p>
        <p>
            <input type="submit" name="btnTest" value="Click Me"
id="btnTest" accesskey="C" title="Click this button to test the
application." />
        </p>
    </form>
</body>
</html>
```

Figure 10-2. The AssociatedLabel control outputs special HMTL text.

Notice that this `<label>` tag has the `for` attribute. The `for` attribute binds the AssociatedLabel to the requested control—txtOutput in this case. When you press Alt-B, the txtOutput control highlights as if this control had the AccessKey property set (it doesn't). In sum, the AssociatedLabel control makes your Web-based application easier to use by assigning a quick access key to controls that don't normally provide this feature.

The normal limitations for HTML pages also apply when using the AssociatedLabel control. For example, assigning an AssociatedLabel control to a standard Label control won't make the resulting `<label>` tag accessible. The AssociatedLabel control only works with controls that would normally provide an AccessKey property.

You might also notice a problem with this control. For some odd reason, it doesn't always display a list of controls from the current page in the AssociatedControlID property, as shown in Figure 10-3. When this happens, simply type the name of the control you want to use in the AssociatedControlID property. The control will work as normal.

Figure 10-3. Avoid the error in the AssociatedControlID property by typing the name of the associated control manually.

Using the HyperLinkList Control

We've all used list boxes to present information in Web forms. Using a list box serves two purposes. First, it helps the developer display more information in less space. The list box only consumes one line on the Web form until the user accesses it. Second, a list box helps the user ignore information that isn't useful at the moment. The list box keeps its data hidden until the user actually needs to make a choice.

NOTE *At the time of this writing, the HyperLinkList control has a known bug that the developer plans to fix. If you find that even after you populate the control with entries it doesn't display any selections, then you've run into the bug.*

The problem with list boxes is that you can only place text within them. The choice doesn't do anything until the user submits the form. The HyperLinkList control changes this functionality by making it possible to store links in a list box, rather than simple text items. When the user selects an option from the list box, they're actually selecting a hyperlink that will take them to another location without a lot of additional clicking.

To use this control, all you need to do is provide a list for the Items collection. Click the ellipses next to this field, and you'll see a List Item Collection Editor dialog box similar to the one shown in Figure 10-4. Notice that you provide a text link in the Text field and the actual URL in the Value field. If you supply a short URL, such as the one shown in the figure, ASP.NET assumes you want to use the current path as a starting point. Supplying a complete URL enables you to create links for anywhere on the Internet.

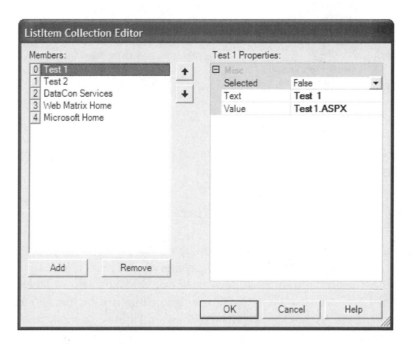

Figure 10-4. Use short URLs for relative links and long URLs for absolute links.

You can also set up this control to use a database connection. In this case, it will work as any other bound control works. All you need to provide are values for the DataSource, DataTextField, and DataValueField properties. Using a database means that you can save time updating the application—update the database instead.

Working with the Performance Console

At some point in the development process, you'll want to know how fast your application works. To determine application speed, you need some means of monitoring the application and how it affects the system. The Performance console shown in Figure 10-5 contains the System Monitor Microsoft Management Console (MMC) snap-in for monitoring applications in real time and the Performance Logs and Alerts MMC snap-in for monitoring applications long term. (MMC is a COM container application that accepts specialized components named *snap-ins*. The snap-in normally provides some type of monitoring or administration function.) This second form of monitoring creates a log that you can view later and use for documentation and/or historical auditing purposes.

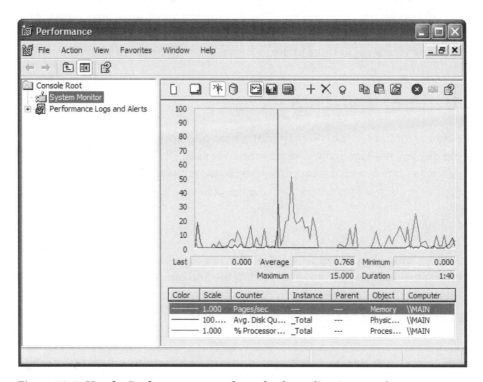

Figure 10-5. Use the Performance console to check application speed.

TIP *Performance monitoring can also work as a diagnostic to help you locate problems in your system. An errant application will often leave a trail of performance indicators that you can use to aid diagnosis. Of course, nothing replaces a good debugger, but any clue you can get is certainly helpful.*

The two performance monitoring snap-ins found in the Performance console look quite simple, but can actually perform complex monitoring tasks. Both snap-ins rely on the use of counters. A *counter* is a little application designed to keep track of specific performance statistics.

The following sections provide you with an overview of performance monitoring. We won't discuss every detail of the MMC snap-ins because that could require an entire chapter or a small book. However, you'll learn how to perform both short- and long-term performance monitoring, and use all of the displays. You'll also learn about some of the most important performance counters.

System Monitor Usage

System Monitor is a short-term performance-monitoring tool. It provides all of the displays used for analysis of performance data. The following sections describe some essential areas of System Monitor usage.

Using Counters

A monitoring session begins with the selection of performance counters. The easiest method to add counters is to click the Add button (the plus sign) on the toolbar. You'll see an Add Counters dialog box like the one shown in Figure 10-6.

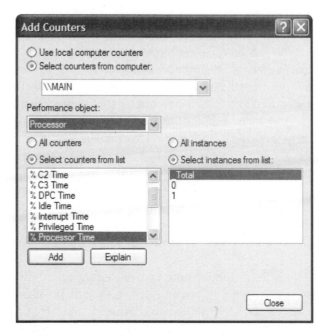

Figure 10-6. The Add Counters dialog box is the starting point for every System Monitor session.

The dialog box shows that you can choose four levels of performance monitoring. The following list describes each level.

Machine: The machine you choose to monitor depends on the circumstances. For example, one performance-monitoring scenario is to compare two machines with the same characteristics and application load. If one machine performs substantially slower than the other, the statistics might indicate the presence of a problem on the slower machine. When working with applications, you'll want to monitor the client for some statistics and the server for other statistics. For example, client monitoring will include browser statistics, while server statistics might include those generated by SQL Server.

Performance object: This is the name of an application containing counters. There's a performance object for each major category of device or application on your machine. For example, Figure 10-6 shows the Processor object. You'll also find objects for the physical and logical disk drive, memory, and network. Applications appear in objects such as browser, job, and thread.

Counter: This entry represents a specific performance-measuring thread within the object. The counter is the portion of the performance monitor that acquires the data. The term *counter* is accurate in this case. The counters actually do count the number of occurrences of an event within a given time interval. For example, when determining the percentage of CPU cycles used to handle user requests, the counter counts both the total processor clock cycles and those used to handle user needs. It then performs a mathematical computation to calculate the percentage.

Instance: In some cases, saying you want to count something doesn't define the problem. For example, if you have two processors and want to determine the percentage of user time, you have to indicate whether you want the user time for one or both processors. You also need to indicate which processor you want to work with if you choose only one.

As you can see, the potential number of performance-monitoring combinations for a single system is immense. A typical system provides a minimum of 40 performance objects. Each of these objects have a number of counters (2 is a minimum and 30 is common). Many of these counters have at least two instances and a _Total instance (the combination of all instances of a counter). In addition, many applications such as SQL Server add their own counters to the mix. If you add multiple machine scenarios into the mix, you can see that System Monitor has a lot to offer.

TIP   *Click Explain in the Add Counters dialog box if you want to know the meaning behind a particular counter. The explanation is relatively short, but usually helpful. It will always provide you with enough information to conduct additional research into the counter.*

This brings up an important point. You don't want to overload a single display with too many counters. Tracking five or six of these counters is difficult on some displays. Adding more than that makes the information hard to track. Select the counters you want to see carefully. If you find that you've selected too many counters, remove a few by highlighting them in the listing and clicking Delete (the X next to the Add button).

After you add the counters, click Close. You'll return to the Performance console and see the counters you selected displaying data. Figure 10-5 shows a typical example of a Performance console display. The line extending from the top to the bottom of the chart area is the current drawing position.

Choosing Counters

Because there are so many counters to choose from, you'll have to exercise some discretion in which counters you track. Sometimes it's a matter of choosing a precise counter based on some application requirement. In other cases, it's a matter of locating the correct counter. Some counters will help almost anyone writing an application. For example, the .NET Framework has a series of counters that you can use to monitor the managed environment. You can learn about everything from memory to network bandwidth usage. There's even a special Interop performance object you can use to measure the cost of including unmanaged components in your application.

Sometimes you'll need to monitor the browser. Interestingly enough, there's an actual Browser performance object, but it has nothing to do with Internet Explorer or any other browser, for that matter. The performance object you want is Process. You'll choose a performance statistic, such as IO Data Bytes/sec next. Finally, you'll choose the application from the instance list. This is one time when it pays to have only one copy of Internet Explorer running, or you'll have a hard time choosing the correct instance.

As previously mentioned, most major applications also install performance objects and associated counters. For example, you'll want to view all of the performance objects that SQL Server provides. Note that you have full access to these counters even if you're using MSDE. However, with MSDE you can't easily access the user settings provided by the SQL Server: User Settable performance object. You have full access to all other SQL Server performance objects including those that monitor the cache.

Interestingly enough, you can't access any IIS statistics using the Web Matrix server. This is another reason that it's more realistic to use a two-machine setup. The Internet Information Services Global performance object contains a number of counters that help you tune the caching for your application. For example, you can monitor the Total Files Cached counter to see how many resources an application uses. It's also interesting to watch the File Cache Hits, File Cache Misses, and File Cache Flushes counters. You can learn a lot about your application by monitoring it first under controlled conditions and then in a production environment.

Setting Graph Properties

Graph appearance is important. For example, you might want to add horizontal or vertical graph lines. Click Properties if you want to change any of the settings. Figure 10-7 shows the General tab of the System Monitor Properties dialog box.

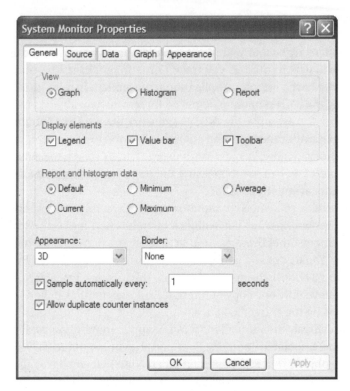

Figure 10-7. The General tab allows you to set graph elements such as the graph type.

As you can see, this tab allows you to select a view. System Monitor supports three views including graph, histogram, and report. You can also select a view using the appropriate button on the toolbar.

Below the views are three options to display with the information: Toolbar, Value Bar, and Legend. The toolbar contains all of the buttons we've discussed to this point. The Value Bar contains a list of all the vital statistics for the counter highlighted in the Legend. For example, you can learn the minimum, maximum, and average values for a particular counter. The Legend lists the selected counters. Each counter entry includes the instance, parent, object, and computer information.

The report and histogram views support only instantaneous data values. Sometimes it's beneficial to see something other than the default data. For example, you might want to see the average data value. The next section of the General tab allows you to change the histogram and report view values. The default setting displays the current (instantaneous) values.

The Sample automatically every setting permits you to update the display more or less often than the default setting of 1 second. Clearing this entry will freeze the display. The Allow duplicate counter instances option tells System Monitor that it's okay to display more than one instance of the same data. This feature comes in handy in report view, but is actually detrimental in other views.

The Data tab shown in Figure 10-8 helps you configure the data display. You begin by selecting one of the entries in the Counters list. This view allows you to change the color of the data, along with the width and style of the line. The scale determines how the lines scale in comparison with the rest of the lines on screen. Using a larger scale can often bring out details about the data, especially if variations are small.

Figure 10-8. Use the Data tab to change the appearance of the data on screen.

The Graph tab contains settings that change graph display elements. This includes the use of a vertical and horizontal grid. You can also give your graph a title and assign a name to the vertical element (the horizontal element is always time). The Vertical Scale properties offer another chance to optimize the graph display. You can set the graph so it displays the data a little larger or smaller than the default settings allow.

Finally, the Appearance tab contains settings that change the colors used to display certain elements such as the graph background and time bar. This tab also enables you to choose a new font for the display. The use of a different font may make information more legible or easier to print.

Creating Custom Consoles

Once you find settings that you like, you can save the settings to disk and reopen them later. Begin by using the File Options command to display the Options dialog box shown in Figure 10-9. This dialog box changes the name and icon for the console. It also contains a Console mode field. The setting in this field determines how much another user of your console can change. In some cases, you might want to set the console to one of the user modes to protect the settings. Using Author mode, as shown in the figure, allows anyone to make any changes they want to the settings.

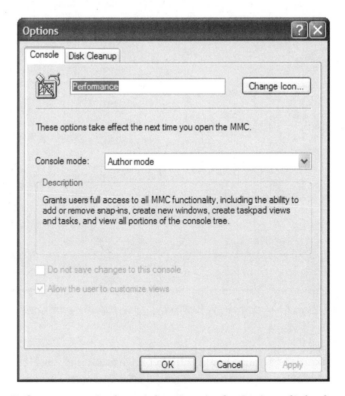

Figure 10-9. Define any required special options in the Options dialog box.

You can also study the settings if you want because the Microsoft Console (MSC) files are actually eXtensible Markup Language (XML) in disguise. If you open one such file in Internet Explorer as shown in Figure 10-10, you can learn a lot about the way Microsoft structures these files. In some cases, you might be able to tweak a console setting after the fact to make the console more appealing.

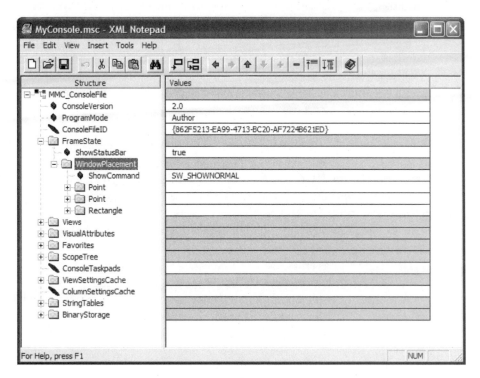

Figure 10-10. MSC files actually contain XML data.

Performance Logs and Alerts

The Performance Logs and Alerts snap-in performs long-term event monitoring. This snap-in performs three different tasks, using three folders: Counter Logs, Trace Logs, and Alerts.

> **Counter Logs:** Performs essentially the same task as System Monitor. It relies on the same counters as System Monitor, but stores the data it collects on disk, rather than displaying it immediately. Of the three tasks that the Performance Logs and Alerts snap-in can perform, this task is the most useful for developers because it allows long-term application monitoring.

Trace Logs: Performs detailed system monitoring. You can choose the types of events it monitors. A trace log can help you see the flow of data on a system or determine when an application is creating too many threads. This part of the snap-in creates special logs that you have to convert into human readable format using the TraceRpt utility. You can read the resulting output in System Monitor or within an application such as Excel (the preferred method in this case).

Alert: Warns you of system conditions. For example, you can use it to warn you that system memory or hard drive space is low. An alert can create event log entries, send you a console message, or run an application as part of the alerting process.

We'll only discuss the Counter Logs option in this chapter. You begin creating a log by right-clicking Counter Logs and choosing either New Log Settings or New Log Settings From. If you choose New Log Settings From, you'll see an Open dialog box from which you can choose an HTM or HTML file containing the appropriate settings. You'll generate this HTM or HTML file by right-clicking an existing Counter Log entry, then selecting Save Settings As from the context menu.

The New Log Settings entry displays a New Log Settings dialog box. Type a name for the counter log and click OK. You'll see a properties dialog box like the one shown for MyLog in Figure 10-11. You'll need to add counters to the Counters field before you can use the counter log to gather statistics.

Figure 10-11. Use the report view to organize large numbers of counters into an easy-to-read report.

The counters and objects used with the counter logs are the same as those used for System Monitor. In fact, when you click Add Counters, you'll see the same Add Counters dialog box as shown in Figure 10-6. Click Add Objects, and you'll see a dialog box that only allows you to select a machine and a performance object. If you select a counter, then you're selecting just that counter or even a counter instance. When you select an object, it includes all the counters within that object.

After you select some objects or counters, you can set the sampling interval. Short intervals produce more data, so you'll get results that are more precise. However, using short intervals also makes the impact of performance monitoring more severe. Again, it's a matter of balancing system resources and performance against the performance monitoring requirements.

After you set everything up, click OK. If you're using the default Start Log settings, the Performance Logs and Alerts snap-in will begin the logging immediately. Otherwise, you'll need to start the logging manually by right-clicking the Counter Log object and selecting Start, or waiting until the predefined conditions occur.

To view the content of a log file, open System Monitor and click View Log Data (the icon that looks like a database symbol). You'll see the Source tab of the System Monitor Properties dialog box. Click Log Files (or database, if you saved the data in that form). Click Add, and then select the log file(s) you want to view. Note that you can add more than one log file to the list to see a longer interval. Make certain that all the logs come from the same counter log. If you think you might want to limit the interval viewed on screen, click Time Range. Figure 10-12 shows an example of the Source tab with the Time Range feature enabled.

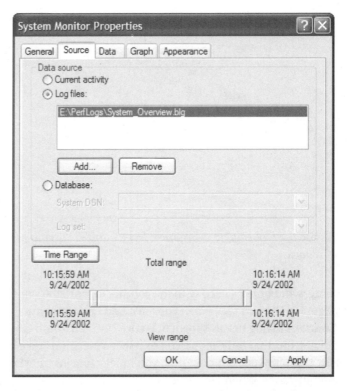

Figure 10-12. Selecting a log to view is as easy as changing the data source for System Monitor.

Click OK and you'll see the static data collected in the log. Of course, this means you won't see the time bar moving across the screen—System Monitor only uses the time bar when it has active data to read. All of the other options that you use for active data apply when working with a log. For example, you can display a graph, histogram, or report version of your log.

Understanding Output Caching

To some extent, we've already discussed the issue of output caching in the "Using the Output Caching Page" section of Chapter 8. However, Web Matrix also provides a separate section of caching pages in the Output Caching category. You can see these pages in the Add New File dialog box shown in Figure 10-13.

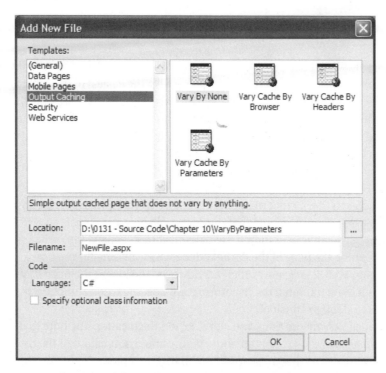

Figure 10-13. Select one of the caching options from the Add New Files dialog box.

Each of these pages has something different to offer in the way of performance enhancement. The following sections will show you how to use each page and describe how each page differs. Based on the information in these subsections, you can choose a caching option that meets your specific needs. Theoretically, each of these pages is actually just a prototype, and you do have other options. Realistically, they reflect some of the better options at your disposal, and you'll do well to try them out for a while. Each of the example pages is a mini-application in its own right, so you can see the effects of caching with relative ease.

TIP *All of these pages rely on some form of the ASP.NET @outputcache directive. You can learn more about this directive and all its parameters at* http://msdn.microsoft.com/library/en-us/cpgenref/html/cpconoutputcache.asp.

Using the Vary By None Page

The Vary By None page provides "fair" output caching in that every client will receive the same page until it expires. This is also the easiest of the caching schemes to implement because it only requires two settings. Here's the line of code you'd add to the All tab of the editor if you wanted to implement the "vary by none" scheme in your project.

```
<%@ outputcache duration="10" varybyparam="none" %>
```

As you can see, all that this scheme requires is that you decide on a valid output cache duration—the time that the cache will hold the current page in seconds. Use a longer duration if the data on your Web page won't change very often. Keeping the page in the cache reduces the wait time for the user and also makes your Web server more efficient. However, the longer the page stays in the cache, the more outdated the its information becomes. Consequently, there's always a tradeoff to consider.

Besides varying the time, you can also add the location attribute to the @ outputcache directive. This attribute determines the location of the cache. The default value places the cache anywhere that's convenient. Generally, this means the cache will appear on the client, but it could also appear on a proxy server, a requesting server, or even the server that processed the request. By creating the cache in a specific location, you affect the usefulness of the cache to a group of people. For example, a cache located on the client won't store information from other sources.

Given that this caching scheme sends the same page to every client, it's not optimized for specific client needs. In general, this means that the client might not display the page optimally. Whether this caching technique represents a problem for your Web application depends on the type of clients that you expect to visit. You'll find that this type of caching works well in situations where you know the kind of clients that will visit in advance. For example, if you run a local company intranet, you have full control over the client the user has installed and can therefore make maximum use of this page.

Using a single-client cache does have disadvantages, but it also has advantages. If the application only stores one copy of the page that will serve every client, it saves memory and other server resources. In short, this scheme has the advantage of being extremely efficient with server resources, in addition to being the easiest caching scheme to implement. Figure 10-14 shows sample output from the default caching application.

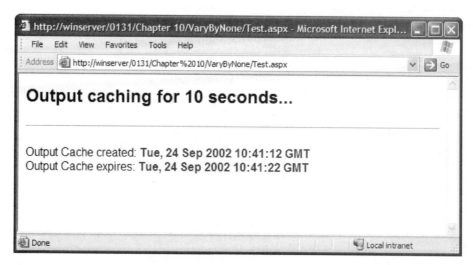

Figure 10-14. Try refreshing this display several times to see the effect of generic caching.

Using the Vary Cache By Browser Page

The Vary By Browser page does what its name implies—it caches individual pages based on the browser type. As you might imagine, using a location attribute for this type of caching will increase the benefit derived from the caching. Storing one version of the page for each browser that requests information from a proxy server would mean that the individual clients wouldn't need to store the information. The @ outputcache directive for this page looks like this:

```
<%@ outputcache duration="10" varybyparam="none" varybycustom="browser" %>
```

Notice that the varybyparam attribute value is the same as the "vary by none" scheme, but in this case, we've added a varybycustom attribute. This attribute determines the type of custom caching the page will perform. The only value you can supply for the varybycustom entry is browser, as shown. If you want to provide another custom value, you must override the HttpApplication.GetVaryByCustomString() method in the Global.ASAX file. We

won't discuss such complex alterations in this book, but you can find out
more at http://msdn.microsoft.com/library/en-us/cpguide/html/
cpconcachingversionsofpagebasedoncustomstrings.asp.

It's important to realize that this form of caching does use more memory. For
example, if you anticipate serving pages to two types of browsers, you'll use twice
the memory of the "vary by none" scheme. However, the additional memory provides a benefit by helping ensure that every page the server sends out is
optimized for that type of browser. Given that browser compatibility is still an
issue, this form of caching will keep users happier.

This form of caching also brings a new object into play, Request.Browser.
This object tells you about the browser making the request. The example provided by Web Matrix displays the browser's name and major version number.
However, this object has a lot more to provide. For example, you can learn if the
browser supports Java applets or JavaScript. You can learn more about this
object at http://msdn.microsoft.com/library/en-us/cpguide/html/
cptskdetectingbrowsertypesinwebforms.asp. Listing 10-1 also shows a modified
version of the default example that includes many of the Request.Browser values.

Listing 10-1. Summarizing the Requesting Browser Capabilities

```
public void Page_Load(Object sender, EventArgs e)
{

    // Display all of the browser statistics.
    BrowserDetails.Text =
        "</br>Type: " + Request.Browser.Type +
        "</br>Browser: " + Request.Browser.Browser +
        "</br>Version: " + Request.Browser.Version +
        "</br>Major Version: " + Request.Browser.MajorVersion.ToString() +
        "</br>Minor Version: " + Request.Browser.MinorVersion.ToString() +
        "</br>Platform: " + Request.Browser.Platform +
        "</br>Is this a beta? " + Request.Browser.Beta +
        "</br>Is this a crawler? " + Request.Browser.Crawler +
        "</br>Is this AOL? " + Request.Browser.AOL +
        "</br>Is this a Win16 machine? " + Request.Browser.Win16 +
        "</br>Is this a Win32 machine? " + Request.Browser.Win32 +
        "</br>Does the browser support frames? " + Request.Browser.Frames +
        "</br>Does the browser support tables? " + Request.Browser.Tables +
        "</br>Does the browser support cookies? " +
            Request.Browser.Cookies +
        "</br>Does the browser support VB Script? " +
            Request.Browser.VBScript +
        "</br>Does the browser support JavaScript? " +
            Request.Browser.JavaScript +
        "</br>Does the browser support Java applets? " +
```

```
        Request.Browser.JavaApplets +
    "</br>Does the browser support ActiveX Controls? " +
        Request.Browser.ActiveXControls;


    // Display the time stamp information.
    TimestampCreated.Text = DateTime.Now.ToString("r");
    TimestampExpires.Text = DateTime.Now.AddSeconds(10).ToString("r");
}
```

As you can see, the Request.Browser object can provide you with a significant amount of information about the client. Now that you have an idea of how this example will work, let's look at it. Figure 10-15 shows the output of the slightly modified Vary By Browser example. Notice the amount of information that this example provides about the browser.

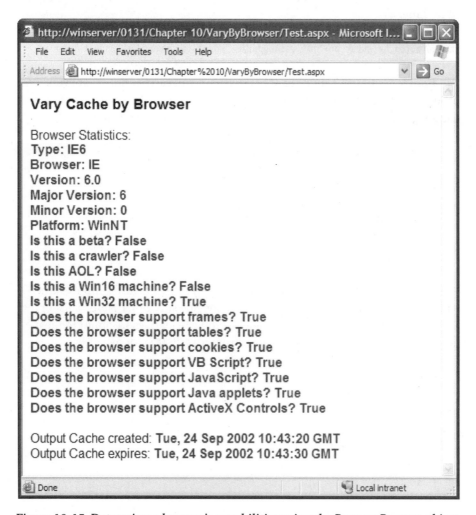

Figure 10-15. Determining a browser's capabilities using the Request.Browser object.

Using the Vary Cache By Headers Page

The headers provided as part of a client request tell a lot about a client, but not the actual client type. For example, client requests can vary by language. The Accept-Language header tells you which languages the client will accept. By checking for this header, you know more about the user making the request, even though you don't know anything more about the browser the user is using. ASP.NET can work with any of the standardized headers. In addition, you can request that it track multiple headers. The server will cache one copy of the page for each header combination. Obviously, requesting more than a few headers could become quite expensive from a resource usage perspective. However, the output provided by the server would be customized for specific user needs. This is one situation when you might consider caching the pages on the client, rather than on the server. Here's an example of the @ outputcache directive for this type of caching.

```
<%@ outputcache duration="10" varybyparam="none" varybyheader="Accept-Language" %>
```

Browsers support a number of headers, but you can't be sure that every browser will support every header you might request. Besides the Accept-Language header, most browsers will include the following headers:

- Authorization

- From

- If-Modified-Since

- User-Agent

In addition to these common headers, many browsers also support some standard headers that you'll find helpful in specific situations. Here's a list of the standard, but less supported, headers. (You can learn more about request headers at http://www.w3.org/pub/WWW/Protocols/HTTP/1.0/spec.txt.)

- Connection

- Accept

- Accept-Encoding

- Host

Along with the @ outputcache directive attributes, this caching scheme also has a special object, Request.Headers. You work with the Request.Headers object using a string as an index into a list of headers that the client provides. Listing 10-2 contains a modified version of the default Vary By Headers page that lists a few additional header values.

Listing 10-2. Summarizing the Request Headers

```
void Page_Load(Object sender, EventArgs e)
{

    // Obtain the header details.
    HeaderDetails.Text =
        "Accept-Language: " + Request.Headers["Accept-Language"] +
        "</br>Authorization: " + Request.Headers["Authorization"] +
        "</br>From: " + Request.Headers["From"] +
        "</br>If-Modified-Since: " + Request.Headers["If-Modified-Since"] +
        "</br>User-Agent: " + Request.Headers["User-Agent"] +
        "</br>Connection: " + Request.Headers["Connection"] +
        "</br>Accept: " + Request.Headers["Accept"] +
        "</br>Accept-Encoding: " + Request.Headers["Accept-Encoding"] +
        "</br>Host: " + Request.Headers["Host"];

    // Display the timestamp information.
    TimestampCreated.Text = DateTime.Now.ToString("r");
    TimestampExpires.Text = DateTime.Now.AddSeconds(10).ToString("r");
}
```

As you can see, each of the Request.Header entries uses a standard index to request the header information. When you try this example, you might notice that the browser you use doesn't include all of the information the example is capable of providing. When the application requests information that Request.Headers can't provide, it returns a blank (empty) string. Figure 10-16 shows typical output from this application.

Figure 10-16. Use the Request.Header object to gain access to header information.

Using the Vary Cache By Parameters Page

The last of the pages we'll discuss is the Vary Cache By Parameters page. This page differentiates between clients by a specific parameter. You can use any data value that the client is expected to provide as a cache value. For example, it's possible to cache pages by location or by customer type. The example page uses a parameter named Category as shown by the following @ outputcache directive.

```
<%@ outputcache duration="100" varybyparam="Category" %>
```

The parameter must arrive along with the rest of the request data. Normally, it appears as a piece of data sent with a form, as in the case of this example. The `<asp:DropDownList>` shown here has the Category ID.

```
<asp:DropDownList id="Category" runat="server">
```

When the user selects a category, and then clicks a button to submit the form, the data goes to the server along with the rest of the request. At the server, the server caches pages according to the category requested. This particular caching technique can use as little or as much memory as you want to devote to a particular need. Unlike caching by the header or the browser value, this caching technique can only have so many page types, and you're in control of them. Consequently, it's easier to determine the application caching resource requirements. Figure 10-17 shows typical output from this application.

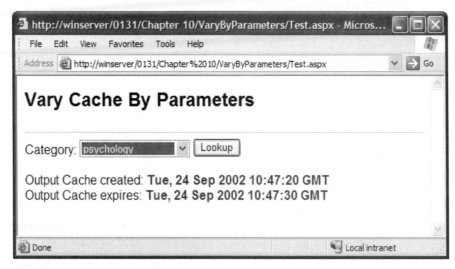

Figure 10-17. Learn the effects of using parameters with this example.

Putting It All Together

We've studied each of the caching methodologies as a separate topic. In many cases, all that you need to provide for an application is one form of caching to ensure that every client receives the type of page they need in a timely manner. However, as your application becomes more complex, you might find that you need additional caching to provide good performance. In these cases, you can combine caching types (exercising care to ensure you have the required resources). For example, you might want to cache pages by both request header type and browser type. You might want to cache a page for each browser used by every language.

Choosing the location for the cache is important too. If you're using generic caching, as we did for the Vary By None page, then the location of the cache isn't as important, but it does become important as your caching scheme becomes more complex. For example, if you're caching by a specific header value, you might want to use the client machine for cache storage to ensure the server doesn't get bogged down. However, when working with a relatively generic cache value such as the type of browser, you might want to use the server for storage.

The important consideration is monitoring. As you learned in the "Working with the Performance Console" section of the chapter, you don't know what effects a cache will have on performance until you monitor the results. In many cases, you'll need to monitor the cache over an extended timeframe to fine-tune the settings. Setting the duration of the cache before it expires can require long-term monitoring to ensure you select the best overall value and don't set the cache for a value that works best during only one part of the day.

An important concept to remember is that developing a cache strategy should come after you've debugged and optimized your application. Using a cache represents a tradeoff—you're trading resources for improved performance. At some point, your application will run out of resources, and the effects of the cache will diminish. Tuning your application is always a pure performance enhancement—tuning often results in lower resource usage. Consider the cache your last tuning step.

Summary

This chapter has helped you understand many elements of performance monitoring—at least when it comes to Web Matrix applications. We've discussed how to use the downloadable controls to create a better user environment, and you've learned about the various features Web Matrix installs to improve performance. Finally, we've discussed the issue of performance monitoring as both a diagnostic tool and a yardstick for measuring application performance.

By now, you should have a few new ideas on how to improve the performance of your applications. It's a good time to look at your applications again, but this time from a performance angle. Use the ideas you've garnered from the chapter to build a faster application—one that does the same work as before, but does it more efficiently. And don't forget to listen to your users—and monitor your logs! Have fun, and best of luck!

You're at the end of the book! Hopefully you'll find that Web Matrix is going to be as important a part of your toolbox as I have in my explorations. Of course, there are still many ways to use Web Matrix that we haven't touched on in the book, and I'd like to hear your ideas about them. Be sure to contact me at JMueller@mwt.net with your latest Web Matrix task idea.

The fun isn't over quite yet. You'll find an appendix at the end of this book that provides you with 52 additional ways to improve your Web Matrix experience. The appendix will make your Web Matrix experience more enjoyable and rewarding.

Part Three

Glossary and Appendix

Glossary

This book includes a glossary so that you can find terms and acronyms easily. It has several important features of which you need to be aware. First, every acronym in the entire book is listed here—even if there's a better-than-even chance you already know what the acronym means. This way, you'll find everything you need to use the book properly.

Second, these definitions are specific to the book. In other words, when you look through this glossary, you're seeing the words defined in the context in which the book uses them. This might or might not always coincide with current industry usage, since the computer industry changes the meaning of words so often.

Finally, the definitions here use a conversational tone in most cases. This means they might sacrifice a bit of puritanical accuracy for the sake of better understanding. The purpose of this glossary is to define the terms in such a way that there's less room for misunderstanding the intent of the book as a whole.

While this glossary is a complete view of the words and acronyms in the book, you'll run into situations when you need to know more. No matter how closely I look at terms throughout the book, there's always a chance I'll miss the one acronym or term that you really need to know. In addition to the technical information found in the book, I've directed your attention to numerous online sources of information throughout the book, and few of the terms the Web site owners use will appear here unless I also chose to use them in the book. Fortunately, many sites on the Internet provide partial or complete glossaries to fill in the gaps:

Acronym Finder: http://www.acronymfinder.com/

Acronym Search: http://www.acronymsearch.com/

The Acronym Database: http://www.ucc.ie/acronyms/

Microsoft Encarta: http://encarta.msn.com/

University of Texas Acronyms and Abbreviations:
http://www-hep.uta.edu/~variable/e_comm/pages/r_dic-en.htm

Webopedia: http://Webopedia.internet.com/

yourDictionary.com (formerly A Web of Online Dictionaries):
http://www.yourdictionary.com/

Let's talk about these Web sites a little more. Web sites normally provide acronyms or glossary entries—not both. An acronym site only tells you what the letters in the acronym stand for; it doesn't provide definitions to explain what the acronym means concerning everyday computer use. The two extremes in this list are Acronym Finder (acronyms only) and Webopedia (full-fledged glossary entries).

The owner of Acronym Finder doesn't update the site as often as the University of Texas updates theirs, but Acronym Finder does have the advantage of providing an extremely large list of acronyms from which to choose. At the time of this writing, the Acronym Finder sported 164,000 acronyms. The University of Texas Acronyms and Abbreviations site receives updates often and provides only acronyms (another page at the same site includes a glossary).

Most of the Web sites that you'll find for computer terms are free. In some cases, such as Microsoft's Encarta, you have to pay for the support provided. However, these locations are still worth the effort because they ensure you understand the terms used in the jargon-filled world of computing.

Webopedia has become one of my favorite places to visit because it provides encyclopedic coverage of many computer terms and includes links to other Web sites. I like the fact that if I don't find a word I need, I can submit it to the Webopedia staff for addition to their dictionary, making Webopedia a community-supported dictionary of the highest quality.

One of the interesting features of the yourDictionary.com Web site is that it provides access to more than one dictionary and in more than one language. If English isn't your native tongue, then this is the Web site of choice for you.

Word List

TERM	MEANING
A	
Active Server Pages (ASP)	A special type of scripting language environment used by Windows servers equipped with Internet Information Server (IIS). This specialized scripting language environment helps the developer create flexible Web applications that include server scripts written in a number of languages such as VBScript, JavaScript, JScript, and PerlScript. The use of variables and other features, such as access to server variables, helps the developer create scripts that can compensate for user and environmental needs as well as security concerns. ASP uses HTML to display content to the user. Recent extensions to ASP in the form of Active Server Pages eXtended (ASPX) provide a broader range of application support functionality, improved debugging, new features such as "code behind," and improved performance.
ActiveX Control	*See* **OCX**
Application	The complete program or group of programs. An application is a complete environment for performing one or more related tasks.
Array	A structure that acts like an in-memory database. An array provides random or sequential access to each element by number (also called a *subscript*). Arrays normally contain a single dimension. In some cases, arrays provide multidimensional access to data. A multidimensional array has the same number of elements in each subarray in a given dimension. Jagged arrays treat each dimension as a separate subarray, which means that each subarray can contain a different number of elements.
ASP	*See* **Active Server Pages**

TERM	MEANING
B	
Binary	1. A numbering system that only uses two digits: 0 and 1. 2. A method used to store worksheets, graphic files, and other nontext information. The data store can appear in memory, but most often appears in a file on disk. While you can use the DOS TYPE command to send these files to the display, the contents of the file remain unreadable. Other binary files include programs with extensions of EXE, DLL, or COM.
Biometrics	A statistical method of scanning an individual's unique characteristics, normally body parts, to ensure that they are who they say they are. Some of the scanned elements include voiceprints, irises, fingerprints, hands, and facial features. The two most popular elements are irises and fingerprints because they're the two that most people are familiar with. The advantages of using biometrics are obvious. Not only can't the user lose their identifying information (at least not very easily), but with proper scanning techniques the identifying information can't be compromised either.
Browser	A special application such as Internet Explorer, Opera, or Netscape, normally used to display data downloaded from the Internet. The most common form of Internet data is the HyperText Markup Language (HTML) page. However, modern browsers can also display various types of graphics and even standard desktop application files such as Word for Windows documents directly. The actual capabilities provided by a browser vary widely depending on the software vendor and platform.

TERM	MEANING
C	
CAB	*See* **Cabinet File**
Cabinet File (CAB)	1. A compressed-format file similar to the ZIP files used to transfer code and data from one location to another. Only developers who work with Microsoft language products normally use the CAB format, but any developer working in the Windows environment could use them. 2. A single file created to hold a number of compressed files. A related set of cabinet files can be contained in a folder. During installation of a program, the compressed files in a cabinet are decompressed and copied to an appropriate directory for the user.
Cascading Style Sheets (CSS)	A method for defining a standard Web page template. This may include headings, standard icons, backgrounds, and other features that would tend to give each page at a particular Web site the same appearance. The reason for using CSS includes improving the speed of creating a Web site (it takes less time if the developer doesn't have to create an overall design for each page) and consistency. Changing the overall appearance of a Web site also becomes as easy as changing the style sheet instead of each page alone. CSS is also a standards-supported technology, so it represents an easy method for developers to create Web pages that will work in standards-compliant browsers.
cHTML	*See* **Compact HyperText Markup Language**
Client	The requestor and recipient of data, services, or resources from a file or other server type. This term can refer to a workstation or an application. Often used in conjunction with the term *server*, this is usually another PC or an application.
CLR	*See* **Common Language Runtime**

TERM	MEANING
Code Behind	A type of Web page scripting technology most closely associated with Active Server Pages eXtended (ASPX) that separates the user interface of the Web page from the code required to make the page functional. The advantage of this approach is that the developer spends less time looking for application code—reducing the time of some tasks such as debugging. The code behind portion contains all of the functions and methods that the Web page uses to control various display elements and to perform programming tasks in the background such as opening a database connection. The code behind file normally has the same name as the ASPX page, with the programming language suffix appended. For example, if the user interface portion of the application is Default.ASPX, the code behind portion might appear in the Default.ASPX.CS file when using C# as the coding language.
Code Builder	A specialized application component (also known as a wizard) for programming language Integrated Development Environments (IDEs) or other developer-oriented tools that requests input from the developer and uses this input to generate application code. The use of a code builder ensures that the developer can create consistent code in the shortest time possible. Wizards of this type automate many error-prone, repetitive coding tasks—making the code easier to read and reducing errors. Many of these benefits are derived from the fact that the code builder always produces the same output for a given input.
COM	*See* **Component Object Model**

TERM	MEANING
Common Language Runtime (CLR)	The engine used to interpret managed applications within the .NET Framework. All Visual Studio .NET languages that produce managed applications can use the same runtime engine. The major advantages of this approach include extensibility (you can add other languages) and reduced code size (you don't need a separate runtime for each language).
Compact HyperText Markup Language (cHTML)	A form of HyperText Markup Language (HTML) especially designed for mobile device use. Pages creating using cHTML have the same appearance as HTML. However, cHTML doesn't support Joint Pictures Experts Group (JPEG) images, tables, image maps, multiple fonts or font styles, background colors or images, frames, Cascading Style Sheets (CSS), or more than two colors. All user tasks in cHTML rely on the use of the following four buttons, rather than on a full keyboard: cursor forward, cursor backward, select, and back/stop. The Japan-based Access Company originated cHTML for use with i-mode devices. The protocol is used less now that most companies are developing around the eXtensible HyperText Markup Language (XHTML).
Component Object Model (COM)	A Microsoft specification for a binary-based, object-oriented code and data encapsulation method and transference technique. It's the basis for technologies such as Object Linking and Embedding (OLE) and ActiveX (the replacement name for OCXs—an object-oriented code library technology). COM is limited to local connections. Distributed Component Object Model (DCOM) is the technology used to allow data transfers and the use of OCXs within the Internet environment. However, difficulties in making DCOM work over the Internet have made the text-based eXtensible Markup Language (XML) technologies such as the Simple Object Access Protocol (SOAP) popular.

TERM	MEANING
Console	1. A type of character-mode application that normally runs at the DOS (command) prompt. A console application normally performs a simple or utilitarian task that doesn't require the Graphical User Interface (GUI) associated with most application development today. 2. The generic term for a workstation used to monitor server status information. In most cases, the workstation and server are the same device. Most people associate consoles with a character mode interface, but this isn't a requirement.
Cookie	One or more special files used by an Internet browser to store site-specific settings or other information specific to Web pages. The purpose of this file is to store the value of one or more variables so that the Web page can restore them the next time the user visits a site. A Webmaster always saves and restores the cookie as part of some Web page programming task using a programming language such as JavaScript, Java, VBScript, or CGI. In most cases, this is the only file that a Webmaster can access on the client site's hard drive. The cookie could appear in one or more files anywhere on the hard drive, depending on the browser currently in use. Microsoft Internet Explorer uses one file for each site storing a cookie and places them in the Cookies folder that normally appears under the main Windows directory or within a user specific directory (such as the \Documents and Settings folder). Netscape Navigator uses a single file named COOKIE.TXT to store all of the cookies from all sites. This file normally appears in the main Navigator folder.

TERM	MEANING
Counter	1. An application designed to measure performance on a Windows system. The counter is part of a performance object. It's normally stored with other counters associated with the same performance object within a Dynamic Link Library (DLL) on the host machine. A counter may allow monitoring of one or more instances of the same type of device or other object as individual performance statistics. 2. A specialized programming structure used to track application data. In some cases, the counter is a specialized object the developer adds to the application for the purpose of statistical data collection.
Cracker	A hacker (computer expert) who uses their skills for misdeeds on computer systems where they have little or no authorized access. A cracker normally possesses specialty software that allows easier access to the target network. In most cases, crackers require extensive amounts of time to break the security for a system before they can enter it. Some sources call a cracker a *black hat hacker*.
CSS	*See* **Cascading Style Sheets**

D

Data Stream	One of several methods to send or access information that resides either in local or remote storage. A data stream consists of a series of bits taken from any location within a data storage unit (such as a file). The information can flow continuously (as in an Internet transfer for music) or in blocks (as occurs when reading data from a file on the local hard drive). The reading and writing sequence need not use blocks of any given size, and the transfer often works with individual bits rather than characters or words.

TERM	MEANING
Database Management System (DBMS)	A method for storing and retrieving data based on tables, forms, queries, reports, fields, and other data elements. Each field represents a specific piece of data, such as an employee's last name. Records are made up of one or more fields. Each record is one complete entry in a table. A table contains one type of data, such as the names and addresses of all the employees in a company. It's composed of records (rows) and fields (columns), just like the tables you see in books. A database may contain one or more related tables. It may include a list of employees in one table, for example, and the pay records for each of those employees in a second table. Sometimes also referred to as a Relational Database Management System (RDBMS), which includes products such as SQL Server, Access, and Oracle.
DBMS	*See* **Database Management System**
DCOM	*See* **Distributed Component Object Model**
DDE	*See* **Dynamic Data Exchange**
DISCO	*See* **Discovery of Web Services**
Discovery of Web Services (DISCO)	A service associated with the Internet that's designed to make it easier to locate and use SOAP services. This particular service is SOAP specific and a single vendor, Microsoft, currently supports it. The DISCO service relies on a special protocol named SOAP Contract Language (SCL) to allow the discovery of services by remote computers.

TERM	MEANING
Distributed Application	An application that resides on more than one machine; normally a client and server, but is not necessarily limited to this configuration. The application could include multiple levels of clients and servers, commonly referred to as tiers. The application is composed of multiple interchangeable elements. For example, a server component could service more than one application type. The application elements are loosely coupled (both systems only require access to self-describing messages), and the developer can replace each element with updates as needed as long as the new element provides the same interface to the client.
Distributed Component Object Model (DCOM)	A transport protocol that works with the component object model (COM), and is used for distributed application development. This protocol enables data transfers across the Internet or other nonlocal sources, but is usually limited to a Local Area Network (LAN) or Wide Area Network (WAN) environment. DCOM adds the capability to perform asynchronous, as well as synchronous, data transfers between machines. The use of asynchronous transfers prevents the client application from becoming blocked as it waits for the server to respond. See COM for more details.
DLL	*See* **Dynamic Link Library**
Document Type Definition (DTD)	A document that defines how an application should interpret markup tags within an HTML, XML, or SGML document. In some cases, such as HTML, the DTD is an actual specification. In other cases, such as XML, the DTD is an external document supplied by the user or the vendor. A DTD can define every characteristic of a document as long as those characteristics are specified using standard tags and attributes.
DTD	*See* **Document Type Definition**

TERM	MEANING
Dynamic Data Exchange (DDE)	1. The capability to place data from one application on the Windows clipboard and paste it from the clipboard into another application. A user can cut a graphics image created with a paint program, for example, and paste it into a word processing document. After it's pasted, the data doesn't reflect the changes made to it by the originating application. The source and target applications must provide DDE functionality for this technology to work. They must also support the data formats required for the information exchange. 2. A method for communicating with an application that supports it and requesting data or services. The communication parameters include the application, the topic of the conversation, and a DDE message. In most cases, the DDE message consists of a series of menu or macro sequences that perform the desired task.
Dynamic Link Library (DLL)	A specific form of application code loaded into memory by request. It's not executable by itself like an EXE is. A DLL does contain one or more discrete routines that an application may use to provide specific features. For example, a DLL could provide a common set of file dialogs used to access information on the hard drive. More than one application can use the functions provided by a DLL, reducing overall memory requirements when more than one application is running. DLLs have a number of purposes. For example, they can contain device-specific code in the form of a device driver. Some types of COM objects also rely on DLLs.

E

Encryption	The act of making data unreadable unless the reader provides a password or other key value. Encryption makes data reasonably safe for transport in unsecured environments like the Internet.

TERM	MEANING
eXtensible HyperText Markup Language (XHTML)	A cross between XML and HTML specifically designed for Internet devices such as Personal Digital Assistants (PDAs) and cellular telephones, but also usable with desktop machine browsers. Since this language relies on XML, most developers classify it as an XML application builder. The language relies on several standardized namespaces to provide common data type and interface definitions. XHTML creates modules that are interpreted based on a specific platform's requirements. This means that a single document can serve the needs of many display devices.
eXtensible Markup Language (XML)	1. A method used to store information in an organized manner. The storage technique relies on hierarchical organization and uses special statements called *tags* to separate each storage element. Each tag defines a data attribute and can contain properties that further define each data element. 2. A standardized Web page design language used to incorporate data structuring within standard HTML documents. For example, you could use XML to display database information using something other than forms or tables. It's actually a lightweight version of Standard Generalized Markup Language (SGML) and is supported by the SGML community. XML also supports tag extensions that allow various parts of a Web-based application to exchange information. For example, once a user makes a choice within a catalog, that information could be added to an order entry form with a minimum of effort on the part of the developer. Since XML is easy to extend, some developers look at it as more of a base specification for other languages, rather than a complete language.

TERM	MEANING
eXtensible Style Language (XSL)	This term is also listed as eXtensible Stylesheet Language by some sources. XSL is a technology that separates the method of presentation from the actual content of either an eXtensible Markup Language (XML) or HyperText Markup Language (HTML) page. The XSL document contains all of the required formatting information so that the content remains in pure form. This is the second style language submitted to the World Wide Web Consortium (W3C) for consideration. The first specification was for Cascading Style Sheets (CSS). XSL documents use an XML-like format.
eXtensible Style Language Transformation (XSLT)	The language used within the eXtensible Style Language (XSL) to transform the content provided in an eXtensible Markup Language (XML) file into a form for display on screen or printing. An XSL processor combines XML content with the formatting instructions provided by XSLT and outputs a new document or document fragment. XSLT is a World Wide Web Consortium (W3C) standard.

F

| File Transfer Protocol (FTP) | One of several common data transfer protocols for the Internet. This particular protocol specializes in data transfer in the form of a file download or upload. The site presents the user with a list of available files in a directory list format. An FTP site may choose DOS or UNIX formatting for the file listing, although the DOS format is extremely rare. Unlike HTTP sites, an FTP site provides a definite information hierarchy using directories and subdirectories, much like the file directory structure used on most workstation hard drives. Generally, FTP transfers require a special application, but some browsers now include this capability. FTP transfers occur without encryption, so security is an issue unless the owner of the FTP site encrypts the individual files. |

TERM	MEANING
Folder	When used in context of Windows, a specialized area for storing files on the hard drive. Folders help you manage both data and applications by breaking them up into smaller, easier-to-recognize groups. The DOS equivalent term for folders is *directories*—the same term used by many other operating systems. Sometimes referred to as a subdirectory and viewed with Explorer.
FTP	*See* **File Transfer Protocol**

G

GAC	*See* **Global Assembly Cache**
Global Assembly Cache (GAC)	A central repository used by the .NET Framework for storing public managed components. The GAC contains only components with strong names, ensuring the integrity of the cache. In addition, the GAC can hold multiple versions of the same component, which ensures that applications can access the version of a component that they need, rather than the single version accessible to all applications.
Graphical User Interface (GUI)	1. A method of displaying information that depends on both hardware capabilities and software instructions. A GUI uses the graphics capability of a display adapter to improve communication between the computer and its user. Using a GUI involves a large investment in both programming and hardware resources. 2. A system of icons and graphic images that replace the character-mode menu system used by many older machines including "green screen" terminals that are connected to mainframes and sometimes to cash registers. The GUI can ride on top of another operating system (such as DOS, Linux, and UNIX) or reside as part of the operating system itself (such as the Macintosh OS and Windows). Advantages of a GUI are ease of use and high-resolution graphics. Disadvantages include cost, higher workstation hardware requirements, and lower performance over a similar system using a character mode interface.

TERM	MEANING
GUI	*See* **Graphical User Interface**

H

Hacker	An individual who works with computers at a low level (hardware or software), especially in the area of security. A hacker normally possesses specialty software or other tools that allow easier access to the target hardware or software application or network. The media defines two types of hackers that include those that break into systems for ethical purposes and those that do it to damage the system in some way. The proper term for the second group is *crackers* (see **Cracker** for details). Some people have started to call the first group *ethical hackers* or *white hat hackers* to prevent confusion. Ethical hackers normally work for security firms that specialize in finding holes in a company's security. However, hackers work in a wide range of computer arenas. For example, a person who writes low-level code (like that found in a device driver) after reverse engineering an existing driver is technically a hacker. The main emphasis of a hacker is to work for the benefit of others in the computer industry.
Handheld Device Markup Language (HDML)	A technology that predates most standardized efforts, such as the Wireless Access Protocol (WAP), for transmitting Internet content to cellular telephones. It's a proprietary language that users can only view using Openwave browsers. The associated transport protocol is the Handheld Device Transport Protocol (HDTP). A user types a request into the phone, which is transferred to a gateway server using HDTP. The gateway server translates the request to HTTP, which it sends to the Web server. The Web server provides specialized HDML content, which the gateway server transfers to the cellular telephone using HDTP. To use this protocol, the Web server must understand the text/x-hdml MIME type.

TERM	MEANING
Handheld Device Transport Protocol (HDTP)	A specialized set of rules for sending requests and receiving responses using a mobile device such as a cellular telephone or Personal Digital Assistant (PDA). This transport provides the same services as HTTP, but with the needs of mobile devices in mind.
Handle	A pointer to a resource allocation. The handle provides a method for the application to "grasp" and use the resource. Handles are used for a variety of programming tasks, including gaining access to a window. If an application wants to allow an external function to manipulate a resource it owns, it usually passes the resource handle to allow the external function access.
HDML	*See* **Handheld Device Markup Language**
HDTP	*See* **Handheld Device Transport Protocol**
Hierarchical	1. A method of arranging data within a database that relies on a tree-like node structure, rather than a relational structure. 2. A method of displaying information on screen that relies on an indeterminate number of nodes connected to a root node. 3. A chart or graph in which the elements are arranged in ranks. The ranks usually follow an order of simple to complex or higher to lower.
Histogram	A special variation of the bar graph that shows the frequency with which a data point appears within a specific range.
HTM/HTML File	A file containing the tags, scripts, and comments normally associated with Web content formatted using the HyperText Markup Language (HTML). The version of HTML contained in the file is important. HTML comes in a number of versions, each of which adds functionality to the previous version. The version of HTML supported by a browser often affects the functionality of that browser and could determine the compatibility issues faced by the users of that browser. The World Wide Web Consortium (W3C) manages changes to the HTML specification.

TERM	MEANING
HTML	*See* **Hypertext Markup Language**
HTTP	*See* **Hypertext Transfer Protocol**
Hypertext Markup Language (HTML)	1. A scripting and data presentation (markup) language for the Internet that depends on the use of tags (keywords within angle brackets <>) to display formatted information on screen in a non–platform-specific manner. The non–platform-specific nature of this scripting language makes it difficult to perform some basic tasks such as placement of a screen element at a specific location. However, the language does provide for the use of fonts, color, and various other enhancements on screen. There are also tags for displaying graphic images. Scripting tags for using more complex scripting languages such as VBScript and JavaScript are available, although not all browsers support this addition. Another tag addition allows the use of ActiveX controls. 2. One method of displaying text, graphics, and sound on the Internet. HTML provides an ASCII-formatted page of information read by a special application called a *browser*. Depending on the browser's capabilities, some key words are translated into graphics elements, sounds, or text with special characteristics, such as color, font, or other attributes. Most browsers discard any keywords they don't understand, allowing browsers of various capabilities to explore the same page without problem. Obviously, there's a loss of capability if a browser doesn't support a specific keyword.

TERM	MEANING
HyperText Transfer Protocol (HTTP)	One of several common data transfer protocols for the Internet. HTTP normally transfers textual data of some type. For example, the HyperText Markup Language (HTML) relies on HTTP to transfer the Web pages it defines from the server to the client. The eXtensible Markup Language (XML) and Simple Object Access Protocol (SOAP) also commonly rely on HTTP to transfer data between client and server. It's important to note that HTTP is separate from the data it transfers. For example, it's possible for SOAP to use the Simple Mail Transfer Protocol (SMTP) to perform data transfers between client and server.

I

IDE	*See* **Integrated Development Environment**
IETF	*See* **Internet Engineering Task Force**
IIS	*See* **Internet Information Server**
Import	The process of obtaining information stored in some type of permanent storage such as a file on disk. The information can come from data exported by the target application for later use. However, the most common reason for an import is to gain access to data created by another application. Import files normally rely on standard data formats, with plain text and delimited text being the most popular. Delimited text files normally contain information stored in a database with the delimiters showing field and record boundaries. The main requirement for an import is that the source and target applications both understand the same common form of data storage. In addition, the source application should provide some type of export functionality, and the target application should provide some type of import functionality.

TERM	MEANING
Integrated Development Environment (IDE)	A programming language front end that provides all the tools you need to write an application through a single editor. The IDE normally includes support for development language help, access to any tools required to support the language, a compiler, and a debugger. Some IDEs include support for advanced features such as automatic completion of language statements and balloon help showing the syntax for functions and other language elements. Many IDEs also use color or highlighting to emphasize specific language elements or constructs. Older DOS programming language products provided several utilities—one for each of the main programming tasks. Most (if not all) Windows programming languages provide some kind of IDE support.
Internet Engineering Task Force (IETF)	The standards group tasked with finding solutions to pressing technology problems on the Internet. This group can approve standards created both within the organization itself and outside the organization as part of other group efforts. For example, Microsoft has requested the approval of several new Internet technologies through this group. If approved, the technologies would become an Internet-wide standard performing data transfer and other specific kinds of tasks.
Internet Information Server (IIS)	Microsoft's full-fledged Web server that normally runs under the Windows Server operating system. IIS includes all the features that you'd normally expect with a Web server: FTP and HTTP protocols, along with both mail and news services. Older versions of IIS also support the Gopher protocol; newer versions don't provide this support because most Web sites no longer need it.

TERM	MEANING
Internet Server Application Programming Interface (ISAPI)	A set of function calls and interface elements designed to make using Microsoft's Internet Information Server (IIS) easier. Essentially, this set of API calls provides the programmer with access to the server itself. This technology makes it easier to provide full server access to the Internet server through a series of ActiveX controls, without the use of a scripting language. There are two forms of ISAPI: filters and extensions. An extension replaces script-based technologies like CGI. Its main purpose is to provide dynamic content to the user. A filter can extend the server itself by monitoring various events like user requests for access in the background. You can use a filter to create various types of new services like extended logging or specialized security schemes. Most developers use technologies such as Active Server Pages (ASP) in place of ISAPI because these technologies are easier to use. For example, ASP makes it easy to modify a file without the need to recompile it. However, ISAPI is still used for speed-critical applications such as the Simple Object Access Protocol (SOAP) listener used by some SOAP implementations.
ISAPI	*See* **Internet Server Application Programming Interface**

J

Joint Photographic Experts Group (JPEG) File Format	One of several graphics file formats used on the Internet. This is a vector file format normally used to render high-resolution images or pictures. (The current version of the file standard supports 16.7 million colors.)
JPEG	*See* **Joint Photographic Experts Group File Format**

TERM	MEANING

L

LAN — *See* **Local Area Network**

Local Area Network (LAN) — Two or more devices connected together using a combination of hardware and software. The devices, normally computers and peripheral equipment such as printers, are called *nodes*. A network interface card (NIC) provides the hardware communication between nodes through an appropriate medium (cable or microwave transmission). The actual connection is provided through cables in many cases, but can also rely on radio waves, infrared, and other technologies. There are two common types of LANs (also called *networks*). Peer-to-peer networks allow each node to connect to any other node on the network with shareable resources. This is a distributed method of files and peripheral devices. A client-server network uses one or more servers to share resources. This is a centralized method of sharing files and peripheral devices. A server provides resources to clients (usually workstations). The most common server is the file server, which provides file-sharing resources. Other server types include print servers and communication servers.

M

MAN — *See* **Metropolitan Area Network**

Metropolitan Area Network (MAN) — A partial extension and redefinition of the WAN, a MAN connects two or more LANs together using a variety of methods. A MAN usually encompasses more than one physical location within a limited geographical area, usually within the same city or state. (A WAN can cover a larger geographical area, and sometimes includes country-to-country communications.) Most MANs rely on microwave communications, fiber optic connections, or leased telephone lines to provide the internetwork connections required to keep all nodes in the network talking with each other.

TERM	MEANING
Microsoft Database Engine (MSDE)	This term also appears as Microsoft Desktop Engine and Microsoft Data Engine in various publications. MSDE is a miniature form of SQL Server that enables developers to create test database applications. Microsoft designed this engine for use by one person, usually the developer, although you can potentially use it for up to five people. The developer accesses MSDE through a programming language Integrated Development Environment (IDE) or using command line utilities. In some cases, MSDE is also used to provide access to a remote copy of SQL Server. Some third-party products, such as MSDE Query, provide a Graphical User Interface (GUI) for MSDE.
Microsoft Management Console (MMC)	A special application that acts as an object container for Windows management objects like Component Services and Computer Management. The management objects are actually special components that provide interfaces that allow the user to access them within MMC to maintain and control the operation of Windows. A developer can create special versions of these objects for application management or other tasks. Using a single application like MMC helps maintain the same user interface across all management applications.
Microsoft Mobile Internet Toolkit (MMIT)	A free add-on toolkit for the .NET development environment that enables a programmer to create applications for alternative computing devices such as cellular telephones and Personal Digital Assistants (PDAs). The tools include special applications, coding examples, projects, and other programming language embellishments. This toolkit addresses the needs of Internet application development for the most part.
MIME	*See* **Multipurpose Internet Mail Extensions**

TERM	MEANING
MMC	*See* **Microsoft Management Console**
MMIT	*See* **Microsoft Mobile Internet Toolkit**
MSDE	*See* **Microsoft Database Engine**
Multipurpose Internet Mail Extensions (MIME)	The standard method for defining the content of Internet messages. This standard allows computers to exchange objects, character sets, and multimedia using e-mail without regard to the computer's underlying operating system. MIME is defined in the IETF RFC1521 standard.

O

Object Linking and Embedding (OLE)	The process of packaging a filename or data, server name (generally an application), and any required parameters into an object, and then placing this object into the file created by another application. For example, a user could place a graphic object within a word processing document or spreadsheet. OLE supports both linking (placing a pointer to the source data in permanent storage in the target file) and embedding (placing the actual data into the target file). When you look at the object, it appears as if you simply pasted the data from the originating application into the current application, which is similar to Dynamic Data Exchange (DDE). However, the data object created by OLE automatically changes as you change the data in the original object (provided you use the linking portion of the technology). It also contains the intelligence to know which application created the data. Generally, you can start the originating application and automatically load the required data by double-clicking the object.
OCX	*See* **OLE Custom eXtension**
OLE	*See* **Object Linking and Embedding**

TERM	MEANING
OLE Custom eXtension (OCX)	A component or control designed to make adding various capabilities to an application easier for the programmer. Essentially, an OCX is a DLL with added programmer and Component Object Model (COM) interfaces. Component technology has evolved to encompass a wide variety of uses including both client-side and server-side application elements. A component differs from a control in that a component is usually used for a processing task and lacks a user interface. Controls include application elements such as pushbuttons and textboxes.

P

Patch	When applied to software, a term that normally defines a small piece of code designed to provide an upgrade. (Some vendors are stretching the size of some patches so they're almost as large as the actual application.) In most cases, a patch will repair a programming error of some type. It could also improve security or add application features. The methods of creating a patch include complete executable replacement or executable modification using an external application. Patches can also affect application data and support files.
Path	1. A series of directory entries separated by backslashes (or other separators) that point to the location of a file or other resource on disk. 2. The complete location information to find a file or other resource. 3. The route used for data or other transfers between nodes of a network. 4. The route used to locate a specific piece of information in a hierarchical data file such as XML.
PDA	*See* **Personal Digital Assistant**

TERM	MEANING
Personal Digital Assistant (PDA)	A small handheld device such as a Palm Pilot or Pocket PC. These devices are normally used for personal tasks such as taking notes and maintaining an itinerary during business trips. Some PDAs rely on special operating systems and lack any standard application support. However, newer PDAs include some level of standard application support, because vendors are supplying specialized compilers for them. In addition, you'll find common applications included, such as browsers and application office suites that include word processing and spreadsheet support.
Protocol	A set of rules used to define a specific behavior. For example, protocols define how networks and the Internet transfer data. Other protocols define how data is formatted within files. Most protocols rely on some type of standardization process to achieve development community support.

R

TERM	MEANING
RAM	*See* **Random Access Memory**
Random Access Memory (RAM)	The basic term used to describe volatile storage within a computer system. RAM comes in a variety of types, each of which has specialized features. These special features make the RAM more acceptable for some storage tasks than others.
RCW	*See* **Runtime Callable Wrapper**
Runtime Callable Wrapper (RCW)	A proxy for unmanaged applications that enables the unmanaged code to call managed code functions. The RCW makes it appear that the managed code is actually unmanaged code to the calling application. The purpose of the RCW is to enable interoperability between the managed and unmanaged environments.

TERM	MEANING
S	
Schema	A formal method for describing the structure of a database, storage technology, or data transfer technique such as XML. The schema defines the requirements for constructing the object in question. For example, a schema for a relational database would include information on the structure of tables, fields, and relations within the database.
SCL	*See* **SOAP Contract Language**
SDK	*See* **Software Development Kit**
Server	An application or workstation that provides services, resources, or data to a client application or workstation. The client usually makes requests in the form of OLE, DDE, COM (through DCOM), COM+, HTML, or other command formats. The server response to a request is service, resource, or data, an error message, or an access denied message.
Simple Mail Transfer Protocol (SMTP)	One of the most commonly used protocols to transfer text (commonly mail) messages between clients and servers. This is a stream-based protocol designed to allow query, retrieval, posting, and distribution of mail messages. Normally, this protocol is used in conjunction with other mail retrieval protocols like Point Of Presence (POP). However, not all uses of SMTP involve e-mail data transfer. Some Simple Object Access Protocol (SOAP) applications have also relied on SMTP to transfer application data.
Simple Object Access Protocol (SOAP)	A Microsoft-sponsored protocol that provides the means for exchanging data between COM and foreign component technologies like Common Object Request Broker Architecture (CORBA) using XML as an intermediary. SOAP is often used as the basis for Web services communication. However, a developer could also use SOAP on a LAN or in any other environment where machine-to-machine communication is required and the two target machines provide the required infrastructure.

TERM	MEANING
SMTP	*See* **Simple Mail Transfer Protocol**
Snap-ins	Component technologies allow one application to serve as a container for multiple subapplications. A snap-in refers to a component that's designed to reside within another application. The snap-in performs one specific task out of all of the tasks that the application as a whole can perform. The Microsoft Management Console (MMC) is an example of a host application. Network administrators perform all Windows 2000/XP management tasks using snap-ins designed to work with MMC.
SOAP	*See* **Simple Object Access Protocol**
SOAP Contract Language (SCL)	A description of the capabilities of a Web service written in eXtensible Markup Language (XML). The description defines the messages that the Web service is able to either send or receive. Developers will find the Simple Object Access Protocol (SOAP) Discovery specification contains the rules used to create this description.
Software Development Kit (SDK)	A special add-on to an operating system or an application that describes how to access its internal features. For example, an SDK for Windows would show how to create a File Open dialog box. Programmers use an SDK to learn how to access special Windows components such as the Component Object Model (COM) or the Media Player.
SQL	*See* **Structured Query Language**
SQL Script	*See* **Structured Query Language Script**

TERM	MEANING
Structured Query Language (SQL)	Most DBMSs use this language to exchange information. Some also use it as their native language. SQL provides a method for requesting information from the DBMS. It defines which table or tables to use, what information to get from the table, and how to sort the information. A typical request will include the name of the database, table, and columns needed for display or editing purposes. SQL can filter a request and limit the number of rows using special features. Developers also use SQL to manipulate database information by adding, deleting, modifying, or searching records. IBM research center designed SQL between 1974 and 1975. Oracle introduced the first product to use SQL in 1979. SQL originally appeared on mainframe and minicomputers. Today it's a favorite language for most PC DBMSs as well. There are many versions of SQL, the most recent of which was approved by the American National Standards Institute (ANSI) in 1991.
Structured Query Language Script (SQL Script)	The implementation of the Structured Query Language in script form as an application. A SQL script defines a series of actions that an interpreter will perform to complete specific database-related tasks. The script language allows both queries and flow control, as well as other elements normally associated with a development language.
Stylesheet	A method of storing the formatting parameters of a document in an easy-to-change file or other permanent storage media. By changing the format definition for a paragraph, character, or division in a stylesheet, the user can instantly change the appearance of the entire document. Stylesheets come in forms for applications, as well as for the Internet. Some stylesheets appear as part of the application data, but newer forms, such as Cascading Style Sheets (CSS), appear in a separate file.

TERM	MEANING
Syntax	The expression of a thought, concept, or idea in an organized format for parsing by an application. The syntax normally includes both the spelling and grammar of the formal expression and therefore constitutes a language. Computer languages rely on syntax to define the formal spelling and grammar of keywords used to express the developer's ideas. For example, the syntax for the SQL language's SELECT statement provides a blueprint for constructing SQL statements. Likewise, all formal languages such as VBScript and C# have a syntax that defines the language.

T

Template	A special file that stores the settings and standard entries (also known as *boilerplate*) to create a specialized final document. For example, graphics designers often use templates to store the general settings used in creating charts and graphs for a presentation. Application developers also use templates to store the standard code used to create an application. By adding variables to the template, the developer can create a specialized form of a more generic application. Using a template reduces the time required to create the final document because many of the settings are already established. In addition, using templates tends to add consistency to a group of documents and can reduce originator error. Many programs use template files to store initial project settings, and templates created for one application generally aren't interchangeable with another.

U

UDDI	*See* **Universal Description, Discovery, and Integration**

TERM	MEANING
Uniform Resource Identifier (URI)	A generic term for all names and addresses that reference objects on the Internet. A URL is a specific type of URI. See **Uniform Resource Locator**.
Uniform Resource Locator (URL)	A text representation of a specific location on the Internet. URLs normally include the protocol (http:// for example), the target location (World Wide Web or www), the domain or server name (mycompany), and a domain type (com for commercial). It can also include a hierarchical location within that Web site. The URL usually specifies a particular file on the Web server, although there are some situations when a Web server will use a default filename. For example, asking the browser to find http://www.mycompany.com would probably display the DEFAULT.HTM or INDEX.HTM file at that location. The actual default filename depends on the Web server used. In some cases, the default filename is configurable and could be any of a number of files. For example, Internet Information Server (IIS) offers this feature, so the developer can use anything from an HTM, to an ASP, to an XML file as the default.
Universal Description, Discovery, and Integration (UDDI)	A standard method of advertising application and other software-related services online. The vendor offering the service registers at one or more centralized locations. Clients wishing to use the service add pointers to the service to their application.
URI	*See* **Uniform Resource Identifier**
URL	*See* **Uniform Resource Locator**
W	
W3C	*See* **World Wide Web Consortium**
WAI	*See* **Web Accessibility Initiative**
WAN	*See* **Wide Area Network**
WAP	*See* **Wireless Access Protocol**

TERM	MEANING
Web Accessibility Initiative (WAI)	An initiative launched by the World Wide Web Consortium (W3C) in 1997 to ensure that everyone has fair and equal access to the Internet, even those with special needs. WAI defines standards that affect the usability of a Web site. The areas of consideration include visual, hearing, physical, and neurological issues. For example, WAI considers the needs of users who might need to use large text to view a Web site or a screen reader to hear the content found on a Web site. Developers will also find that WAI provides for captioning, use of special input devices, and other interface needs. It also considers the effects of strobes and the complexity of the presentation. Some developers are under the misconception that WAI is only for those with disabilities. However, WAI helps everyone. For example, even if you have great hearing, you might need captioning to enjoy a presentation in a crowded office where sound would disturb those around you.
Web Services Description Language (WSDL)	A method for describing a Web-based application that's accessible through an Internet connection, also known as a *service*. The file associated with this description contains the service description, port type, interface description, individual method names, and parameter types. A WSDL relies on namespace support to provide descriptions of common elements such as data types. Most WSDL files include references to two or more resources maintained by standards organizations to ensure compatibility across implementations.

TERM	MEANING
Wide Area Network (WAN)	An extension of the Local Area Network (LAN), a WAN connects two or more LANs together using a variety of methods. A WAN usually encompasses more than one physical site, such as a building. Most WANs rely on microwave communications, fiber optic connections, or leased telephone lines to provide the internetwork connections required to keep all nodes in the network talking with each other.
Wireless Access Protocol (WAP)	A method of providing secure access for mobile devices of all types to Web-based application content through a gateway. The underlying technology works much like Handheld Device Markup Language (HDML), but using standardized and secure access techniques. This technology supports most mobile networks including Cellular Digital Packet Data (CDPD), Code-Division Multiple Access (CDMA), Global System for Mobile Communications (GSM), and Time Division Multiple Access (TDMA). Supported mobile device operating systems include PalmOS, EPOC, Windows CE, FLEXOS, OS/9, and JavaOS. The technology can support pages in either Wireless Markup Language (WML) or HyperText Markup Language (HTML) format, although WML is preferred because it better supports mobile device requirements.
Wireless Markup Language (WML)	An XML-based language used to communicate with Wireless Access Protocol (WAP) devices such as cellular telephones or Personal Digital Assistants (PDAs). Most cellular telephones provide support for WML. The pages are served in a manner similar to that used by the Handheld Device Markup Language (HDML).
WML	*See* **Wireless Markup Language**

TERM	MEANING
World Wide Web Consortium (W3C)	A standards organization essentially devoted to Internet security issues, but also involved in other issues such as the special <OBJECT> tag required by Microsoft to implement ActiveX technology. The W3C also defines a wealth of other HTML and XML standards. The W3C first appeared on the scene in December 1994, when it endorsed Secure Sockets Layer (SSL). In February 1995, it also endorsed application-level security for the Internet. Its current project is the Digital Signatures Initiative—W3C presented it in May 1996 in Paris.
WSDL	*See* **Web Services Description Language**
X	
XHTML	*See* **eXtensible HyperText Markup Language**
XML	*See* **eXtensible Markup Language**
XSL	*See* **eXtensible Style Language**
XSLT	*See* **eXtensible Style Language Transformation**

52 Ways to Improve the Web Matrix Experience

You've learned a lot about Web Matrix in this book, and I've suggested some do-it-yourself projects you can try to improve your knowledge. We've also discussed many ways to improve the Web Matrix experience in the form of Notes and Tips. This appendix provides you with 52 additional ways to enjoy your Web Matrix experience. All of these tips are short bits of information that you can think about as you use Web Matrix. If you have a tip that you'd like to share with me, contact me at JMueller@mwt.net.

1. Always complete the user interface design of your project before you begin coding. Using this technique reduces the probability of coding errors and forces you to think about how the user will interact with the application.

2. Web Matrix makes an excellent tool for creating small database applications, but you'll want to use a tool such as Visual Studio .NET for large or complex applications.

3. Store components and controls in the Global Assembly Cache (GAC) when you plan to use them in multiple projects.

4. Make any IDE customization changes before you begin serious work with Web Matrix. See the "Creating Your Own Toolbox Tab" section of Chapter 6 for details.

5. Web Matrix can open and edit any text document—even those that don't specifically appear on its list of standard documents.

6. Keep all of the files related to an application in a single folder to create pseudo-projects.

7. Use the Web Matrix walkthrough found at http://www.asp.net/webmatrix/tour/ as a starting point for your Web Matrix experience.

8. Use the Code Builders, whenever possible, to automate some of your coding. In fact, this is one area of expansion you might want to explore for Web Matrix.

9. Create Web pages using a combination of eXtensible Markup Language (XML) and eXtensible Stylesheet Language Transformations (XSLTs) whenever you need the ultimate in flexibility. All you need do to change the appearance of the Web site is create a different XSLT page to display it.

10. Remember to test your mobile applications thoroughly using a combination of Personal Digital Assistant (PDA) and cellular telephone emulators. Each device is likely to have special needs. If nothing else, each device will have a different screen size.

11. Always create the summary view of your database application first when using Web Matrix because this is the one area where Web Matrix provides some automation. Once you have the connection in place, you can create detail views and reports.

12. Use the Vary By None page as an example of generic caching. This project helps you create a caching setup with good overall balance and a minimal resource requirement.

13. Always reset the `<customErrors>` setting in WEB.CONFIG before you install your application in a production environment. Failure to take this precaution could expose the internal mechanisms of your application to the outside world.

14. You can find an interesting article about PHP, a unique open source solution for Web development, at `http://hotwired.lycos.com/webmonkey/01/48/index2a.html`. (Another good source is The PHP Resource Index at `http://php.resourceindex.com/`.) Because PHP relies on pure text files, you can easily work with the files using Web Matrix.

15. The Web Matrix online book, *Inside ASP.NET Web Matrix*, located at `http://www.asp.net/webmatrix/web%20matrix_doc.pdf`, contains extended user interface documentation not found in this book. This online book also explains some of the projects that come with Web Matrix in a little more detail.

16. Because SQL scripts are pure text, you can create and fine-tune them using Web Matrix. Of course, you'll still need to test the script using an application such as MSDE Query. (See the "Configuring MSDE Using MSDE Query" section of Chapter 5 for details.)

17. Use specialized mobile code as needed to overcome display or functionality problems with mobile devices. You write specialized code using Customization Mode and by selecting a target device.

18. Ensure you keep security at the forefront of your development efforts. Web Matrix provides pages that you can use to create log-in and log-out options for the user.

19. When creating a Web service, always try testing the service using direct browser access first. This technique displays a simple test page that you can use to enter data and invoke the method. Once you're sure the Web service will work as anticipated, you can perform more extensive testing using a Web page.

20. Store components and controls in a local /bin folder when you plan to use them only for a single application to keep the GAC uncluttered.

21. Never assume that the visitors to your site will be happy sharing their personal information. Always ask if they would mind sharing this information first. Make sure you publish a public privacy statement and adhere to other standardized privacy requirements as well.

22. Make sure you update your Microsoft Mobile Internet Toolkit (MMIT), now called ASP.NET Mobile Controls, regularly. Microsoft is constantly releasing support for new mobile devices through updates.

23. You can add new templates to Web Matrix at any time—making it an extremely flexible tool.

24. Use XML Notepad (`http://msdn.microsoft.com/library/en-us/dnxml/html/xmlpadintro.asp`) to edit XML files whenever possible. This free utility organizes the data in a way that Web Matrix can't.

25. Always use a two-machine setup for testing your applications. Otherwise, an application that runs fine on a single machine may fail when placed on the production system.

26. Use ASPX pages when dynamic content delivery is the most important consideration for your Web page. The programmable nature of ASP.NET helps you create content that can change by user.

27. Use the Vary Cache By Browser page when you need to cache a different version of your page for each browser, but want to keep overall resource requirements down.

28. Use Cascading Style Sheets (CSS), whenever possible, to enhance the usability of your Web pages. Placing the formatting information in a CSS file makes it easier for users with special needs to access the page. In the future, CSS might also enable users to customize a page to their specifications.

29. You can find an interesting Cold Fusion tutorial at `http://hotwired.lycos.com/webmonkey/99/03/index1a.html`. While this solution isn't free, it does use pure text files, so you can easily edit your applications using Web Matrix.

30. Make sure you look at the Control Gallery Web site at `http://www.asp.net/ControlGallery/` for additional application controls and components.

31. Have fun with Web Matrix! Adjust the IDE to meet your needs and create new templates as you see fit. Web Matrix isn't only a useful tool, it's a fun tool to experiment with.

32. Attempt to write your mobile applications so they will work on desktop browsers as well. This technique reduces the time and resources required to write the application, as well as debugging time.

33. Use MSDE Query (`http://www.msde.biz/download.htm`) to make your experience using MSDE as a database engine better. This tool replicates many of the functions performed by Query Analyzer.

34. Use the Vary Cache By Headers page as an example of how to cache pages based on specific users needs. Unfortunately, this is one of the most resource-intensive ways of caching files because you can't easily control the number of caching scenarios.

35. Test the effects of CSS settings using HTML pages whenever possible. The use of HTML helps you see the effects of a style setting more quickly. Once you fine-tune the settings, you can move them to other environments such as ASP.NET or XSLT.

36. Choose a security strategy that matches the importance of the data that you want to share. In many cases, a simple log-in page isn't enough. You'll want to use some form of Windows authentication or even rely on certificates.

37. Remember to add a `<mobileControls>` element to the WEB.CONFIG file for mobile applications to ensure they operate as anticipated. One of the most important properties for this element is `sessionStateHistorySize`. Set this property value high enough so the mobile application behaves as anticipated and doesn't run out of resources.

38. Always create a strong name for components or controls that you intend to place in the GAC using the SN utility. This utility generates a key pair when used with the –k switch.

39. Keep track of which mobile device users visit your site most often so that you can perform targeted application testing. Always test your application using the devices that the majority of visitors to your site use. Emulators often work well for less-used devices.

40. Use Design Time ActiveX Control Pad (`http://msdn.microsoft.com/downloads/sample.asp?url=/msdn-files/027/000/228/msdncompositedoc.xml`) to create the `<OBJECT>` tags required for your Web Matrix application.

41. Try designing your projects with accessibility in mind. Many of the people who visit your site will have special needs that the United States Government's Section 508 (`http://www.section508.gov/`) requirements and the Web Accessibility Initiative, WAI, (`http://www.w3.org/WAI/`) answer.

42. Use the Vary Cache By Parameters page as an example of the best technique for custom caching. This method relies on specific content on your page to determine which page to serve.

43. Make sure you explore the Online Gallery regularly for new components and controls to use with Web Matrix. You can access this feature by right-clicking the Toolbox and selecting Add Online Toolbox Components from the context menu.

44. Use the TLbImp utility to create assemblies from components and the AXImp utility to create assemblies from controls. Both utilities accept a key-pair file created with the SN utility to generate an assembly with a strong name.

45. Stored procedures represent one of the easiest methods of controlling the data sent by a Web Matrix application to a SQL Server. Using a stored procedure also allows you to implement the same code in other applications. The only problem with stored procedures is that you need a method for testing them completely—something that MSDE Query or a full version of SQL Server can provide.

46. Web services that require a SOAP header can't be tested using the default Web page. You can view the XML generated by the Web service, but will need to create a Web page for testing purposes.

47. Keep your application secure by removing access to resources that the user will never need. You can do this by setting local security on files and adding security through IIS.

48. Use generalized code whenever possible in mobile applications to ensure your applications provide the same overall experiences for all users. You write generalized code using All Device Mode.

49. It's always a good idea to experiment with multiple caching strategies for an application. Sometimes you need to combine caching techniques to obtain a good result. In other cases, server settings or cache duration becomes more important.

50. Never rely on emulator testing alone when working with mobile applications. You must use hardware testing, as well, to ensure the application will actually run on the target device.

51. Don't forget that Web Matrix can create HTML pages. Although HTML pages are best used for static content, they still provide a valuable means of presenting data on screen.

52. Make sure you become part of the community effort to support Web Matrix. This isn't a Microsoft project—even though many developers at Microsoft started it. This is your project. Web Matrix is an editor that provides extreme flexibility, and the price is right.

Index

Apress Titles

ISBN	PRICE	AUTHOR	TITLE
1-893115-73-9	$34.95	Abbott	Voice Enabling Web Applications: VoiceXML and Beyond
1-59059-061-9	$34.95	Allen	Bug Patterns in Java
1-893115-01-1	$39.95	Appleman	Dan Appleman's Win32 API Puzzle Book and Tutorial for Visual Basic Programmers
1-893115-23-2	$29.95	Appleman	How Computer Programming Works
1-893115-97-6	$39.95	Appleman	Moving to VB .NET: Strategies, Concepts, and Code
1-59059-023-6	$39.95	Baker	Adobe Acrobat 5: The Professional User's Guide
1-59059-039-2	$49.95	Barnaby	Distributed .NET Programming in C#
1-59059-068-6	$49.95	Barnaby	Distributed .NET Programming in VB .NET
1-59059-063-5	$29.95	Baum	Dave Baum's Definitive Guide to LEGO MINDSTORMS, Second Edition
1-893115-84-4	$29.95	Baum/Gasperi/Hempel/Villa	Extreme MINDSTORMS: An Advanced Guide to LEGO MINDSTORMS
1-893115-82-8	$59.95	Ben-Gan/Moreau	Advanced Transact-SQL for SQL Server 2000
1-893115-91-7	$39.95	Birmingham/Perry	Software Development on a Leash
1-893115-48-8	$29.95	Bischof	The .NET Languages: A Quick Translation Guide
1-59059-041-4	$49.95	Bock	CIL Programming: Under the Hood™ of .NET
1-59059-053-8	$44.95	Bock/Stromquist/Fischer/Smith	.NET Security
1-893115-67-4	$49.95	Borge	Managing Enterprise Systems with the Windows Script Host
1-59059-019-8	$49.95	Cagle	SVG Programming: The Graphical Web
1-893115-28-3	$44.95	Challa/Laksberg	Essential Guide to Managed Extensions for C++
1-893115-39-9	$44.95	Chand	A Programmer's Guide to ADO.NET in C#
1-59059-034-1	$59.99	Chen	BizTalk Server 2002 Design and Implementation
1-59059-015-5	$39.95	Clark	An Introduction to Object Oriented Programming with Visual Basic .NET
1-893115-44-5	$29.95	Cook	Robot Building for Beginners
1-893115-99-2	$39.95	Cornell/Morrison	Programming VB .NET: A Guide for Experienced Programmers
1-893115-72-0	$39.95	Curtin	Developing Trust: Online Privacy and Security
1-59059-014-7	$44.95	Drol	Object-Oriented Macromedia Flash MX
1-59059-008-2	$29.95	Duncan	The Career Programmer: Guerilla Tactics for an Imperfect World
1-59059-057-0	$29.99	Farkas/Govier	Use Your PC to Build an Incredible Home Theater System
1-893115-71-2	$39.95	Ferguson	Mobile .NET
1-893115-90-9	$49.95	Finsel	The Handbook for Reluctant Database Administrators
1-893115-42-9	$44.95	Foo/Lee	XML Programming Using the Microsoft XML Parser
1-59059-024-4	$49.95	Fraser	Real World ASP.NET: Building a Content Management System
1-893115-55-0	$34.95	Frenz	Visual Basic and Visual Basic .NET for Scientists and Engineers
1-59059-038-4	$49.95	Gibbons	.NET Development for Java Programmers
1-893115-85-2	$34.95	Gilmore	A Programmer's Introduction to PHP 4.0

ISBN	PRICE	AUTHOR	TITLE
1-893115-36-4	$34.95	Goodwill	Apache Jakarta-Tomcat
1-893115-17-8	$59.95	Gross	A Programmer's Introduction to Windows DNA
1-893115-62-3	$39.95	Gunnerson	A Programmer's Introduction to C#, Second Edition
1-59059-030-9	$49.95	Habibi/Patterson/ Camerlengo	The Sun Certified Java Developer Exam with J2SE 1.4
1-893115-30-5	$49.95	Harkins/Reid	SQL: Access to SQL Server
1-59059-009-0	$49.95	Harris/Macdonald	Moving to ASP.NET: Web Development with VB .NET
1-59059-091-0	$24.99	Hempel	LEGO Spybotics Secret Agent Training Manual
1-59059-006-6	$39.95	Hetland	Practical Python
1-893115-10-0	$34.95	Holub	Taming Java Threads
1-893115-04-6	$34.95	Hyman/Vaddadi	Mike and Phani's Essential C++ Techniques
1-893115-96-8	$59.95	Jorelid	J2EE FrontEnd Technologies: A Programmer's Guide to Servlets, JavaServer Pages, and Enterprise JavaBeans
1-59059-029-5	$39.99	Kampa/Bell	Unix Storage Management
1-893115-49-6	$39.95	Kilburn	Palm Programming in Basic
1-893115-50-X	$34.95	Knudsen	Wireless Java: Developing with Java 2, Micro Edition
1-893115-79-8	$49.95	Kofler	Definitive Guide to Excel VBA
1-893115-57-7	$39.95	Kofler	MySQL
1-893115-87-9	$39.95	Kurata	Doing Web Development: Client-Side Techniques
1-893115-75-5	$44.95	Kurniawan	Internet Programming with Visual Basic
1-893115-38-0	$24.95	Lafler	Power AOL: A Survival Guide
1-59059-066-X	$39.95	Lafler	Power SAS: A Survival Guide
1-59059-049-X	$54.99	Lakshman	Oracle9*i* PL/SQL: A Developer's Guide
1-893115-46-1	$36.95	Lathrop	Linux in Small Business: A Practical User's Guide
1-59059-045-7	$49.95	MacDonald	User Interfaces in C#: Windows Forms and Custom Controls
1-893115-19-4	$49.95	Macdonald	Serious ADO: Universal Data Access with Visual Basic
1-59059-044-9	$49.95	MacDonald	User Interfaces in VB .NET: Windows Forms and Custom Controls
1-893115-06-2	$39.95	Marquis/Smith	A Visual Basic 6.0 Programmer's Toolkit
1-893115-22-4	$27.95	McCarter	David McCarter's VB Tips and Techniques
1-59059-040-6	$49.99	Mitchell/Allison	Real-World SQL-DMO for SQL Server
1-59059-021-X	$34.95	Moore	Karl Moore's Visual Basic .NET: The Tutorials
1-893115-27-5	$44.95	Morrill	Tuning and Customizing a Linux System
1-893115-76-3	$49.95	Morrison	C++ For VB Programmers
1-59059-092-9	$34.99	Mueller	Web Matrix Developer's Guide
1-59059-003-1	$44.95	Nakhimovsky/Meyers	XML Programming: Web Applications and Web Services with JSP and ASP
1-893115-80-1	$39.95	Newmarch	A Programmer's Guide to Jini Technology
1-893115-58-5	$49.95	Oellermann	Architecting Web Services
1-59059-020-1	$44.95	Patzer	JSP Examples and Best Practices
1-893115-81-X	$39.95	Pike	SQL Server: Common Problems, Tested Solutions
1-59059-017-1	$34.95	Rainwater	Herding Cats: A Primer for Programmers Who Lead Programmers
1-59059-025-2	$49.95	Rammer	Advanced .NET Remoting (C# Edition)

ISBN	PRICE	AUTHOR	TITLE
1-59059-062-7	$49.95	Rammer	Advanced .NET Remoting in VB .NET
1-59059-028-7	$39.95	Rischpater	Wireless Web Development, Second Edition
1-893115-93-3	$34.95	Rischpater	Wireless Web Development with PHP and WAP
1-893115-89-5	$59.95	Shemitz	Kylix: The Professional Developer's Guide and Reference
1-893115-40-2	$39.95	Sill	The qmail Handbook
1-893115-24-0	$49.95	Sinclair	From Access to SQL Server
1-59059-026-0	$49.95	Smith	Writing Add-ins for Visual Studio .NET
1-893115-94-1	$29.95	Spolsky	User Interface Design for Programmers
1-893115-53-4	$44.95	Sweeney	Visual Basic for Testers
1-59059-035-X	$59.95	Symmonds	GDI+ Programming in C# and VB .NET
1-59059-002-3	$44.95	Symmonds	Internationalization and Localization Using Microsoft .NET
1-59059-010-4	$54.95	Thomsen	Database Programming with C#
1-59059-032-5	$59.95	Thomsen	Database Programming with Visual Basic .NET, Second Edition
1-893115-65-8	$39.95	Tiffany	Pocket PC Database Development with eMbedded Visual Basic
1-59059-027-9	$59.95	Torkelson/Petersen/Torkelson	Programming the Web with Visual Basic .NET
1-59059-018-X	$34.95	Tregar	Writing Perl Modules for CPAN
1-893115-59-3	$59.95	Troelsen	C# and the .NET Platform
1-59059-011-2	$59.95	Troelsen	COM and .NET Interoperability
1-893115-26-7	$59.95	Troelsen	Visual Basic .NET and the .NET Platform: An Advanced Guide
1-893115-54-2	$49.95	Trueblood/Lovett	Data Mining and Statistical Analysis Using SQL
1-893115-68-2	$54.95	Vaughn	ADO.NET and ADO Examples and Best Practices for VB Programmers, Second Edition
1-59059-012-0	$49.95	Vaughn/Blackburn	ADO.NET Examples and Best Practices for C# Programmers
1-893115-83-6	$44.95	Wells	Code Centric: T-SQL Programming with Stored Procedures and Triggers
1-893115-95-X	$49.95	Welschenbach	Cryptography in C and C++
1-893115-05-4	$39.95	Williamson	Writing Cross-Browser Dynamic HTML
1-59059-060-0	$39.95	Wright	ADO.NET: From Novice to Pro, Visual Basic .NET Edition
1-893115-78-X	$49.95	Zukowski	Definitive Guide to Swing for Java 2, Second Edition
1-893115-92-5	$49.95	Zukowski	Java Collections
1-893115-98-4	$54.95	Zukowski	Learn Java with JBuilder 6

Available at bookstores nationwide or from Springer Verlag New York, Inc. at 1-800-777-4643; fax 1-212-533-3503. Contact us for more information at sales@apress.com.

books for professionals by professionals™

apress™

About Apress

Apress, located in Berkeley, CA, is a fast-growing, innovative publishing company devoted to meeting the needs of existing and potential programming professionals. Simply put, the "A" in Apress stands for *"The Author's Press™"* and its books have *"The Expert's Voice™"*. Apress' unique approach to publishing grew out of conversations between its founders Gary Cornell and Dan Appleman, authors of numerous best-selling, highly regarded books for programming professionals. In 1998 they set out to create a publishing company that emphasized quality above all else. Gary and Dan's vision has resulted in the publication of over 50 titles by leading software professionals, all of which have *The Expert's Voice™*.

Do You Have What It Takes to Write for Apress?

Apress is rapidly expanding its publishing program. If you can write and refuse to compromise on the quality of your work, if you believe in doing more than rehashing existing documentation, and if you're looking for opportunities and rewards that go far beyond those offered by traditional publishing houses, we want to hear from you!

Consider these innovations that we offer all of our authors:

- **Top royalties with *no* hidden switch statements**
  Authors typically only receive half of their normal royalty rate on foreign sales. In contrast, Apress' royalty rate remains the same for both foreign and domestic sales.

- **A mechanism for authors to obtain equity in Apress**
  Unlike the software industry, where stock options are essential to motivate and retain software professionals, the publishing industry has adhered to an outdated compensation model based on royalties alone. In the spirit of most software companies, Apress reserves a significant portion of its equity for authors.

- **Serious treatment of the technical review process**
  Each Apress book has a technical reviewing team whose remuneration depends in part on the success of the book since they too receive royalties.

Moreover, through a partnership with Springer-Verlag, New York, Inc., one of the world's major publishing houses, Apress has significant venture capital behind it. Thus, we have the resources to produce the highest quality books *and* market them aggressively.

If you fit the model of the Apress author who can write a book that gives the "professional what he or she needs to know™," then please contact one of our Editorial Directors, Dan Appleman (dan_appleman@apress.com), Gary Cornell (gary_cornell@apress.com), Jason Gilmore (jason_gilmore@apress.com), Simon Hayes (simon_hayes@apress.com), Karen Watterson (karen_watterson@apress.com), or John Zukowski (john_zukowski@apress.com) for more information.

52 WAYS TO IMPROVE THE WEB MATRIX EXPERIENCE

(1) Always complete the user interface design of your project before you begin coding. Using this technique reduces the probability of coding errors and forces you to think about how the user will interact with the application.

(2) Web Matrix makes an excellent tool for creating small database applications, but you'll want to use a tool such as Visual Studio .NET for large or complex applications.

(3) Store components and controls in the Global Assembly Cache (GAC) when you plan to use them in multiple projects.

(4) Make any IDE customization changes before you begin serious work with Web Matrix. See the "Creating Your Own Toolbox Tab" section of Chapter 6 for details.

(5) Web Matrix can open and edit any text document—even those that don't specifically appear on its list of standard documents.

(6) Keep all of the files related to an application in a single folder to create pseudo-projects.

(7) Use the Web Matrix walkthrough found at **http://www.asp.net/ webmatrix/tour/** as a starting point for your Web Matrix experience.

(8) Use the Code Builders, whenever possible, to automate some of your coding. In fact, this is one area of expansion you might want to explore for Web Matrix.

(9) Create Web pages using a combination of eXtensible Markup Language (XML) and eXtensible Stylesheet Language Transformations (XSLTs) whenever you need the ultimate in flexibility. All you need do to change the appearance of the Web site is create a different XSLT page to display it.

(10) Remember to test your mobile applications thoroughly using a combination of Personal Digital Assistant (PDA) and cellular telephone emulators. Each device is likely to have special needs. If nothing else, each device will have a different screen size.

(11) Always create the summary view of your database application first when using Web Matrix because this is the one area where Web Matrix provides some automation. Once you have the connection in place, you can create detail views and reports.

(12) Use the Vary By None page as an example of generic caching. This project helps you create a caching setup with good overall balance and a minimal resource requirement.

(13) Always reset the **<customErrors>** setting in WEB.CONFIG before you install your application in a production environment. Failure to take this precaution could expose the internal mechanisms of your application to the outside world.

(14) You can find an interesting article about PHP, a unique open source solution for Web development, at **http://hotwired.lycos.com/ webmonkey/01/48/index2a.html**. (Another good source is The PHP Resource Index at **http://php.resourceindex.com/**.) Because PHP relies on pure text files, you can easily work with the files using Web Matrix.

(15) The Web Matrix online book, *Inside ASP.NET Web Matrix,* at **http://www.asp.net/webmatrix/web%20matrix_doc .pdf**, contains extended user interface documentation not found in this book. This online book also explains some of the projects that come with Web Matrix in a little more detail.

(16) Because SQL scripts are pure text, you can create and fine-tune them using Web Matrix. Of course, you'll still need to test the script using an application such as MSDE Query. (See the "Configuring MSDE Using MSDE Query" section of Chapter 5 for details.)

(17) Use specialized mobile code as needed to overcome display or functionality problems with mobile devices. You write specialized code using Customization Mode and by selecting a target device.

(18) Ensure you keep security at the forefront of your development efforts. Web Matrix provides pages that you can use to create log-in and log-out options for the user.

(19) When creating a Web service, always try testing the service using direct browser access first. This technique displays a simple test page that you can use to enter data and invoke the method. Once you're sure the Web service will work as anticipated, you can perform more extensive testing using a Web page.

(20) Store components and controls in a local /bin folder when you plan to use them only for a single application to keep the GAC uncluttered.

(21) Never assume that the visitors to your site will be happy sharing their personal information. Always ask if they would mind sharing this information first. Make sure you publish a public privacy statement and adhere to other standardized privacy requirements as well.

(22) Make sure you update your Microsoft Mobile Internet Toolkit (MMIT), now called ASP.NET Mobile Controls, regularly. Microsoft is constantly releasing support for new mobile devices through updates.

(23) You can add new templates to Web Matrix at any time—making it an extremely flexible tool.

(24) Use XML Notepad (**http://msdn.microsoft.com/library/ en-us/dnxml/html/xmlpadintro.asp**) to edit XML files whenever possible. This free utility organizes the data in a way that Web Matrix can't.

(25) Always use a two-machine setup for testing your applications. Otherwise, an application that runs fine on a single machine may fail when placed on the production system.

(26) Use ASPX pages when dynamic content delivery is the most important consideration for your Web page. The programmable nature of ASP.NET helps you create content that can change by user.

27. Use the Vary Cache By Browser page when you need to cache a different version of your page for each browser, but want to keep overall resource requirements down.

28. Use Cascading Style Sheets (CSS), whenever possible, to enhance the usability of your Web pages. Placing the formatting information in a CSS file makes it easier for users with special needs to access the page. In the future, CSS might also enable users to customize a page to their specifications.

29. You can find an interesting Cold Fusion tutorial at **http://hotwired.lycos.com/webmonkey/99/03/index1a.html**. While this solution isn't free, it does use pure text files, so you can easily edit your applications using Web Matrix.

30. Make sure you look at the Control Gallery Web site at **http://www.asp.net/ControlGallery/** for additional application controls and components.

31. Have fun with Web Matrix! Adjust the IDE to meet your needs and create new templates as you see fit. Web Matrix isn't only a useful tool, it's a fun tool to experiment with.

32. Attempt to write your mobile applications so they will work on desktop browsers as well. This technique reduces the time and resources required to write the application, as well as debugging time.

33. Use MSDE Query (**http://www.msde.biz/download.htm**) to make your experience using MSDE as a database engine better. This tool replicates many of the functions performed by Query Analyzer.

34. Use the Vary Cache By Headers page as an example of how to cache pages based on specific users needs. Unfortunately, this is one of the most resource-intensive ways of caching files because you can't easily control the number of caching scenarios.

35. Test the effects of CSS settings using HTML pages whenever possible. The use of HTML helps you see the effects of a style setting more quickly. Once you fine-tune the settings, you can move them to other environments such as ASP.NET or XSLT.

36. Choose a security strategy that matches the importance of the data that you want to share. In many cases, a simple log-in page isn't enough. You'll want to use some form of Windows authentication or even rely on certificates.

37. Remember to add a **<mobileControls>** element to the WEB.CONFIG file for mobile applications to ensure they operate as anticipated. One of the most important properties for this element is **sessionStateHistorySize**. Set this property value high enough so the mobile application behaves as anticipated and doesn't run out of resources.

38. Always create a strong name for components or controls that you intend to place in the GAC using the SN utility. This utility generates a key pair when used with the –k switch.

39. Keep track of which mobile device users visit your site most often so that you can perform targeted application testing. Always test your application using the devices that the majority of visitors to your site use. Emulators often work well for less-used devices.

40. Use Design Time ActiveX Control Pad (**http://msdn.microsoft.com/downloads/sample.asp?url=/msdn-files/027/000/228/msdncompositedoc.xml**) to create the **<OBJECT>** tags required for your Web Matrix application.

41. Try designing your projects with accessibility in mind. Many of the people who visit your site will have special needs that the government's Section 508 requirements and the Web Accessibility Initiative (WAI) answer.

42. Use the Vary Cache By Parameters page as an example of the best technique for custom caching. This method relies on specific content on your page to determine which page to serve.

43. Make sure you explore the Online Gallery regularly for new components and controls to use with Web Matrix. You can access this feature by right-clicking the Toolbox and selecting Add Online Toolbox Components from the context menu.

44. Use the TLbImp utility to create assemblies from components and the AXImp utility to create assemblies from controls. Both utilities accept a key-pair file created with the SN utility to generate an assembly with a strong name.

45. Stored procedures represent one of the easiest methods of controlling the data sent by a Web Matrix application to a SQL Server. Using a stored procedure also allows you to implement the same code in other applications. The only problem with stored procedures is that you need a method for testing them completely—something that MSDE Query or a full version of SQL Server can provide.

46. Web services that require a SOAP header can't be tested using the default Web page. You can view the XML generated by the Web service, but will need to create a Web page for testing purposes.

47. Keep your application secure by removing access to resources that the user will never need. You can do this by setting local security on files and adding security through IIS.

48. Use generalized code whenever possible in mobile applications to ensure your applications provide the same overall experiences for all users. You write generalized code using All Device Mode.

49. It's always a good idea to experiment with multiple caching strategies for an application. Sometimes you need to combine caching techniques to obtain a good result. In other cases, server settings or cache duration becomes more important.

50. Never rely on emulator testing alone when working with mobile applications. You must use hardware testing, as well, to ensure the application will actually run on the target device.

51. Don't forget that Web Matrix can create HTML pages. Although HTML pages are best used for static content, they still provide a valuable means of presenting data on screen.

52. Make sure you become part of the community effort to support Web Matrix. Even though many developers at Microsoft started it, this isn't a Microsoft project—it's your project. Web Matrix is an editor that provides extreme flexibility, and the price is right.